P9-DOC-511

Moosewood Restaurant Celebrates

Contributors to This Book Include

Joan Adler, Laura Branca, Susan Harville, David Hirsch, Sara Wade Robbins, Wynelle
Stein, Myoko Maureen Vivino, Lisa Wichman, and Kip Wilcox.

Other Books from The Moosewood Collective

New Recipes from Moosewood Restaurant

Sundays at Moosewood Restaurant (James Beard Award Nominee)

The Moosewood Restaurant Kitchen Garden

Moosewood Restaurant Cooks at Home (James Beard Award Winner)

Moosewood Restaurant Cooks for a Crowd (James Beard Award Nominee)

Moosewood Restaurant Low-fat Favorites (James Beard Award Winner)

Moosewood Restaurant Book of Desserts

Moosewood Restaurant Daily Special

Moosewood Restaurant New Classics (James Beard Award Nominee)

Contact The Moosewood Collective at their website, www.moosewoodrestaurant.com

Moosewood Restaurant Celebrates

Festive Meals for Holidays and Special Occasions

the
moosewood
collective

Clarkson Potter/Publishers
New York

Copyright © 2003 by Moosewood, Inc.

All rights reserved. No part of this book may be reproduced or transmitted
in any form or by any means, electronic or mechanical, including
photocopying, recording, or by any information storage and retrieval system,
without permission in writing from the publisher.

Published by Clarkson Potter/Publishers, New York, New York
Member of the Crown Publishing Group, a division of Random House, Inc.
www.randomhouse.com

CLARKSON N. POTTER is a trademark and POTTER and colophon are
registered trademarks of Random House, Inc.

Printed in the United States of America

Design by Jan Derevjanik
Illustrations by Christopher Corr

Library of Congress Cataloging-in-Publication Data
Moosewood Restaurant Celebrates: Festive Meals for Holidays and Special
Occasions / The Moosewood Collective. — 1st ed.
Includes index.
1. Holiday cookery. I Moosewood Collective.
TX739.M66 2003
641.5'68—dc21   2003055177

ISBN 0-609-60911-4 (hardcover); 0-609-80811-7 (paperback)

10 9 8 7 6 5 4 3 2 1

First Edition

To those who help us all keep it together and to those
who support us even when it all falls apart:
Celebrate with us the spirit of aging gracefully—
the crux of which is staying open to change. We dedicate
this book to living fully without needing to ask why.

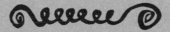

acknowledgments

Saying thank you is a wonderful thing. Doing it, we feel grateful for the invisible net of connection among all of us and bask in the inseparable wholeness of life as it is. Pausing to reflect, we notice that Moosewood, Inc., has become a churning entity, the whole somehow mysteriously bigger than the sum of us, its parts.

As we look back on our last thirty years of tremendous good fortune and steadfast support from workers, diners, readers, fans, and critics, one thing is clear: We are an ever-growing community that thrives on exchange. When we write a cookbook, we reach out like spokes of a wheel, searching all around for new dishes. We don our intuitive thinking caps, cook like crazy, and then distill the best of what we've made and learned, and pour that into our books.

Although nine names appear as authors of this book, some ideas and recipes came from other Moosewood Collective members. There's not one of us that didn't help in some way. We authors wish to thank our other fellow Collective members by name: Aneda Asta, Michael Blodgett, Tony Del Plato, Linda Dickinson, David Dietrich, Penny Goldin, Nancy Lazarus, Neil Minnis, Eliana Parra, and Jenny Wang.

Next, we wish to express appreciation for our agents Arnold and Elise Goodman for practical guidance and ongoing encouragement. We are further indebted to Pam Krauss, our editor, for her insightful polishing of our manuscript. As always, our interaction with the hardworking, efficient staff at Clarkson Potter has been invigorating. We especially want to extend warm thank-yous to Jan Derevjanik, our designer, and Christopher Corr, our artist, for their creativity and aesthetic expertise.

At Moosewood, we never forget you readers and cooks, who use our books to revitalize your passion for preparing good food. Your extraordinarily cheerful messages remind us how eagerly you await the publication of our newest recipes. It's you who put these pages to use, feeding and connecting with the meaningful people in your life. Your labors make our work come alive. So though we might never meet in person, we are joined ineffably by our mutual labors of love.

We hope this book of celebrations helps wake up many palates to the cherished tastes of diverse cultures around the world. May we all increasingly explore our global world with its enormous potential for sharing and learning. And may all of you, whoever you are, who find and use this book or have found a niche in your heart for Moosewood, know that we thank you—truly thank you—for celebrating with us.

contents

CELEBRATIONS BY SEASON

summer

autumn

winter

spring

any time of year

recipes by festive menu

caribbean jerk grill for father's day

A Caribbean menu with an emphasis on grilled vegetables, seafood, fish, tempeh, and tofu using jerk sauces and rubs. Fire up the summer season fast.

Two Super Rubs

Mojo Sauce

Jerk Sauce

Cilantro Almond Pesto

Caribbean Rice & Bean Salad

Piña Colada Slush

juneteenth

An informal celebratory buffet for this African American independence day.

Shrimp Jambalaya

Tofu Skewers with Peanut Sauce

Crabmeat Corn Spread

Black-eyed Pea Salad

Tropical Fruit Salad

Cashew Butterscotch Bars

summer solstice

A dinner party with a Chesapeake Bay menu.

Crab Cakes

Versatile Sour Cream Sauce

Red Cabbage Slaw

Quick Cucumber Pickle

dessert buffet

A dessert buffet in strawberry season that is perfect for a graduation, a special birthday, anniversary, or informal wedding.

Chocolate Soufflé Cake

Lemon Curd Layer Cake

Cheese-Filled Crêpes with Mango Sauce

Strawberry Mascarpone Tart

wedding or commitment celebration

A grand selection of sweet, spicy, and savory appetizers for a buffet in a country setting.

Stuffed Tomato & Cucumber Bites

Chipotle Shrimp or Tofu

Summer Rolls with Peanut Sauce

Umeboshi Sushi

Sushi-Stuffed Mushrooms

Tropical Fruit Kabobs

Greens & Cheese Frittatini

Cheddar Shortbread Hearts

Tomato Lime Pesto

Classic Southern Italian Dried Figs

Grapes & Gorgonzola

fourth of july

Americana menu with a twist.

Portabello Burger Fireworks

Boston Bean Salad

Blue Cheese Potato Salad

Red, White & Blue Parfait

rainy day picnic on the porch

A family picnic to salvage a summer downpour.

- Bedeviled Eggs
- Tomatoes & Arugula on Toast
- Cornmeal Lemon Shortbread
- Peach Fizz

heat wave dinner party

A spur-of-the-moment dinner party for the sultriest of summer days.

- Saucy Asian Noodle Salad
- Summer Cucumber Melon Soup
- Lime Frozen Yogurt
- Raspberry Fizz

labor day get-together

An eclectic pot luck picnic for sharing new recipes and old favorites.

- Roasted Russets with Chipotle Aioli
- Barbecued Tofu & Vegetables
- Spicy Grilled Corn on the Cob
- Grilled Curried Corn on the Cob
- Jenny's Mom's Eggplant
- Fruit Cobbler
- Two Summer Citrus Coolers

tapas party

A smörgasbord of little dishes from Spain.

- Spanish Chickpeas
- Cauliflower Green Olive Salad
- Manchego Potato Frittata
- Stuffed Mushrooms
- Cheese Crisps

halloween

A dinner party for grown-ups who love this celebration, too!

- October Bitter Sweet Salad
- Sautéed Broccoli Rabe
- Pumpkin & Mushroom Lasagna
- Cranberry Sorbet
- Bone Cookies
- Lickety Split Face Paints

day of the dead

Delicious food for families and their ancestors.

- Potato Leek Soup
- Stuffed Chayotes
- Mango Jicama Salad
- Pan de Muerto

eastern european dinner party

A dinner party that borrows flavors from Hungary, Poland, and the Czech Republic.

- Braised Polenta Cabbage Rolls
- Baked Beets on Greens
- Plum (or Pear) Torte

diwali

To celebrate this Hindu festival of lights, set the table with flowers, fruit, and candles, and enjoy a selection of unique Indian dishes.

- Curried Squash & Apple Soup
- Mango Cranberry Chutney
- Indian Vegetable Pancakes
- Red Lentils & Rice
- Greens with Cashews
- Kheer

sports night supper

A Mexican dinner for family and friends gathering to watch the World Series.

Black Bean & Chocolate Chili
Shrimp & Mango Quesadillas
Creamy Mushroom Quesadillas
Roasted Squash with Corn & Beans
Mexican Lime Cumin Slaw

two thanksgiving dinners

Two menus that offer equally delicious options for vegans and vegetarians, as well as traditionalists.

Vegetarian

Cracked Wheat Rolls
"Jazzed Up" Cranberry Sauce
Polenta Dome
Roasted Autumn Vegetables
Crisp Autumn Salad
Honey Roasted Pears
Pumpkin Maple Pie

Vegan

Harvest Nuts & Seeds
Red Cabbage with Cranberries
Mushroom Filo Pastries
Mashed Potatoes & Parsnips
Caramelized Onion Gravy
Roasted Winter Squash
Apple Pecan Crumble

ramadan

A hearty menu to culminate the Muslim holy month of fasting and prayer.

Sambusas
Spinach Almond Beureks
Shorba
Moroccan Salad
Preserved Lemons
Semolina Almond Cookies

hanukkah

Crispy foods loved by children and adults alike mark this Jewish Festival of Lights.

Potato Latkes to Celebrate Your Roots
Homemade Applesauce
Poppyseed Cookies

holiday cookie exchange

Special cookies to make and share with friends during the winter holiday season.

Cherry Chocolate Rugalach
Cranberry Cornmeal Biscotti
Lemon Cookies
Oatmeal Chocolate Chip Cookies
Orange & Fig Cookies
Peanut Butter Cookies
Spiced Coconut Date bars

christmas

Choose a menu from a selection of vegetarian and vegan dishes that suits the desires of your family and guests.

> Salmon Baked in Parchment
>
> Vegetable Pot Pie
>
> Brussels Sprouts with Chestnut Beurre Blanc
>
> Stuffed Yams
>
> Pearl Onions Braised in Wine
>
> Roasted Chestnuts
>
> Chocolate Cranberry Tart

kwanza karamu buffet

A harvest festival menu bringing together African influences from the South and the Caribbean.

> Harvest Stuffed Squash
>
> Sweet Potato Stuffed Eggplant
>
> Spinach Callaloo with Crabmeat
>
> Curried Coconut Green Beans
>
> Collard Greens & Red Beans
>
> Apple Brown Betty

first night

Dishes to celebrate a family-oriented New Year's Eve.

> Cauliflower Fritters
>
> Tomato Bean Soup
>
> Escarole Pie
>
> Orange Gratin

new year's day brunch buffet

Satisfying and festive foods to welcome the New Year.

> Best Dressed Shrimp Salad
>
> Sweet Potato & Zucchini Hash
>
> Savory Flan
>
> Good Luck Lentil Salad
>
> Campari Compote
>
> Buttery Blueberry Coffee Cake

setsubun (japanese bean day)

To celebrate "devils out, happiness in" as spring begins in Japan: A light meal to contrast and balance the rich holiday menus.

> Japanese Stuffed Peppers
>
> Asian Turnips with Wasabi
>
> Gingered Carrots with Hijiki
>
> Nori Rice Balls

southwest dinner party

The warm, sunny flavors of the Southwest United States are especially appreciated this time of year.

> Tomatillo Fish Soup
>
> Light Southwestern Potato Salad
>
> Avocado Citrus Salad
>
> Calabacitas

chinese new year

Cook-in instead of take-out.

> Mandarin Hot & Sour Soup
>
> Tea Eggs
>
> Chinese Long Beans
>
> Mu Shu Vegetables

valentine's day

Chocolates tenderly made for those you love.

> Special Day Chocolates
> Chocolate-Filled Dried Figs
> Chocolate Crunch
> Chocolate Apricots
> Espresso Truffles
> Hazelnut Truffles

tibetan-american losar dinner

Tibetans in Ithaca add their own flavors to Moosewood's cross-cultural cuisine.

> Tibetan-style Seitan Burritos
> Choklay's Home Fries
> Tibetan Hot Sauce
> Spicy Cabbage Salad
> Tibetan-style Chai

new orleans mardi gras dinner

Turn down the lights and turn up the sound of your favorite jazz recording.

> Baked Creole Ratatouille
> Olive Butter Spread
> Cajun Dirty Rice
> Puff Pastry with Strawberries

birthday breakfast in bed

A special breakfast or brunch for a lazy morning.

> Chai Smoothie
> Chocolate Waffles with Strawberry Sauce

pizza & sundae party

A reliable party favorite for a birthday, graduation, or casual celebration with young people.

> Homemade Pizza Crust & Toppings
> Classic Caramel Sauce
> Bittersweet Chocolate Sauce
> Wet Walnuts
> Whipped Cream
> Sundry Sundae Toppings

greek easter dinner party

An early spring meal for a vegetarian Easter.

> Greenest Green Salad
> Roasted Baby Artichokes
> Vegetable Pastitsio
> Baklava with Hazelnuts

passover seder

Traditional dishes with a Moosewood touch.

> Matzo Ball Soup
> Haroset
> Matzo Casserole
> Hazelnut Chocolate Torte
> Passover "Brown Bubbie"

mother's day tea

A vegetarian meal for health-conscious mothers to herald the month of May.

> Smoked Salmon Spread
> Spring Green Salad
> Bell Pepper & Asparagus Frittata
> Green Beans with Shallots
> Chocolate Angelfood Cake

cinco de mayo

Sweet and spicy foods to welcome spring.

> Tamale Pie
>
> Stewed Cardoons
>
> Nopalitos Salad
>
> Black Bean & Citrus Salad
>
> Strawberry Chocolate Quesadillas

appetizers, dips & dressings

Tasty nibbles for any time of year.

> Light Saffron Fish Soup
>
> Avocado Orange Soup
>
> Two Olive Herb Spreads
>
> Baked Eggplant Dip
>
> Asian Bean Curd Spread
>
> Green Skordalia
>
> Filo Bites
>
> Two Dipping Sauces
>
> Sweet Potato Pot Stickers
>
> Vegetable-Wrapped Sushi Rolls
>
> Tofu Almond Balls
>
> Puffed Pastry Cheese Straws
>
> Fried Sage Leaves
>
> Cashew Cream
>
> Anchovy Dressing
>
> No-Egg Caesar Dressing
>
> Dressings for Every Season

eight more cakes

Just in case.

> Winemaker's Grape Cake
>
> Brown Sugar Poundcake
>
> Chocolate Ganache Birthday Cake
>
> White Chocolate & Fig Poundcake
>
> Vegan Chocolate Gingerbread
>
> Frosted Carrot Cupcakes
>
> Almond Cake with Peaches
>
> Chocolate Pudding Cake

food as a gift

Take it next door, give it away on your travels, or ship it across the continent!

> Pear Raspberry Preserves
>
> Winter Squash Butter
>
> Salt & Pepper Sampler
>
> Stout Irish Gingerbread
>
> Best Vegan Date Nut Bread
>
> Currant & Walnut Biscuits
>
> Dog Biscuits
>
> Also see the lists on page 386

introduction

WHY CELEBRATE? Gratitude may be one of the very best reasons. It's certainly the most important ingredient for experiencing a state of abundance. To have fun, rejoice in plenty, praise an achievement or victory, honor and commemorate the past, or get the future off to a good start—all of these are great reasons to celebrate. January 2003 ushered in thirty years of continuous operation for Moosewood, so we consider this cookbook our toast to continued good food and festivity.

In America, one of the most frequently heard complaints in businesses and organizations is how seldom time is set aside to recognize and appreciate contributions, accomplishments, and successes. It's become the norm to focus on shortfalls, mistakes, and disappointments, and overlook opportunities to enjoy the things that are going just fine. Contrast that with the attitude in places such as San Miguel de Allende, Mexico, where the citizens agreed to *cut back* to forty official festivals a year because they thought they might not be getting enough ordinary work done! With that example, we should all be able to find one or two more days each year to make more joyous.

Over the course of the year, we usually celebrate days that are special to us with food. Moosewood has a long tradition of devoting our Sunday menu to the foods of a particular ethnic or regional cuisine, and sometimes we tie the menu to a particular holiday or historical event. In this book, we have recipes for traditional holidays and seasonal festivities, and suggestions for all kinds of occasions. We also serve up a little history and some thoughts about how people's treasured foods outlast many other cultural changes.

So, when shall we celebrate? How about right now? In addition to the customary celebrations, we hope you'll find ways to enjoy *whatever* your life presents. You can find plenty of excuses to create unexpected special occasions not tied to tradition, the calendar, or shopping rituals. Recognize and mark the everyday triumphs. Celebrate your nephew's beautiful smile following five grueling, expensive years of orthodontic torture. Don't wait to graduate from college—celebrate passing Statistics 101. Throw a party when your garden produces its first luscious, sun-ripened tomatoes. Celebrate that you and your best friend have actually made it to the gym three times a week for a full month. Create a celebration more often, just because you feel like having a good time.

New vegetarians and their friends and relatives often wonder how to replace the meat and poultry so often featured at holidays. We've created good meatless versions of many traditional dishes, given plenty of suggestions for adding your personal flair, and offered myriad options for devising fully satisfying vegetarian feasts for any time at all.

Some, but certainly not all of these recipes feature an unusual ingredient or require a little extra time and care to prepare. Although many can be prepared for any day, some are just not the sort of dishes you can whip together from the usual things on hand. But we haven't gone overboard on complex procedures and obscure ingredients.

The foods we've developed and written about reflect both our personal experience and our current interests and explorations. The selection of topics and festivities that we've chosen to highlight here is by no means comprehensive. It's only a sampling of the amazing culinary diversity and creativity available to us today.

A special meal doesn't have to be a major opus. We cook and cater for big gatherings and have the honor of feeding people on some of the most significant occasions in their lives. So here we share some tips on how to feed a crowd and get out of the kitchen and into the party. We think it's especially essential for cooks to join the fun, so all of our menus include suggestions for cooking in advance and orchestrating the food preparation sanely and sensibly. Ultimately, the food is less important than the gathering of people and the opportunity to enjoy one another's company.

We're certain, beyond the shadow of a doubt, that there's enough festive food between the covers of this book to keep you partying all year long. May your meals be gorgeous, exciting, scrumptious, and memorable, and may your celebrations be an opportunity for gratitude and sharing joy in abundance.

out of the kitchen & into the party
(tips for the fun-loving cook)

By planning ahead and remembering a few tricks, you can prepare many of the dishes for a celebration in advance and only have to finish the flourishes as the guests arrive. Then you can party with the best of them—carefree and undistracted, as if the food just appeared out of nowhere. Here's a checklist to help you. But, remember, if it all starts to fall apart for one reason or another, drag your favorite guests into the kitchen and turn your minor disasters into part of the party.

* Make a *complete* shopping list so there's no running back to the market for some forgotten essential ingredient.

* Make sure you have plenty of large sealable plastic bags and airtight containers on hand. If you clearly label storage containers and organize them in the refrigerator, you will help maintain your sanity as the preparations proceed.

* Start out with a clean, organized work space. Gather serving bowls, platters, dishes, and utensils in advance, so that they're right there when you need them. Liberate those crucial vessels filled with leftovers in the refrigerator, so you're fully equipped. For a large party, take stock of your wares and put the call out to friends for decorative serving dishes, tablecloths, vases, and baskets.

* Prepare time-consuming recipes (or parts of them) as much in advance as possible. Many casseroles and other main dishes can be assembled, partially baked or not, and then frozen. Freeze in a container that is also appropriate for baking. Ceramic or glass pans are the most versatile, especially if microwaving is an option. Allow enough time for thawing and remember that frozen or cold dishes take additional time to bake.

* Prepare dishes that will be served cold or at room temperature a day ahead or early in the day. Keep salads made of fruit or fresh greens separate from their dressings to prevent oversaturation or wilting; toss them together just before serving. Be sure to store them covered or in sealed containers for freshness.

* Soups and sauces often can be prepared ahead, refrigerated, and reheated. Remember to remove them from the fridge early enough that you can reheat them gently. For creamy soups and sauces, use a heat diffuser and stir often.

* On the day of the event, set the table early or delegate the task to a helper; then you can give your full attention to the food when it's time to serve.

* Carefully time dishes that should be freshly boiled, steamed, grilled, sautéed, or served hot from the oven so they're ready to eat when you are. It's best to plan no more than two or three dishes that need to be cooked the same way.

* Remember to allow some time to assemble the finished dishes on serving platters and garnish them. Many dishes are fine at room temperature once arranged, but some aren't. Don't let greens, herbs, and cheeses sit in a hot kitchen wilting or melting: Refrigerate them or put them on ice.

* Rinse garnishes ahead and grate, slice, or dice them while the main dishes are simmering or baking. Cover them so they don't dry out and store them in a convenient spot so they'll be close at hand at serving time. Don't let your piping hot centerpiece lose its steam while you're frantically trying to complete the finishing touches.

* If you plan to serve large quantities of hot foods buffet-style, make sure you have enough fuel on hand for chafing dishes and/or warming trays suitable for the buffet table.

* Invest in or plan to rent two or three thermal carafes for keeping coffee and other hot drinks ready to serve. If you intend to leave containers of milk or half-and-half sitting out next to the coffee and tea, be sure to place them on ice.

* Take a substantial break at some time shortly before the guests arrive or before the meal is ready to eat. Figure out in advance when a good time for the break might be in the overall scheme of things, and don't let yourself skip it. A short but refreshing "breather" makes all the difference in the world. Then have a PARTY!

* People like to be helpful. When someone at the party asks if there's anything they can do, pause for a moment before reflexively saying, "Not really" or "I don't think so." If there actually *is* something they can do, let them do it and thank them.

* Accept compliments. No matter whether the celebration food meets your highest standards or not, you did a lot, and now's the time to enjoy it. Save the critical analysis for later, and a good time will be had by all.

about the recipes

It's always helpful for those using our cookbooks to understand what we cooks had in mind as we wrote the instructions. Cooks develop a touch of intuition and a "feel" for the food; trying to capture this not-strictly-scientific art with words on paper can be a daunting task at times. But that's our job, so we do our best. Here are a few things that might help you avoid pitfalls as you explore the dishes in this book.

Most of our recipes list the quantity of prepared vegetables (such as chopped or sliced) in cups. When the exact amount of a vegetable isn't crucial, however, we just call for "1 vegetable" and we mean a medium-sized one (not a teensy-weensy one nor a gargantuan one). If you're unsure of just how much is the perfect amount, remember two things. First, nothing's perfect and, thankfully, there's a gracious bit of latitude in most cooking . Secondly, you can always add more, but you can seldom remove an ingredient once it's gone into the pot or bowl.

Peeling is mostly a matter of personal taste. Whether the vegetable or fruit is organic and its eventual use in a specific dish can be determining factors. We always peel carrots, parsnips, turnips, sweet potatoes, and beets. Cucumbers, eggplant, potatoes, and fruit are sometimes peeled, sometimes not: We decide case by case. You can follow our lead or strike out on your own.

When we call for scallions, we expect you to use both the green and white parts unless otherwise indicated. When no particular type of potato is specified, any non-baking potato will do. With canned tomatoes, you can buy whole ones and either chop them with a knife right in the can or squeeze them by hand into the pot—or use already diced tomatoes, sometimes labeled "fresh cut." However, when we call for canned tomatoes, we hope you won't use tomato paste or purée instead. You'll end up with a very different final product—one that would probably make all of us collectively wince.

When fresh herbs in the ingredient list are followed by a dried equivalent in parentheses, either is fine, but we preferred the fresh herb. If only the fresh herb is listed, we don't recommend using dried at all. In some recipes, we call for dried herbs, but you may always use fresh if you prefer: Just triple the dried amount and add the fresh herb near the end of the cooking process.

Optional ingredients and garnishes (without quantities) are really just that—optional. We liked the additions, but thought they weren't crucial to the success of the dish. We leave it up to you. Just take the plunge and decide to use them or not. If you're not happy with the results, write yourself a note about what to do next time in the margin of the recipe page: Live and learn. When the procedure mentions, "oil a baking pan," no amount of oil is given since this will vary depending on the type of pan used and whether the oil is brush-applied or sprayed.

Dairy products are another area of free choice. If we think that a particular dish cries out for a full-fat product, we let you know. Otherwise, it's up to you. Often 2% milk works just fine in any recipe that calls for milk. Skim milk is another story: It can work, but the result is likely to be more watery and less creamy. These days, we almost always use nonfat yogurt, reduced-fat coconut milk, Neufchâtel rather than cream cheese, and low-fat sour cream rather than their full-fat counterparts. But sometimes there's just no way around the heavy cream or half-and-half if you want a super rich and velvety result.

CHART OF MEASURES

Here's a handy list of commonly used American standard equivalencies—just in case you have one those moments of forgetfulness.

3 teaspoons	=	1 tablespoon		
4 tablespoons	=	¼ cup		
5⅓ tablespoons	=	⅓ cup		
8 tablespoons	=	½ cup	=	1 gill
10⅔ tablespoons	=	⅔ cup		
12 tablespoons	=	¾ cup		
16 tablespoons	=	1 cup	=	2 gills
1 fluid ounce	=	2 tablespoons	=	30 milliliters
2 ounces	=	¼ cup	=	60 milliliters
4 ounces	=	½ cup	=	120 milliliters
8 ounces	=	1 cup	=	240 milliliters
2 cups	=	1 pint	=	480 milliliters
4 cups (32 quarts)	=	1 quart	=	960 milliliters (.96 liter)
1.06 quarts	=	34 ounces	=	1 liter
4 quarts	=	1 gallon	=	3.84 liters
1 ounce (by weight)	=	28 grams		
¼ pound (4 ounces)	=	115 grams		
1 pound (16 ounces)	=	454 grams		
2.2 pounds	=	1 kilogram (1000 grams)		

pairing wine & food

A favorite cartoon of ours depicts two gentlemen sampling wine. One says to the other, "It's a good wine, not a great wine . . . but I think you'll be amused by its impudence." Although it's easy to be intimidated by the wealth of wine lore and its terminology, the best advice is simply to trust one's own taste.

Finding wines that contrast with or complement food is the goal. For a meatless cuisine, our concerns center around whether foods are light, dense, rich, mild, spicy, full-flavored, or delicate. The richer and more full-flavored a dish, the "bigger" the wine we serve with it.

These are the wines we offer at Moosewood, but there are many other excellent varieties available. Use the list as a very basic primer.

barolo is a "big" red wine that stands up to rich or hearty stews, pastas, roasted or grilled vegetables.

cabernet sauvignon is a hearty red wine to go with rich casseroles, bean dishes, and cheeses.

chardonnay is a versatile, popular dry white wine that provides good balance for lighter salad plates or for creamy cheese or egg dishes, such as quiche or frittata.

gewürtztraminer is a semidry white wine that tames the heat of spicy dishes and contrasts well with dishes that have a fruity flavor.

merlot is a red wine good with cheese-based casseroles, pasta, or beans.

riesling is an aromatic white wine. Dry types pair with spicy foods, light salads, or seafood dishes.

pinot grigio is a white wine with good acidity that balances fish or spicy dishes.

pinot noir is a red wine that resonates with highly flavored dishes full of herbs and spices, beans, earthy vegetable stews, and seafood.

shiraz is a red wine with similar uses to Pinot Noir.

Always be aware of sulfites. If you've ever suddenly become short of breath, flushed, or experienced a rash or stomach upset after drinking wine, you may be sensitive to sulfites. It's impossible to produce sulfite-free wine, but if you're sulfite-sensitive, drinking wines with no added sulfites is definitely the way to go. Sweet white wines usually have a higher sulfite content than most red wines, and aged wines such as Zinfandel generally have a higher sulfite content than wines that are not aged, such as Chardonnay. Organic wines may be the best choice.

in praise of food as a medium of culture

Food, beyond meeting our basic need for nourishment, is a profoundly significant instrument of cultural identity. Through food we experience abundance, nurturing, generosity, pride, and fulfillment. It connects us to our past, reorients and centers us in the haste of the present, and is a practical, beautiful means of renewing, sharing, and passing on our ethnic, regional, national, even ideological identities.

The aromas and tastes of familiar foods anchor us and command our loyalty. Almost every natural food has a story or folktale about its discovery, cultivation, harvest, and symbolic place of honor. People have composed songs about herbs and waged war over spices. We mark personal rites of passage and historic turning points of a population with special foods year after year.

While some people continue to steward ancestral lands in a sacred relationship with the past and the future, others left their homelands for opportunity, for refuge, or against their will. For many of us, reproducing traditional dishes heals the spirit, brings joy to the heart, and transmits our love and history from one generation to another.

Culture is fluid, dynamic. So within every ethnic, regional, or family cuisine, there is room for individuality and variation. Through subtle differences in the choice of ingredients and proportion of seasonings, we can distinguish the cooking of our mothers and fathers from that of our aunts and uncles.

When family members return home for a holiday, we can detect in their cooking the influences of time spent away from home. When new friends, lovers, and partners become kin, our cultural boundaries are stretched and redrawn again and again. That urge to share something new with those we love feeds the explorer in all of us.

As we've moved into this new century, both restaurant chefs and home cooks have plunged into developing cross-cultural cuisine, shuffling elements of various ethnic styles and ingredients into some truly remarkable concoctions. The array of innovations is staggering, and while not all of it works, a lot of it is exciting, delicious, and wonderfully creative.

Ithaca, New York—the home of Moosewood Restaurant—has breathtaking landscapes of waterfalls, gorges, and rolling green hills. But it's also well-known for its seemingly stubborn, cloudy, gray skies that dismay many who come here from sunnier places. Our friend Gary Esolen aptly coined the humorous phrase "land of the midday gloom" to describe our less-than-sunny weather. Winter here can sometimes last until mid-May, which leaves us with only a glimpse of spring. So, when summer arrives in early June and our world bursts into glorious bloom, we want to get outside to celebrate!

During the first weekend in June, our town kicks off the summer season with a gigantic party, the Ithaca Festival. The festival is a time to greet friends and appreciate the many talented artists in our unique community. We revel in the sunshine, buy beautiful handmade crafts, and stuff ourselves with delicious treats from the food vendors. Even though we usually have one torrential downpour during the festival, we are nonetheless convinced once again that we live in one of the most wonderful places on earth. After three days of partying, we have left behind our winter blues. Spirits are lifted and we revel in the splendor of long, hot days!

In summer, just-picked fruit, vegetables, and herbs are abundant in our gardens, and at farmers' markets and roadside stands. Moosewood menu offerings showcase this fresh produce, and at our summer parties, the food is sumptuous and beautiful. Here we share with you some warm-weather menus that we have enjoyed at our favorite party places in Ithaca, such as Lavender Hill and Penny and Jenny's lake house.

We also offer scrumptious ideas for traditional occasions like Father's Day and July Fourth as well as inventive celebrations for Summer Solstice, Juneteenth, and even a Heat Wave Dinner Party. These celebratory menus capture the best of summer's goodness in recipes that are brimming with fresh ingredients: succulent tomatoes, aromatic herbs, multicolored peppers, sweet corn, ripe berries, and juicy melons.

Maybe you will be inspired to have a Dessert Buffet in strawberry season or to host a lavish buffet for a Wedding or Commitment Celebration that we help you to create step by step. We even include a "porch picnic" for a rainy day.

So gather together good company for a summer party, and we promise that the menu will be fabulous.

CARIBBEAN JERK GRILL FOR FATHER'S DAY

Two Super Rubs: Herbed Garlic & Curried Spice
Mojo Sauce
Jerk Sauce
Cilantro Almond Pesto
Caribbean Rice & Bean Salad
Piña Colada Slush

Here in Ithaca, the first warm, balmy nights in June give us the feeling of being transported to somewhere in the tropics after our long season of cool weather. We like to celebrate Father's Day by starting up the grill and evoking the lively, aromatic cuisine of the sun-infused Caribbean.

The popular conception that men like to grill leads us to conclude that men also like to eat grilled foods. Since this is Dad's day, it seems only fair to have another family member prepare the food, a task that's easily dispatched by using the grilling advice that follows. Of course, if Dad just loves to grill, why stop him?

The two rubs and two sauces provide lots of spicy, flavorful options for marinating or seasoning grilled vegetables, tempeh, tofu, fish, or seafood. Because grilling will require the cook's full attention, the accompanying bean and rice salad and Cilantro Almond Pesto can be prepared ahead of time. The fruit slush ingredients can also be chilled ahead and simply blended at the last minute. The pesto makes a vibrant spread that is a good match for the Caribbean-inspired marinades offered here. Use it as an appetizer with crackers or chips or spread it on bread or rolls topped with foods fresh from the grill. If you're fortunate enough to have any grilled leftovers, they make a mean sandwich, especially with the pesto for added gusto.

TWO SUPER RUBS

These two rubs can be used to heighten the flavor of grilled foods, roasted vegetables, and baked or broiled fish and seafood. You can apply them just before cooking or, for more pronounced flavor, rub them on 1 to 3 hours before cooking. Always marinate perishable foods like tofu, tempeh, fish, and seafood in the refrigerator.

The 1 cup yield will provide plenty of seasoning for a meal that serves 4 to 6 people. Use about ¼ cup of rub per pound of sliced tofu or tempeh, and 1 to 2 tablespoons per 6-ounce fish fillet. A light coating is sufficient for cut vegetables: Use about ½ cup of rub per 4 to 5 cups of sliced vegetables.

HERBED GARLIC RUB

Assertive herbs, garlic, and vinegar give zest to this versatile rub.

- ¼   CUP MINCED OR PRESSED GARLIC CLOVES
- ½   TEASPOON GROUND BLACK PEPPER
- 2   TABLESPOONS MINCED FRESH ROSEMARY (1 TABLESPOON DRIED)
- 2   TABLESPOONS CHOPPED FRESH OREGANO (2 TEASPOONS DRIED)
- 2   TEASPOONS DRIED THYME
- ⅓   CUP OLIVE OIL
- ⅓   CUP BALSAMIC VINEGAR
- ½   TEASPOON SALT, OR TO TASTE

YIELDS 1 CUP
TOTAL TIME: 10 MINUTES

Combine all of the ingredients in a bowl. Let sit for at least 5 minutes so the flavors develop. Rub the mixture directly on the foods to be grilled.

In a tightly covered container in the refrigerator, Herbed Garlic Rub will keep for 2 to 3 weeks.

CURRIED SPICE RUB

While curries are very popular all throughout the Caribbean, they are especially notable in Trinidad and Tobago, where much of the population has East Indian ancestors.

YIELDS 1 CUP
TOTAL TIME: 10 MINUTES

3 or 4 FRESH CHILES, SEEDED FOR A MILDER "HOT"

8   LARGE GARLIC CLOVES

⅓   CUP GRATED FRESH GINGER ROOT

1½   TABLESPOONS GROUND CUMIN

1½   TEASPOONS TURMERIC

1½   TEASPOONS GROUND CARDAMOM

1½   TEASPOONS SALT

3   TABLESPOONS FRESH LEMON OR LIME JUICE

3   TABLESPOONS VEGETABLE OIL

VEGETABLE OIL FOR BRUSHING

Place all of the ingredients in the bowl of a mini-food processor and whirl until well combined. Or, by hand, mince the chiles and garlic, and stir together in a bowl with the remaining ingredients. Lightly brush vegetable oil on the food to be grilled before applying the rub; this will help it cling.

Curried Spice Rub will keep for 2 to 3 weeks, tightly covered, in the refrigerator.

MOJO SAUCE

This lively sauce could be considered plenty of excitement for one evening. Heated oil is infused with piquant seasonings to provide a zesty marinade for grilled or roasted foods. A little of this potent hot sauce will perk up almost any dish.

Mojo Sauce will keep in the refrigerator in a closed container for 2 to 3 weeks.

YIELDS 1¾ CUPS
TOTAL TIME: 15 MINUTES

3   TABLESPOONS GRATED FRESH GINGER ROOT

3   TABLESPOONS MINCED OR PRESSED GARLIC

2   TABLESPOONS MINCED FRESH JALAPEÑOS

1   CUP OLIVE OIL

½   CUP ORANGE JUICE

6   TABLESPOONS FRESH LIME JUICE

1   TEASPOON SALT

In a heatproof 1-quart bowl, combine the ginger, garlic, and jalapeños. In a small saucepan, heat the oil just until it begins to smoke. Carefully pour the hot oil over the ingredients in the bowl: They will foam when the hot oil hits. Whisk in the orange juice, lime juice, and salt.

Allow the sauce to cool before using. For best flavor, marinate foods in the Mojo Sauce for at least 30 to 60 minutes in the refrigerator. Additional sauce that was not used for marinating may be served as a hot sauce to pass at the table with the meal.

JERK SAUCE

Yah Mon! This is a spicy sweet version of the classic Caribbean cooking sauce. For best flavor, marinate tofu, tempeh, vegetables, fish, or shrimp in the jerk sauce for at least 30 to 60 minutes in the refrigerator before grilling. If desired, brush additional Jerk Sauce onto foods as they're being grilled.

Jerk Sauce will keep in the refrigerator for 2 to 3 weeks. Keep a batch in your refrigerator and jazz up backyard barbecues or grill-fests in a snap.

YIELDS 1 GENEROUS CUP
TOTAL TIME: 10 TO 15 MINUTES

1	TABLESPOON GRATED FRESH GINGER ROOT
4	GARLIC CLOVES, CHOPPED
1	CUP CHOPPED RED ONIONS
1 to 2	RED OR GREEN FRESH CHILES, SEEDED FOR A MILDER "HOT"
1½	TEASPOONS DRIED THYME
1½	TEASPOONS GROUND CINNAMON
½	TEASPOON GROUND ALLSPICE
⅛	TEASPOON GROUND CLOVES
3	TABLESPOONS VEGETABLE OIL
2	TABLESPOONS UNSULPHURED MOLASSES
1	TABLESPOON RED WINE VINEGAR
1	TABLESPOON SOY SAUCE
½	TEASPOON SALT

Combine all of the ingredients in a food processor or blender and purée until smooth. Add more salt to taste, if desired.

grilling basics

Grills have become commonplace fixtures in backyards and on balconies every-where, and grilling seems naturally to evoke a festive air. For some unexplainable reason, food always tastes better outdoors. The cook gets out of the kitchen, and there's no heating up the house with the oven. Delectable, smoky flavors and suc-culent sealed-in juices are surefire results of good grilling. Who can resist?

Grilled foods can go straight from the grill to the mouth, or they can become part of a fancier dish. Toss them with grains or pasta for a wonderful array of sal-ads. Top a pizza or a tossed salad, or add them to a pasta sauce. Mound them in a split baguette or on focaccia topped with crisp lettuce and drizzled with herbed vinaigrette, or tuck them into a pita.

Charcoal braziers, kettles, and hibachis all make good grills that heat up in about 45 minutes. Wood will impart a genuine smoky taste, and aromatic chips such as mesquite give a good consistent burn. Hickory, fruitwood (apple, plum, pear), maple, and sprigs of rosemary infuse the food with some of our favorite, distinctive flavors. After adding twigs, wood chips, or sprigs to the charcoal, wait until the flames burn out and coals form before putting foods on the grill. Alterna-tively, soak wood chips in water for at least 30 minutes before grilling time: The wet chips will make aromatic smoke but no flames.

Self-lighting briquettes and starter fluids make fires that leave nasty-smelling petroleum residues, so we avoid them. Instead, we use a "chimney"—a cylinder about the size of a large coffee can—to facilitate good air flow and get briquettes burning with just a couple of pieces of newspaper. Chimneys are readily available where grilling supplies are sold and are worth the small investment.

If you intend to do a lot of grilling, you're probably more likely to do it with a gas grill. After a quick twist of the wrist, most grills heat up in just 10 minutes. Lava or ceramic elements radiate the heat, which can be adjusted by dials. Charcoal and gas grills both provide ample dry heat to give food a distinctive grilled quality, but a gas grill won't produce any smoked flavor without the addi-tion of wood chips. For this reason, many gas grills come with a chip-box holder or smoker pouch. If yours didn't, you can place a perforated metal pie plate filled with soaked wood chips directly on the elements.

We think a portable grill rack, which sits right on the grill, is an indispensable accessory. Its enamel-coated metal surface has a grid of small openings that keep cut foods from falling into the fire. Tofu, tempeh, fish fillets, and smaller cut vegetables are almost impossible to cook on a conventional grill without a rack. Preheat the rack on the grill for 10 minutes, lightly oil it to prevent sticking, then grill to your heart's content. If you are preparing a modest amount of food, the entire rack can be lifted and brought to the table.

marinades, rubs & basting

Because vegetables have little or no fat, they must be "slicked up" before grilling. Oil promotes browning and prevents drying out, charring, and sticking. Most vegetables are quite tasty when simply brushed with oil and grilled, but the additional flavor of an oil-based rub, basting mixture, or marinade can be even better.

About an hour of marinating is a good rule of thumb. However, mushrooms, eggplant, and bland foods such as tofu and tempeh can benefit from 2 to 3 hours of marinating, if you have the time. Always marinate perishable foods such as fish, seafood, tofu, or tempeh in the refrigerator.

Herbs used in basting mixtures and marinades should be assertive enough to withstand the high heat of the grill. Resinous, woody herbs like rosemary, oregano, savory, thyme, sage, and marjoram work best. Leafy green herbs, such as cilantro, parsley, dill, tarragon, and basil, are better for dressings, sauces, or salsas that are added at the completion of grilling.

Charcoal-grilled foods, cooked properly, will have a natural smoky quality. Overcooked, they'll be worse than burnt toast. If oil or other fat drips onto live coals or heating elements, flames shoot up, resulting in a bitter, black char. To avoid charred food, be sure to brush only *lightly* with oil and thoroughly drain marinated items before placing them on the grill.

a few tips for the grillmaster

* When planning your menu, remember that grilled vegetables take time and space on the grill. They're better suited to a small group than a large crowd. Or you may grill them ahead of time and serve them at room temperature.

* Use a wide pastry brush to baste foods. A natural one made of bound-together herb sprigs, such as parsley and rosemary, or a 3-inch natural-bristle paintbrush reserved for the purpose will both work well.

* Most foods are best when grilled over high heat. With a charcoal fire, the coals should be at the gray-ash stage. If you can comfortably hold your hand by the grilling rack for no longer than 4 to 5 seconds, the fire is ready to go.

* For crispness, salt vegetables after grilling and keep the grill lid open (unless it rains, of course).

* For kabobs, cut vegetables in same-size pieces and marinate them in a nonreactive dish. Before grilling, skewer together those with similar cooking times. Use wooden skewers soaked in water to make them flame resistant. Metal ones cook the vegetables from the inside and negate the desired effects of the grill.

* When grilling in batches, keep finished vegetables warm or let them cool to room temperature. Don't cover them tightly, which can make them soggy.

* Keep tongs and platters nearby to facilitate turning and quick removal from the grill. Have a fork handy to test for tenderness.

* Grilling can subdue the vivid natural color of raw vegetables, so get out your festive serving platters to enhance the presentation.

* Salmon, tuna, mahimahi, mako, monkfish, halibut, sea bass, swordfish, tilapia, catfish, and trout are all good grillers. Thicker cuts are easier to handle than thin fillets. Leave the scales on whole fish to seal in juices and to reduce sticking; just peel back the skin and scales before serving. Always marinate fish or seafood or lightly brush it with oil. To avoid tearing the skin when turning fillets, use a two-pronged fork to carefully lift the fish, place it on a spatula, and flip it over. The rule of thumb is to grill each side for 4 to 5 minutes per inch of thickness.

* Jumbo shrimp can go straight on the grill, but skewers work best for regular shrimp and scallops. Cut pieces of fish or select shellfish that are similarly sized to ensure even cooking. To make flipping easy, pierce each piece of seafood on the kabob with two parallel skewers.

* Never use a marinade for raw fish later as a sauce without cooking it first. Either discard the uncooked marinade or simmer it on the stove top until somewhat reduced and drizzle over that day's meal.

CILANTRO ALMOND PESTO

This vegan pesto is extremely versatile. Besides its role in this menu, it's a wonderful flavor booster for bean dishes, soups, dressings, salsas, burritos, enchiladas, or as a simple spread for tortillas or crackers.

½   CUP TOASTED WHOLE ALMONDS*

1½ CUPS LOOSELY PACKED FRESH CILANTRO LEAVES

1   LARGE GARLIC CLOVE, MINCED OR PRESSED

½   CUP CRUMBLED FIRM TOFU (2 OUNCES)

3   TABLESPOONS FRESH LIME JUICE

2   TABLESPOONS OLIVE OIL

½   TEASPOON SALT, MORE TO TASTE

1   SMALL FRESH GREEN CHILE, COARSELY CHOPPED,
    SEEDED FOR A MILDER "HOT"

YIELDS 1 GENEROUS CUP
TOTAL TIME: 20 MINUTES

* Toast almonds in a single layer on an unoiled baking tray at 350° for 5 to 6 minutes until lightly browned.

Using a food processor, chop the almonds until they are finely ground. Add the remaining ingredients and process until fairly smooth.

The pesto will keep in a covered container in the refrigerator for 3 or 4 days.

grilling at a glance

asparagus Snap off and discard the tough bottom stems. Brush the tender tops with oil or marinate them. For easier turning, spear an asparagus near its tip with one skewer and near its bottom with a second skewer. Add 5 or 6 more spears to the 2 skewers, spacing them evenly. Grill for 5 to 8 minutes, turning frequently.

corn See page 106.

eggplant Cut unpeeled into ¼- to ½-inch-thick slices (cut regular eggplant crosswise, Asian-style ones lengthwise). Marinate or brush with oil. Grill for 7 to 8 minutes per side.

fennel Remove and discard the outermost layer. Cut lengthwise into ½-inch-thick wedges so that a section of the core holds each wedge together. Brush with oil or marinate. Grill for 8 minutes per side.

leeks Use young, tender leeks. Remove dark green outer leaves. Cut the bulb in half lengthwise and rinse scrupulously. Brush with oil or marinate. Grill for 5 minutes per side.

mushrooms Rinse well and let dry. Use smaller mushrooms whole; halve or quarter larger ones. Remove and discard the stems of portabellos and shiitake. Marinate or brush with oil. Grill 10 minutes or more, until tender and juicy—up to 20 minutes for portabellos.

onions Peel. Skewer small onions whole vertically through the stem end. Cut larger onions crosswise into ½-inch-thick slices and skewer through the concentric, nested rings to hold the slices together. Marinate or brush with oil. Grill small whole onions for 10 minutes; grill slices for 7 minutes per side.

peppers Core, seed, and cut bell peppers lengthwise into halves or quarters. Leave small chiles whole, but halve and seed larger ones. Marinate or brush with oil. Grill for 5 minutes per side. For smooth texture, peel the darkened skin before serving.

potatoes Peel and cut large boiling potatoes into ¼- to ½-inch-thick slices or use unpeeled, scrubbed, whole new potatoes. Parboil slices for about 5 minutes, until almost tender but not fully cooked. Brush with oil or marinate. Grill slices for 4 to 5 minutes per side; new potatoes for 6 to 8 minutes.

radicchio Cut heads through the stem end into halves or quarters, depending on the size. Brush with oil or marinate. Grill for 8 minutes per side.

sweet potatoes Peel and cut sweet potatoes into ¼- to ½-inch-thick slices. Parboil about 5 minutes, until almost tender but not fully cooked. Brush with oil or marinate. Grill for 4 to 5 minutes per side.

tempeh An ideal, firm-textured soy product for grilling. Most tempeh comes in ½-inch-thick squares or rectangles. Slice these into 1- or 2-inch-wide strips: The cut surfaces will absorb more marinade. Soak in a liberally seasoned marinade for at least 30 minutes. Use a well-oiled grill rack to prevent sticking. Grill for 10 to 12 minutes, turning often.

tofu Use firm or extra-firm tofu. For best texture, press the tofu (page 67). Cut into ½-inch-thick slices or 1-inch cubes, marinate for at least 30 minutes. Use a well-oiled grill rack to prevent sticking. Grill for 10 to 12 minutes, turning frequently.

tomatoes Skewer cherry tomatoes. Cut large tomatoes into ½-inch-thick slices or cut crosswise in half and scoop out the seeds. Brush with oil or marinate. Grill cherry tomatoes for 4 minutes per side. Grill slices for 4 minutes on the first side and 1 or 2 minutes on the second side. Grill halves for 10 minutes, turning often.

winter squash Peel, seed, and cut crosswise into ½-inch-thick slices. Parboil until barely tender. Brush with oil or marinate. Grill for 4 to 5 minutes per side.

zucchini & summer squash Trim the ends. Cut unpeeled and lengthwise into ½-inch-thick slices. Marinate or brush with oil. Skewer lengthwise and grill for 6 minutes per side.

CARIBBEAN RICE & BEAN SALAD

Here's an attractive salad with a bright, refreshing flavor and interesting textures. This is a fine way to use up leftover rice, and the complement of beans and rice provides a good source of protein. If you have no leftover rice and no time to cook any either, you can often find cooked rice at supermarket deli counters these days. One quick stop and 15 minutes of prep at home, and you've got a great meal for a hot summer day.

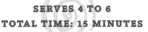

3	CUPS COOKED RICE
1½	CUPS COOKED BLACK BEANS (15-OUNCE CAN, DRAINED)
1	CUP FINELY CHOPPED CELERY
½	CUP DICED RED OR GREEN BELL PEPPERS
½	CUP CHOPPED FRESH PARSLEY
2	TABLESPOONS CHOPPED SCALLIONS
2	TABLESPOONS OLIVE OIL
2	TEASPOONS MINCED FRESH THYME,
½	TEASPOON TURMERIC
½	TEASPOON PAPRIKA
½	TEASPOON SALT
½ to ⅔ CUP FRESH LIME JUICE	
1	TEASPOON TABASCO OR OTHER HOT PEPPER SAUCE, OR TO TASTE

In a large bowl, combine the rice, black beans, celery, bell peppers, parsley, scallions, oil, thyme, turmeric, paprika, salt, ½ cup of the lime juice, and Tabasco sauce. Mix well and add more salt, lime juice, and/or Tabasco sauce to taste.

Serve the salad chilled or at room temperature.

PIÑA COLADA SLUSH

Fruit slushes can be as wildly diverse as the fruits and flavorings found in summer. They are like a gourmet snow cone, bordering on a soft sorbet. Use combinations of frigidly cold fruits, herbs, and juices, and add a little rum for a festive touch.

Make the simple syrup ahead to have on hand. It will keep for 1 month. Use the smaller quantity of syrup given in the recipe and add more to taste, depending upon the sweetness of the fruit and your personal yen for a sweeter flavor.

simple syrup

2   CUPS WATER
1   CUP SUGAR

6   CUPS FRESH PINEAPPLE CHUNKS (1-INCH PIECES)*
4½   CUPS FRESH MANGO CHUNKS (1-INCH PIECES)*
12   ICE CUBES
¾   CUP REDUCED-FAT COCONUT MILK (PAGE 397)
½ to 1 CUP SUGAR SYRUP
1   TABLESPOON FRESH LIME JUICE
     RUM TO TASTE
     SEVERAL PINCHES OF SALT TO TASTE

     PINEAPPLE CHUNKS AND THIN SLICES OF LIME

* One pineapple and two or three mangos will be sufficient for this recipe.

SERVES 6
YIELDS 7½ CUPS
PREPARATION TIME: 20 TO
30 MINUTES
CHILLING TIME: 30 MINUTES

In a small heavy pot on medium heat, simmer the water and sugar until the syrup leaves a thin coating on a spoon, about 10 minutes. You should have about 1¾ cups of syrup. Cool the syrup and store it in a glass jar in the refrigerator until ready to use.

Spread the pineapple and mango chunks on a large tray or several plates and place them in the freezer for 30 minutes.

In a blender or food processor, crush the ice cubes, then scoop them out and set aside. In batches, combine the crushed ice, fruit chunks, coconut milk, sugar syrup, and lime juice and purée or process until smooth, thick, and slushy. Stir together in a bowl and add rum and salt to taste.

Ladle into a dessert dish, parfait glass, or wineglass. Garnish with pineapple pieces and slivers of lime. Serve immediately.

JUNETEENTH

Shrimp Jambalaya on rice
Tofu Skewers with Peanut Sauce
Crabmeat Corn Spread on crackers or in puff pastry
Black-eyed Pea Salad
Tropical Fruit Salad
Cashew Butterscotch Bars

Juneteenth is an African-American holiday that commemorates the 1865 emancipation of enslaved Africans in Galveston, Texas. Although traditionally celebrated on June 19, the ambiguity in its name is telling. Abraham Lincoln issued the Emancipation Proclamation in January 1863, but people in bondage in Texas were kept ignorant of their emancipation for an astounding two and a half years. It wasn't until mid-June of 1865 that slaves learned the truth and wasted no time in exercising their freedom. Many dropped what they were doing and walked, ran, or danced right out of the fields, never looking back. Juneteenth is a celebration of black culture, liberation, and independence, and of the triumph of the human spirit over oppression.

Juneteenth was declared a Texas state holiday in 1979. It's celebrated all over the United States, much like Independence Day. These gatherings are for every generation of the community, every member of the family. In a city, Juneteenth can be celebrated with a great block party like the one over at the Southside Community Center here in Ithaca, or a festival in a big park with a bandstand and fireworks. In rural areas, kick it off with a parade down Main Street, then gather for a feast wherever church socials and outdoor barbecues are held.

People come together to enjoy live jazz, blues, R&B, gospel, rap, African music, drumming, dance, fashion shows, storytelling, poetry, and performance. People exhibit their arts and cook up a storm. Everyone stuffs themselves silly. It's June, and beautiful young vegetables and fresh herbs and flowers are flourishing everywhere, so you can celebrate with the very best ingredients.

What to cook? If you want to tap those African roots, you'll be well on your way with rice, peppers, millet, green onions, tender okra, roasted peanuts, sweet potatoes, or yams. Our Juneteenth menu works well as either an informal buffet or a sit-down meal. While the menu is comprised of six dishes, four (or even five) of these can be prepared in advance, so you don't need to spend the whole day cooking.

Begin at the end by making dessert. Cashew Butterscotch Bars can be baked a day or two ahead and stored. The spicy syrup that tops our Tropical Fruit Salad can be made several days before serving and stored covered in the refrigerator. Black-eyed Pea Salad will keep for up to 5 days if well covered and refrigerated. The Crabmeat Corn Spread takes only ½ hour to make, so you may prefer to make it fresh, but it can be made a day ahead and kept cold. Shrimp Jambalaya and Tofu Skewers with Peanut Sauce are really best if cooked and immediately served hot, but even the jambalaya can be made the day before and stored chilled—just don't add the shrimp until you are ready to serve.

On Juneteenth, prepare the fruit for the Tropical Fruit Salad and keep it cold. Warm the Crabmeat Corn Spread in a microwave oven or bake it in puff pastry shells in a toaster oven. If you'd like to serve the jambalaya on rice, start brown rice after you assemble the ingredients for the Tofu Skewers, or start white rice, which takes half the time to cook, when you put the skewers in the oven. Make the Tofu Skewers with Peanut Sauce. While the tofu bakes, reheat the jambalaya and, right before serving, cook the shrimp in the hot stew. Dress the fruit salad with the already prepared spicy syrup.

Offer strong coffee flavored with chicory and cinnamon, brewed iced tea, and fresh lemonade. Tired already? Never attempt to cook this kind of big meal by yourself! Get help, and you'll have a ball. Set the buffet or table, raise your glasses to freedom, and enjoy a fabulous feast.

SHRIMP JAMBALAYA

At Moosewood Restaurant, we serve jambalaya over rice. This version is a big, robust Creole vegetable stew with shrimp, but you can make it without shrimp and use vegetable stock in place of the shrimp stock. Okra is a traditional ingredient, but it really can be optional in this already ample recipe.

If using dried thyme and marjoram, stir them into the jambalaya a bit earlier than when the fresh herbs are added—around the time you add the tomatoes would be good.

1	POUND FRESH OR FROZEN SHRIMP
¼	CUP PLUS 2 TABLESPOONS VEGETABLE OIL
⅓	CUP UNBLEACHED WHITE FLOUR
2	CUPS CHOPPED ONIONS
2	GARLIC CLOVES, MINCED OR PRESSED
2	BAY LEAVES
½	TEASPOON GROUND ALLSPICE
1½	CUPS PEELED AND CHOPPED CARROTS
2	CUPS BITE-SIZED GREEN BEAN PIECES
1	CUP DICED CELERY
2	CUPS FRESH OR UNDRAINED CANNED CHOPPED TOMATOES
5	CUPS WATER OR SHRIMP SHELL STOCK*
2	CUPS SLICED YELLOW SQUASH**
2	CUPS SLICED ZUCCHINI**
4	CUPS CHOPPED BELL PEPPERS**
8	OUNCES FROZEN CUT OKRA (OPTIONAL)
2	TEASPOONS MINCED FRESH THYME (1 TEASPOON DRIED)
1	TEASPOON MINCED FRESH MARJORAM (½ TEASPOON DRIED)
¼	CUP MINCED FRESH BASIL
1	TEASPOON TABASCO OR OTHER HOT PEPPER SAUCE
1	TABLESPOON WORCESTERSHIRE SAUCE
	SALT TO TASTE
	CHOPPED FRESH PARSLEY
	LEMON WEDGES

* If you have shrimp with shells, use the shells to make a flavorful stock: Bring 4 cups of water to a boil, simmer the shells for 10 minutes, and strain. Add enough water to the strained cooking liquid to make 5 cups of stock.

** Cut the yellow squash and zucchini into ¼-inch-thick semicircles and chop 3 bell peppers (red, green, and yellow) into 1-inch pieces.

Peel and devein the shrimp and chill until needed.

Heat ¼ cup of the oil in a heavy nonstick skillet until hot but not smoking. (At the right temperature, a pinch of flour sprinkled in will float away into the oil.) Add the flour and stir well. Cook the roux on low heat for about 15 to 20 minutes, stirring frequently, until it is nut brown and smooth. It darkens slowly, so stir and be patient—the aroma becomes spectacular.

While the roux cooks, heat the remaining 2 tablespoons of oil and sauté the onions, garlic, and bay leaves for 10 minutes, until the onions are translucent. Add the allspice and carrots, cover, and cook for about 4 minutes. Add the green beans and celery and cook for 3 minutes.

Stir in the tomatoes, the water or stock, the yellow squash, zucchini, bell peppers, and the okra, if using. Cook for 5 to 10 minutes, until the vegetables are tender. Add the fresh herbs, Tabasco, and Worcestershire sauce. Stir in the shrimp. When the shrimp turn pink, stir in the roux and cook just until thickened. Add salt to taste.

Serve garnished with chopped parsley and lemon wedges, and with extra hot sauce on the side.

MARJORAM

BASIL

THYME

TOFU SKEWERS WITH PEANUT SAUCE

Our peanut sauce harkens back to West African flavors that are perfect for a Juneteenth meal, and these skewers have converted the tofu-phobic and pleased the masses. We served this dish to connoisseurs at the James Beard Society and they couldn't stop raving.

Sixteen-ounce cakes of tofu work best here, and eighteen 10-inch bamboo skewers are perfect for this recipe. Most supermarkets carry 1-pound tofu cakes, often vacuum-packed in water and refrigerated.

tofu

SERVES 8 TO 12
YIELDS 18 OR 27 SKEWERS
PREPARATION TIME: 25 MINUTES
BAKING TIME: 20 TO 25 MINUTES

¼   CUP SOY SAUCE
¼   CUP VEGETABLE OIL
3   CAKES FIRM TOFU (ABOUT 3 POUNDS)

peanut sauce

2   TABLESPOONS SOY SAUCE
2   TABLESPOONS HONEY OR 2 TO 3 TABLESPOONS BROWN SUGAR
6 to 8 TABLESPOONS FRESH LIME JUICE OR WHITE VINEGAR
½   TEASPOON TABASCO OR OTHER HOT PEPPER SAUCE, MORE TO TASTE
1   TEASPOON GROUND CUMIN (OPTIONAL)
½   CUP PEANUT BUTTER

Preheat the oven to 450°. Lightly spray or oil a large baking sheet.

In a large shallow bowl, stir together the soy sauce and oil. Cut a cake of tofu in half crosswise (like a layer cake), stack the two halves back together, and position the tofu so you can cut parallel to its long side. Slice down through both layers eight times to make a total of 18 thin pieces. Put the tofu pieces into the bowl and coat well with the soy sauce mixture.

To thread the tofu lengthwise onto skewers, stand a tofu piece on its thin edge so that the long side is parallel to the countertop edge. Poke the skewer away from you straight through the tofu near its right end. Bend the rest of the tofu piece up and to the right and poke through near the middle, then curve the tofu back to the left to make a backward S-shape and poke through the other end (see Note). Gently push the piece down the skewer to the center and thread one more piece onto each end, for three pieces per skewer. Or, if you prefer, thread only two pieces per skewer, one on each end. Continue using the coated tofu pieces to make five more three-piece skewers or eight more two-piece skewers. Place the finished skewers edge-side down on the prepared baking sheet.

Repeat this process for the other two cakes of tofu. (Practice makes perfect, not to mention speedier.)

Bake for 20 to 25 minutes, until sizzling and browned.

Meanwhile, combine all of the sauce ingredients in a blender and purée until smooth. If the sauce is too thick to pour, add a little water. Set aside.

When the tofu skewers are baked, place them on a serving platter and generously drizzle with peanut sauce. Serve hot or at room temperature. Pass any extra sauce at the table.

note

If you find it easier to begin poking the left side of the tofu piece and curving up and left first, then curving right to form a true S-shape, that's just fine.

TOFU PIECE · FIRST POKE → BACKWARD S-SHAPE → 2 PER SKEWER

CRABMEAT CORN SPREAD

This recipe makes a delicious spread with crab and shrimp to put on crackers or toasted rounds of French bread or pumpernickel. For a savory appetizer, fill puff pastry shells with the mixture and bake until golden brown and crisp.

2	TABLESPOONS BUTTER, MELTED
½	CUP CHOPPED SCALLIONS
2	CUPS DICED CELERY
2	CUPS FRESH OR FROZEN CORN KERNELS
2	TEASPOONS OLD BAY SEASONING
1	TEASPOON WORCESTERSHIRE SAUCE
	GROUND BLACK PEPPER TO TASTE
1	TEASPOON MINCED FRESH THYME (OPTIONAL)
1	CUP NEUFCHÂTEL OR CREAM CHEESE
16 to 20	SHRIMP, PEELED AND DEVEINED (12 OUNCES)
8	OUNCES LUMP OR SHREDDED CRABMEAT, PICKED OVER FOR SHELLS OR CARTILAGE
	FRESH LEMON JUICE TO TASTE (OPTIONAL)

YIELDS 5 CUPS
TOTAL TIME: 30 TO 35 MINUTES

In a saucepan, combine the butter, scallions, and celery, cover, and cook for 5 minutes without browning. Add the corn, Old Bay Seasoning, Worcestershire sauce, pepper, and thyme, if using. Cover and cook on low heat for 5 minutes. Add the Neufchâtel and stir until melted. Remove from the heat, cover, and set aside.

Meanwhile, bring about a quart of water to a boil and cook the shrimp until they turn pink, about 3 minutes. Drain. Cut the shrimp and the crabmeat into bite-sized pieces and combine in a bowl. Stir the cream cheese mixture into the seafood. Add lemon juice to taste.

Serve warm or at room temperature.

BLACK-EYED PEA SALAD

In this salad, the crunch of bell peppers makes a nice counterpoint to the texture and distinctive flavor of the black-eyed peas. Moosewood cook Nancy Lazarus invented this dish when black-eyed peas were seldom seen in salads in Northeastern U.S. cooking. The recipe makes enough for a simple lunch or supper, served with a puréed soup, corn on the cob, or with wholegrain bread and a sharp cheese. Its tanginess makes it a perfect side dish next to a sweet potato salad or creamy potato salad.

If you can get fresh black-eyed peas, by all means use them. But frozen black-eyed peas work fine—they retain their shape and absorb the flavors of the dressing nicely. Canned or dried black-eyed peas may also be used, but we much prefer frozen or fresh. Covered and refrigerated, the salad will keep for up to 4 or 5 days.

1½ CUPS LIGHTLY SALTED WATER

16 OUNCES FROZEN BLACK-EYED PEAS (ABOUT 3½ CUPS)

1 CUP MINCED GREEN BELL PEPPERS

½ CUP MINCED SCALLIONS

¼ CUP MINCED FRESH CILANTRO

¼ CUP FRESH LIME JUICE

¼ CUP OLIVE OIL

½ TEASPOON SALT, OR TO TASTE

¼ TEASPOON GROUND BLACK PEPPER

SERVES 6 TO 8
PREPARATION TIME: 30 MINUTES
MARINATING TIME: AT LEAST 30 MINUTES

In a covered saucepan, bring the water to a boil. Stir in the black-eyed peas, return to a boil, cover, lower the heat, and simmer for 20 to 30 minutes, or until tender.

Meanwhile, in a bowl, combine the bell peppers, scallions, and cilantro. When the black-eyed peas are done, drain them briefly in a colander. Add the hot beans to the bowl without stirring and set aside for 5 minutes: The heat from the beans will soften the peppers, scallions, and cilantro just enough.

In a small bowl, stir together the lime juice, olive oil, salt, and black pepper. Pour the dressing over the peas, stir well, and set aside to marinate for at least 30 minutes before serving.

Serve at room temperature or chilled.

TROPICAL FRUIT SALAD

A light, spicy, sweet syrup glazes the fresh tropical fruit in this bright and sunny tropical salad. Imagine these island spices wafting on a gentle Caribbean breeze! When stored in the refrigerator, the syrup will keep for several weeks. It may begin to crystallize when stored longer than that.

spiced syrup

SERVES 6 TO 8
TOTAL TIME: 35 MINUTES

2	CUPS WATER
8	SLICES PEELED FRESH GINGER ROOT (⅛ INCH THICK)
1	CUP SUGAR
3	WHOLE CLOVES
½	TEASPOON ANISE SEEDS
1	WHOLE CINNAMON STICK
½	TEASPOON WHOLE BLACK PEPPERCORNS
¼	TEASPOON GROUND CARDAMOM

tropical fruit salad

½	RIPE CANTALOUPE, CUT INTO BITE-SIZED CHUNKS OR MELON BALLS
½	FRESH PINEAPPLE, PEELED, CORED AND CUT INTO BITE-SIZED CHUNKS
1	MANGO, PEELED, PITTED AND CUT INTO BITE-SIZED CHUNKS
	EDIBLE ROSE PETALS, VIOLETS, OR MINT SPRIGS

To make the syrup, bring the water, ginger root, sugar, and spices to a boil in a small, uncovered saucepan. Reduce the heat to low and simmer for 20 to 25 minutes, until the syrup coats a spoon with a sticky film. Cool for about 10 minutes and strain into a glass jar. You should have about 1¼ cups of syrup.

Assemble the fruit chunks in a large bowl. Drizzle about ¼ cup of the cooled syrup over the fruit and toss gently. Top with roses, violets, or mint sprigs. Serve immediately.

Store the extra syrup in the refrigerator and use for other fruit salads or mix to taste with sparkling water as a beverage.

CASHEW BUTTERSCOTCH BARS

Are you hankering for a rich, sultry taste from down South? Sink your teeth into this chewy dessert bar: Sweet butterscotch interlaced with salty toasted cashews. Browning the butter before mixing in the other ingredients intensifies the buttery flavor. Straining the butter once is plenty; don't worry about removing all of the brown particles (the milk solids).

1½ CUPS RAW UNSALTED CASHEWS

1 TEASPOON SALT

½ CUP BUTTER

½ CUP BROWN SUGAR, PACKED

1 EGG

2 TEASPOONS PURE VANILLA EXTRACT

1¾ CUPS UNBLEACHED WHITE FLOUR

YIELDS 24 BARS
PREPARATION TIME: 35 MINUTES
BAKING TIME: 25 TO 30 MINUTES

syrup

3 TABLESPOONS BUTTER

⅓ CUP SUGAR

2 TABLESPOONS WATER

Preheat the oven to 350°. Butter and flour a 9 x 13-inch baking pan.

Toast the cashews on an unoiled baking sheet for 7 to 10 minutes, until golden; then chop, toss with ¾ teaspoon of the salt, and set aside to cool.

In a heavy skillet or saucepan, heat the butter until it begins to bubble, turn amber colored, and leave tiny brown particles on the bottom of the pan. Strain through a fine-mesh sieve and refrigerate for 10 minutes.

Beat the brown sugar, egg, and vanilla into the cooled butter until creamy. Sift in the remaining ¼ teaspoon of salt and half of the flour; mix until blended. Sift in the rest of the flour and mix until the dough is stiff and forms a ball. Press the dough evenly into the bottom of the prepared pan and set aside.

For the syrup, warm the butter and sugar on medium-low heat in a saucepan just until the mixture bubbles vigorously and the sugar begins to melt. Add the water and stir until most of the sugar has melted into syrup. Toss the cashews in the syrup and spread evenly over the dough.

Bake for about 25 minutes, until just golden and firm. Cool and then cut into 24 bars—6 rows x 4 columns. Store in a container with a tight-fitting lid.

SUMMER SOLSTICE: A CHESAPEAKE DINNER

Crab Cakes with Versatile Sour Cream Sauce
Corn on the Cob (page 106)
Red Cabbage Slaw
Quick Cucumber Pickle
Iced Tea, Lemonade, or Peach Fizz (page 23)
The sweetest melon of the season

By connection or coincidence, six of Moosewood's nineteen collective members hold the Chesapeake Bay close to their hearts. Each of the six share vivid memories of hot, sticky summers graciously relieved by boating on the bay or by the cooling breezes and temperate climate of Maryland's Eastern Shore. All recall with great relish intoxicating meals of the sweetest sweet corn, the most succulent tomatoes and seafood, and remarkably juicy melons.

Moosewood and Maryland also share a geological tie that is of special interest to food lovers. When the Ice Age glaciers melted in central New York, the sediment from the area washed down the Susquehanna river and collected to form what became Maryland's Eastern Shore, the peninsula that created the Chesapeake Bay. This mineral-rich silt, the mild temperatures, and the moisture from the Bay gave rise to a superb agricultural terrain that yields some of the finest produce on the East Coast. The Chesapeake's shallow, brackish waters also provided the perfect ecosystem for the region's most renowned delicacy, the blue-fin crab. Indeed, the word *Chesapeake* comes from a Native American expression meaning "waters that abound with hard-shelled fish."

These days, with fresh fish and excellent produce shipped to markets everywhere, most everyone can enjoy a Chesapeake-style dinner, no matter where they live.

To prepare this meal with the least last-minute effort, make the sour cream sauce, the quick pickle, and the slaw early in the day or the night before. The pickles only get better with time. When it comes to the crab cakes, you have some choices. If you're proficient working a number of skillets simultaneously—or if you have an extra pair of helper's hands—the crab cakes can be fried twice as fast.

Spread the table with your easiest oilcloth and paper plates. Bring out the iced tea, lemonade, or Peach Fizz . . . and relax.

CRAB CAKES

Chesapeake Bay inhabitants, though generally an unassuming lot, can become truly haughty when the subject of crab cakes is raised. Fortunately, two members of our Moosewood Collective are Baltimore natives, so naturally we turned to one of them, Dave Dietrich, to develop our crab cakes. His recipe adheres to classic principles but adds some nice innovations.

Now we'll address a few of the controversial fine points of crab cake making. To begin with, what kind of crabmeat should be used? Bluefin crabmeat, whether from Texas, Maryland, or Thailand, is really the only choice. It comes packed in several grades, the most common being special, lump, and backfin. Backfin is both the highest priced and most highly touted; special is the most modestly priced—but let's face it, all crab is rather expensive. Is taking the high road worth it? We doubt it.

Restaurants brag about their backfin crab cakes made without filler. In the neighborhoods, however, the crabmeat often comes from leftover steamed crabs, so the bread crumb filler helps hold the cakes together and extends the yield. We'll side with the time-honored traditions of the local residents.

Our crab cake mixture can be prepared a few hours ahead of time and kept in the refrigerator until ready to shape and cook. In Baltimore, crab cakes are served plain with a knife and fork or eaten as sandwiches on crackers or bread. But for those who are drawn to creamy toppings, serve these cakes with our Versatile Sour Cream Sauce (opposite).

1	EGG
¼	TEASPOON DIJON MUSTARD
1½	TEASPOONS SOY SAUCE
2	TABLESPOONS OLIVE OIL
2	TEASPOONS FRESH LEMON JUICE
1	CUP BREAD CRUMBS*
1	TEASPOON BAKING POWDER, SIFTED
1	POUND CRABMEAT
2	TEASPOONS CHOPPED FRESH PARSLEY
1	TEASPOON CHOPPED SCALLIONS
½	TEASPOON OLD BAY SEASONING

SERVES 4
PREPARATION TIME: 15 MINUTES
COOKING TIME: 10 TO 25 MINUTES

* Pulverize stale or lightly toasted bread in a blender or food processor. Use a white flour bread such as an Italian or French loaf.

In a small bowl, whisk together the egg, mustard, soy sauce, olive oil, and lemon juice. In a separate bowl, first combine the bread crumbs and baking powder and then add the crabmeat, parsley, scallions, and Old Bay Seasoning. Stir in the egg mixture and blend thoroughly. Shape the mixture into eight cakes about ¾ inch thick and 3 inches across. (Or, if you prefer, make four jumbo cakes.)

To pan-fry, heat one or two lightly oiled cast iron or other heavy pans or griddles. Cook the crab cakes for about 7 minutes on each side, until golden and crisp.

To broil, preheat the broiler. Place the crab cakes on an oiled broiler pan. Broil for 6 minutes on the first side. Turn the crab cakes over and broil for 4 minutes more.

note

Total cooking time depends on the size of your broiler pan or griddle and how many you use. If you can cook all of the cakes at once, pan-frying will take about 15 minutes and broiling 10 minutes.

VERSATILE SOUR CREAM SAUCE

This topping can add verve to any fish cake, potato cake, or potato pancake. Or serve it as a dip for crudités, chips, or crackers. At home, we use roasted red peppers from a jar for the sake of time and convenience. One cup of sauce will generously top eight crab cakes.

1½ TABLESPOONS MINCED ROASTED RED PEPPERS

2 TEASPOONS MINCED SCALLION GREENS OR CHIVES

2 TEASPOONS FRESH LIME JUICE

1 TEASPOON PRESSED GARLIC

1 TEASPOON SUGAR

1 CUP SOUR CREAM

¼ to ½ TEASPOON SALT, OR TO TASTE

YIELDS 1¼ CUPS
TOTAL TIME: 10 MINUTES

Gently but thoroughly, stir together all of the ingredients in a small bowl. Refrigerate until serving. The sauce will keep for 5 days in a closed container in the refrigerator.

RED CABBAGE SLAW

The dressing for this slaw was inspired by cole slaws that Moosewood cook Lisa Wichman grew up eating at home in Baltimore. The translucent, cooked mayonnaise strikes a near perfect balance between sour and sweet and adds a shiny gloss to the fuchsia red cabbage and scarlet peppers. We offer a range of both sugar and vinegar, so you can start with the smaller amounts and then adjust the dressing to taste.

We at Moosewood thank Vera George, Lisa's mom, for feeding her family so well.

8   CUPS FINELY SLICED RED CABBAGE*

cooked mayonnaise dressing

¼   CUP VEGETABLE OIL

¼ to ⅓ CUP SUGAR

1   TEASPOON DRY MUSTARD

½   TEASPOON SALT

⅓ to ½ CUP CIDER VINEGAR

1   LARGE EGG, BEATEN

1   RED BELL PEPPER, SEEDED AND CORED
    SALT TO TASTE

* Half of a large head of red cabbage will yield about 8 cups.

SERVES 4 TO 6
PREPARATION TIME: 25 TO 30 MINUTES
CHILLING TIME: 45 TO 60 MINUTES

Bring a large pot of salted water to a boil. Add the cabbage and blanch on high heat for 1 minute. Drain and set aside.

In a small saucepan, combine the oil, sugar, mustard, salt, and vinegar. Add the beaten egg and cook on medium-low heat, stirring constantly for about 5 minutes, until the dressing thickens slightly and just begins to simmer (see Note). Remove from the heat and set aside.

Julienne the bell pepper into 2½ x ⅛-inch strips. Place in a serving bowl and add the drained cabbage. Stir in the dressing and toss well. Refrigerate for 45 to 60 minutes, until cold, stirring once or twice. Add salt to taste. Serve immediately.

note

If the egg cooks too quickly and curdles, whirl the mayonnaise in a blender for 1 minute, until smooth.

QUICK CUCUMBER PICKLE

These delicious pickles are a snap to throw together, and the flavor improves if you let them sit in the refrigerator overnight. We use English cucumbers for this recipe: They are available in markets almost year-round and are fresh-tasting, thin-skinned, and seedless—good character traits for making yummy pickles.

If you have kirby cucumbers in your garden, they will also work wonderfully. Just pick enough to make 8 cups of sliced cucumbers. Be careful to slice off and discard the blossom end of the cucumbers; they can make pickles soggy.

3	TWELVE-INCH ENGLISH CUCUMBERS
1	MEDIUM ONION, CUT INTO QUARTERS AND THINLY SLICED CROSSWISE
¼	CUP LOOSELY PACKED FRESH DILL SPRIGS
3 or 4	GARLIC CLOVES, THINLY SLICED
2	CUPS DISTILLED WHITE OR RICE WINE VINEGAR
1	TABLESPOON CORIANDER SEED
½	TEASPOON GROUND MUSTARD
2	TEASPOONS WHOLE BLACK PEPPERCORNS
2	BAY LEAVES, CRUMBLED
1½	TABLESPOONS SALT, PREFERABLY COARSE KOSHER SALT
¼	CUP SUGAR

YIELDS 8 CUPS
PREPARATION TIME: 20 MINUTES
CHILLING TIME: 1 HOUR OR OVERNIGHT

Cut the unpeeled cucumbers crosswise into ¼-inch slices and place them in a large heatproof bowl along with the sliced onions, dill, and garlic. Place the vinegar, coriander, mustard, peppercorns, bay leaves, salt, and sugar in a nonreactive saucepan and bring the mixture to a boil. Stir until the sugar and salt dissolve.

Pour the hot mixture over the vegetables in the bowl and mix gently. Let stand for at least 1 hour or refrigerate overnight for optimal flavor.

Serve chilled or at room temperature. The cucumber pickles will keep pickling in a sealed container in the refrigerator for 2 to 3 weeks.

DESSERT BUFFET

Chocolate Souffle Cake
Lemon Curd Layer Cake
Cheese-Filled Crêpes with Mango Sauce
Strawberry Mascarpone Tart

In western New York, June is shamelessly lush—with a profusion of sunlight and flowers in every nook and cranny of the landscape. After months of seemingly endless wintry days, we are almost giddy with delight at the sudden, magical change in the weather. We head to the nearest parks, get down on our elbows and knees in the garden, and festoon our porches with baskets and pots of flowering plants. When the first strawberries arrive, it's time to set out for the fragrant U-Pick fields, filling our bellies and buckets until they can hold no more of summer's first bounty.

If we were to choose a month for wanton festivity, it would be June. It's the perfect time for weddings, anniversaries, graduations, reunions, picnics, and garden parties. Days are long and nights are short. It's the month to cast off restraint and embrace whim and fancy. When life is this sweet, why not lavish yourself with a multitude of indulgences, including your most sought-after and dreamt-about desserts?

Here, in contrasting colors and flavors, are a few of our Moosewood favorites: bright pink strawberry tart, creamy mango crêpes, and two cakes—one that is lemony tart and another that is dark, rich, and chocolaty. Serve one, two, or all four desserts on a table set up in the garden and decorated with just-picked flowers, bowls of fresh hulled strawberries, and several cool, refreshing beverages. All of the desserts can be made a day ahead except the mango sauce and crêpe filling, both of which are easy to prepare a few hours before the guests arrive.

CHOCOLATE SOUFFLÉ CAKE

Here's a light and melty chocolate cake that mimics your favorite soufflé. It has a lovely, moist, spongy texture and just the right amount of orange flavor coming through. Fresh orange slices or orange sections make a perfect garnish.

1	CUP SEMI-SWEET CHOCOLATE CHIPS
1	TABLESPOON UNSWEETENED COCOA FOR DUSTING
6	EGGS, SEPARATED*
¼	TEASPOON CREAM OF TARTAR
	PINCH OF SALT
2	TABLESPOONS PLUS ½ CUP SUGAR
1	CUP BUTTER, AT ROOM TEMPERATURE
1	TEASPOON FRESHLY GRATED ORANGE PEEL
	CONFECTIONERS' SUGAR (OPTIONAL)

SERVES 12
PREPARATION TIME: 20 MINUTES
BAKING TIME: 40 MINUTES
COOLING TIME: AT LEAST
45 MINUTES

* Crack each egg in half crosswise and carefully slip its yolk (without breaking it) from one half of the shell to the other, as the whites drain off into a bowl.

Melt the chocolate chips in a double boiler, or use a microwave oven or a heatproof bowl perched over a pot of simmering water. Set aside to cool. Meanwhile, preheat the oven to 350°, butter a 9-inch springform pan, and dust it with cocoa; tap out the excess.

In a deep bowl, beat the egg whites until foamy. Add the cream of tartar and salt and continue to beat until the whites begin to thicken. Gradually beat in the 2 tablespoons of sugar; the whites will become shiny and form soft peaks. Continue to beat for another minute or two, until the whites form perky peaks that almost stand erect; then set aside.

In a medium bowl, cream together the butter and the remaining ½ cup of the sugar for 2 to 3 minutes, until light and fluffy. Add the egg yolks and grated orange peel, and continue to beat for several more minutes, until the batter is pale yellow and fluffy. Scrape the cooled chocolate into the butter mixture and beat until blended. Gently fold the chocolate mixture into the whites; then pour the batter into the prepared pan.

Bake for about 40 minutes in the middle of the oven, until a toothpick inserted 2 inches from the edge comes out clean. The center of the cake will still be soft. Cool for 15 minutes on a wire rack. The cake will collapse slightly. Run a knife between the edge of the springform pan and the cake before carefully releasing the sides of the pan. Cool for at least another ½ hour before serving. If you like, top with a light dusting of confectioners' sugar.

LEMON CURD LAYER CAKE

Lemon curd tastes lots better than it sounds! Its velvety smooth texture and concentrated lemon flavor make the perfect filling for this lavish four-layer cake. Our cake batter uses heavy cream instead of butter—so easy—and it neatly employs the reserved egg whites from the lemon curd.

lemon curd

4	EGG YOLKS*
1	TABLESPOON FRESHLY GRATED LEMON PEEL
⅓	CUP FRESH LEMON JUICE
⅔	CUP SUGAR
½	CUP UNSALTED BUTTER, AT ROOM TEMPERATURE

cake

2¼	CUPS UNBLEACHED WHITE FLOUR
1⅓	CUPS SUGAR
2	TEASPOONS BAKING POWDER
½	TEASPOON BAKING SODA
¾	TEASPOON SALT
4	EGG WHITES*
1	CUP HEAVY CREAM
½	CUP BUTTERMILK OR MILK
1	TABLESPOON FRESHLY GRATED LEMON PEEL
1	TEASPOON PURE VANILLA EXTRACT

frosting

1	CUP HEAVY CREAM
3	TABLESPOONS CONFECTIONERS' SUGAR
1	TEASPOON PURE VANILLA EXTRACT
1	TEASPOON FRESHLY GRATED LEMON PEEL

SERVES 8 TO 10
PREPARATION TIME: 30 MINUTES
BAKING TIME: 30 MINUTES
COOLING TIME: 30 TO 40 MINUTES
ASSEMBLY TIME: 10 MINUTES
CHILLING TIME: 30 MINUTES

* Crack each egg in half crosswise and carefully slip its yolk (without breaking it) from one half of the shell to the other, as the whites drain off into a bowl.

Whisk together the egg yolks, lemon peel, lemon juice, and sugar in a saucepan. Cook the mixture on medium heat, whisking constantly, until the lemon curd thickens and becomes foamy, 5 to 6 minutes. Remove from the heat and whisk in the butter a tablespoon at a time, until the curd is smooth and uniform. Cover and refrigerate the curd until you're ready to fill the cake.

Preheat the oven to 350°.

Butter two 9-inch round cake pans and dust them with flour; tap out the excess. In a medium bowl, sift together the flour, sugar, baking powder, baking soda, and salt. Beat the reserved egg whites in a separate bowl until they begin to form stiff peaks; set aside. In a large bowl, whip the heavy cream with an electric mixer or whisk until soft peaks form. Gently stir the buttermilk, lemon peel, and vanilla into the whipped cream; then fold in the egg whites. Add the flour mixture in thirds and stir just until the batter is uniform. Pour half of the batter into each of the prepared pans.

Bake until the cakes begin to pull away from the edges of the pans and a knife tests clean in the center, about 30 minutes. Cool the cakes in the pans for 10 minutes; then turn them out onto a rack to cool completely.

With a long serrated knife, use a sawing motion to carefully slice each cake in half horizontally to form four layers in all. Place one layer on a serving plate and spread it with one-third of the lemon curd. Stack the second layer on top and spread with another one-third of the curd. Repeat for the third layer, and then top the cake with the fourth layer. Set aside.

Whip the heavy cream for the frosting with an electric mixer or whisk until soft peaks form. Fold in the confectioners' sugar, vanilla, and lemon peel and continue to whip *just* until stiff peaks begin to form. Frost the top and sides of the cake. Chill for at least 30 minutes before serving.

CHEESE-FILLED CRÊPES WITH MANGO SAUCE

These lemony crêpes freeze well, so they can easily be made ahead of time. To freeze the crêpes, first cool them to room temperature; then layer waxed paper between each crêpe, wrap the whole stack tightly in plastic wrap, and freeze for up to a week. The creamy cheese filling and mango sauce are quick and simple to prepare and should be made fresh on the spot.

crêpes

¾	CUP MILK
¾	CUP WATER
2	EGGS
2	TABLESPOONS SUGAR
1	TEASPOON FRESHLY GRATED LEMON PEEL*
1	CUP UNBLEACHED WHITE FLOUR
	PINCH OF SALT

cream cheese filling

½	CUP PLUS 2 TABLESPOONS HEAVY CREAM
½	CUP NEUFCHÂTEL OR CREAM CHEESE, SOFTENED
3	TABLESPOONS CONFECTIONERS' SUGAR
1	TEASPOON FRESHLY GRATED LEMON PEEL*
1	RIPE MANGO, PEELED, PITTED AND CUBED**

mango sauce

2	RIPE MANGOS, PEELED, PITTED AND CUBED**
½	CUP SUGAR
	PINCH OF SALT
1	TEASPOON FRESH LEMON JUICE
1	TEASPOON FRESHLY GRATED LEMON PEEL*
¼	CUP UNSWEETENED GRATED COCONUT, TOASTED***

YIELDS 12 CRÊPES & 1¾ CUPS SAUCE
PREPARATION TIME: 1 HOUR
COOKING & ASSEMBLY TIME:
ABOUT ½ HOUR

* For ease, just grate 1 full tablespoon of grated lemon peel at the start and you'll have all you'll need.

** Mangos have large pits and the pulp is slippery. A shallow slice from end to end along the two broad, flat sides works best. Score the mango flesh of each slice into ½-inch pieces and pare them away from the skin. Peel the remaining skin around the pit, then carefully cut the tender pulp away from the pit and dice it.

*** To toast grated coconut, spread it on an unoiled baking tray and bake at 350° in any style oven for 2 to 3 minutes, until lightly golden.

Use just a few strokes to whisk together all of the crêpe batter ingredients in a deep bowl. The batter will be mostly smooth with a few small lumps. Refrigerate for 30 minutes.

Meanwhile, prepare the filling. In a large bowl, whip ½ cup of the heavy cream with an electric mixer or whisk until soft peaks form. In a separate bowl, beat together the remaining 2 tablespoons of heavy cream, the Neufchâtel, confectioners' sugar, and lemon peel. Fold the whipped cream into the cheese mixture and stir in the mango. Set aside in the refrigerator.

Combine all of the Mango Sauce ingredients in a blender or food processor and whirl until smooth. Chill until ready to use.

Heat a small 6- to 7-inch well-seasoned crêpe pan or heavy skillet until water dances when sprinkled on its surface. Coat the pan lightly with oil using a paper towel or cooking spray. Pour ¼ cup of batter onto the hot skillet and swirl the batter around the bottom of the pan to make a well-rounded crêpe. When the edges begin to curl, which takes about 1½ minutes, lift the crêpe quickly with your fingers or a spatula and flip over. Toast the other side for 30 to 45 seconds, remove from the pan, and transfer to a platter. The crêpe should be a creamy white color with some light brown spots. Repeat with the rest of the batter: Oil the skillet as needed and stack the finished crêpes on the platter.

Cool the crêpes and use within a day, or freeze for later use.

To serve, spread about 3 tablespoons of filling on one half of each crêpe and roll into a cylinder. Repeat with the rest of the filling and crêpes. Arrange the filled crêpes on a serving platter and offer Mango Sauce and toasted coconut alongside.

STRAWBERRY MASCARPONE TART

We all swooned when Moosewood cook Laura Branca sweetened up one of our long, tedious meetings with a taste of her final version of this melt-in-your-mouth tart.

Indulge in this rich, luscious dessert when you find ripe, sweet, beautiful, fresh strawberries. Mascarpone is an incredibly smooth, soft Italian cheese. Don't even think about the fat or calories—life's too short and this tastes too good.

SERVES 8
TOTAL TIME: 1 HOUR

sweet pastry shell

2	TEASPOONS FRESHLY GRATED ORANGE PEEL
¼	CUP SUGAR
½	CUP CHILLED BUTTER, CUT INTO PATS
¼	TEASPOON SALT
1½	CUPS UNBLEACHED WHITE PASTRY FLOUR
1	LARGE EGG YOLK
1	TEASPOON PURE VANILLA EXTRACT
1 to 2	TABLESPOONS COLD WATER (OPTIONAL)

mascarpone filling

2	PINTS FRESH STRAWBERRIES, RINSED AND HULLED
1	POUND MASCARPONE CHEESE (PAGE 398)
6	TABLESPOONS SIFTED CONFECTIONERS' SUGAR
2	TABLESPOONS AMARETTO, GRAND MARNIER, OR FROZEN ORANGE JUICE CONCENTRATE*

glaze

1	TEASPOON CORNSTARCH
1	TABLESPOON COLD WATER
2	TABLESPOONS FROZEN ORANGE JUICE CONCENTRATE
3	TABLESPOONS CONFECTIONERS' SUGAR
1	TABLESPOON AMARETTO OR GRAND MARNIER*

* Amaretto is an almond-flavored liqueur; Grand Marnier, an orange-flavored one.

In a bowl, stir together the orange peel and sugar. Add the butter, salt, and flour. Working quickly with your fingers, rub together the ingredients until the mixture is crumbly. Work in the egg yolk until the dough is pale yellow. Sprinkle on the vanilla and mix with your hands until the dough holds together. Add some of the water, if needed. Form the dough into a ball, cover with plastic wrap, and chill for at least ½ hour.

Preheat the oven to 350°.

On a lightly floured surface, roll out the dough. Lift it into a 10-inch pie plate, flute the edges, and prick the bottom in three or four places with a fork to prevent the pastry from bubbling. Bake for 15 minutes, until light golden; then set aside to cool.

While the pastry shell bakes, halve or slice the strawberries unless they're very small. Combine the mascarpone, confectioners' sugar, and liqueur in a bowl. Gently fold half of the strawberries into the mascarpone mixture, and refrigerate the filling.

Meanwhile, dissolve the cornstarch in the water and combine it with the orange juice concentrate and confectioners' sugar in a small saucepan. Heat the liquid until it bubbles; then stir on low heat for 1 to 2 minutes, until it thickens to a syrup. Cool the syrup to room temperature, and then stir in the amaretto or Grand Marnier. Coat the remaining strawberries with the glaze.

Spread the mascarpone filling evenly in the pastry shell. Arrange the glazed strawberries in one or two rings around the edge of the tart, reserving four large strawberry halves for the center. Drizzle on any remaining glaze. Chill the tart until ready to serve.

variation

For individual tartlets, preheat the oven to 350°. Divide the pastry dough into eight equal pieces. Roll each piece of dough to fit a 3-inch tart pan and prick the bottom with a fork. Bake for 10 to 12 minutes, until lightly golden. Spread each tart with the mascarpone filling and decorate with glazed berries.

If you don't have tart pans, but like this idea, many supermarkets sell disposable, 3-inch foil tart pans at very reasonable prices. At our local markets, eight foil tart pans cost less than two dollars.

WEDDING OR COMMITMENT CELEBRATION

Stuffed Tomato & Cucumber Bites
Chipotle Shrimp or Tofu
Summer Rolls with Peanut Sauce
Umeboshi Sushi
Sushi-Stuffed Mushrooms
Tropical Fruit Kabobs
Greens & Cheese Frittatini
Cheddar Shortbread Hearts with Tomato Lime Pesto
Classic Southern Italian Dried Figs
Grapes & Gorgonzola

Weddings and commitment celebrations are joyous times that should be fun for everyone. For such an occasion, we've chosen a menu of diverse appetizers that offer variety and a chance to foray into the exotic. These hors d'oeuvres are elegant, yet possible for the home cook and a few of his or her friends to whip up. Our appetizers fall into several popular ethnic culinary categories with a balance of complementary tastes and textures. We've taken into account the varied tastes and dietary needs of a large group of people, so at this party, vegetarians, vegans, and none-of-the-above will all eat, and eat well.

And as a bonus, there's no need to worry about linens, silverware, and dishes for different courses. Usually, an ample supply of small plates, stemware, and cocktail napkins is all that is needed, although large cloth napkins are a nice touch to consider, because they can double as "place mats" on your guests' laps.

Be sure the serving area is roomy enough for the guests to move about and eat without being crowded or jostled. For parties of seventy-five or more, consider a double-line buffet. Arrange the tables in an L or U shape in an area where there is good traffic flow and an easy exit at the end. For a smaller buffet, use one or two rectangular or round tables situated so that there is access from all sides. Place the plates, utensils, and napkins at the beginning of the tables and trash bins at the end, so guests can easily dispose of toothpicks, skewers, and plates. The tables can be cleared and refreshed with a clean tablecloth when it's time for the cake.

Many people like to hire specialty cake bakers to make a traditional layer cake because it's such a conspicuous centerpiece at the party. However, if you and your friends are bakers, you could make several of our cakes in place of a single cake. The Chocolate Ganache Birthday Cake (page 376), the Lemon Curd Layer Cake (page 56), and the White Chocolate & Fig Poundcake (page 378) work well together and can be lavishly decorated with fresh, edible flowers. Or, if you want to make your own wedding cake, see the Festive Celebrations Cake in *Moosewood Restaurant Book of Desserts* (pages 96–97).

The best advice for any celebration is to do as much as you can days, even weeks, ahead of time. Here's a quick guide to what can be prepared in advance.

* Stuffed Tomato & Cucumber Bites: Filling can be made up to 3 days ahead and stored refrigerated. Stuff the tomatoes and cucumbers right before serving.
* Chipotle Shrimp or Tofu: Sauce can be made up to 3 days ahead and chilled.
* Summer Rolls: Filling can be made a day ahead. Store refrigerated.
* Tropical Fruit Kabobs: Chill the melons overnight. Make the marinade a day ahead.
* Greens & Cheese Frittatini: Wrappers can be made, filled, and rolled as much as 24 hours ahead. Store in plastic wrap in the refrigerator; slice just before serving.
* Cheddar Shortbread Hearts: Bake up to a week ahead; store in sealed containers.
* Tomato Lime Pesto: Make up to 3 days before serving and store refrigerated.
* Grapes & Gorgonzola: Can be made a day before the event and stored in the refrigerator. Roll the grapes in additional ground almonds before serving.

Like any virtuoso performance, the presentation of food for a wedding or commitment celebration needs a beautiful set, stage management, and interesting lighting. To set the stage, we invite you to imagine a celebration late in the afternoon on a glorious summer day. Buffet tables are set up in a backyard or park. Drinks are self-serve, in a shady area near fragrant flower gardens. The centerpiece is a vase filled with an impressive arrangement of garden and wild flowers, surrounded by bunches of grapes and Queen Anne cherries. Next to the bouquet is a silver frame with a calligraphed menu. Wood, porcelain, glass, silver, and copper, as well as baskets, decorative mats, and fans are used to display the food.

Dishes are grouped together by cuisine, and platters and decorations imaginatively reflect the different cultures. The snowy rice paper Summer Rolls are arranged on a bed of crimson aduki beans, the Tropical Fruit Kabobs are on a platter lined with banana leaves. Purple kale, arugula, fresh herbs, local and tropical fruits and vegetables, and edible flowers are abundant. The table linens, in keeping with the romantic theme, are strewn with rose petals and red candy hearts.

After the guests are satiated and are lingering contentedly over the last sips of wine and coffee, evening softly falls. Strands of twinkle lights strung near the tables light up. Candles along the garden path are set aglow. In this romantic, peaceful setting, love abounds.

Make lavish use of the following edible flowers as garnishes, to decorate a summer buffet table and set a festive tone.

* **Carnations** or **Clove Pinks** Clove-flavored petals; cinnamon fragrance.

* **Chrysanthemums** Used in Asian cuisine; pungent flavor.

* **Daylilies** Wide variety of multihued, showy blooms.

* **Hollyhocks** Graceful, elegant garnishes.

* **Marigolds** Can be used whole, or the petals sprinkled over platters.

* **Nasturtiums** Popular decorations; peppery flavor and floral fragrance.

* **Pansies, Violets, Violas** Light, sweet taste, perfect for pressing into icing.

* **Roses** Can be used in bud, full flower, or as petals. Delicious added to drinks.

* **Sunflowers** Large showy petals; use as a bed for desserts or fruit.

STUFFED TOMATO & CUCUMBER BITES

The filling in this recipe is briny and intensely flavored and has a lovely purple-black hue. It's a delicious stuffing for bite-sized, hollowed-out cherry tomatoes and pastel-green cucumbers.

2½ CUPS GRATED FETA CHEESE

2 CUPS PITTED, COARSELY CHOPPED KALAMATA OLIVES

2 GARLIC CLOVES, MINCED OR PRESSED

¼ CUP OLIVE OIL

28 to 30 ROUND CHERRY TOMATOES (NOT GRAPE TOMATOES)

3 LARGE CUCUMBERS

LEAVES OF ASSORTED GREENS (OPTIONAL)
CHOPPED FRESH PARSLEY OR PARSLEY SPRIGS

YIELDS ENOUGH FILLING FOR ABOUT 30 CHERRY TOMATOES AND 30 CUCUMBER SEGMENTS
TOTAL TIME: 30 MINUTES

Place the feta, olives, garlic, and olive oil in a food processor and pulse until you have a fairly smooth paste. Depending on the capacity of your food processor, it may be necessary to do this in batches. Set the filling aside.

Slice off the tops of the cherry tomatoes and use a teaspoon to carefully remove the pulp and seeds. If necessary, use a paring knife to gently cut through the pulp, but be sure to leave the tomato shell intact. Stuff each tomato shell with about 2 teaspoons of the filling.

Peel the cucumbers, cut them in half lengthwise, and scoop out the seeds with a spoon. Fill each cucumber shell with the cheese and olive filling and then slice crosswise into 1-inch-thick pieces.

Arrange the stuffed tomatoes and cucumber segments on large, colorful serving platters, or on platters covered with assorted greens. Top with chopped parsley or parsley sprigs.

CHIPOTLE SHRIMP OR TOFU

This is elegant party food that tastes exotic but is easy to prepare. The flavors of cumin and smoky-hot chipotle peppers add a delicious dimension to the roasted vegetable sauce. We love the sauce on both shrimp and tofu, so we include a tofu variation. If you want to please everyone, vegetarians and non-vegetarians alike, replace 1½ pounds of the shrimp with about 24 ounces of tofu, and serve both!

If the appetizer will not be served immediately after preparation, keep it warm in a chafing dish. To serve, arrange the shrimp, or tofu, on a colorful platter, ring with avocado slices and jicama matchsticks, and drizzle with fresh lemon juice. The smooth and crunchy garnishes will cool the taste buds in between bites of spicy appetizer. For more decoration, add cherry tomatoes, chopped scallions, and minced fresh cilantro.

3	LARGE TOMATOES, CUT INTO WEDGES (ABOUT 4 CUPS)
2	ONIONS, SLICED (ABOUT 2 CUPS)
6	GARLIC CLOVES, COARSELY CHOPPED
	PINCH OF SALT
3	TABLESPOONS EXTRA-VIRGIN OLIVE OIL OR OLIVE OIL
1	TABLESPOON CUMIN SEEDS
¼	TEASPOON GROUND CLOVES
1 to 2	CANNED CHIPOTLE PEPPERS IN ADOBO SAUCE, OR TO TASTE*
3	POUNDS MEDIUM SHRIMP, PEELED AND DEVEINED
	SALT TO TASTE

SERVES UP TO 24
TOTAL TIME: 1 HOUR FOR
SHRIMP, 1¾ HOURS FOR TOFU

* Look for canned chipotles in adobo sauce in small jars or cans in the ethnic section of supermarkets. Chipotles are smoked hot peppers and adobo sauce is a spicy thick tomato purée flavored by the peppers.

Preheat the oven to 450°. Lightly oil a nonreactive baking sheet.

Spread the tomato wedges and the onion slices on the baking sheet. Sprinkle with the garlic and salt, drizzle with 2 tablespoons of the oil, and toss well. Roast for about 30 minutes, stirring every 10 minutes, until the tomatoes are tender and the onions are brown at the edges (see Note).

Meanwhile, toast the cumin seeds in an unoiled frying pan just until fragrant, about 1 minute. Grind to a powder with a mortar and pestle or in a spice grinder.

When the vegetables are roasted, place them in a blender or food processor with the ground cumin, cloves, and the remaining tablespoon of oil and purée to make a smooth sauce. Add the chipotle peppers one at a time, to taste, puréeing briefly after each addition.

Transfer the sauce to a sauté pan and warm on medium heat, stirring constantly. When hot, add the shrimp, stir well, and cook until opaque, about 5 minutes. Add salt to taste.

note

We like the flavor of the roasted vegetables but, if you want to save time, simmer them on the stove top for 10 to 15 minutes.

variation

To replace the shrimp with tofu, sandwich three 16-ounce cakes of firm tofu between two baking trays and rest a heavy can or book on the top tray. Press for 15 to 20 minutes and then drain the expressed liquid.

While the tofu is pressing, roast the tomatoes and onions, and make the sauce as above. Set aside. Reduce the oven to 375°. Slice each cake of pressed tofu horizontally into thirds. Stack the slices and then cut through all three layers on the two diagonals, making an X. This will yield 12 triangular pieces of tofu per cake. In a small bowl, whisk together ¼ cup of soy sauce, ¼ cup of vegetable oil, and ¼ cup of water. Arrange the tofu triangles on an oiled baking sheet, and toss with the soy sauce mixture. Bake until the tofu is crisp around the edges, 45 to 60 minutes, gently turning the tofu at 15-minute intervals. Heat the reserved sauce in a large skillet and add the baked tofu. Toss gently and add salt to taste.

SUMMER ROLLS WITH PEANUT SAUCE

These lovely little packets are a hybrid of much of what we love about Southeast Asian cookery. Crisp vegetables, fresh herbs, and a sultry dipping sauce that recalls favorite Thai and Vietnamese meals.

Rice paper discs or wrappers generally can be found in the ethnic section of well-stocked supermarkets, usually in boxes of thirty. They are very fragile and sometimes split while handling, so it's a good idea to have extras on hand. If you don't have a lot of countertop space, you can soften and fill the wrappers one at a time.

We like to tie these rolls with scallion greens or chives and display them on a brilliantly colored platter festooned with scallion brushes. See the note at the end for directions on tying the rolls and making scallion brushes.

**YIELDS 48 ROLLS,
2 CUPS OF DIPPING SAUCE
SERVES UP TO 24
TOTAL TIME: 1 HOUR**

peanut dipping sauce

6	TABLESPOONS PEANUT BUTTER
¾	CUP HOISIN SAUCE
½	CUP FRESH LIME JUICE
½ to ¾	TEASPOON CAYENNE

filling

½	CUP MINCED SCALLIONS
¼	CUP CHOPPED FRESH BASIL
¼	CUP CHOPPED FRESH CILANTRO
¼	CUP CHOPPED FRESH MINT
16	OUNCES TOFU-KAN OR OTHER SEASONED TOFU (PAGE 402), FINELY DICED
3	CUPS PEELED, SEEDED AND FINELY CHOPPED CUCUMBERS
3	CUPS PEELED AND GRATED CARROTS
3	CUPS FINELY SLICED OR SHREDDED NAPA CABBAGE OR ROMAINE LETTUCE, OR FRESH MUNG BEAN SPROUTS

55 to 60 RICE PAPER DISCS, 8 INCHES ACROSS

FRESH CHIVES (AT LEAST 4 OUNCES) OR SCALLIONS (SEE NOTE)

In a small bowl, whisk together all of the dipping sauce ingredients until smooth and set aside.

In a large bowl, gently toss together all of the filling ingredients. Dampen a large clean dish cloth and lay it flat on a work surface.

Fill a large bowl with hot water. Holding a rice paper disc by the edge, gently lower one side of it into the hot water—it will soften as it absorbs water. Slowly turn the disc in the water until it has completely softened, taking care not to force it or it may tear or crack. Place the disc on the damp towel and flatten it out. Soften several more discs and lay them side by side on the towel; don't overlap them or they'll stick together.

Mound ¼ cup of the filling just below the center of each disc (above the 6 o'clock position on a clock face). Fold the two side edges of the wrapper over the filling to form a rectangular shape with curved ends. Tightly roll up from the bottom to make a neat little 3-inch package. Place, seam side down, on a platter. Repeat until all of the filling is used. Cover with plastic wrap and chill for no more than 5 hours before serving or the rice paper becomes gummy.

note

To make ties for the rolls, bring a small pot of water to a boil. If you are using scallions, slice off the white part and reserve for the scallion brushes, and cut the green parts in half lengthwise. In batches, blanch for 10 seconds enough chives, or scallion greens, to tie all of your rolls. Immediately transfer them to a bowl of ice water for 10 seconds, remove, and drain well. Tie each summer roll around the middle with a chive or scallion ribbon and, if it's too long, snip off the ends.

To make scallion brushes, slice the roots from the reserved whites. With a sharp knife, vertically score the white of each scallion just shy of its center in 3 to 5 places, rotating the scallion each time you score it. Immerse in ice water and watch it open.

UMEBOSHI SUSHI

Many sushi bars in this country (and some abroad) have begun to serve sushi rolls with purely vegetarian fillings. Often called *nori-maki* on the menu, these rolls have the appeal of traditional sushi without the fish and eggs.

The dark, chewy nori wrapper, made from seaweed, is filled with sweet sticky rice and slivers of colorful crisp vegetables and served with a spicy or mild sauce. Each piece looks like a miniature mosaic. Nori rolls are virtually fat-free, so they are nutritious as well as delicious, and especially beautiful when surrounded by nasturtiums or marigolds.

A bamboo rolling mat, or *sudore,* available in Asian food stores, facilitates easy assembly, but it's not impossible to make the rolls using a smooth dish towel or just your hands.

This recipe uses regular short-grain brown rice rather than the traditional white sushi rice. Short-grain white rice can also be used. The key is to use freshly cooked moist rice that is neither dry nor mushy. Umeboshi vinegar (*umesu*) and umeboshi paste are made with Japanese pickled plums that derive their color from the red shiso leaves used in the pickling process. Both are a deep fuschia with a complex flavor that is at once sweet, sour, and salty. They are available bottled in natural foods stores. The Macrobiotic Company of North Carolina imports them from Japan and supplies them to groceries and food co-ops for bulk purchase.

YIELDS 48 PIECES
SERVES UP TO 24
TOTAL TIME: 1½ HOURS

rice mixture

2   CUPS SHORT-GRAIN BROWN RICE
3½ CUPS WATER
1   SIX-INCH PIECE OF KONBU (OPTIONAL)*
¼   CUP UMEBOSHI VINEGAR OR RICE VINEGAR
½   CUP MIRIN

filling

30 to 35 SPINACH LEAVES, THICK STEMS REMOVED
1   RED BELL PEPPER, CUT INTO 1 X ¼-INCH MATCHSTICKS
1   RIPE HASS AVOCADO**
2   TEASPOONS FRESH LEMON JUICE
     DASH OF SALT
8   SHEETS OF NORI
3   TABLESPOONS UMEBOSHI PLUM PASTE

dipping sauce

2   TEASPOONS WASABI POWDER (OPTIONAL)***
2 to 4 TEASPOONS WATER
¼   CUP SOY SAUCE
2 to 4 TEASPOONS SAKE OR RICE VINEGAR

 * Use dried konbu seaweed, also called kelp. It has long, thick, olive-brown leaves and
   is available in Asian and natural food stores.

** Slice around the avocado lengthwise, twist the halves apart, and coax the pit out with
   the tip of a spoon. Be sure to use a ripe avocado. It should yield slightly to pressure.

*** Made from a Japanese radish root of the same name, this spicy hot condiment is
    available in Asian and natural food stores and wherever sushi is sold.

In a pot, combine the rice, water, and konbu, if using. Cover and bring to a
boil, then lower the heat and simmer for about 45 minutes, until the rice is
soft and has absorbed the water. Meanwhile, stir together the vinegar and
mirin and set aside.

While the rice cooks, blanch the spinach in a small amount of boiling water
for 1 minute. Drain and chop coarsely. Blanch the bell pepper pieces in boiling water for about 2 minutes, until crisp-tender and bright red. Drain and
set aside. Scoop the flesh from the avocado halves and slice through the
stem end into ¼-inch-wide pieces. Sprinkle the avocado with lemon juice
and salt to retard discoloration and set aside. Lightly toast the nori by waving it over a very low open flame for about 30 seconds. Mix the umeboshi
plum paste, which is sometimes lumpy, until it is smooth and spreadable.

In a small bowl, mix the wasabi powder and water to form a paste. In
another bowl, combine the soy sauce and sake or rice vinegar. Set aside.

When the rice is ready, remove the konbu and stir in the reserved vine-
gar/mirin mixture. Spread the rice on a platter to cool slightly. If you wish,
fan it vigorously while mixing with a flat wooden spatula until it shines.
Now you're ready to assemble the nori rolls.

Place a nori sheet on the *sudore* and align the bottom edges. Moisten your
hands with water and a little vinegar. Evenly spread about ½ cup of rice on
the nori, leaving an inch of the top and bottom borders uncovered. About
one-third of the way up from the bottom, make a horizontal ½-inch-wide
depression in the rice. Spread 1 teaspoon of the umeboshi paste along it,

cover it with a thin layer of spinach, and arrange julienned peppers and avocados side by side in a single layer on the spinach.

Lift up the *sudore* at the bottom edge (closest to you) and begin to roll. Tuck the nori wrapper under as if making a jelly roll, but be sure to keep the bottom edge of the *sudore* free of the roll. Continue rolling to the top edge of the *sudore*, pressing down gently, evenly, and steadily with the palms of both hands to form a firm, well-shaped nori roll. Moisten the uncovered top edge with a little water to help seal the roll.

When you finish making all eight rolls, use a sharp, wet knife to trim the ends of the rolls; then slice each roll into six equal pieces. Stir the wasabi paste into the soy sauce mixture just before serving. Arrange the sushi rolls cut side up on a platter and serve with the bowl of dipping sauce in the center.

SUSHI-STUFFED MUSHROOMS

Here is an appetizer that makes use of the Umeboshi Sushi recipe, but doesn't require the nori wrappers or the *sudore* rolling technique. Smaller mushroom caps are good for appetizers, but larger mushroom caps, such as portabellos, can make a nice dinner centerpiece.

1	RECIPE UMEBOSHI SUSHI INGREDIENTS (PAGE 70)
48	MUSHROOMS (ABOUT 2 POUNDS), STEMMED
2	TABLESPOONS VEGETABLE OIL

SERVES 16 TO 24
TOTAL TIME: 1¼ HOURS

Make the rice mixture as described on page 71. Meanwhile, blanch and chop the spinach. Dice the bell pepper and avocado (forget about match-sticks) and blanch the bell pepper pieces for about 2 minutes, until bright red. Stir the lemon juice, umeboshi plum paste, and all of the chopped vegetables into the cooked rice mixture. Set aside.

Lightly grill or sauté the mushroom caps in oil for about 10 minutes, until tender and juicy. Fill them with balls of the sushi filling. Drizzle on the dipping sauce and serve immediately.

TROPICAL FRUIT KABOBS

A honey-pineapple glaze, laced with a hint of rum, enhances the refreshing taste of ripe summer melons. These multihued fruit kabobs are a colorful addition to any buffet table. Since melon tends to express its juice while sitting, prepare and skewer the fruit right before serving.

¼	CUP MILD HONEY
3	TABLESPOONS LIGHT RUM
2	TEASPOONS FRESHLY GRATED LIME PEEL, OR TO TASTE
3	TABLESPOONS UNSWEETENED PINEAPPLE JUICE*
1	TABLESPOON CORNSTARCH
1	RIPE CANTALOUPE, PEELED AND SEEDED
1	RIPE HONEYDEW MELON, PEELED AND SEEDED
½	SEEDLESS WATERMELON

24 to 30 TEN-INCH BAMBOO SKEWERS

YIELDS 24 TO 30 KABOBS
SERVES UP TO 24
TOTAL TIME: 30 MINUTES

* Pineapple juice is available canned in the juice aisle of most supermarkets and also as frozen concentrate. Dilute the concentrate in a 3:1 ratio of water to pineapple concentrate.

In a small saucepan, whisk together the honey, rum, lime peel, and 2 tablespoons of the pineapple juice. Bring to a simmer on low heat. In a small bowl, whisk together the remaining tablespoon of pineapple juice with the cornstarch. Add it in a steady stream to the honey mixture and cook, whisking constantly, just until the mixture begins to bubble and thicken. Remove from the heat and allow to cool.

Cut the cantaloupe, honeydew, and watermelon into 1-inch cubes. You should have 45 to 75 pieces of each melon depending on the size of the fruit. Using paper towels, pat and dry the cubes while tossing the fruit together. Drizzle on the cooled honey glaze and toss again to evenly coat the fruit.

Alternate types of melon, placing 5 to 7 assorted pieces on each bamboo skewer. You should get 24 to 30 finished skewers. Arrange the pastel-colored kabobs side by side on a large platter. Make a second layer with the skewers perpendicular to the first layer. Continue this crisscross pattern until all of the skewers have been used. Serve immediately.

GREENS & CHEESE FRITTATINI

We discovered that beaten eggs cook up as perfect wrappers that can be rolled and sliced crosswise into delicious bite-sized pinwheels with spirals of green or pink filling. No, we didn't use food coloring—ruby chard makes a slightly outrageous pink-colored filling and spinach makes a deep green one.

Arrange the frittatini slices on pretty platters and garnish with red grapes, red pepper strips, cherry tomatoes, and sprigs of fresh dill for a colorful presentation.

wrapper

YIELDS 5 WRAPPERS, 60 TO 65 PINWHEELS
PREPARATION TIME: 45 MINUTES
CHILLING TIME: AT LEAST 1 HOUR
AND UP TO 24 HOURS

10	LARGE EGGS
10	TEASPOONS WATER
1¼	TEASPOONS SALT
1¼	TEASPOONS GROUND BLACK PEPPER
2 to 4	TABLESPOONS OLIVE OIL

filling

10	OUNCES FRESH SPINACH OR 1 LARGE BUNCH RUBY CHARD (ABOUT 8 CUPS COARSELY CHOPPED)*
2	TEASPOONS OLIVE OIL
2	GARLIC CLOVES, MINCED OR PRESSED
¼	TEASPOON SALT
½	CUP NEUFCHÂTEL OR CREAM CHEESE, SOFTENED (4 OUNCES)
⅔	CUP GRATED PARMESAN CHEESE
1	TABLESPOON CHOPPED FRESH DILL

* We like the taste of the filling with either spinach or chard, but ruby chard will give a pink hue to the filling.

For each wrapper, beat 2 eggs at a time in a small bowl with 2 teaspoons water, ¼ teaspoon salt, and ¼ teaspoon pepper. Heat 2 teaspoons of oil in a large 10-inch cast iron or nonstick skillet until water sprinkled on the surface dances. (The skillet really must be this large to get five wrappers of the right size and thickness). Pour in the egg mixture and tilt the pan to spread it evenly. Cover the skillet and cook on medium-high heat for 2 to 3 minutes, until the eggs are firm and the edges are getting dry. Carefully lift the wrapper with a spatula and turn it over. Cook for 1 minute or less, until the second side has light brown spots. Turn out onto a large plate that's covered with a paper towel.

Add 1 to 2 teaspoons of oil to the skillet (the amount will depend on how well-seasoned your skillet is) and repeat the process to make four more wrappers, placing a paper towel between each wrapper to absorb any extra oil. Set aside while you make the filling.

Rinse the spinach or chard and tear or chop the leaves. Warm the oil in a large pot and cook the garlic for about a minute, stirring constantly so that it doesn't burn. Add the greens with whatever water clings to them, and the salt, and cook on high heat, stirring often until they are wilted, about 2 to 3 minutes. When cool enough to handle, squeeze out the water, transfer to a cutting board, and finely chop. Place the Neufchâtel in a bowl and add the cooked greens. Mix well. Stir in the Parmesan cheese and dill.

To assemble, evenly spread about ⅓ cup of filling over each wrapper. Roll into tight cylinders and wrap well with plastic wrap. Place on a platter and refrigerate until thoroughly chilled, at least an hour and up to 24 hours. Remove the plastic wrap and cut each cylinder crosswise into slices about ½ inch thick. Use a sharp knife and a back-and-forth sawing motion for neat slices. The end pieces will be too flimsy and raggedy to use, so they are perfect "tasting samples." Arrange cut side down on serving platters and serve cold or at room temperature.

CHEDDAR SHORTBREAD HEARTS

These wonderful wafers are our version of the "goldfish" crackers that we all secretly know and love. The dough is extremely pliable and easy to work. For a romantic presentation, we cut it with a heart-shaped cookie cutter and top with Tomato Lime Pesto (opposite). Arrange on a platter surrounded by nasturtiums and violets or Johnny-jump-ups, and they're sure to elicit *oohs* and *ahhhs*.

The shortbread is especially good when fresh from the oven, but can be stored in an airtight container and kept at room temperature for up to a week, or frozen for about a month.

4	CUPS GRATED SHARP CHEDDAR CHEESE
½	CUP UNSALTED BUTTER, CUT INTO SMALL CHUNKS
1½	TABLESPOONS OLD BAY SEASONING (PAGE 399)
2	CUPS UNBLEACHED WHITE FLOUR

YIELDS ABOUT 4 DOZEN 2½-INCH HEARTS
PREPARATION TIME: 20 TO 25 MINUTES
BAKING TIME: 10 MINUTES

Preheat the oven to 400°.

In a food processor or standing mixer, blend together the cheese, butter, and Old Bay Seasoning until smooth. Gradually add the flour and mix thoroughly to form a dough. (If you use a small food processor, blend in the flour by hand.) Shape the dough into a ball; if it's crumbly, you may need to squeeze it with your hands.

On a lightly floured surface, flatten the ball and use a rolling pin to roll the dough into a ¼-inch thickness. Cut out shapes with the cookie cutter of your choice and place on an unoiled baking sheet about an inch apart. Bake for 10 minutes, or until lightly browned on the edges and bottom. Remove from the oven and cool on a wire rack.

TOMATO LIME PESTO

This simply made pesto has a multitude of uses. We love it on top of Cheddar Shortbread Hearts (opposite) for an elegant appetizer. But a dollop in a soup or stew that needs a little zip is perfect, too. Or try some on pasta, or spread a little on crostini and top with a bit of fresh mozzarella.

1	CUP PACKED SUN-DRIED TOMATOES (NOT OIL-PACKED)*
1	CUP ALMONDS
1	FRESH CHILE PEPPER, COARSELY CHOPPED, SEEDED FOR A MILDER "HOT"
1	CUP CHOPPED FRESH TOMATOES
¼	CUP FRESH LIME JUICE, MORE TO TASTE
	SALT TO TASTE

YIELDS ABOUT 2 CUPS
TOTAL TIME: 20 MINUTES

* We prefer the ones preserved with salt, not sulfites. Their red color is not as bright but their flavor is superior. The only caveat is to add salt judiciously.

In a small heatproof bowl, cover the sun-dried tomatoes with boiling water and set aside to soften for 10 to 15 minutes.

Meanwhile, toast the almonds in a single layer on an unoiled baking tray at 350° for 8 to 10 minutes, until fragrant and golden brown. Cool for a few minutes, then coarsely chop them. When the sun-dried tomatoes are soft, drain them well.

Place all of the ingredients in a food processor and pulse until you have a fairly smooth paste. Add additional lime juice and/or salt to taste.

Stored in an airtight container and refrigerated, this pesto will keep for 3 or 4 days.

CLASSIC SOUTHERN ITALIAN DRIED FIGS

This treat, with its winning texture combo of chewy *and* crunchy, has been made for generations in southern Italy. The natural sweetness of the figs is offset by the intriguing flavors of lemon, fennel, bay, and almond. Prepare the figs at least a week before serving to allow the flavors to deepen and thoroughly mingle.

32	ALMONDS (ABOUT ¼ CUP)
32	PLUMP DRIED CALIMYRNA OR SMYRNA FIGS (ABOUT 1 POUND)
2	TABLESPOONS FRESHLY GRATED LEMON PEEL
2	TEASPOONS FENNEL SEEDS
16 to 20	WHOLE BAY LEAVES

YIELDS 32 FIGS
PREPARATION TIME: 25 MINUTES
BAKING TIME: 10 MINUTES
COOLING TIME: 15 MINUTES
CHILLING TIME: AT LEAST 1 WEEK

Preheat the oven to 400°.

Toast the almonds on a baking sheet for 6 to 8 minutes, stirring once, until lightly browned and fragrant. Meanwhile, cut a slit in the side of each fig with a small paring knife and pull each fig slightly open with your fingers.

When the almonds are toasted, remove them from the oven, but keep the oven on. Insert a pinch of grated lemon peel into the slit of each fig and push a toasted almond in after. Press the sticky sides of the figs closed again.

Bake the figs on an unoiled baking tray for 10 minutes. Allow to cool thoroughly.

In a small crock or wide-mouthed mason jar, layer the figs, sprinkling each layer with fennel seeds and placing bay leaves between layers. Cover tightly and store in the refrigerator for at least a week before serving.

fresh fig flowers

If you are able to find fresh figs at the market, serve them raw in their natural glory. A lovely way to present them is to score each fig into six or eight wedges, cutting just through the skin from the stem end down to the widest part. Peel the skin back, but don't remove it, so that the "skin wedges" look like flower petals surrounding the glistening center. Peel the figs into the flower shapes just before serving. Decorate the serving plate with thin orange slices, fresh raspberries, or fresh mint leaves, if desired—or don't mess with perfection at all and serve the figs unadorned.

GRAPES & GORGONZOLA

Treat your taste buds to a tempest of sensations when you bite into these sweet, succulent grapes rolled in creamy, salty Gorgonzola cheese and a dusting of toasted almonds. Choose red or green seedless grapes that are firm, sweet, and juicy, the bigger the better.

Grapes & Gorgonzola is great paired with other savory appetizers or served as an end-of-the-meal confection. They look beautiful on a white platter surrounded by sliced fresh apricots, nectarines, and kiwis.

¼	CUP NEUFCHÂTEL
½	CUP GORGONZOLA CHEESE*
1½	CUPS ALMONDS**
1	POUND SEEDLESS GRAPES
⅓	CUP BUTTERMILK

YIELDS ABOUT 4 DOZEN GRAPES
TOTAL TIME: 30 MINUTES

* Roquefort, Stilton, or blue cheese are other options.

** Pecans, pistachios, or walnuts can also be used.

Bring the Neufchâtel and the Gorgonzola to room temperature. Meanwhile, spread the almonds in a single layer on an unoiled tray and toast on the "medium toast" setting of a toaster oven until fragrant, about 5 minutes. Or toast them in a regular oven at 350° for 8 to 10 minutes. When cool, grind the nuts in a food processor to the texture of coarse meal. Pour the ground nuts onto a baking tray or large platter and set aside. Rinse the grapes and thoroughly pat dry with a clean cloth or paper towel.

When the cheeses reach room temperature, mash the Neufchâtel and crumble the Gorgonzola. Place in a food processor or mixing bowl, add the buttermilk, and process or beat with an electric mixer until smooth. Or, if you prefer, mash the cheeses together with a fork until smooth, and then whisk in the buttermilk.

Fold all of the grapes into the cheese mixture with a rubber spatula, coating each grape completely. Spoon a grape onto the tray of ground nuts and roll it in the nuts until evenly coated. Transfer to a tray or platter lined with wax paper. Repeat with all of the grapes.

Cover the finished platter loosely with plastic wrap and refrigerate. Reserve extra ground nuts in case any grapes need a final "roll" before serving. Chilled grapes taste best.

FOURTH OF JULY

Portabello Burger Fireworks
Boston Bean Salad
Blue Cheese Potato Salad
Salad Greens with a Dressing for the Season (page 263)
Red, White & Blue Parfait

Fourth of July is a joyous day celebrated coast to coast in the United States. It immediately brings up images of fireworks, picnics, get-togethers, and hilltop views of the colorfully exploding night sky. This holiday comes as a welcome midsummer break in our everyday workweek, and it's a chance to enjoy the hot, sultry weather. What a wonderful time to pack up food and travel to your favorite park or fireworks viewing spot (or to your backyard) to revel in the day off.

It can also be an opportunity to pause and reflect on the origins of this auspicious day. On June 11, 1776, the Second Continental Congress appointed a committee of Thomas Jefferson, John Adams, Benjamin Franklin, Roger Sherman, and Robert Livingstone to draft a formal statement declaring independence from Great Britain. Thomas Jefferson composed it, the committee and Congress altered it during three days of meetings, and they signed it on July 4, 1776. By August 2, fifty-six representatives from all thirteen colonies had signed the document, which now resides in the National Archives in Washington, D.C.

It may be hard to relate the fun we have watching fireworks to the feelings people in 1776 surely had. Even so, we may feel gratitude for those who began this country based on principles of individual freedom and a government answerable to its people. Remembering why we celebrate what we celebrate can be a very good thing.

So here's a midsummer menu that will work inside or out with a finale bursting with the symbolic red, white, and blue. Portabello Burgers are our new twist on the ubiquitous American burger. The Boston Bean Salad and Blue Cheese Potato Salad are fresh takes on traditional July Fourth picnic foods. The salad greens with dressing are a lovely foil for the other salads, but not essential to the menu—you decide. The scrumptious dessert parfait is a gorgeous display of color and makes great use of fresh berries of the season.

We suggest you make part of this menu ahead of time, so that your holiday is more relaxing. Marinate the portabello mushrooms and tofu, if using, on July 3 or very early the following day. If you like, make the bean salad and potato salad a day ahead as well. For the parfait, prepare the creamy cheese mixture and the fruit layers and store them separately until ready to serve the parfait. When you're ready to eat, grill the burgers, set out the finished salads and condiments for the burgers, toss the greens with the dressing of your choice, and assemble the parfait.

PORTABELLO BURGER FIREWORKS

Here are two great marinades, four burger fillings, six hefty buns or rolls, and eight condiment ideas. Choose from among the Pizza Burger, Bleu Burger, Classic Burger, or Tofu Spinach Burger. We love them just as they are, but why not experiment with adding your favorite condiments for an explosion of flavor? Set your taste buds ablaze with ketchup, mustard, mayonnaise, barbecue sauce, roasted red pepper aioli, Worcestershire sauce, or olivada.

Select "bun-sized" portabello mushrooms. It's best if their caps are slightly larger than the buns you use. The marinades will keep refrigerated in a sealed container for at least a week.

6   WHOLE PORTABELLO MUSHROOMS
     DASH OF SALT

SERVES 6
TOTAL TIME: 40 MINUTES

dijon marinade

1   CUP OLIVE OIL
½   CUP BALSAMIC VINEGAR
2   TABLESPOONS SALT
2   TABLESPOONS DIJON MUSTARD
     GROUND BLACK PEPPER TO TASTE

pesto marinade

1   CUP OLIVE OIL
½   CUP CIDER VINEGAR
2   TABLESPOONS SALT
6   GARLIC CLOVES, MINCED OR PRESSED
1   CUP CHOPPED FRESH BASIL
½   TEASPOON SALT
1   TEASPOON GROUND BLACK PEPPER

Choose one of the following burgers

tofu spinach burger with dijon marinade

½   CUP GRATED FETA CHEESE (OPTIONAL)
3   OUNCES SPINACH, RINSED AND WELL DRAINED
1   CAKE FIRM TOFU (16 OUNCES), CUT CROSSWISE INTO 6 THIN SLICES*

bleu burger with dijon marinade

½   CUP CRUMBLED BLUE CHEESE
18   THIN SLICES OF ROASTED RED PEPPERS

pizza burger with pesto marinade

⅔   CUP GRATED MOZZARELLA CHEESE

2   TOMATOES, THICKLY SLICED, OR ⅓ CUP THICK TOMATO SAUCE

classic burger with pesto marinade

1   RED ONION, THINLY SLICED INTO ROUNDS

18   DILL OR SWEET PICKLE SLICES

12   FRESH LETTUCE LEAVES

6   BURGER BUNS OR ROLLS

* If you're making the Tofu Spinach Burgers, marinate the tofu slices overnight in about ⅓ of the Dijon Marinade. If space allows, grill or broil the tofu slices at the same time that you grill or broil the portabello caps.

Rinse and stem the portabello mushrooms. Pat the caps dry with a paper towel, lightly sprinkle with salt, and set aside. Discard the stems or save them for stock.

If you're making the Tofu Spinach Burger or the Bleu Burger, whisk together all of the ingredients for the Dijon Marinade. If you're making the Pizza Burger or Classic Burger, whisk together all of the ingredients for the Pesto Marinade.

Brush the portabello caps with marinade, place them in a single layer in a large nonreactive baking pan, and pour on the rest of the marinade. Marinate for at least 10 minutes at room temperature or, for fuller flavor, cover and refrigerate overnight.

Grill or broil the portabello caps hollowed stem side down for 5 to 7 minutes. Turn over and cook for another 4 to 7 minutes, until juicy and tender. Pay close attention so everything cooks to perfection. Remove from the grill or broiler and allow to cool just enough to handle them.

Divide your remaining burger ingredients equally among the six portabellos and stuff the caps by layering the ingredients in the order listed. Grill or boil the stuffed portabellos until the cheese melts and/or the filling is hot.

Transfer to a platter and serve with your favorite buns or rolls and your choice of condiments.

BOSTON BEAN SALAD

These simple, homey beans are the perfect match for our Blue Cheese Potato Salad (opposite). Or just eat them along with dill pickles or bread-and-butter pickles, whichever you like best.

We suggest you make an effort to buy canned beans that contain no EDTA, such as Flora, Goya, or Eden all-natural brands. Then you get the best of four values: convenience, speed, flavor, and healthfulness.

3   CUPS COOKED CANNELLINI BEANS
     (TWO 15-OUNCE CANS, RINSED AND DRAINED)
2   CUPS CHOPPED FRESH TOMATOES
¼   CUP MINCED SCALLIONS
¼   CUP CHOPPED FRESH PARSLEY

SERVES 4 TO 6
PREPARATION TIME: 10 MINUTES
CHILLING TIME (OPTIONAL):
20 MINUTES

dressing

2   TABLESPOONS MILD HONEY
2   TABLESPOONS DIJON MUSTARD
2   TABLESPOONS CIDER VINEGAR
2   TABLESPOONS VEGETABLE OIL
¼   TEASPOON SALT, MORE TO TASTE
¼   TEASPOON FRESHLY GROUND PEPPER, OR TO TASTE

Combine the beans, tomatoes, scallions, and parsley in a large bowl. Whisk together all of the dressing ingredients and pour into the beans. Gently stir to mix. Add more salt and pepper to taste.

Serve immediately or chill for at least 20 minutes and serve cold.

BLUE CHEESE POTATO SALAD

Party potato salad served on a blue platter with a cherry tomato garnish is a creamy, delicious classic with a twist. What could be more fitting for the Fourth?

To be most efficient timewise, prepare the rest of the ingredients while the potatoes cook. That way everything will be ready to toss together at the same time—with no waiting around at all.

6	CUPS BITE-SIZED CUBED RED-SKINNED POTATOES (2 POUNDS)
1	TEASPOON SALT
1	CUP DICED CELERY
½ to 1	CUP FINELY CHOPPED RED ONIONS, SCALLIONS OR CHIVES
¼	CUP CHOPPED FRESH PARSLEY
¼	CUP RED WINE VINEGAR
3	TABLESPOONS OLIVE OIL
½	TEASPOON FRESHLY GROUND BLACK PEPPER
1	CUP CRUMBLED BLUE CHEESE*
	SALT TO TASTE

SERVES 6 TO 8
PREPARATION TIME: 30 MINUTES
CHILLING TIME (OPTIONAL):
20 MINUTES

* Roquefort, Gorgonzola, Stilton, Danish Blue or a mixture

Place the potatoes in a large saucepan with water to cover. Add the salt, cover, and bring to a boil; then reduce the heat to low and simmer until just tender, about 10 minutes. Drain well.

In a large mixing bowl, combine the hot potatoes, celery, red onions, and parsley. Stir in the vinegar, oil, and pepper and allow to cool to room temperature. Gently toss in the blue cheese. Add salt to taste.

Serve immediately or chill for at least 20 minutes and serve cold.

RED, WHITE & BLUE PARFAIT

Without a doubt, fresh berries are best in the summer. Here at Moosewood we always take advantage of their exquisite goodness while the opportunity lasts. Lucky folks in Florida, Texas, southern California, and other warm climes can make our U.S.A. parfait with fresh fruit year-round, but if you live in colder conditions, don't fret: Frozen fruit that has been thawed works like a charm, too.

This very pretty dessert looks especially festive presented as individual servings in clear wine or parfait glasses or served homestyle in a large glass or crystal bowl.

SERVES 6
TOTAL TIME: 20 MINUTES

2	CUPS QUARK* OR DRAINED NONFAT YOGURT (SEE NOTE)
1	CUP NEUFCHÂTEL OR CREAM CHEESE
2	TEASPOONS PURE VANILLA EXTRACT
¼	CUP SUGAR OR PURE MAPLE SYRUP
1	TABLESPOON FRESH LEMON JUICE
	PINCH OF FRESHLY GRATED LEMON PEEL (OPTIONAL)
2	CUPS PREPARED STRAWBERRIES, CHERRIES OR RASPBERRIES**
2	CUPS BLUEBERRIES, BLACKBERRIES OR BLACK RASPBERRIES**
	SUGAR OR PURE MAPLE SYRUP TO TASTE

* Quark, or *kvarg,* is a low-fat or nonfat unripened soft cheese popular in Germany and other parts of Europe. Made of cow's milk, it has a thick, creamy consistency like yogurt cheese and a flavor much like sour cream. Less tangy than yogurt and richer in texture, quark is commonly used in cheesecakes, dips, and sauces.

** Rinse fresh strawberries, cherries, and blueberries. Gently soak fresh raspberries, blackberries, and black raspberries in water and drain well. Stem and slice the strawberries or pit the cherries. Use the other berries whole. Reserve six whole berries or cherries for topping.

In a blender, food processor, or with an electric mixer, combine the quark or drained yogurt, Neufchâtel, vanilla, sugar, lemon juice, and, if using, the lemon peel until the cheese mixture is creamy, smooth, and free of lumps. Set aside.

Place the prepared red and blue fruits in separate bowls and stir sugar or maple syrup into each fruit to reach the degree of sweetness you desire.

In each of six parfait glasses or glass custard cups, layer ⅓ cup of red fruit, about ¼ cup of the cheese mixture, ⅓ cup of the blue fruit, another ¼ cup of the cheese mixture, and top with one of the reserved whole berries or cherries. Chill or serve immediately.

note

To drain yogurt, line a colander with overlapping paper coffee filters or several layers of cheesecloth. Place the colander in a large bowl. Spoon in 3 to 4 cups of yogurt, cover with plastic wrap, and weight the top with a plate plus a heavy can. Refrigerate for 2 hours; then discard the liquid collected in the bowl. The yogurt will thicken considerably and will yield 2 to 3 cups.

RAINY DAY PICNIC ON THE PORCH

Bedeviled Eggs
Tomatoes & Arugula on Toast
Cornmeal Lemon Shortbread
Peach Fizz

You've got big plans for a long summer's day outside with the kids but, out of the blue, it's pouring buckets and your plans are ruined. The only thing darker than the sky is the gloomy mood in the house. As disappointment gives way to boredom and irritability, with whining close on the horizon, it's up to you to save the day.

With some summer produce, a few pantry staples, and a little finesse, you can turn that rainy day into a memorable event—a kid-friendly feast fest. Enlist their help or, better yet, surprise them with a picnic on the porch. Suddenly, the day starts to brighten with unforeseen promise, and you become a magical wizard of fun.

Now, don't turn on the TV or do anything else predictable and ordinary. Dig out an adventure book to read, unearth an old board game, dress up and act out a story, or hold an indoor treasure hunt. If you don't have a porch, go to the pavillion in the nearest park for your picnic. Wear bathing suits under your raincoats.

All of the dishes we suggest for this spur-of-the-moment picnic are quick and easy to make and use some of the abundant produce you might expect to find in the summer kitchen, such as fresh tomatoes. The delicious golden shortbread is made solely from stock pantry items and needs just a quick patting into the pan before baking as one gigantic cookie to cut apart.

And, of course, if it doesn't rain, or stops raining abruptly, this menu works perfectly well (perhaps even better) for a sunny day picnic.

BEDEVILED EGGS

We've downed our share of deviled eggs at Moosewood over the years, as we're quite sure you have, and usually the scenario is familiar: After eating one or two stuffed halves, satisfaction sets in and you move on. But these eggs surprised us. Their bright lemony flavor with a kiss of fresh basil bewitch the unsuspecting person planning to try just one, and it's almost impossible to stop eating them—until they're gone. Don't say we didn't warn you.

Once you have beautiful hard-boiled eggs, the deviling's easy. To help prevent eggs from cracking during cooking, bring them to room temperature before simmering them and follow our tips below.

6	LARGE EGGS, AT ROOM TEMPERATURE
3	TABLESPOONS MAYONNAISE
¼	TEASPOON FRESHLY GRATED LEMON PEEL
2	TEASPOONS FRESH LEMON JUICE
2	TABLESPOONS MINCED FRESH BASIL
	PINCH OF SALT AND GROUND BLACK PEPPER, OR TO TASTE
12	SMALL WHOLE FRESH BASIL LEAVES

SERVES 4 TO 6
TOTAL TIME: 25 MINUTES

Arrange the eggs in a pot in a single layer and add water to cover by about an inch. Bring to a rapid simmer (not an all-out boil) on medium-high heat, and then remove from the heat and allow to sit for 10 to 15 minutes. Drain and cool with very cold or iced water; then peel.

Slice each egg in half lengthwise. Gently scoop the yolks into a small bowl and mash them with a fork. Add the mayonnaise, grated lemon peel, lemon juice, basil, salt, and pepper and mix until smooth and creamy.

Mound the whites with the yolk filling and top each half with a fresh basil leaf. Arrange on a platter and serve.

TOMATOES & ARUGULA ON TOAST

The combination of mildly peppery arugula, creamy sharp feta, and sun-drenched tomatoes makes a superb summer munchie on crispy toast brushed with olive oil. Cut enough tomato and feta slices to cover the bread.

8 SLICES OF BREAD	
¼ to ⅓ CUP OLIVE OIL	
24 to 32 ARUGULA LEAVES, RINSED AND DRIED*	
4 LARGE RIPE TOMATOES, SLICED	
10 OUNCES FETA CHEESE, THINLY SLICED	
FRESHLY GROUND BLACK PEPPER TO TASTE	
DRIZZLE OF EXTRA-VIRGIN OLIVE OIL (OPTIONAL)	

YIELDS 8 OPEN-FACED SANDWICHES
SERVES 4 TO 6
TOTAL TIME: 20 MINUTES

* If the kids don't like arugula, replace it with a milder-tasting lettuce.

Toast the bread. Brush each slice with the oil and top with 3 or 4 arugula leaves. Layer on the tomato and feta slices. Sprinkle with pepper and, if you like, drizzle with the extra-virgin olive oil. A small feast appears.

variations

When ripe tomatoes are in season, it's hard to get enough of them. On the opposite page are more of our favorite tomato combos, so you're never at a loss for something new to do with those succulent juicy red orbs.

Try a sandwich of tomato slices with any of these combinations:

* Slices of fresh mozzarella cheese, strips of pimientos, chopped fresh basil, a drop of olive oil, salt, and pepper.

* Chèvre spread thickly on the bread and topped with minced fresh herbs.

* Avocado slices, chipotle mayonnaise (stir ½ teaspoon of adobo sauce into regular mayonnaise), alfalfa sprouts.

* Prepared olive tapenade spread on the bread and topped with fresh spinach or watercress.

CORNMEAL LEMON SHORTBREAD

Kids will demolish this buttery, crumbly shortbread in the time it takes you to pour them a glass of milk. A single wedge served with a modest scoop of ice cream or sorbet and accompanied by a hot beverage, such as espresso with a twist of lemon, makes a simple and elegant dessert for the adults in the crowd. Stored in a sealed container, the shortbread will keep for about a week.

1	CUP UNSALTED BUTTER, AT ROOM TEMPERATURE
¾ to 1	CUP CONFECTIONERS' SUGAR
1	TABLESPOON FRESH LEMON JUICE
2	TEASPOONS PURE VANILLA EXTRACT
1	TEASPOON SALT
1	TEASPOON FRESHLY GRATED LEMON PEEL
1½	CUPS UNBLEACHED WHITE FLOUR
½	CUP CORNMEAL

YIELDS 16 WEDGES
PREPARATION TIME: 15 MINUTES
CHILLING TIME: 15 MINUTES
BAKING TIME: 25 TO 30 MINUTES

Preheat the oven to 350°. Line a baking tray with parchment paper (page 399).

In a medium bowl, cream the butter and sugar together until smooth and fluffy. Add the lemon juice, vanilla, salt, and lemon peel. Beat well. Fold in the flour and cornmeal until the dough forms a sticky ball.

Chill the dough for 15 minutes in the refrigerator.

Cut the chilled dough in half and, with lightly floured hands, press each half into a smooth disk about 6 inches in diameter and ¼ inch thick. Place each disk about 2 inches apart on the prepared baking tray and score into eight equal pie-shaped wedges.

Bake for 25 to 30 minutes, until firm and slightly golden. Cool for a few minutes; then carefully cut through the score marks and let the shortbread rest until it's room temperature and firm in texture.

Serve immediately or promptly hide in a cookie jar.

PEACH FIZZ

In Ithaca, New York, it rains so frequently that, as a rule, you can't let it put a damper on your effervescence—otherwise you'd be semi-permanently down in the dumps. Some long-term Ithacans even develop a fondness for rain in all its astounding presentations: warm drizzle, steady downpour, freezing torrent, light shower, thundering deluge, intermittent pitter-patter, driving sheets. But if you need a little extra sparkle some rainy day, picnic or no picnic, try this sweet, bubbling beverage and it's sure to cheer you up.

We prefer a "fruit-juice-sweetened" peach juice—not a peach nectar, which would be overly sweet for this fizz.

2	CUPS CHILLED PEACH JUICE
¼	CUP SUGAR
1	TEASPOON PURE VANILLA EXTRACT OR PURE ALMOND EXTRACT
2	CUPS PEELED, PITTED AND SLICED FRESH RIPE PEACHES THAT HAVE BEEN FROZEN, OR 2 CUPS PACKAGED FROZEN SLICED PEACHES*
8	ICE CUBES
8	OUNCES SPARKLING WATER, CHILLED

**SERVES 4
YIELDS 1 QUART
TOTAL TIME: 10 TO 15 MINUTES**

* Sliced fresh peaches spread on a tray will take about 30 minutes to freeze.
One 16-ounce package of frozen sliced peaches will yield 2 cups.

Combine the peach juice, sugar, and vanilla or almond extract in a blender and purée until the sugar dissolves completely. Add the frozen peaches and continue to blend until the mixture is smooth and creamy, about 2 minutes.

Place a couple of ice cubes in each of the four large glasses and pour about ¾ cup of the peach purée into each glass. Add about 2 ounces of sparkling water to each glass, stir briskly, and serve immediately.

HEAT WAVE DINNER PARTY

Saucy Asian Noodle Salad
Summer Cucumber Melon Soup
Lime Frozen Yogurt
Raspberry Fizz

Usually, we rejoice that it's summertime and the livin' is easy. But sometimes it's too darn hot—unrelentingly hot for days on end. The oppressive air shimmers with waves of heat rising from baked sidewalks and wilted cornfields. Everyone's got fever in the morning and fever all through the night and it takes tremendous effort simply to go about the everyday business of living. The idea of going near a hot stove is like a bad joke. Is this any time to think about entertaining?

It could be. People who live in tropical climates certainly haven't stopped eating or celebrating. They've developed cuisines that wisely use light foods, chosen for their cooling properties. We think that this menu is a remarkably good antidote to harsh heat and it involves almost no cooking. Cucumber and honeydew melon quickly replenish water and minerals lost in perspiration. Buttermilk and yogurt are low-fat coolers to ease the burn. And there's the mentholated relief of fresh mint. The spicy hot ginger and chili paste in the Saucy Asian Noodle Salad retain their vivid integrity even though the salad's served chilled, and they work their cooling miracle as well. Lime is always crisp and refreshing and especially so in our nonfat frozen dessert.

Three of the four dishes on the menu can be made ahead of time. In fact, the syrup, or "shrub," for the Raspberry Fizz *must* be made ahead, since it needs to steep for 24 hours. Both the Lime Frozen Yogurt and the raspberry shrub are long-term keepers, and you can whip them up as soon as the heat hits. The noodle salad is fine made a day or two ahead; give it a fresh squeeze of lemon and a few drops of sesame oil right before serving. The soup is the one dish that's truly at its best when served as soon as it's ready. Blend it as the party is about to begin.

If the urge to entertain suddenly strikes, however, and you decide to make the menu in one fell swoop, here are a few tips. Start by pressing the tofu for the noodle salad and combine the marinade ingredients. While the tofu is pressing, prepare the lime frozen yogurt mixture and get it churning in the ice cream maker. Next marinate the tofu. While you wait for the pot of water for the noodles to boil, prepare the rest of the salad ingredients. Then while the noodles and cabbage cook, you may have time to cube the honeydew and cucumber for the soup. Place them in separate bowls, cover with plastic wrap, and chill until ready to make the soup. Finally, finish the noodle salad, cover it, and store in the refrigerator. If you like, stir together the coriander, nutmeg, salt, and pepper for the soup in a tiny bowl, so it's at-the-ready for the moment of blending. With almost everything measured and chopped, the soup will come together in a flash. So, why not call your friends, the ones who have no chance right now of finding tropical breezes on a balmy beach, and offer them cool enticements to gently revive flagging appetites and refresh spirits. Easy does it. Just keep it cool, boy. Real cool.

SAUCY ASIAN NOODLE SALAD

Looking for a new noodle? Soba noodles have been popular in Japan since the 1600s and they're gaining popularity here in the 2000s for good reason. Buckwheat flour, the noodle's main ingredient, imparts a distinctive nutty taste and plenty of protein to boot. Most groceries now stock soba noodles, but look for the more flavorful Japanese imports in Asian markets. If you're out of soba, linguine or udon noodles will do in a pinch.

To make the most efficient use of time, press the tofu while you assemble the rest of the ingredients for the recipe, and marinate it while you prepare the cabbage, carrots, and radish. It's nice to reserve a small amount of the grated radish and some mung sprouts to garnish the dish at the end.

1	CAKE FIRM OR SILKEN TOFU (16 OUNCES), PRESSED* AND CUT INTO BITE-SIZED CUBES

SERVES 6
TOTAL TIME: 40 TO 45 MINUTES

lemony soy marinade

¼	CUP SOY SAUCE
¼	CUP FRESH LEMON JUICE
1	TABLESPOON DARK SESAME OIL
1	TABLESPOON WHITE VINEGAR
3	TABLESPOONS BROWN SUGAR, PACKED
2	TEASPOONS GRATED FRESH GINGER ROOT
1	TEASPOON CHINESE CHILI PASTE

8	OUNCES UNCOOKED SOBA NOODLES (½ POUND)
2	CUPS RINSED AND FINELY SHREDDED BOK CHOY OR OTHER CHINESE CABBAGE
1	CUP RINSED AND FINELY SHREDDED TENDER MUSTARD GREENS**
2	CUPS MUNG BEAN SPROUTS
2	CUPS PEELED AND GRATED CARROTS
¼	CUP GRATED RADISH, RED OR DAIKON
½	CUP PEANUT BUTTER

2 to 4 TABLESPOONS WATER AND SOY SAUCE IN EQUAL PROPORTIONS

MUNG BEAN SPROUTS
A FEW NASTURTIUMS AND/OR TOASTED SESAME SEEDS (OPTIONAL)

* To press tofu, sandwich it between two plates and rest a heavy can or book on the top plate. Press for 15 to 20 minutes; then drain the expressed liquid.

** Or use spinach, arugula, watercress or baby greens.

Bring 3 quarts of water to a boil in a large pot.

Meanwhile, place the tofu cubes in a single layer in a nonreactive pie pan or shallow baking dish. Whisk together all of the marinade ingredients and pour over the tofu. Set aside.

When the water boils, cook the soba noodles for 8 to 10 minutes, until al dente. Add the shredded cabbage for the final 1 to 2 minutes of noodle cooking. Drain the noodles and cabbage and rinse with cold water. Drain again.

In a serving bowl, mix together the noodles, cabbage, greens, sprouts, carrots, and grated radish. Reserving the marinade, remove the tofu with a slotted spoon and add it to the noodle mixture.

Put the remaining marinade in a blender with the peanut butter and add enough water and soy sauce to purée the mixture to a smooth sauce. Pour the sauce over the noodle salad and toss gently to mix. Top with mung sprouts and decorate with nasturtiums and toasted sesame seeds, if you wish.

Serve immediately at room temperature or cover and refrigerate to serve later.

SUMMER CUCUMBER MELON SOUP

If you start with cold honeydew melon and cold cucumbers and frosty cold buttermilk, this soup is so quick to make that you won't need to chill it before serving. It will be refreshing and soothingly cool right away—perfect for one of those unbearably hot summer days we all know and dread.

SERVES 6
TOTAL TIME: 20 MINUTES

½   HONEYDEW MELON, PEELED, SEEDED AND CUBED
     (4 TO 5 CUPS)

3   CUPS BUTTERMILK

2   TABLESPOONS CHOPPED FRESH MINT

½   TEASPOON GROUND CORIANDER

⅛   TEASPOON FRESHLY GRATED NUTMEG

½   TEASPOON SALT

⅛   TEASPOON GROUND BLACK PEPPER, OR TO TASTE

2   CUCUMBERS, PEELED, SEEDED AND DICED INTO ¼-INCH PIECES
     (3 CUPS)

     DASH OF FRESHLY GRATED NUTMEG
     CHOPPED FRESH CILANTRO (OPTIONAL)

In batches in a blender, combine the melon, buttermilk, mint, coriander, nutmeg, salt, and pepper and purée until smooth. Stir in the cucumbers.

Serve immediately with a dusting of nutmeg and, if you like, a bit of cilantro.

LIME FROZEN YOGURT

This incredibly easy-to-make, creamy treat is fat free! You'll be blissfully unaware of the blistering heat—at least while your mouth's full.

YIELDS 1 QUART FROZEN YOGURT
SERVES 6
PREPARATION TIME: 5 TO 10 MINUTES
FREEZING TIME: ABOUT 30 MINUTES
IN MOST ICE CREAM MAKERS

2   CUPS NONFAT PLAIN YOGURT

6   TABLESPOONS FRESH LIME JUICE

¼   TEASPOON FRESHLY GRATED LIME PEEL

1   CUP SUGAR

Beat together the yogurt, lime juice, lime peel, and sugar in a bowl for about 2 minutes, until the sugar dissolves. Pour the mixture into an ice cream maker and freeze according to the manufacturer's directions.

Store in the freezer in a covered container until ready to serve.

RASPBERRY FIZZ

If you were thirsty in the eighteenth or nineteenth centuries, you might have drunk a "shrub," a refreshing beverage flavored with fruit, cider vinegar, and sugar syrup. In the twenty-first century, we can revive this tradition by using sparkling water to add fizz.

It's important to use a fine sieve or cheesecloth for straining or the pesky raspberry seeds will slip through. You can also use our raspberry shrub (the raspberry syrup concentrate without the sparkling water) as a sweet-acidic fruit flavoring in marinades, sauces, and glazes that are especially fine for roasted vegetables, grilled fish, and salads.

shrub concentrate

YIELDS 2 CUPS CONCENTRATE
PREPARATION TIME: 10 MINUTES
STEEPING TIME: 24 HOURS

1   CUP CIDER VINEGAR
1   CUP FRESH OR FROZEN RED RASPBERRIES
½   CUP SUGAR

SPARKLING WATER AS NEEDED

Purée the vinegar, raspberries, and sugar in a blender or food processor and pour into a nonreactive saucepan. Bring to a boil; then reduce the heat to low and simmer for 3 to 4 minutes.

Transfer the mixture to a glass or ceramic bowl or jar. Cover and let sit at room temperature for 24 hours. Then strain (in batches, if necessary) through a fine sieve or colander lined with cheesecloth, urging the liquid through by stirring with a wooden spoon. Be patient: It takes awhile to strain all of the liquid from the seeds and pulp. When you finish straining the shrub, discard the seeds and pulp.

For a quick, fruity soda, combine 2 tablespoons of shrub with 6 ounces of sparkling water and a couple of ice cubes, and there you have it: a glass of Raspberry Fizz.

Bottled and refrigerated, the shrub will keep for up to 1 month.

LABOR DAY GET-TOGETHER

MENU

Roasted Russets with Chipotle Aioli
Barbecued Tofu & Vegetables
Spicy Grilled Corn on the Cob
Grilled Curried Corn on the Cob
Jenny's Mom's Eggplant
Fruit Cobbler
Two Summer Citrus Coolers
Your Favorite Iced Green Tea

Labor Day is one of the few holidays when we close the restaurant. Because Moosewood is open throughout the day and evening, Collective members have few opportunities to party together. So we've had a Moosewood tradition now for at least 10 years to have a big bash at Penny and Jenny's beautiful lakeside home to mark the end of our super busy summer season.

Labor Day is almost always bittersweet. We're sad to see the days get shorter and chillier but relieved to have our worklife pace return to a somewhat gentler rate. The lake house is a perfect place for this annual event, with its wide, wraparound porches and expansive view of Cayuga Lake. By early September, the lake is about as warm as it gets, and after a refreshing dip, our appetites are ready to indulge.

The menu changes every year. In addition to food prepared by Penny and Jenny, other Moosers will bring a dish to pass, more often than not recipes that are being developed for one of our cookbooks. The result is a multiethnic mishmash that works just fine.

The menu here includes dishes that have recently debuted on Labor Day as well as three perennial favorites, corn on the cob, Jenny's Mom's Eggplant, and Fruit Cobbler. Sweet corn may be the ultimate summer vegetable. It's as if the warmth and goodness of this bright season have been made three-dimensional, and our enjoyment of corn is like a communion with the sun. You can easily guess our rapture over corn by the sheer number of ways we cook and top it, including three tasty options for grilled corn. If you have leftover corn, try Tamale Pie (page 340), Crabmeat Corn Spread (page 44), Roasted Squash with Corn & Beans (page 160), or Black Bean & Citrus Salad (page 344).

This at-home picnic can be pulled together more easily if you make the Roasted Russets, Chipotle Aioli, and Barbecued Tofu & Vegetables ahead of time. The potatoes are good either warm or at room temperature. The aioli should be kept refrigerated until serving time. The tofu dish can be served warm, hot, at room temperature, or even chilled, and should be kept refrigerated once cooked. Reheat it just before serving, if you wish. The Fruit Cobbler can also be made a day ahead, but it's best served warm, either fresh from the oven or briefly reheated.

That leaves the corn and eggplant for last-minute preparation. The toppings for the boiled corn can be assembled ahead of time. However, the grilled corn recipes will require attention during grilling, so an additional cook or helper will be needed to stand guard over the corn while you make Jenny's Mom's Eggplant.

ROASTED RUSSETS WITH CHIPOTLE AIOLI

This recipe was inspired by one of our favorite Ithaca restaurants—Just a Taste Wine & Tapas Bar. We love munching crisp potatoes out back on their flagstone patio. We've adapted their treat by slicing the potatoes into easy-to-eat wedges and oven-roasting rather than frying them.

Russets are good-sized baking potatoes with coarse, tasty skins. Our aioli made with chipotle peppers in adobo sauce and fresh garlic is pretty spicy. At home, most of us make our own mayonnaise, but this throw-together recipe uses prepared mayo, so you can labor less on Labor Day. Leftover aioli keeps for a week or more when tightly covered and refrigerated.

potatoes

SERVES 6 TO 8
TOTAL TIME: 45 MINUTES

6	RUSSET POTATOES, EACH SCRUBBED AND CUT LENGTHWISE INTO 6 TO 8 WEDGES
¼	CUP VEGETABLE OIL OR COOKING SPRAY
⅛	TEASPOON SALT

chipotle aioli

½ to ⅔	CUP PREPARED MAYONNAISE
1 to 2	TABLESPOONS CHIPOTLES IN ADOBO SAUCE*
3	TABLESPOONS FRESH LIME JUICE
1	LARGE GARLIC CLOVE, MINCED OR PRESSED
⅛	TEASPOON SALT

* These spicy hot, smoky peppers are available preserved in tangy adobo sauce. Look for jars or cans of them in the produce section of large supermarkets. Adobo sauce is a thick, spicy purée of tomatoes, vinegar, onions, sugar, and spices.

Preheat the oven to 400°. Lightly oil a large baking sheet.

In a large bowl, coat the potato wedges with oil, sprinkle with the salt, and spread them evenly in a single layer on the prepared baking sheet. Roast for 20 minutes, or until light brown on one side. Turn them over with a spatula and roast for about 15 minutes more, until browned.

Meanwhile, place ½ cup of the mayonnaise, 1 tablespoon of the chipotles, the lime juice, garlic, and salt in a mini-food processor or blender and whirl until smooth and well combined. Blend in more chipotles and/or mayonnaise to taste. Spoon the aioli into a small bowl and chill until serving time.

When the russets are roasted, arrange them on a platter with the aioli in the center and serve hot.

BARBECUED TOFU & VEGETABLES

Barbecue sauces are as much a defining element of summer cooking as tofu dishes are a mainstay of the Moosewood repertoire. Here they're united in a flavorful, easily prepared dish. Our recipe yields 2 cups of sauce.

tofu and vegetables

SERVES 8
PREPARATION TIME: 30 MINUTES
BAKING TIME: 40 TO 45 MINUTES

2	CAKES EXTRA-FIRM TOFU (16 OUNCES EACH)
8	CUPS CUBED RED AND/OR GREEN BELL PEPPERS
16	SMALL ONIONS, PEELED AND QUARTERED
8	CUPS RINSED AND HALVED MUSHROOMS, PATTED DRY
2	TABLESPOONS VEGETABLE OIL

hearty barbecue sauce

½	CUP TOMATO PASTE
½	CUP BALSAMIC VINEGAR
¼ to ⅓	CUP UNSULPHURED MOLASSES*
½	CUP HOISIN SAUCE
¼	CUP SOY SAUCE
4 to 6	GARLIC CLOVES, MINCED OR PRESSED
2	TEASPOONS TABASCO OR OTHER HOT PEPPER SAUCE, MORE TO TASTE

* For a sweeter sauce, use the full ⅓ cup of molasses.

Cut the tofu into ½-inch slices and put them on a baking tray. Place another baking pan on top, and rest two heavy cans or books on the pan. Press for 15 to 20 minutes. When the tofu is pressed, drain the expressed liquid and pat dry with a paper towel; then cut the tofu into ½-inch cubes.

Preheat the oven to 400°.

In a large bowl, toss together the peppers, onions, mushrooms, tofu cubes, and oil and spread onto several large baking pans. Bake for 15 minutes; then stir and bake for another 10 minutes. Meanwhile, combine all of the sauce ingredients in a bowl. Brush the tofu and vegetables with a generous amount of the sauce and return to the oven for 10 minutes. Stir and brush with more sauce and bake until the vegetables are tender, 5 to 10 minutes more.

Serve with additional sauce, if desired.

SPICY GRILLED CORN ON THE COB

You'll really enjoy the sweet mystique of grilled corn sprinkled either with our heady, aromatic North African Spice Mix or with our Jamaican Jerk Spice Mix, which augments the corn's sweetness with cinnamon, nutmeg, and allspice and adds kick with the pepper.

It only takes a small amount of olive oil or butter to help the spices cling to the kernels, and the result is enormously finger-licking good.

SERVES 3 TO 6
PREPARATION TIME: 15 MINUTES
GRILLING TIME: 10 TO 20 MINUTES

Choose one of the following spice mixes:

north african spice mix

2	TEASPOONS GROUND CUMIN
2	TEASPOONS GROUND CORIANDER
½	TEASPOON GROUND GINGER
½	TEASPOON GROUND CINNAMON
	DASH OF GROUND CLOVES
½	TEASPOON CRUSHED DRIED OREGANO
½	TEASPOON SALT
½	TEASPOON GROUND BLACK PEPPER

jamaican jerk spice mix

1	TEASPOON GROUND ALLSPICE
½	TEASPOON GROUND CINNAMON
½	TEASPOON DRIED THYME
½	TEASPOON GROUND BLACK PEPPER
½	TEASPOON SALT
	DASH OF CAYENNE
	DASH OF GROUND NUTMEG

6 UNHUSKED EARS OF CORN
1 TABLESPOON OLIVE OIL OR MELTED BUTTER

Prepare the grill.

Combine the spice mix ingredients in a small bowl or jar. Pull the husks back from the ears of corn without detaching them from the stem ends. Remove the silk. Brush the kernels with the oil or melted butter and sprinkle with the spice mix. Pull the husks back up over the kernels, tie together at the top with an extra strand of husk, and dampen slightly under running water. Grill (page 106), turning frequently, until the husks are dried out and the kernels are tender, 10 to 20 minutes.

Serve immediately.

GRILLED CURRIED CORN ON THE COB

The slightly smoky, sweet flavor of grilled corn is even better when basted with curried coconut milk. At Moosewood we always use freshly ground spices and coconut milk that has no preservatives. Curry powder and garam masala are best when fresh, as their flavor fades over time. If yours have been sitting for a long time on the shelf, it's definitely worth replacing them.

When grilling or broiling the corn, be careful not to let the husks burn. The cooking time will depend on how hot the grill or oven is, so keep watch.

6	UNHUSKED EARS OF CORN
¼	CUP COCONUT MILK*
1	TABLESPOON CURRY POWDER OR GARAM MASALA
2	TABLESPOONS MINCED FRESH CILANTRO
½	TEASPOON SALT

SERVES 4 TO 6
PREPARATION TIME: 20 MINUTES
GRILLING TIME: 15 TO 25 MINUTES

* If you open the can of coconut milk without shaking it, skim off the thick part that rises to the top and use it. The baste will cling better to the corn.

Prepare the fire in the grill or preheat the oven broiler.

Carefully peel back the husks of the corn without detaching them from the stem end. Remove the corn silk. In a small bowl, stir together the coconut milk, curry powder, cilantro, and salt. Brush the kernels of each ear of corn with the curry baste and then pull the husks back to the top.

Grill (page 106) or broil the corn for 15 to 25 minutes, turning often, until the husks are dry and the kernels are tender and just beginning to brown. Remove the husks carefully—hot steam may escape.

Serve immediately.

cooking sweet corn on the cob

boiling

Bring a large pot of water to a vigorous boil on high heat. No salt in the water, please, because salt toughens the skins of the kernels. Hold the sugar, too—if the corn's tough or starchy, sweetened water won't help. Cook the husked corn a few ears at a time, keeping the water at a steady boil. Cook tender young ears just until hot, a minute or less. More mature corn needs no more than 3 to 5 minutes.

steaming (stovetop & microwave)

Remove the coarse outer husks, but not the inner ones. The hot husks help to steam the kernels and also intensify the corn flavor. Don't bother removing the silk. Most of it will stick to the husks when you pull them off later.

In a conventional steamer, place the ears in an uncrowded single layer or stand them loosely upright. Usually it takes 5 to 10 minutes for corn to get "steaming hot," but it varies with the size of the steamer and how packed the ears are.

A microwave is handy for cooking just an ear or two. Place the unhusked corn in the microwave at the highest setting. The rule of thumb is 2 minutes per ear, but it depends on your microwave.

grilling

Choose large ears of corn with plump kernels. Let your bed of coals become glowing and covered with ash. Place the corn on the grill and turn it several times during cooking. Grill bare ears for 3 to 5 minutes and unshucked ears for 8 to 10 minutes.

Is it best to remove the husks and silk before grilling corn? Some argue that husks keep kernels moist and unscorched. Husk-off grillers say that exposing the kernels to the live coals brings out the sweetness by caramelizing the sugars. We suggest you experiment and decide for yourself.

To spread seasoned oil or butter on the ears before grilling, pull back the husks, remove the silk, spread on the butter, and then pull the husks back up to the tops.

oven roasting

This is a good method when you're cooking for a crowd. Preheat the oven to 450°. Peel back the husks, remove the silk, spread on softened butter or oil, and pull the husks back up. Bake in a roasting pan covered with foil for 20 to 25 minutes.

JENNY'S MOM'S EGGPLANT

Jenny Wang's mom, Pilwun, brought this dish to a Moosewood Labor Day party one year, and it became an instant hit. Simply prepared, this stir-fried eggplant makes a succulent side dish for all manner of foods and is also delicious served with rice.

Salting the eggplant causes it to "sweat" and keeps it from soaking up all of the oil the moment it touches the hot skillet. We use balsamic vinegar in our version of Pilwun's hit, but you may choose to use Chinese black vinegar for a truly authentic touch.

12	CUPS CUBED EGGPLANT (¾-INCH CUBES)*
1½	TABLESPOONS SALT
3	TABLESPOONS VEGETABLE OIL
4	LARGE GARLIC CLOVES, MINCED OR PRESSED
½	CUP DRY SHERRY OR CHINESE RICE WINE**
1 to 2	TABLESPOONS WATER (OPTIONAL)
6	SCALLIONS, SLICED ON THE DIAGONAL INTO 1-INCH PIECES
2	TABLESPOONS SOY SAUCE
2	TABLESPOONS BALSAMIC VINEGAR

SERVES 6 TO 8
SITTING TIME: AT LEAST 30 MINUTES
PREPARATION TIME: 15 MINUTES
COOKING TIME: 25 MINUTES

* Two large or 3 medium eggplant will yield about 12 cups cubed. The eggplant may be peeled or not, as you wish.

** A flavorful Asian wine that is somewhat drier than most white cooking wines.

Place the eggplant cubes in a colander, and set it in either a sink or a bowl.

Sprinkle the cubes with a generous tablespoon of the salt and mix well. Let sit for at least 30 minutes or up to 2 hours. When you're ready to cook, rinse the eggplant and gently squeeze the cubes to remove as much liquid as possible. The eggplant will be reduced in volume.

Warm the oil in a wok or large heavy skillet until hot. Add the garlic and swirl it in the wok for 1 minute to season the oil. Add the eggplant and stir-fry on medium-high heat for about 5 minutes. Pour in the sherry and continue to cook for 2 to 3 minutes, until the sherry is somewhat reduced. Cover the wok, lower the heat to medium, and cook for 6 to 8 minutes, until the eggplant is almost tender: Be sure to stir a few times, adding 1 to 2 tablespoons of water, if needed, to keep the eggplant from scorching— but avoid making it soupy.

Add the scallions and the remaining teaspoon of salt. Cover and continue to cook until the eggplant is soft and tender but still holds its shape, 5 to 10 more minutes. Splash on the soy sauce and vinegar, stir well, and remove from the heat. Serve immediately.

FRUIT COBBLER

If you like homey, deep-dish desserts, this cobbler—filled with a potpourri of luscious fruits—is sure to become a mainstay of your repertoire. The topping is a twist on a classic biscuit recipe. We just fluffed it up with an egg and added a little sugar and a splash of vanilla.

The fruit combo we suggest is quite yummy, but other berries could be good, too. Whatever you choose, use a total of 8 cups, and if frozen fruit is all that's available, it will work fine.

fruit filling

SERVES 8
PREPARATION TIME: 30 MINUTES
FINAL BAKING TIME:
20 TO 25 MINUTES

- 4   CUPS FRESH PEACHES, PEELED, PITTED AND SLICED
- 3   CUPS FRESH PLUMS, PITTED AND SLICED
- 1   CUP FRESH RASPBERRIES
- ¾   CUP SUGAR
- 1   TEASPOON FRESH LEMON JUICE
- 2 to 3 TABLESPOONS UNBLEACHED WHITE FLOUR

biscuit crust

- 1   CUP UNBLEACHED WHITE FLOUR
- 2   TABLESPOONS SUGAR
- 1   TEASPOON BAKING POWDER
- ¼   TEASPOON BAKING SODA
- ¼   TEASPOON SALT
- ¼   CUP BUTTER, AT ROOM TEMPERATURE
- ⅓   CUP BUTTERMILK
- 1   EGG
- ½   TEASPOON PURE VANILLA EXTRACT

Preheat the oven to 400°.

Combine all of the fruit filling ingredients in a 7 x 11-inch or 9-inch-square baking dish. Cover with aluminum foil and bake for 20 minutes.

Meanwhile, sift together the flour, sugar, baking powder, baking soda, and salt in a large bowl. With a pastry cutter or knife, cut the butter into the flour mixture until the size of small peas. In a separate bowl, beat together the buttermilk, egg, and vanilla. Quickly stir the wet ingredients into the dry ingredients and mix briefly to make a soft dough. When the fruit is baked, drop the dough in eight equal, evenly spaced spoonfuls on top.

Bake, uncovered, for 20 to 25 minutes, until golden brown. A toothpick inserted in the center of the biscuit topping should test clean. Serve warm.

TWO SUMMER CITRUS COOLERS

The desire for refreshing summer drinks is endless, and of course the options are endless, too. The best ones are cool or cold, not too sweet, and subtly flavored. Here are two sit 'n' sip beverages that can be made on the spot and enjoyed at leisure.

Ginger Lemonade

½ CUP PEELED, CHOPPED FRESH GINGER ROOT

2 WHOLE LEMONS, PEELED AND CHOPPED, SEEDS REMOVED

⅔ CUP SUGAR

1 CUP WATER

2 LITERS SPARKLING WATER

¼ CUP FRESH MINT LEAVES

YIELDS 1¾ CUPS CONCENTRATE
TOTAL TIME: 10 TO 15 MINUTES

Combine the ginger root, chopped lemons, sugar, and water in a blender and purée until well macerated. Pour the concentrate through a sieve into a small glass or ceramic pitcher.

To serve, pour 3 tablespoons of the concentrate into each glass. Add ice cubes and sparkling water, stir, and garnish with fresh mint.

Serve immediately.

Orange Limeade with a Twist

3 VERY RIPE BANANAS

¾ CUP FROZEN ORANGE JUICE CONCENTRATE

¾ CUP FRESH LIME JUICE

¼ CUP PURE MAPLE SYRUP

6 CUPS COLD WATER

1 to 1½ TEASPOONS GROUND NUTMEG*

* If you have whole nutmeg, freshly grated nutmeg is even better.

YIELDS 1¾ QUARTS
SERVES 8
TOTAL TIME: 15 MINUTES

Combine all of the ingredients in batches in a blender and purée until smooth and frothy. Pour over ice in tall glasses and serve immediately. Cheers!

AUTUMN

In New York State, fall, like spring, is a time of seasonal transition. While April gives a sense of beginnings, September foreshadows endings. Both seasons have their own kind of anticipation, their surprises, their unsettledness, and, most assuredly, their good food. Although most of us can get almost any kind of produce any time of year, fruits and vegetables are still a barometer of seasonal activity. When bushels of butternut squash arrive at the market, we think about shaking out the down comforter, planting bulbs, and planning for Thanksgiving dinner.

In autumn, nature delivers the fruits of her labor with the kind of generosity and loyalty we wish we could find more often in our own species. Producing and preserving seem to be the raisons d'être of September, October, and November. While plants pour their energy into bearing their fruits and vegetables, many of us are vigorously gathering the last of the harvest. And as the plants produce seeds and thrust roots farther into the ground, we, too, settle into the shelter of our homes.

The fruits and vegetables of fall have a decidedly different character than those of spring or summer. They are a bit less juicy and delicate, with stronger flavors, darker colors, and a meatier texture. They lend themselves to rich stews and soups as well as sweet and savory roasted and baked dishes. In the northeastern United States, the produce of fall matches the colors of the turning leaves. Golden onions, purple plums, orange squash and pumpkins; green collards and kale; and red beets, potatoes, apples, and late raspberries all blend into a blur of autumn colors against the changing foliage of red oak, poplar, larch, sugar maple, and Japanese maple.

Fall is a cooking time of year, full of the urge to bake pies and make soups and stews. Brisk days stimulate appetites, and early darkness sends people indoors. Suddenly, the kitchen becomes the place where everyone gathers.

In this chapter, you'll discover menu ideas for small, intimate dinners, a large vegan Thanksgiving feast, an unusual Halloween supper, and delightful meals to celebrate Diwali and the Day of the Dead. Whether you traditionally observe these occasions or not, the dinners in themselves reflect the spirit and ambience of this colorful season of harvest and warmth, friendship and family closeness.

TAPAS PARTY

The Spanish word *tapa* means "cover" or "lid." In many small bars or bistros in Spain—called *tascas*—it was customary to give the customer who had ordered a glass of wine a small dish of appetizers on the house. This little plate would be placed on top of the glass, like a cover, when the glass was either brought to the table or served at the bar. Now the word *tapas* has come to mean any appetizers or small foods enjoyed as a first course with a drink. Penelope Casas, who has written about tapas in several fine cookbooks, gives her expert opinion: "*Tapas* are not necessarily a particular kind of food; rather, they represent a style of eating and a way of life. . . . Anything served in small portions can be a *tapa*."

In Spain, the tapas tradition is an integral part of life. For as much as a couple of hours before a late dinner (which typically won't be served until about ten o'clock), Spaniards gather with their friends to have wine, sample tapas, talk, argue, and laugh. Even the tiniest bar in the smallest village will have one or two tapas offerings and big city tapas bars may display an incredible, opulent array. A group of friends may spend an entire evening socializing and moving from *tasca* to *tasca.* Whatever the gathering place, there is usually a spirited, open, friendly atmosphere.

In America, most towns don't have even one tapas bar and most people are accustomed to eating supper much earlier than 10 or 11 P.M. Still, the lively spirit and colorful aura of the tapas tradition can be duplicated at home and will create a relaxing occasion, so much more interesting than the typical cocktail party fare.

Everyone will enjoy eating together and sampling a variety of bite-sized foods prepared to complement each other.

Our tapas menu is a balanced group of small dishes, most of which can be prepared well ahead. You may wish to augment our selection with some purchased foods, such as bread, cheeses, cornichon pickles, olives, or nuts. Or add a few very simply prepared foods, such as hard-boiled eggs or roasted red peppers. See the list below for other dishes in this book that we recommend for tapas.

A tapas party may consist of a small array of dishes, which serve as appetizers to a late dinner; or it might be a lavish spread of ten or fifteen (or even more!) little foods, which replaces a more formal meal altogether.

Tapas can be served with red and/or white wine, beer, sangria (alcoholic or not), or—best of all—with a dry fino sherry, the most traditional accompaniment to tapas. Of course, Spanish wines are the most appropriate. Try an amontillado sherry, such as the one by Valdespino, or go for a Spanish red, like an aged "Crianza" rioja, and you won't go wrong.

Here is a list of other dishes that make great tapas. Be sure to consider color, texture, and ingredients as you plan your party. Go for a balance of light and heavy dishes, sweet and sour flavors, and simple and fancy foods.

SPANISH CHICKPEAS

Here we mix highbrow saffron with the humble chickpea for a fragrant dish that's enticingly spicy and smoky. These beans are tangy and saucy enough to convince even those dubious about chickpeas that they're a good thing after all. If you like, serve them with basmati rice, couscous, or some thick slices of bread for soaking up the juices.

3	CUPS CHOPPED FRESH TOMATOES
4	GARLIC CLOVES, MINCED OR PRESSED
½	CUP FRESH LEMON JUICE
2	TABLESPOONS SOY SAUCE
2	TEASPOONS ADOBO SAUCE*
1	TABLESPOON PAPRIKA
	LARGE PINCH OF SAFFRON
2	CUPS CHOPPED RED ONIONS
1	TABLESPOON EXTRA-VIRGIN OLIVE OIL
3	CUPS COOKED CHICKPEAS (TWO 15-OUNCE CANS, RINSED AND DRAINED)

SERVES 8 TO 10
TOTAL TIME: 20 MINUTES

* Adobo sauce is a thick, spicy purée of tomatoes, vinegar, onions, sugar, and spices available in the Hispanic or ethnic sections of well-stocked supermarkets.

Combine the tomatoes, garlic, lemon juice, soy sauce, adobo sauce, paprika, and saffron in a blender. Purée to a sauce and set aside.

In a nonreactive saucepan, sauté the red onions in the oil for about 10 minutes on medium heat, until softened. Add the chickpeas and the tomato sauce and simmer for 10 minutes, stirring often, until the chickpeas are hot.

Serve immediately.

CAULIFLOWER GREEN OLIVE SALAD

The sharp-flavored combo of garlic, lemon, red onions, and Spanish olives makes this a bracing, bright note to a tapas meal, and it nicely offsets our simple creamy potato frittata and spicy chickpeas. Because the olives are salty, the dressing requires very little salt.

This salad is delicious prepared ahead: Store in a closed container in the refrigerator until ready to eat, then bring it to room temperature and dig in. Serve it in a large shallow bowl or platter with bread for dipping in the dressing. Yum!

dressing

½   CUP EXTRA-VIRGIN OLIVE OIL
2   GARLIC CLOVES, MINCED OR PRESSED
¼   CUP FRESH LEMON JUICE
2   TABLESPOONS CHOPPED FRESH PARSLEY
     PINCH OF SALT TO TASTE

SERVES 8 TO 10
PREPARATION TIME: 25 MINUTES
COOKING TIME: 15 MINUTES
SITTING TIME: AT LEAST 10 MINUTES

vegetables

6   CUPS BITE-SIZED CAULIFLOWER FLORETS
1   RED OR YELLOW BELL PEPPER, SEEDED AND CUT INTO ¼-INCH-THICK STRIPS
1   CUP CHOPPED CELERY, SLICED CROSSWISE ON THE DIAGONAL INTO
     ¼-INCH-THICK PIECES
1   CUP THINLY SLICED RED ONIONS
1   CUP PITTED GREEN OR SPANISH OLIVES, RINSED*

     SALT AND CRACKED OR GROUND BLACK PEPPER TO TASTE

* We prefer sweet, mild olives in this dish, but use more piquant ones, if you prefer.
If using large olives, halve or coarsely chop them.

Bring a large pot of salted water to a boil. Meanwhile, use a whisk or blender to combine all of the dressing ingredients. Set the dressing aside.

When the water boils, cook the cauliflower florets for 4 to 5 minutes, until just tender; then transfer them with a slotted spoon or sieve to a large platter or shallow bowl. Add the bell pepper strips to the boiling water and cook for about 1 minute, until crisp-tender. Drain well and add them to the cauliflower. Gently stir in the celery, red onions, and olives.

Pour the dressing over the vegetables and toss well. Allow to sit for at least 10 and up to 60 minutes before serving—the longer the salad sits, the deeper the flavor. Add salt and black pepper to taste and serve.

MANCHEGO POTATO FRITTATA

Manchego is a wonderful Spanish cheese with a distinctive, delicious flavor. It has a consistency that's slightly softer than Parmesan and it's easy to grate. Although imported cheeses can be a bit pricey, try Manchego here for that authentic Spanish touch. We've found it in the cheese section of well-stocked supermarkets and think it's worth the splurge.

To save time, you can prepare the bell peppers in the recipe while the sliced potatoes are cooking. A nonstick skillet is best for this frittata. If you don't have one, add a little extra oil to the pan before pouring the eggs over the vegetables.

SERVES 8 TO 10
TOTAL TIME: 1 HOUR

1½	TABLESPOONS VEGETABLE OIL
3	POTATOES, THINLY SLICED (ABOUT 4 CUPS)*
1	TEASPOON SALT
1	CUP PEELED AND SLICED SHALLOTS
2	CUPS DICED RED BELL PEPPERS
½	TEASPOON DRIED THYME
½	TEASPOON DRIED MARJORAM
⅛	TEASPOON GROUND BLACK PEPPER
1	TABLESPOON DRY SHERRY (OPTIONAL)
8	EGGS, LIGHTLY BEATEN
1½	CUPS GRATED PEPPER JACK CHEESE
1½	CUPS GRATED MANCHEGO CHEESE

* Cut the potatoes lengthwise into quarters, then slice crosswise into ⅛-inch-thick wedges.

Warm 1 tablespoon of the oil in a medium skillet. Add the potatoes, sprinkle with ½ teaspoon of the salt, stir to coat with the oil, cover, and sauté on high heat for 5 minutes. Uncover and stir almost constantly for 5 more minutes. Reduce the heat to low and continue to cook, covered, for 15 to 20 minutes, until tender and moist.

Meanwhile, heat the remaining ½ tablespoon of oil on medium heat in a 12- or 13-inch skillet (preferably nonstick). Add the shallots, bell peppers, thyme, marjoram, pepper, and the remaining ½ teaspoon of salt and sauté for 5 minutes. Add the sherry, if using, and continue to cook for another 5 minutes.

Transfer the cooked potatoes to the nonstick skillet. Use a spatula to mix together the potatoes and other vegetables and distribute them evenly in the skillet. Pour the eggs evenly over all and sprinkle on the grated cheeses. Cover and cook on low heat for 5 to 10 minutes, until the eggs are set (see Note).

Cut into wedges and serve hot.

variation

Use 3 cups Manchego and no pepper jack cheese for a milder frittata, or go spicy hot with all pepper jack instead!

note

For a golden-crusted top, finish the frittata under the broiler. Preheat the broiler when you begin to sauté the shallots and bell peppers. After the eggs and cheese are added to the skillet, place in the broiler with the top an inch or so below the flame. Broil for 5 to 10 minutes, until the cheese is golden brown and bubbling.

CELEBRATE

STUFFED MUSHROOMS

When made with small, bite-sized moonlight mushrooms, one of our stuffed mushrooms is a perfect hors d'oeuvre (just exactly a mouthful). If you prefer to use larger moonlight or cremini mushrooms, halve the number of mushrooms and bake a bit longer, until tender. For a more daring dab of color, don't mix the chèvre into the filling; decorate each mushroom with a bright white cube of cheese instead. Omit the chèvre for a vegan version.

8 to 10 SUN-DRIED TOMATO HALVES (NOT OIL-PACKED)

1   CUP DICED ONIONS

1 to 2 TABLESPOONS VEGETABLE OIL

24 to 30 MUSHROOMS (ABOUT 1 POUND), STEMS REMOVED AND RESERVED

1   TEASPOON DRIED THYME

1½   TEASPOONS DRIED BASIL (2 TABLESPOONS FRESH)

½   TEASPOON SALT

4   CUPS RINSED, STEMMED AND CHOPPED SPINACH

¾   CUP CHÈVRE OR GOAT CHEESE, CRUMBLED

2   TABLESPOONS DRY SHERRY

SERVES 8 TO 10
PREPARATION TIME: 30 MINUTES
BAKING TIME: 25 TO 30 MINUTES

Preheat the oven to 375°.

Place the sun-dried tomatoes in a heatproof bowl, pour boiling water over them, cover, and let sit for at least 15 minutes.

Meanwhile, sauté the onions in 2 teaspoons of the oil in a saucepan on medium heat, stirring now and then, for 7 minutes. Between stirs, brush the mushroom caps with as much of the remaining oil as needed and set aside in an unoiled 9 x 13-inch baking pan. Chop the mushroom stems. Add them with the thyme, basil, and salt to the sautéed onions and continue to cook, uncovered, for another 5 minutes, stirring once or twice. Add the spinach and toss lightly. Drain and mince the sun-dried tomatoes: There should be about ½ cup. Add them to the saucepan, cover, and cook for 2 to 3 minutes, stirring, until the spinach is reduced but still quite green.

Remove the saucepan from the heat and mix in the chèvre. Pour the sherry into the bottom of the baking pan. Mound each mushroom cap with filling and arrange the stuffed mushrooms in the pan in a single layer. Cover with aluminum foil and bake for 10 minutes. Uncover and bake for 15 to 20 minutes more, until completely tender. Serve the mushrooms hot, at room temperature, or chilled.

CHEESE CRISPS

Also known as fricos, these lacy snacks are a delicious complement to glasses of sherry. They couldn't be simpler to make, whether do-ahead or last-minute.

2   CUPS FRESHLY GRATED MANCHEGO* CHEESE OR
    PARMIGIANO-REGGIANO

2   TABLESPOONS UNBLEACHED WHITE FLOUR

YIELDS 24
PREPARATION TIME: 5 MINUTES
BAKING TIME: 8 TO 10 MINUTES
COOLING TIME: 10 MINUTES

* Look for this Spanish cheese in the cheese section of well-stocked supermarkets. We think it's worth the splurge.

Preheat the oven to 350°. Line two large or three medium baking trays with parchment paper or, if you prefer, lightly butter the trays.

Stir together the grated cheese and flour. Drop the mixture in tablespoons onto the prepared baking trays to make about 24 mounds. Space the spoonfuls about 4 inches apart. Spread with your fingers into 3-inch rounds or ovals. Push any stray pieces of cheese back toward the center of the rounds.

Bake until the cheese is melted, bubbling, and brown on the edges, 8 to 10 minutes. Cool the crisps on the baking tray for about 10 minutes and remove with a spatula.

Cheese crisps will keep for up to 3 days when stored in a sealed container at room temperature.

HALLOWEEN

October Bitter Sweet Salad with Cranberry Vinaigrette
Sautéed Broccoli Rabe
Pumpkin & Mushroom Lasagna
Cranberry Sorbet
Bone Cookies

Special bonus recipe: Lickety Split Face Paint

Many of our most venerable American celebrations descend to us from the ancient Celtic tribes of Europe. And present-day Halloween has its roots in one of the four main traditional Celtic days that welcome each season. After the fall harvest, the Celts marked the waning of the sun by the feast of Samhain. It was believed that the spirits of those who had died returned to be among the living and awaited judgment by Samhain, the lord of the dark. At the end of the festival, villagers wearing masked disguises escorted the spirits out of town.

The early Christian church did its best to appropriate the pagan holiday into the liturgy by substituting All Saints' Day or All Hallows' Day (for Samhain) on November 1, and following it with All Souls' Day on November 2—both days to honor the dead. But old habits survived, especially on Hallows' E'en (short for *even*, which is Middle English for the eve or night before All Hallows' Day). On October 31, costumed processions and harvest feasts expressing thanks for nature's bounty continued year after year.

The great Canadian writer Robertson Davies, who knew a thing or two about Celtic and pagan ways, believed that modern-day Halloween has been trivialized and that it should not properly be a holiday for children at all, but rather a day of reflection and respect for our ancestors—a time to offer tribute in some way. He wrote, "There have always been people who give no regard to their forebears, and it was they who were thought in the days of the old Celtic religion to suffer on Halloween. That was the night when the spirits of the neglected or affronted dead took vengeance on their unworthy descendants."

Perhaps we should take a look back and give thought to those who went before us, lest our dreams be haunted and our futures blighted. Accordingly, we've planned an adult dinner party that includes mushrooms and broccoli rabe—foods most children haven't learned yet to appreciate—and our harvest meal is filled with tastes of both bitter and sweet, like life (and death). We highly recommend a few toasts to the dead as treats for the tricksters in your family line.

OCTOBER BITTER SWEET SALAD

This unusual combination of bitter and sweet, crisp and juicy, is delicious and very attractive with its glistening red vinaigrette. Choose whatever combination of salad greens appeals to you, but with an emphasis on the sharper-tasting ones, such as arugula, watercress, or mizuna. Peppery frisée, with its lacy leaves, is ideal. A large head of frisée will yield about 6 cups of greens.

cranberry vinaigrette

SERVES 8
TOTAL TIME: 20 MINUTES

½ CUP EXTRA-VIRGIN OLIVE OIL

3 TABLESPOONS CIDER VINEGAR OR WHITE WINE VINEGAR

2 TEASPOONS SUGAR

¼ CUP DRIED CRANBERRIES (CRAISINS)

1 TEASPOON SALT

¼ TEASPOON GROUND BLACK PEPPER

salad

8 CUPS MIXED FIELD GREENS, RINSED

2 to 3 FIRM BUT RIPE BARTLETT PEARS, CORED AND THINLY SLICED (ABOUT 4 CUPS)

3 TABLESPOONS FRESH LEMON JUICE

2 CUPS PEELED AND SHREDDED OR THINLY SLICED TURNIPS OR 2 CUPS CELERY HEART STALKS, SLICED ON THE DIAGONAL

¼ CUP DRIED CRANBERRIES (CRAISINS)

¼ CUP CRUMBLED GOAT CHEESE OR BLUE CHEESE (OPTIONAL)

Combine the vinaigrette ingredients in a blender or food processor and whirl until the dried cranberries are finely minced and suspended in the dressing. Set aside.

Tear the salad greens into bite-sized pieces and arrange on individual plates or on a large platter. Toss the pear slices and lemon juice together in a bowl to evenly coat the pears and prevent discoloration; then arrange them on the greens. Top with the turnip or celery heart slices and sprinkle on the cranberries. Finish with the crumbled cheese, if using.

Shake up or stir the Cranberry Vinaigrette and drizzle it evenly over the salad just before serving.

SAUTÉED BROCCOLI RABE

For almost all of our recipes that used broccoli rabe, we used to write apologies and disclaimers about its bitterness, and we'd explain how it was an acquired taste. But now we just want to say, "Oh, grow up. If you haven't tried it, you really should."

Broccoli rabe is also known as Italian broccoli, rapini, and brocoletti di rape—but should not be confused with broccolini. Broccoli rabe *is* peppery and assertive and a delicious counterpoint to sweet pumpkin. If you *must,* parboil it for about 2 minutes before sautéing to reduce the bitterness a bit.

2   POUNDS BROCCOLI RABE (ABOUT 2 BUNCHES)
2   TABLESPOONS OLIVE OIL
3 or 4 GARLIC CLOVES, MINCED OR PRESSED
1   TEASPOON SALT
     CRACKED BLACK PEPPER TO TASTE
     PINCH OF RED PEPPER FLAKES (OPTIONAL)
1   TABLESPOON WATER (OPTIONAL)

SERVES 8
TOTAL TIME: 20 MINUTES

Trim and discard any tough or hollow portions of the broccoli rabe stems. Rinse the rabe well and drain. Chop the bunches of rabe coarsely into 1½- to 2-inch lengths.

In a large heavy skillet, heat the olive oil and add the broccoli rabe. Sauté on medium-high heat for about 5 minutes. Stir in the garlic and sauté for another 5 minutes, until the garlic is tender and the broccoli rabe is bright green. Add the salt, black pepper and, if desired, the red pepper flakes. If the broccoli rabe is not quite done, add the water and stir for 1 to 2 minutes, until tender but not mushy.

Serve hot.

PUMPKIN & MUSHROOM LASAGNA

Having long admired a traditional Italian dish of pumpkin-filled ravioli with sage butter, we wanted to use that marvelous combination in a pasta dish better suited to making ahead for a crowd. With earthy mushrooms, fresh sage, and salty ricotta salata to temper the sweetness of the pumpkin filling, this lasagna is unusual, lighter than most, and completely satisfying.

The assembly is easy. We layer on DeCecco dried lasagna noodles right out of the box and eliminate the tedious, messy boiling of the noodles. The mushy no-boil type of noodle is not necessary and, in fact, not nearly as good as regular noodles.

4	CUPS CHOPPED ONIONS
1	TABLESPOON OLIVE OIL
6	CUPS CHOPPED PORTABELLOS OR OTHER MUSHROOMS
¼	CUP CHOPPED FRESH SAGE LEAVES
1	TEASPOON SALT
1	CUP MARSALA, VEGETABLE STOCK OR A COMBINATION
2	EGGS, LIGHTLY BEATEN
3½	CUPS CANNED PUMPKIN (29-OUNCE CAN)*
3	CUPS RICOTTA CHEESE
¼	TEASPOON GROUND BLACK PEPPER
¼	TEASPOON GROUND NUTMEG
¾	POUND UNCOOKED LASAGNA NOODLES
1½	CUPS CRUMBLED RICOTTA SALATA
½	CUP GRATED PECORINO ROMANO CHEESE

SERVES 8 TO 10
PREPARATION TIME: 45 MINUTES TO 1 HOUR
BAKING TIME: 1 HOUR
SITTING TIME: 10 MINUTES

* Or use puréed cooked or frozen butternut squash. Two butternut squash will yield about 3½ cups puréed squash.

In a large pot, sauté the onions in the oil for 5 minutes. Add the mushrooms and sauté for another 5 minutes, until the mushrooms are somewhat wilted. Add the sage, ½ teaspoon of the salt, and the Marsala or stock and simmer on low heat for 5 minutes. Set aside.

In a large bowl, stir together the eggs, pumpkin, ricotta cheese, pepper, nutmeg, and the remaining ½ teaspoon of salt. Set aside.

Preheat the oven to 375°. Lightly oil a 9 x 13-inch baking dish.

Dip out about ½ cup of the liquid from the sautéed mushrooms and pour it into the prepared baking dish. Cover the bottom with a layer of lasagna noodles arranged close together. Evenly spread on half of the pumpkin mixture. Spoon on about a third of the sautéed mushrooms and sprinkle with ½ cup of ricotta salata. Add a second layer of noodles followed by the remaining pumpkin mixture, another third of the sautéed mushrooms, and ½ cup of ricotta salata. Finish with a layer of noodles thoroughly moistened by the last third of the sautéed mushrooms. Evenly sprinkle on ½ cup of ricotta salata and top with the grated Pecorino.

Cover and bake for 50 minutes. Uncover and bake for an additional 10 minutes, until the lasagna is bubbly, the noodles are tender, and the top is browned. Remove from the oven and let stand for about 10 minutes before serving.

jack-o'-lanterns

As the story goes, Irish Jack was a crafty, stingy drunkard who tricked the devil into swearing he would not come after Jack's soul. But when Jack died, he was turned away from heaven's gate, so he went back to the devil to complain. In response, the devil threw at Jack a coal from the fires of hell, which Jack then cleverly tucked into a hollowed-out turnip. Ever since, Jack, with his "jack-o'-lantern" has wandered abroad in the world, lighting the darkness.

When Europeans colonized America, pumpkins replaced turnips because the orange squash were more plentiful, easier to carve, and—like many things in the New World—bigger. But hollowed turnips, with the light of votive candles flickering through the grotesque faces carved in them, are just the right size to make a spooky decoration that's not too big for a table set for an adult Halloween dinner party or to place atop gateposts to frighten off any malevolent spirits. And you can use the insides of the scooped-out turnip in the salad.

CRANBERRY SORBET

Rome's Emperor Nero is sometimes given credit for the invention of ice cream, but historical records indicate that ice cream was actually known much earlier. Evidence from the beginning of recorded history suggests that in ancient China, water ices were being made even before Nero's reign. From China, frozen desserts spread to Arabia, India, and Persia and eventually, Marco Polo introduced them to Italy. In the sixteenth century, Catherine de Medici brought ice cream to France and the innovation quickly spread through the rest of Europe.

Nancy Johnson, an American, invented the hand-crank ice cream maker in 1846. Today electric ice cream machines effortlessly turn out a batch of sorbet, ice cream, frozen yogurt, or sherbet in just 30 to 45 minutes, so anyone can become a homemade ice cream aficionado.

Sorbet (from the Italian *sorbetto*) is a water ice and is sometimes also called sherbet, Italian ice, or fruit ice, although in many cases sherbet contains milk or cream and is technically a milk ice. Sorbets are always dairyless.

Our method couldn't be quicker or easier: It doesn't involve cooking a syrup or waiting around for it to cool. If you're starting with an unopened bottle of room temperature cranberry juice, stir in the sugar before chilling the juice and the sugar will dissolve more easily. The sorbet is a cheery deep pink color with a slightly lemony flavor smacking of cranberry. It's not too sweet—just sweet enough to satisfy. Try blending in ¼ cup of frozen raspberries for an extra touch.

2½	CUPS CRANBERRY JUICE, CHILLED (SEE NOTE)
¼	CUP SUGAR
2	TABLESPOONS CANNED WHOLE BERRY CRANBERRY SAUCE, CHILLED
1	TABLESPOON FRESH LEMON JUICE*

YIELDS 1 QUART
PREPARATION TIME: 10 MINUTES
FREEZING TIME: 30 TO 45 MINUTES IN MOST ICE CREAM MAKERS

* If the cranberry juice you use has lemon juice in it, you can omit this, if you like.

In a blender, purée the cranberry juice, sugar, whole berry cranberry sauce, and lemon juice until smooth. (Be sure to use a blender, because it increases volume and ensures a good sorbet texture.) Pour the cold mixture into an ice cream maker and freeze according to the manufacturer's directions.

Dish up the sorbet right away or store immediately in the freezer in a covered container until ready to serve.

note

Many brands of cranberry juice and cranberry cocktail are laced with large amounts of fructose and corn syrup; some have more water and sugary additives than actual cranberry juice and/or cranberry concentrate.

For the best flavor, look for a brand that has cranberry juice and cranberry concentrate listed as the first ingredients. We like Naturally Cranberry juice by Apple & Eve, which has fresh-pressed cranberry juice as its first ingredient and has no added sugar, fructose, or corn syrup, but a blend of four other juice concentrates instead.

BONE COOKIES

Adapted from a Mario Batali recipe, these crunchy cookies look a bit like bones of the dead and are the perfect shape for dunking into coffee. They need to sit out overnight before baking, so you can't have them on the spur of the moment. Once baked, however, they will keep for several weeks in a sealed container, so they're fabulous for making ahead of time.

3	LARGE EGGS
2	CUPS CONFECTIONERS' SUGAR
2	CUPS UNBLEACHED WHITE FLOUR
1	TEASPOON BAKING POWDER
1	TEASPOON PURE VANILLA EXTRACT OR PURE ORANGE EXTRACT

YIELDS 40 TO 48
PREPARATION TIME: 30 MINUTES
SITTING TIME: AT LEAST 8 HOURS
BAKING TIME: 15 TO 20 MINUTES

With an electric mixer, beat the eggs at high speed for 5 to 6 minutes, until pale yellow and thick. Add the confectioners' sugar and beat for another 5 minutes. In a second bowl, stir together the flour and baking powder and gradually mix it into the egg mixture. The batter will resemble stiff meringue and hold its shape. Fold in the vanilla or orange extract.

Divide the dough by slicing it with a sharp knife into four equal parts. The dough will be soft, sticky, stiff, and somewhat delicate. Flour your hands and a clean working surface. Working with one portion of the dough at a time, use your hands or a spatula to scoop each portion onto the counter. Roll and gently stretch each piece of dough into a ¾-inch-thick rope that is 36 to 42 inches long. Don't try to make smooth, uniform ropes; a few lumps and twists are just right for the eerie nature of these cookies. Slice the ropes into 10 to 12 equal pieces, to make 40 to 48 "bones" in all, each about 3½ inches long.

Arrange the bone cookies on two unoiled baking sheets, cover with a light-weight kitchen towel, and set aside to dry for 8 hours or overnight.

Preheat the oven to 375°.

Remove the towel from the cookies and bake for 15 to 20 minutes, until light golden in color (see Note). Remove from the baking sheets and allow to cool completely on a rack before storing.

note

If you have an electric oven, we recommend baking the cookies in two batches, using only the middle rack. This will prevent scorching the cookie bottoms.

LICKETY SPLIT FACE PAINTS

Although Halloween originated as a very serious adult holiday, these days it's one of the most anticipated and beloved of days for kids, and it's more than just a chance for them to stay up late and eat candy—it's the celebration of fantasy and imagination. Child development experts say that dressing up and pretending to be something you're not is important play for kids. It's exciting and enabling for a child to try on a new image, whether witch, ghost, pirate, superhero, princess, or giant pumpkin.

Often the general chaos of Halloween culminates with door-to-door trick-or-treating, which gives kids a stage and a script for showing off their pretend characters, as well as a ritually sanctioned method of requesting (demanding? extorting?) treats. Although trick-or-treating is often the ultimate annual downfall for nutrition-conscious families, there are relatively healthful treats (such as granola bars, fruit, homemade cookies, fresh-popped popcorn, raisins, craisins, and/or toasted nuts) that you can hand over to the goblins beseechingly looming at your door.

Nontoxic, washable, inexpensive face paints instantly create a festive, makeup mood. They can be made right in your kitchen in a matter of seconds. They're easy enough for the kids to make themselves and safe because they are food-based. We use food coloring in gel form, which is easy to control, makes mixing colors simple, and allows for some very sophisticated shades. Mix yellow coloring with just a bit of red and you'll get a perfect shade of pumpkin. The texture of these paints is creamy, so apply with a finger rather than a brush. Glitter also adheres easily to the creamy base. Go full-face or inventively daub on hearts, stars, or superhero war paint. These paints can be stored in jars and, like superheroes, last forever.

1	TABLESPOON SOLID SHORTENING	YIELDS 1 TABLESPOON
1	TABLESPOON CORNSTARCH	TOTAL TIME: 5 MINUTES
¼	TEASPOON FOOD COLORING	

Combine the shortening and cornstarch in a small bowl and add the food coloring. This tiny amount will produce brilliant color. Mix until creamy and the color is uniform.

A tablespoon of face paint won't cover a large area (such as an entire face), but it will make quite a few decorations. Use the proportions above to mix up as much or as little as you need.

DAY OF THE DEAD

Potato Leek Soup
Stuffed Chayotes
Mango Jicama Salad
Pan de Muerto (page 137) or Bone Cookies (page 128)
Tequila, Cerveza, or a Fruit Juice Spritzer

Every November 1 and 2 the Day of the Dead, or *El Día de los Muertos,* is celebrated throughout Central and South America. It's a time to remember and honor deceased relatives and to acknowledge and embrace the cycle of life.

This festive memorial day keeps the memory of loved ones alive by preparing for annual visits from the departed. Altars to the dead, or *offrendas,* are erected in homes and at gravesites. The shrines are set aglow with candles and incense to guide the spirits home, and some of the deceased's favorite foods are offered as enticement. The brilliant orange marigold is the flower traditionally chosen to beautify homes and cemeteries on the Day of the Dead and to ward off demons with its pungent smell. Following a ritual vigil, the food, drink, and confections set out for the dead are feasted upon by the living. But not to worry: The spirits have not been deprived. It is believed that, at their visitations, they've supped the spiritual essence of the offerings.

Nowhere is this holiday more anticipated and celebrated than in Mexico, where the Day of the Dead is a *mestizo* of Catholic ceremony and ancient Aztec ritual. The timing corresponds exactly with the Catholic holy days for the dead: All Saints' Day and All Souls' Day. Yet making food for spirits, hanging sardonically grinning skeletons, and concocting sugar skulls and candy bones all reflect ancient sacrificial rites, as well as a cosmology that disarms death by befriending and laughing with it.

Food plays a central role in the festivities, and many ingredients of holiday fare such as corn, pumpkin, and squash pay homage to the end of the growing season. The convergence of this holiday with the Mexican harvest, or the end of the living and growth period of vegetation, is both another relic of the pagan past and an ever-present affirmation of the life cycle.

This is a wholly satisfying yet simple meal. We suggest baking the Pan de Muerto early in the day. Although it's not time-consuming to make, it does need time to cool completely before serving. While the bread bakes, prepare the Potato Leek Soup, which can be stored chilled and then gently reheated before serving. The Mango Jicama Salad is a medley of marinated fruits and vegetables on a bed of greens. We suggest a minimum of 30 minutes for marinating, but you can make this a day ahead and it only gets better. The chayotes in this recipe roast for about 30 minutes, an ample amount of time in which to make the filling. Beer, tequila, and atole—a corn-sweetened fruit drink—are classical libations on this day.

Buen Provecho!

POTATO LEEK SOUP

As a choice of potatoes, we like Yukon Golds for their buttery color and creamy texture. Scrubbed, but not peeled, potatoes make a more nutritious soup, but if you use a thick-skinned potato like a russet or want a very smooth soup, peel your potatoes.

Onions could replace the leeks, but the leeks add a more delicate sweetness. For a soup that is lower in fat but still has an appealing creamy quality, replace the half-and-half with evaporated skimmed milk.

1½ TABLESPOONS VEGETABLE OIL

4   CUPS COARSELY CHOPPED LEEKS*

5½ CUPS CUBED POTATOES, PEELED IF YOU PREFER

6   CUPS WATER OR VEGETABLE STOCK

2   TEASPOONS SALT

2   TABLESPOONS CHOPPED FRESH DILL (2 TEASPOONS DRIED)

2   CUPS HALF-AND-HALF

     SALT AND GROUND BLACK PEPPER TO TASTE

     CHOPPED FRESH CHIVES OR SCALLIONS

SERVES 6
PREPARATION TIME:
ABOUT 30 MINUTES
COOKING TIME: 30 MINUTES

* Use only the white and most tender, light green part of the leek near the bulb. Be sure to rinse the chopped leeks well under running water to remove sand and grit. About 4 medium leeks will yield 4 cups when chopped.

Warm the oil in a soup pot on low heat. Gently sauté the leeks, stirring often, for 10 minutes. Add the potatoes, water or stock, and the salt, cover, and bring to a boil. Reduce the heat and simmer for about 30 minutes, until the vegetables are tender.

Add the dill and half-and-half. Working in batches, purée the soup in a blender until smooth. Add salt and pepper to taste, sprinkle with chives or scallions, and serve hot.

unfamiliar vegetables & fruits

There are thousands of species of edible plants in the world—about 4,000 in North America alone. As cooks, we at Moosewood enjoy discovering and experimenting with new vegetables and fruits. Many of these "discoveries" are old favorites in another corner of the world, but they're new to us. We appreciate that one of the benefits of being a nation of immigrants is the vast and constantly changing variety in the marketplace. These days most of us can cruise through the produce section in our grocery store and see fruits and vegetables we've never tasted and sometimes things we can't even name.

Not so terribly long ago in much of the United States, oranges were rare treats that children might find in their Christmas stockings. Only when a sea captain returned from a voyage around the world would his New England neighbors taste pineapple. Twenty years ago, you wouldn't find tomatillos or jicama here in upstate New York, but now they're readily available. In our snowy part of the world, we can even find fresh cactus paddles.

Every few weeks, to make cooking more interesting and maybe give yourself a little geography lesson, try out a new vegetable or fruit from the produce section of your supermarket. But also go out and talk to people. Ask at the Korean market or the Thai restaurant how to cook something new to you. Get the Italian produce manager at the supermarket to tell you how his mom used to cook cardoons. Boldly approach the stranger with interesting-looking things in her shopping cart.

It took a hundred years to convince Europeans to eat the strange new potatoes and tomatoes from the New World. Don't you wait so long to try something new.

STUFFED CHAYOTES

Chayote (chi-OH-tee) is a pear-shaped green summer squash that originated on Mayan and Aztec farms. It has a delicate flavor that resembles a cross between cucumber and zucchini and is prized for its lovely texture, readiness to absorb flavors, and ability to survive long cooking. Jamaicans use it like apples in pies, and in New Orleans it's called mirliton. It is very popular in Mexico and Central America and is becoming more available in large supermarkets in the United States.

Chayotes are firmer than most other squash and therefore need to cook longer. For the most efficient use of time, begin to bake the chayotes; then prepare the rest of the ingredients while they're in the oven. Well wrapped, chayotes will keep for up to a month in the vegetable crisper of the fridge.

6	CHAYOTES (4 OUNCES EACH)
3	TABLESPOONS OLIVE OIL
½	TEASPOON SALT
1	CUP FINELY CHOPPED ONIONS
2	GARLIC CLOVES, MINCED OR PRESSED
1	TEASPOON GROUND CORIANDER
1	TEASPOON GROUND CUMIN
½	TEASPOON DRIED OREGANO
½	CUP CHOPPED FRESH OR CANNED TOMATOES
1	CUP FROZEN, CANNED OR FRESH CORN KERNELS
2	TABLESPOONS CHOPPED FRESH CILANTRO
2	EGGS, BEATEN
1	CUP GRATED SHARP CHEDDAR CHEESE
1 to 2	TABLESPOONS CHIPOTLE PEPPERS IN ADOBO SAUCE*
½	CUP BREAD CRUMBS**

SERVES 6
PREPARATION TIME: 40 MINUTES
FINAL BAKING TIME: 15 MINUTES

* Look for it in small jars or cans in the ethnic section of supermarkets. The chipotles are smoked hot peppers and the adobo sauce is a thick, spicy tomato purée.

** Pulverize stale or lightly toasted whole wheat, sourdough, or French bread in a blender or food processor.

Preheat the oven to 400°. Lightly oil a baking dish.

Cut the chayotes in half lengthwise. Lightly brush the cut surfaces with about a tablespoon of the olive oil and sprinkle with ¼ teaspoon of the salt. Place them cut side down in the prepared baking dish, cover, and bake for 30 minutes.

When the chayotes have baked for 15 to 20 minutes, warm the rest of the oil in a large skillet. Add the onions, garlic, coriander, cumin, oregano, and the remaining ¼ teaspoon of salt and sauté on medium heat, stirring often, for about 10 minutes. Add the tomatoes, corn, and cilantro and bring to a simmer. Add the eggs and stir until scrambled.

Meanwhile, when the chayotes are tender, reduce the oven temperature to 350°, remove the chayotes, and set aside to cool. When cool enough to handle, carefully scoop out the flesh and the edible seeds (reserving the shells) and mash with a potato masher or whirl briefly in a food processor. Stir the mashed chayotes into the skillet and cook for about 5 minutes. Remove from the heat and stir in the cheese and chipotles.

Return the chayote shells to the baking dish. Mound one-twelfth of the filling in each chayote shell. Sprinkle the tops with the bread crumbs. Bake, uncovered, for about 15 minutes, until hot.

MANGO JICAMA SALAD

Crisp, citrus-bright, and colorful, this salad is an ideal partner to spicy, creamy, or grilled fare. It is a semi-composed salad in which marinated fresh fruit and vegetables are served on a bed of arugula or on another peppery green of your choice.

Allow the topping to marinate for at least 30 minutes or make it the day before. Extensive marinating will not disturb the salad's color or texture, and the flavors will continue to marry and mellow. This dish is also a good companion for Black Bean & Chocolate Chili (page 157).

SERVES 6
PREPARATION TIME: 15 MINUTES
MARINATING TIME: 30 MINUTES

zesty orange dressing

1	TEASPOON FRESHLY GRATED ORANGE PEEL
3	TABLESPOONS ORANGE JUICE
3	TABLESPOONS VEGETABLE OIL
2	TABLESPOONS FRESH LEMON JUICE
1	TABLESPOON SUGAR
¾	TEASPOON SALT

salad

1	CUP CUBED MANGO (½-INCH PIECES)*
1	CUP CUBED JICAMA (½-INCH PIECES)
1	CUP CUBED RED BELL PEPPERS (½-INCH CUBES)
2	TABLESPOONS SLICED GREEN OLIVES
2	TABLESPOONS FINELY CHOPPED SCALLION GREENS
8	OUNCES ARUGULA OR MESCLUN

* Mangos have large pits and the pulp is slippery. A shallow slice from end to end along the two broad, flat sides works best. Score the mango flesh of each slice into ½-inch pieces and pare them away from the skin. Peel the remaining skin around the pit, then carefully cut the tender pulp away from the pit and dice it.

Whisk together all of the dressing ingredients in a cup. In a medium bowl, combine the mango, jicama, bell peppers, olives, and scallion greens. Pour the dressing over the mango mixture and marinate for at least 30 minutes.

At serving time, arrange a bed of arugula or mesclun on individual salad plates or alongside the main dish on each person's plate. Spoon the marinated salad onto the greens. Serve soon.

PAN DE MUERTO

The altars and gravesite decorations that are created for the Day of the Dead celebrations in Mexico usually include a round, orange-flavored bread scented with anise. This sweet bread is left at gravesites so that the spirits of departed loved ones can eat the spiritual aspects of the offering, leaving the actual goody for their living relatives to consume.

Pan de Muerto (Bread of the Dead) is a yeasted bread typically decorated with pieces of dough shaped like bones. We've created a rich-tasting, quickbread version of Pan de Muerto—easier to make but with all the delicious traditional flavors. If the spooky aspect of this tradition intrigues you, press Halloween candy (skeletons and skulls) into the bread while it's still warm. Or use white icing and pipe bones and teardrops onto the cooled loaf.

1	ORANGE
1	CUP NONFAT PLAIN YOGURT
1	LARGE EGG
¼	CUP MELTED BUTTER
2½	CUPS UNBLEACHED WHITE FLOUR
¾	CUP SUGAR
1	TEASPOON BAKING POWDER
1	TEASPOON BAKING SODA
1	TEASPOON SALT
1	TEASPOON ANISE SEED

YIELDS ONE 9-INCH ROUND LOAF
PREPARATION TIME: 20 MINUTES
BAKING TIME: 40 MINUTES
COOLING TIME: 15 MINUTES

Preheat the oven to 375°. Lightly butter a 9-inch pie plate.

Zest the orange and set the grated peel aside. Slice the rest of the peel from the orange and separate the sections, discarding any white membranes and seeds. Place the orange sections in a blender or into the bowl of a food processor and whirl for half a minute, until the orange is emulsified. Add the grated orange peel, yogurt, egg, and butter and purée briefly or pulse about 4 times, until the ingredients are thoroughly combined.

Sift the flour, sugar, baking powder, baking soda, and salt into a large bowl. Using a rubber spatula, stir the wet ingredients into the dry ingredients until the batter is well combined. Stir in the anise. Spoon the batter into the prepared pie plate and smooth the top.

Bake for 20 minutes; then reduce the oven temperature to 350° and continue to bake for 15 to 20 minutes, until the bread is golden yellow. Cool on a wire rack for about 15 minutes. Run a knife around the edge and pop the bread out of the pie plate. Serve with the flat side down.

EASTERN EUROPEAN DINNER PARTY

Stuffed Mushrooms (page 118)
Braised Polenta Cabbage Rolls
Baked Beets on Greens
Plum (or Pear) Torte

Eastern Europe has a complex history of shifting political borders, differing religious influences, domination by foreign powers, and a resultant mingling of diverse peoples. Quite a wealth of cultural integrity still permeates Eastern Europe, with its many countries' folk traditions, celebratory rituals, and distinct cookery styles. Food, plentiful and flavorful, is always at the heart of any get-together or festivity, and vegetables often play a large role.

On a normal day, Eastern Europeans often take four meals rather than three: a very early light continental breakfast, a midmorning snack, a main meal between 2 and 3 P.M., and a light meal around 8 P.M.—late by American standards. Shopkeepers often close for several hours for the midafternoon meal and reopen in the evening for a few hours. For any dinner party, you would surely arrive by 3, eat heartily, forget about business for the rest of the day, and eat a modest supper again in midevening to sustain you through the sociable late-night visit.

We time-constrained, rushing Americans might take a lesson in relaxation and enjoyment from these gracious Eastern European traditions that celebrate being together in good company as its own reward and goal, with no hurry to scurry away and finish up some other obligation. Try it for a change. Invite some friends for an "early" dinner that begins in midafternoon. Imagine autumn in Transylvania with that winsome gypsy aura hanging heavy in the air.

Our Braised Polenta Cabbage Rolls served with Baked Beets are absolutely appropriate for *rucak*, the main meal of the day, especially in fall, when root vegetables and cabbage are the natural choices. Although stuffed cabbage is a bit time-consuming (and most people wouldn't take the time to make it for themselves), it's a lovely dish to present to others. And these particular cabbage rolls have a unique twist that will probably be a novelty for your guests.

Start by baking the beets and, while they cook, prepare the cabbage leaves, polenta, and tomato sauce. When the beets are tender, lower the oven temperature, pop in the cabbage rolls, and slip the skins from the beets. As the kitchen becomes warm and cozy, savory aromas fill the air, which instantly arouse everyone's appetites as soon as they arrive. While not difficult, the main dishes will take some time to prepare, so we've added a really easy, breezy cake for dessert.

If you have the time and an inclination to fill out the menu to capacity, you could prepare Stuffed Mushrooms the day before and zap them in the microwave as an appetizer or late night snack.

BRAISED POLENTA CABBAGE ROLLS

These are cabbage rolls with a difference. Instead of the more familiar rice fillings of the Middle East, these cabbage leaves are stuffed with a dressed-up polenta that's both savory and creamy. The preparation time depends on the type of cornmeal used, so check out the Note at the end of the recipe.

We give you a choice of very different cheeses: mild, tangy, or sharp. Inspired by Romanian and Croatian cuisines, which use sauerkraut to great advantage, we've made a tangy tomato sauce as a braising liquid—the rolls simmer to perfection.

cabbage rolls

SERVES 6
PREPARATION TIME: 40 TO 60 MINUTES
BAKING TIME: ABOUT 30 MINUTES

10 to 12 LARGE WHOLE GREEN CABBAGE LEAVES*

1	TABLESPOON OLIVE OIL
2	CUPS DICED ONIONS
2	CUPS WATER (SEE NOTE)
1	TEASPOON SALT
1	CUP CORNMEAL
1	CUP GRATED FONTINA, FARMER CHEESE OR FETA CHEESE
¼	TEASPOON GROUND BLACK PEPPER

tomato sauerkraut sauce

2	TEASPOONS OLIVE OIL
4	GARLIC CLOVES, MINCED OR PRESSED
2½	CUPS TOMATO JUICE
1	CUP SAUERKRAUT, DRAINED
2	TABLESPOONS MINCED FRESH DILL (2 TEASPOONS DRIED)

SOUR CREAM

* If using green cabbage, core it and immerse the whole head in boiling water. After several minutes, as each leaf begins to separate from the head, use tongs to gently pull it completely off the cabbage and set aside to cool. If using Chinese cabbage, cut 12 good leaves from the core and blanch for about 2 minutes, until softened.

Prepare the cabbage leaves.

Heat the olive oil in a heavy saucepan on medium heat and sauté the onions for about 10 minutes, stirring often, until translucent. Lower the heat, add a dash of water to prevent sticking, and continue to cook for 10 minutes, until caramelized and rich golden brown.

Meanwhile, in a separate heavy saucepan, bring the water and the salt to a boil. While whisking briskly so that lumps don't form, pour in the cornmeal in a slow, steady stream. Reduce the heat to low and simmer, stirring occasionally and adding more water if needed, until the polenta is fairly stiff and tastes done (see Note). Stir in the caramelized onions and the cheese and black pepper. Set aside.

For the sauce, warm the oil in a saucepan and sauté the garlic just until golden, stirring constantly. Add the tomato juice and sauerkraut and bring to a simmer. Stir in the dill. Pour the sauce into an unoiled 9 x 12-inch baking pan and set aside.

Preheat the oven to 350°.

To assemble the rolls, put about ⅓ cup of filling at the broad end of each cabbage leaf, fold the side edges toward the center to cover the filling, and then roll up lengthwise. Place the rolls seam side down in the baking pan. Cover with aluminum foil and bake for about 30 minutes, or until hot and steaming.

To serve, spoon some of the tomato sauce over each roll and garnish with a dollop of sour cream.

note

The amount of water needed and the cooking time depend on the cornmeal used. The coarseness of the grind, variety of corn, and whether or not it's roasted all influence the cornmeal/water ratio and cooking time. Finely ground cornmeal might be done after just a few minutes of simmering; coarsely ground and stone-ground cornmeals may need to simmer for up to 45 minutes. Most cornmeals will need more water added during cooking; you can add water to soften the polenta, but you can't easily make the polenta thicker if you start with too much water.

BAKED BEETS ON GREENS

Look for 6 to 8 beets about 2½ inches in diameter for this recipe. Wrapped in foil and baked, the beets retain their distinctive flavor and moisture—and they peel very easily as well: The beet skins slip right off.

Horseradish dressings may have Greek or Eastern European origins. This one is intentionally tangy and provides a zippy contrast to the sweet, earthy taste of the beets and greens. When served together, the beets and greens are best warm or at room temperature, but leftover beets are good chilled as well. The greens are also good with a dash of vinegar.

2	BUNCHES RED BEETS WITH GREENS (6 TO 8 BEETS)
2	TEASPOONS OLIVE OIL
1	GARLIC CLOVE, MINCED OR PRESSED
1	TABLESPOON WATER
	SALT TO TASTE
	GROUND BLACK PEPPER TO TASTE

SERVES 6
PREPARATION TIME: 15 MINUTES
BAKING TIME: 45 TO 75 MINUTES

horseradish dressing

¼	CUP OLIVE OIL
1	GARLIC CLOVE, MINCED OR PRESSED
1	TABLESPOON PREPARED HORSERADISH
5	TEASPOONS RED WINE VINEGAR OR CIDER VINEGAR
½	TEASPOON SALT, MORE TO TASTE
1	TEASPOON MINCED FRESH DILL (OPTIONAL)

Preheat the oven to 400°.

Cut off the beet greens about an inch above the tops of the beets and set aside. Rinse the beets to remove any dirt and cut off the roots. Wrap each beet in foil, folding over the edges to make a good seal. Place them directly on the oven rack with a baking sheet on a lower shelf to catch any drips.

Bake until the center of each beet is easily pierced with a sharp knife, 45 to 75 minutes, depending upon the size and age of the beets. Let cool slightly.

Meanwhile, rinse the beet greens well and, if the leaves are large, cut them into 1-inch strips. About 15 minutes before serving, heat the olive oil in a saucepan and lightly sauté the garlic. Add the beet greens and the water, cover, and steam for 6 to 10 minutes, stirring occasionally, until the greens are wilted and tender. Add salt and pepper to taste. Cover and set aside.

Meanwhile, whisk together all of the dressing ingredients.

Remove the foil from a beet and slip off its skin. Trim off the stem and cut the beet into ½-inch cubes. Repeat with the rest of the beets, unwrapping them one at a time to keep them warm. Place the cubed beets in a bowl and toss gently with the dressing. Add salt to taste.

Arrange the cooked greens in a shallow dish or on a platter and mound the beets on top. Serve warm or at room temperature.

PLUM (OR PEAR) TORTE

This torte was inspired by a recipe from John Campione, a friend of Moosewood's David Hirsch. It uses fresh plums of the "prune plum" type—oval-shaped and deep purple—the variety most often used to make prunes.

Plums were introduced to the orchards of Rome by Pompey the Great in 65 B.C.E. and were spread into Europe by Alexander the Great. Today, plums are the second most-cultivated fruit in the world, second only to apples. There is a new movement by the prune industry to market prunes as dried plums or as plum raisins, in hopes of appealing to younger people.

Our juicy torte can be made ahead and stored in the refrigerator. Just before serving, reheat it briefly in the oven at 300° until warm.

½	CUP BUTTER, AT ROOM TEMPERATURE
¾	CUP BROWN SUGAR, PACKED
2	EGGS
1	CUP UNBLEACHED WHITE PASTRY FLOUR
1	TEASPOON BAKING POWDER
	PINCH OF SALT
3	CUPS HALVED AND PITTED PRUNE PLUMS OR PEELED PEAR SLICES*
1	TABLESPOON SUGAR
1	TEASPOON GROUND CINNAMON
	FRESH WHIPPED CREAM (OPTIONAL)

SERVES 6 TO 8
PREPARATION TIME: 15 MINUTES
BAKING TIME: 60 TO 75 MINUTES
COOLING TIME: 10 TO 15 MINUTES

* Fresh prune plums are not always available, and this is equally delicious with red plums or pears. Use 4 red plums, each cut into 6 thick slices, or use 2 large ripe pears, peeled, cored, and cut into ¼-inch slices. If using pears, we like to add up to 1 teaspoon of freshly grated nutmeg to the sugar and spice sprinkled on top.

Preheat the oven to 350°. Lightly butter or oil a 9-inch springform pan or a 9-inch round glass pie pan.

With an electric mixer, cream together the butter and brown sugar. Add the eggs and beat for 1 minute. Add the flour, baking powder, and salt and mix just until the dry ingredients are smoothly incorporated. Spoon the batter into the prepared pan and spread it evenly to form a thin layer that will rise when baked. Arrange the plum halves cut side down first around the outer edge (starburst fashion) and then fill in the center. Stir together the sugar and cinnamon and sprinkle it evenly over the torte.

Bake for 60 to 75 minutes, depending on the juiciness of the fruit. The batter will rise up and almost cover the fruit. The torte is ready when the top is lightly browned and the sides begin to pull away from the pan.

Cool on a rack for 10 to 15 minutes. Then run a knife between the torte and the sides of the springform pan before releasing the pan; or serve directly from the glass pie pan. Eat warm or at room temperature with whipped cream, if desired.

DIWALI

Curried Squash & Apple Soup
Mango Cranberry Chutney
Indian Vegetable Pancakes
Red Lentils & Rice
Greens with Cashews
Kheer
Spiced Coconut Date Bars (page 213)

In the Northern Hemisphere, festivals of light are especially welcome in November and December, two of the darkest and coldest months of the year. Diwali, along with Hanukkah, the Winter Solstice, Christmas, Kwanza, and the New Year bring families and friends close together to share food, gifts, memories, and a sense of renewal.

Diwali, which literally means "garland of lights" in Sanskrit, is usually a three-day festival celebrated by both Hindus and Sikhs in the month of November. In preparation for the holiday, homes are thoroughly cleaned, windows are opened to let in fresh air, and the rooms are decorated with freshly cut flowers. The first day begins before dawn with fireworks. Everyone dresses up in their new clothes and exchanges gifts along with many kinds of special sweets with their neighbors and relatives. Brightly lit oil lamps and candles welcome Laksmi, the goddess of wealth and prosperity.

The origins of Diwali are drawn from generations of folklore and legend which tell about the return of Lord Ram and his wife, Sita, after having lived in exile for twelve years. Diwali celebrates their homecoming. For children, it is a time to hear stories that teach about such virtues as generosity, knowledge, and hard work. The third day of Diwali corresponds to the beginning of the Lunar New Year.

Food for a Diwali celebration should be bright, warm, and colorful. Our menu features an autumnal harvest of fruits and vegetables in green, red, yellow, and gold. Crispy pancakes contrast nicely with a smooth, slightly sweet squash soup. An eye-catching array of lentils and saffrony rice, sautéed greens, and reddish-orange, sweet-tart mango-cranberry chutney are another reminder that food is meant to be both beautiful to look at and beautiful to eat.

To allow yourself a relaxed pace in preparing the menu, prepare the Curried Squash & Apple Soup, Mango Cranberry Chutney, Kheer, and Spiced Coconut Date Bars a day or two ahead. Not only will these dishes deepen their flavors as they sit, they will also require no last-minute fussing. Simply reheat the soup, and a few hours before dinner is to be served, prepare the Red Lentils & Rice, followed by the Greens with Cashews. Finally, assemble and cook the Indian Vegetable Pancakes so they will be crispy and hot at the table. For a warm, glowing atmosphere, light candles all around the house and enjoy the prosperity of friends and family.

CURRIED SQUASH & APPLE SOUP

Deep-orange squash and juicy, ripe apples characterize the sweet abundance of the autumn harvest. Combined with coriander and cumin, they meld into a beautifully golden, smooth soup that reflects the glowing candlelight of Diwali.

soup

SERVES 6
TOTAL TIME: 1 HOUR

2	CUPS CHOPPED ONIONS
2	TABLESPOONS BUTTER OR VEGETABLE OIL
1	TABLESPOON CUMIN SEEDS
2	TEASPOONS CORIANDER SEEDS
1	TEASPOON SALT
6	CUPS PEELED, SEEDED AND COARSELY CHOPPED BUTTERNUT SQUASH*
2	CUPS PEELED, CORED AND COARSELY CHOPPED APPLES
2	CUPS PEELED AND COARSELY CHOPPED SWEET POTATOES*
4	CUPS WATER

topping

1	TABLESPOON MINCED GARLIC
1	TABLESPOON VEGETABLE OIL
10	OUNCES FRESH SPINACH OR MUSTARD GREENS, RINSED AND CHOPPED

* About 3 pounds of butternut squash and just less than 2 pounds of sweet potatoes will yield the right amount for this recipe.

In a large nonreactive soup pot, sauté the onions in the butter or oil until soft and translucent, about 10 minutes. In a small dry skillet, toast the cumin and coriander seeds on low heat for 3 to 4 minutes, until aromatic and lightly browned. Cool for a few minutes and grind to a powder. Add the ground spices, salt, squash, apples, sweet potatoes, and water to the onions. Bring to a boil, then lower the heat, cover, and simmer on low heat for about 30 minutes, until all of the ingredients are thoroughly cooked and tender.

Meanwhile, in a large skillet, sauté the garlic in the oil for about 1 minute on medium heat, stirring constantly, until soft and just golden. Add the greens and sauté on high heat until the water evaporates and the greens wilt. Remove from the heat and set aside.

Purée the soup in small batches in a blender until smooth, adding about ¼ cup of water if the soup is thicker than you'd like. When ready to serve, gently reheat, ladle into shallow bowls to show off its good looks, and top each serving with some of the the sautéed greens.

MANGO CRANBERRY CHUTNEY

Cranberries add a Northern Hemisphere touch to this favorite tropical condiment. Their tartness provides a nice counterpoint to the sweetness of the mango, while their ruby hue lends an attractive color. The recipe makes a generous amount: Leftovers can be refrigerated for up to 2 weeks or frozen for 4 to 5 months.

1	TABLESPOON VEGETABLE OIL
½	CUP CHOPPED ONIONS
1	WHOLE CINNAMON STICK
1½	TEASPOONS GRATED FRESH GINGER ROOT
1	TEASPOON SALT
½	TEASPOON GROUND CARDAMOM
3	CUPS FRESH OR FROZEN WHOLE CRANBERRIES
⅔	CUP BROWN SUGAR, PACKED
½	CUP WATER
1	TABLESPOON CIDER VINEGAR
1	LARGE RIPE MANGO, PEELED AND DICED INTO ½-INCH CUBES*

YIELDS 3½ CUPS
TOTAL TIME: 35 MINUTES

* **Mangos have large pits and the pulp is slippery. A shallow slice from end to end along the two broad, flat sides works best. Score the mango flesh of each slice into cubes and pare them away from the skin. Peel the remaining skin around the pit, then carefully cut away the tender pulp and dice it.**

Warm the oil in a medium saucepan. Add the onions and sauté for 5 minutes. Stir in the cinnamon, ginger root, salt, and cardamom and cook on moderate heat for 5 more minutes, stirring constantly. Add the cranberries, brown sugar, water, and vinegar, bring to a simmer, and cook, uncovered, for about 10 minutes, until the cranberries pop and soften.

Add the mango and simmer for an additional 3 to 5 minutes, or until the mango is just melting into the chutney. Remove from the heat and adjust the brown sugar to taste.

Serve at room temperature or preferably chilled.

INDIAN VEGETABLE PANCAKES

Here is a mouthwatering potato pancake that has the character of a samosa: a soft, spicy potato and vegetable interior with a crispy fried exterior. It's possible to make the mixture and form the pancakes ahead, and then fry them just before serving. We like them topped with plain yogurt.

4½ CUPS PEELED AND CUBED POTATOES (1-INCH CUBES)	**YIELDS 12 PANCAKES** **TOTAL TIME: 1¼ HOURS**
1½ to 2 TEASPOONS SALT	
⅔ CUP VEGETABLE OIL	
1½ TEASPOONS WHOLE CUMIN SEEDS	
1½ TEASPOONS BLACK MUSTARD SEEDS*	
1 TEASPOON TURMERIC	
1½ CUPS FINELY CHOPPED ONIONS	
1½ CUPS DICED RED BELL PEPPERS	
2 CUPS PEELED AND GRATED CARROTS	
3 to 4 DROPS OF TABASCO OR OTHER HOT PEPPER SAUCE, MORE TO TASTE	
2 CUPS FROZEN PEAS	
1 CUP BREAD CRUMBS	

* Less pungent than yellow mustard seeds, black mustard seeds release their nutty flavor when sautéed until they pop. They are often used in pickling because of their preservative properties.

In a large pot, bring 2 quarts of water to a boil. Add the potatoes and ½ teaspoon of the salt and simmer for 10 to 15 minutes, until tender. Drain the potatoes and reserve some of the cooking liquid. Place the potatoes in a large bowl, moisten them with about 2 tablespoons of the reserved cooking liquid, and mash them with a potato masher.

Warm 2 tablespoons of the oil in a 10-inch skillet on medium heat. Add the cumin and mustard seeds and cook for about 30 seconds, until the mustard seeds begin to pop. Add the turmeric, 1 teaspoon of the salt, and the onions and continue to sauté for 8 to 10 minutes, until the onions are soft. Stir in the peppers and carrots and cook for about 5 minutes more, until crisp-tender, adding a splash of water, if needed, to prevent sticking. Sprinkle on a few drops of Tabasco sauce; then add the peas and stir for 1 to 2 minutes, until the peas soften.

Transfer the vegetables to the bowl of mashed potatoes and stir in ¼ cup of the bread crumbs. Rinse and dry the skillet. Mix together the vegetables and potatoes and, if necessary, adjust the salt and Tabasco sauce to taste. Divide the potato mixture to form twelve round patties, each about 3 inches across. Set aside on a platter. Sprinkle the remaining bread crumbs on the twelve patties, about ½ tablespoon per side.

Meanwhile, warm 3 tablespoons of the oil in the skillet until hot.

Gently slide three patties into the skillet with a wide spatula. Fry on medium heat for about 5 minutes, until crisp on the bottom. Carefully lift each one and turn it over, being careful not to splash the oil. Fry on the second side for 3 to 4 minutes, remove from the skillet, and drain on paper towels. Add a generous tablespoon of the remaining oil, fry three more patties, and drain well. Repeat twice more to make twelve pancakes in all.

Serve immediately or place the pancakes in a heatproof dish and keep them warm in a 300° oven until ready to serve.

RED LENTILS & RICE

This lentil dish, adapted from Ashley Miller's recipe for Lemony Lentils in her book *The Bean Harvest Cookbook,* brings the warm flavors of ginger, cinnamon, and red pepper to any cool-weather meal. It is quick and easy to prepare, since both the lentils and the rice cook in a short amount of time. The lemon wedges and cilantro are not an afterthought, but an integral part of the dish.

rice

SERVES 6
TOTAL TIME: 1 HOUR

- 1½ CUPS WHITE BASMATI RICE, RINSED AND DRAINED
- 2¾ CUPS WATER
- PINCH OF SAFFRON
- ½ TEASPOON SALT

lentils

- 1 CUP CHOPPED ONIONS
- 2 TABLESPOONS VEGETABLE OIL
- 1 TABLESPOON CHOPPED GARLIC
- 1 TABLESPOON PEELED, GRATED FRESH GINGER ROOT
- 1 TABLESPOON FRESHLY GRATED LEMON PEEL
- ½ TEASPOON GROUND CINNAMON
- ⅛ TEASPOON CAYENNE PEPPER OR 1 SMALL SEEDED AND MINCED JALAPEÑO
- 1 CUP PEELED AND CHOPPED CARROTS
- 1 CUP CHOPPED RED BELL PEPPER
- 1½ CUPS RED LENTILS, RINSED AND DRAINED
- 2 CUPS WATER
- 1½ TEASPOONS SALT, OR TO TASTE
- 6 LEMON WEDGES
- ⅓ CUP CHOPPED FRESH CILANTRO, MORE TO TASTE

Place the rice, water, saffron, and salt in a medium pot. Bring to a boil, stir once, cover, reduce the heat to low, and simmer for about 25 minutes, until the rice is tender and all of the water has been absorbed.

Meanwhile, in a large heavy soup pot, sauté the onions in the oil for about 10 minutes, until soft and translucent. Add the garlic, ginger root, lemon peel, cinnamon, and cayenne or jalapeño. Cook for 1 to 2 minutes, stirring constantly, and adding a little water if needed to prevent sticking. Add the carrots and cook for 3 to 4 minutes, until tender. Stir in the peppers and cook for about 2 minutes. Add the lentils, water, and salt; cover and bring to a boil—this will happen quickly, so stay close to the pot. Reduce the heat to low and simmer for 15 to 20 minutes, until the lentils are soft.

Serve the lentils over the saffron rice with lemon wedges and cilantro.

GREENS WITH CASHEWS

Our cashew, coconut, and lime dressing makes this simply prepared side dish highly flavorful. Leftover coconut milk can be frozen for later use or, better yet, just accompany this meal with a nice coconut-fruit smoothie.

SERVES 6
TOTAL TIME: 30 MINUTES

10	OUNCES FRESH SPINACH OR 8 CUPS LOOSELY PACKED KALE OR SWISS CHARD
2	TABLESPOONS VEGETABLE OIL
1½	CUPS CHOPPED ONIONS
2	GARLIC CLOVES, MINCED OR PRESSED
1	SMALL FRESH GREEN CHILE, SEEDED AND MINCED
⅓	CUP TOASTED CASHEWS*
2	TABLESPOONS FRESH LIME JUICE
¾	TEASPOON SALT, OR MORE TO TASTE
½	CUP REDUCED-FAT OR REGULAR COCONUT MILK (PAGE 397)
1	TEASPOON CURRY POWDER

* Toast cashews in a single layer on an unoiled baking tray at 350° for 3 to 5 minutes, until fragrant and golden brown. A toaster oven works well.

Rinse, stem, and coarsely chop the spinach, kale, or Swiss chard and set aside. Heat the oil in a large saucepan and add the onions, garlic, and chile. Cook on medium heat for 10 to 12 minutes, stirring occasionally.

Meanwhile, combine the cashews, lime juice, and salt in a blender or food processor and purée until fairly smooth. Gradually blend in the coconut milk: A few remaining little cashew chunks are fine. Set aside.

Add the curry powder to the saucepan and sauté for 1 minute. Add the greens, cover, and cook on medium-high heat until just tender, stirring often. This will take just 2 to 3 minutes for the spinach or Swiss chard, and about 6 minutes for the kale. Pour in the cashew mixture, stirring to evenly coat the greens. Sprinkle on salt to taste.

Serve warm or at room temperature.

KHEER

In India, kheer is traditionally served during the celebration of Diwali. Kheer is a sweet and slightly salty basmati rice pudding flavored with cardamom and saffron. It's easy to make and a basic recipe can have many variations. Ours omits saffron and adds golden raisins. While the pudding simmers slowly on top of the stove, you can be busy doing other tasks in the kitchen.

1/3	CUP WHITE BASMATI RICE, RINSED
4	CUPS MILK
1	TEASPOON SALT
1/2 to 2/3	CUP SUGAR
1/2	TEASPOON GROUND CARDAMOM
2	TEASPOONS PURE VANILLA EXTRACT
1/4	TEASPOON PURE ALMOND EXTRACT
1/3	CUP CHOPPED GOLDEN RAISINS
1/4	CUP TOASTED SLIVERED ALMONDS* (OPTIONAL)

SERVES 6
PREPARATION TIME: 10 TO 15 MINUTES
COOKING TIME: 1½ HOURS OR MORE

* Toast slivered almonds in a single layer on an unoiled baking tray at 350° for about 5 minutes, until fragrant and golden.

Combine the rice, milk, salt, and sugar in a medium saucepan with a heavy bottom. Stir briefly and warm on medium heat until the pudding starts to simmer. Cover, lower the heat, place the saucepan on a heat diffuser, and simmer the pudding slowly for at least 1½ hours, stirring 4 or 5 times. The pudding is done when the rice breaks down and the mixture thickens to the consistency of creamy oatmeal and begins to stick to the bottom of the pan.

Stir in the cardamom, vanilla and almond extracts, and raisins. Allow the pudding to cool. Serve at room temperature or chilled, topped with almonds, if desired.

SPORTS NIGHT SUPPER

Black Bean & Chocolate Chili
Shrimp & Mango Quesadillas
Creamy Mushroom Quesadillas
Roasted Squash with Corn & Beans
Mexican Lime Cumin Slaw
Beer or Root Beer in frosty mugs
Ice Cream with Classic Caramel Sauce (page 311)

"If you can't get off the couch, you can still eat like a pro."

Whether you're tuning into the Olympics, the Super Bowl, or a gripping game of golf, or even if your idea of a midwinter sport is having friends over for some marathon eating, the fans will go wild over this menu.

We've gone south of the border to warm up those chilly nights and perhaps take your mind to sunnier climes.

This menu is a good balance of elements both spicy and cooling, creamy and crisp. Everything can be prepared ahead of time. The Black Bean & Chocolate Chili will improve with long, slow cooking, and both the roasted squash and the slaw can be made early in the day and refrigerated until show time. Whichever quesadillas you choose will need to be skillet-browned shortly before serving. Either filling can be made and chilled hours in advance. Then just before serving, assemble the quesadillas and pan-fry them until everything is thoroughly hot.

If you must paint your face blue or some other becoming hue, turn to page 129 and take a shot at our recipe for nontoxic face paints.

BLACK BEAN & CHOCOLATE CHILI

Using chocolate in dishes other than desserts may seem odd, but it is not so unusual in countries where cocoa beans are grown. Chocolate's deep flavor provides an ambience in which other tastes can flourish. This chili is rich and unusual. We suggest serving it in smaller portions as a side dish or as part of a buffet.

SERVES 6 TO 8
TOTAL TIME: 50 MINUTES

2	TABLESPOONS VEGETABLE OIL
1½	CUPS CHOPPED ONIONS
4	GARLIC CLOVES, MINCED OR PRESSED
1	CELERY STALK, THINLY SLICED
1	SMALL FRESH CHILE, MINCED
1	TABLESPOON GROUND CUMIN
2	TEASPOONS DRIED OREGANO
½	TEASPOON GROUND CINNAMON
	PINCH OF GROUND CLOVES
1	TEASPOON GROUND CORIANDER
½	TEASPOON GROUND BLACK PEPPER
½	TEASPOON SALT
1½	CUPS CHOPPED BELL PEPPERS
3	CUPS COOKED OR CANNED BLACK BEANS (TWO 15.5-OUNCE CANS, RINSED AND DRAINED)
2	CUPS UNDRAINED CRUSHED CANNED TOMATOES (14.5-OUNCE CAN)
1	TABLESPOON FRESH LEMON JUICE
1	TABLESPOON SOY SAUCE
1½	OUNCES SEMI-SWEET CHOCOLATE, BROKEN INTO SMALL PIECES (ABOUT ¼ CUP)
	CHOPPED SCALLIONS

In a saucepan, warm the oil on medium heat. Add the onions and garlic and sauté until the onions become translucent, about 10 minutes. Add the celery and chile, cover, and cook for about 5 minutes.

Reduce the heat and stir in the cumin, oregano, cinnamon, cloves, coriander, black pepper, salt, and the bell peppers. Cover and cook for 5 minutes, until the bell peppers begin to soften. Stir occasionally to keep the spices from burning. If needed, add a little juice from the canned tomatoes.

Add the black beans, tomatoes, lemon juice, and soy sauce. Bring the chili to a simmer, cover, and cook for 5 to 10 minutes. Stir in the chocolate. When it has melted, adjust the salt, black pepper, and lemon juice to taste.

Garnish with chopped scallions.

SHRIMP & MANGO QUESADILLAS

This dish has an innovative array of ingredients and an intriguing balance of sweet, tart, and spicy flavors. At Moosewood, nothing less than luscious, ripe, fresh mangos will do for this quesadilla. Luckily, they have a reasonably long season in most markets.

If your tortillas are not very pliable, it may be easier to warm them for 20 to 30 seconds on each side in a large dry skillet on medium heat before filling them.

1	CUP CHOPPED ONIONS
2	GARLIC CLOVES, PRESSED OR MINCED
2	LARGE FRESH CHILES, SEEDED AND MINCED
3	TABLESPOONS VEGETABLE OIL
1	POUND RAW SHRIMP, PEELED AND DEVEINED
¼	CUP FRESH LIME JUICE
1	TEASPOON SALT
¼	CUP CHOPPED FRESH CILANTRO
2	CUPS PEELED RIPE MANGO, CUT INTO 1-INCH CUBES*
8	FLOUR TORTILLAS (8 INCHES ACROSS)
2	CUPS GRATED CHEDDAR AND/OR MONTEREY JACK CHEESE
1	CUP YOUR FAVORITE STORE-BOUGHT SALSA

SERVES 8
TOTAL TIME: 45 MINUTES

* Mangos have large pits and the pulp is slippery. A shallow slice from end to end along the two broad, flat sides works best. Score the mango flesh of each slice into cubes and pare them away from the skin. Peel the remaining skin around the pit, then carefully cut away the tender pulp and dice it.

In a skillet or saucepan, sauté the onions, garlic, and chiles in 2 tablespoons of the oil until the onions are soft, about 5 minutes. Stir in the shrimp, lime juice, salt, and cilantro and cook for 2 minutes. Add the mango and continue to cook for another 1 to 2 minutes, until the shrimp turns pink. Remove from the heat and drain any excess liquid.

Spread ½ cup of the shrimp mixture on one half of a tortilla, leaving a ½-inch border around the outer edge. Top the shrimp mixture with ¼ cup of the grated cheese. Fold the tortilla in half to form a semi-circle. Fill the remaining tortillas to make eight quesadillas in all.

Heat a lightly oiled large skillet. Place two quesadillas in the skillet and cook for 1 to 2 minutes on each side, until golden brown. Remove the quesadillas from the skillet and keep them warm while cooking the remaining six in pairs. Use the remaining tablespoon of oil, as needed, to keep the quesadillas from sticking to the skillet. Slice each quesadilla in half and serve warm, topped with a generous spoonful of salsa.

CREAMY MUSHROOM QUESADILLAS

The beauty of this dish is that it looks like it came out of the kitchen of an accomplished caterer, yet it is so simple to make. The tortillas are spread with a creamy mushroom-leek mixture, spiced up with some salsa and olives, and cut into neat triangles.

For convenience, we use a prepared salsa for this recipe. We like the unique rustic color and flavor of tomatillo salsa and recommend the Desert Pepper Trading Company brand. Or, use your own favorite salsa recipe or commercial brand. The tortillas will look especially handsome if you use a grill pan and the grill marks show, but a cast iron or heavy frying pan will work just fine, too.

4	CUPS WELL-RINSED AND CHOPPED LEEKS, WHITE AND TENDER GREEN PARTS (ABOUT 2 LARGE LEEKS)
3	TABLESPOONS VEGETABLE OIL
4	CUPS SLICED MUSHROOMS (12 OUNCES)
8	OUNCES NEÛFCHATEL OR CREAM CHEESE, AT ROOM TEMPERATURE
2	TABLESPOONS MINCED GREEN OLIVES
½	CUP GRATED SHARP CHEDDAR CHEESE
12	NINE-INCH FLOUR TORTILLAS
1	CUP PREPARED SALSA

SERVES 8
TOTAL TIME: 70 MINUTES

To make the filling, sauté the leeks in a large skillet with 2 tablespoons of the oil for about 5 minutes. Add the mushrooms and sauté on medium heat, stirring frequently, until their juices have evaporated. Remove from the heat and stir in the Neûfchatel, olives, and Cheddar cheese.

Heat a grill pan or cast iron skillet over medium heat. Lightly brush one side of each tortilla with the remaining oil. Place a tortilla, oiled side down, in the heated pan and press lightly with a spatula. Cook for about 1 minute, until grill marks show or the tortilla begins to brown. Repeat with the remaining tortillas.

To assemble the quesadillas, lay out 6 tortillas with the grilled side down. Evenly spread 2 tablespoons of salsa and ½ cup of the filling over each. Top each with a second tortilla, with the grilled side showing, and press down gently to seal.

Just before serving, place the quesadillas on a large baking sheet and heat in a 400° oven for about 5 minutes. Cool slightly. Use kitchen scissors or a sharp paring knife to cut each quesadilla into four pie-shaped wedges. Serve immediately.

ROASTED SQUASH WITH CORN & BEANS

For centuries, native cultures in the Western Hemisphere survived on the interdependent cultivation of corn and beans. In the Iroquois tradition of upstate New York, corn, beans, and squash—known as the "three sisters"—were the staple source of food. Grown together, the beans wound their vines around the sturdy corn stalks and the squash leaves shaded the ground, keeping it cool, moist, and free of weeds.

At Cornell University, the department of crop and soil sciences has been cultivating a demonstration garden of corn, beans, and squash to illustrate the caloric and protein advantage of the "three sisters" compared to crops of corn, beans, or squash alone. This garden is open to schools and visitors curious to learn about indigenous cropping systems.

5 to 6 CUPS CUBED BUTTERNUT SQUASH
(BITE-SIZED CHUNKS)

2   CUPS COARSELY CHOPPED RED ONIONS

2   TABLESPOONS MINCED OR PRESSED GARLIC

1   TEASPOON SALT

3   TABLESPOONS OLIVE OR OTHER VEGETABLE OIL

2   TABLESPOONS CHOPPED FRESH SAGE LEAVES

2   TEASPOONS DRIED THYME (2 TABLESPOONS FRESH)

1½   CUPS FRESH OR FROZEN CORN KERNELS

1½   CUPS FROZEN LIMA BEANS*

¼   CUP MINCED FRESH PARSLEY (OPTIONAL)

* Canned lima beans, rinsed and drained, are also fine.

SERVES 8
TOTAL TIME: ABOUT 1 HOUR

Preheat the oven to 450°.

In a large bowl, combine the squash, red onions, garlic, and salt. Evenly coat the vegetables with 2 tablespoons of the oil and spread them on a large baking tray. Bake for 40 to 45 minutes, stirring every 15 minutes, until the vegetables are softened but crisp around the edges.

When the squash has baked for about ½ hour, heat the remaining tablespoon of oil in a large skillet. Add the sage and thyme and simmer for just 4 to 5 seconds. Stir in the corn and lima beans and cook on low heat for about 5 minutes, until tender. Cover and set aside.

In a large serving bowl, toss together the roasted squash and red onions with the seasoned corn and beans. Add parsley, if desired, and serve immediately. This dish is fine to make ahead of time. Store it in a covered container in the refrigerator; then reheat just before serving.

MEXICAN LIME CUMIN SLAW

Mexican cuisine encompasses a wide variety of foods originating from a large geographic area and influenced by other cuisines over a very long time. Here's one recipe, a grain of sand on a beach, that we at Moosewood like a lot.

Our recipe makes a refreshing, mildly hot slaw. If you can't tolerate spicy seasonings, simply reduce or omit the amount of jalapeño pepper or the cayenne. Of course, some like it hot, and in that case this slaw can be made much hotter by adding more hot peppers. *Ay chihuahua!*

slaw

SERVES 6 TO 8
TOTAL TIME: 25 MINUTES

4	CUPS FINELY SHREDDED GREEN CABBAGE
1½	CUPS PEELED GRATED CARROTS
1	RED BELL PEPPER, SEEDED AND DICED
½ to ¾	CUP CHOPPED SCALLIONS
1	JALAPEÑO PEPPER, SEEDED AND MINCED

dressing

2	TABLESPOONS VEGETABLE OIL
2	TEASPOONS FRESHLY GRATED LIME PEEL
3	TABLESPOONS FRESH LIME JUICE
2	TABLESPOONS WHITE BALSAMIC OR CIDER VINEGAR
1	TABLESPOON SUGAR
1	TEASPOON GROUND CUMIN
1	TEASPOON SALT
	PINCH OF CAYENNE

Place all of the slaw vegetables in a serving bowl. In a small bowl, whisk together all of the dressing ingredients. Pour the dressing on the vegetables and toss thoroughly. Taste and, if you wish, add more salt and/or vinegar.

Serve immediately, or refrigerate until serving.

THANKSGIVING

In the fall of 1621, the pilgrims of Plymouth Colony celebrated their first harvest in the New World. William Bradford, the governor of Massachusetts, had proclaimed that all would set aside work for a day to give thanks for the abundant harvest of Indian corn, wheat, beans, squashes, and garden vegetables. Thanks were also due their Native American neighbors, who had generously shared food and seeds and their knowledge of successful farming practices. So, Chief Massasoit and ninety-nine men from the Wampanoag nation also contributed to and celebrated the feast, which included fish and meat, cornbread, plums, leeks, popcorn, and beer. At the Pilgrims' third American Thanksgiving, in 1623, turkey, cranberries, maple syrup, and pumpkin pie were added to the spread.

Two-hundred forty years later, in 1863, President Lincoln made Thanksgiving an official holiday celebrated on the last Thursday of November. Over the decades, with the influx of peoples and influences from around the world, this secular holiday with multiethnic origins has become a shared national ritual for almost everyone, no matter what their own heritage or history. This diversity is what makes it the most American of celebrations.

Today, of course, Thanksgiving is still about people getting together. It's about making connections with family and friends and reaching out to help those in need. It's about stopping everything for a day, or at least a few hours, to enjoy the plenitude of the season. For most of us it's the most anticipated big feast of the year.

Thanksgiving meals can be crowded, noisy, and overstimulating—a challenge for the harried cook. Advance planning is required just to make sure you have enough dishes and chairs, and for such a food-centered holiday, menu planning takes on extra importance. We think it's wonderful to make old family recipes and favorite foods (surely this is a day for nostalgic sentiments), but it's also fine to take some liberties with tradition.

Express who you are on Thanksgiving. Throw out most of the rules, but have at least one dish with corn to honor its historical importance in American culture. And don't forget to include autumn vegetables. Over the years, we've devised many different menus for Thanksgiving meals full of delicious harvest dishes, and we've grouped together here the recipes for two menus. One menu is vegetarian and one is vegan. Feel free to mix and match, devising a menu of your own.

Of course, an extensive menu, prepared for a large gathering, can cause stress for even seasoned cooks. Here's our best advice: Make lists, do as much as you can in advance, and choose some dishes that can be made ahead. Keep some tasks in mind to assign to willing volunteers. Taking part in the preparations can be very satisfying, especially for children. And if the inevitable should occur, remember that this year's mishaps will make great anecdotes in the years to come.

VEGETARIAN THANKSGIVING

While most long-term vegetarians no longer miss that big stuffed bird in the middle of the Thanksgiving table, there may still be some hankering for a front-and-center kind of main dish that attracts attention and gets the requisite number of *oohs* and *ahhhs*. Our Polenta Dome surrounded by colorful Roasted Autumn Vegetables more than fills the bill. Add to that some homemade rolls, an unusually festive-looking salad, fresh cranberry sauce with a twist, and a light fruit dessert plus that special pie, and you've got a Thanksgiving spread that won't be forgotten for years to come.

Many of the dishes on this menu can be made ahead of time, and we suggest you do just that. The "Jazzed Up" Cranberry Sauce takes less than 15 minutes to make and will keep for up to a week and the pumpkin pie stays fresh for several days, so make them early and stash them in the fridge. The day before Thanksgiving, whip up the Cracked Wheat Rolls and the Honey Roasted Pears. The rolls only take about 45 minutes of hands-on time; the rest is rising and baking. During the last rise of the rolls, prepare the pears; then you can pop them both in the oven together. The rolls will be ready about 10 to 15 minutes before the pears are finished. Store the rolls in a bread box and chill the pears. Prepare the dressing and all of the ingredients for the

Crisp Autumn Salad a day ahead too, or do it first thing Thanksgiving morning. Keep each salad ingredient in a separate container and sprinkle a little fresh lemon juice on the apples to keep them from discoloring.

On Thanksgiving Day, set the table and take a deep breath. If you have a very large oven or two ovens, prepare the Polenta Dome first and while it cools make the Roasted Autumn Vegetables just as described in the recipe. When it's time for the second batch of vegetables to go in the oven, put the dome in too. This will take about 2 hours total and everything will be ready at the same time.

However, if you have one standard oven, it will be a tight fit, so here's what to do. About 3 hours before the big meal, whisk together the marinade for the Roasted Autumn Vegetables and prep the first batch of long-cooking vegetables. Get them in the oven; then prepare the polenta dome and finish preparing the rest of the vegetables. Remove the first tray of roasted vegetables from the oven, lower the temperature to 400°, and juggle the second batch of vegetables and the cooled Polenta Dome into the oven. In 30 minutes, they'll both be ready.

Meanwhile, put the cranberry sauce and any other condiments you wish, such as butter and salt and pepper, on the table. Remove the Honey Roasted Pears from the refrigerator. Toss together the Crisp Autumn Salad. When the dome and the second batch of roasted vegetables come out of the oven, you may want to reheat the first tray of vegetables for a few minutes. Decorate the dome with the vegetables. While you finish assembling the dome, wrap the Cracked Wheat Rolls in foil and briefly reheat. Ring the bell for dinner. For dessert, break out the pumpkin pie and serve the pears at room temperature, or cover them and reheat at 400° for about 10 minutes.

For the hardy types who live in cold climes, try taking a brisk walk after dinner and before dessert. Let the pears slowly warm in a 200° oven while you're out. Then come home and revel in the luscious, hot, spicy fruit with its aromatic syrup in a way you never could if you hadn't gone out in the cold for a spell. Happy Thanksgiving!

CRACKED WHEAT ROLLS

Moosewood cook Sara Robbins has a real knack for baking. She can throw together that butter, flour, and sugar just right, and the results never fail to delight. No matter how much food graces your Thanksgiving table, no one will be able to resist these buttery, sweet, wholesome rolls, fresh and steaming from the oven. If you have any left over, they freeze very well.

sponge

1	CUP MEDIUM-GRAIN BULGHUR
1½	CUPS BOILING WATER
2	TABLESPOONS BUTTER
1	TABLESPOON DRY YEAST
½	CUP LUKEWARM WATER (105° TO 115°)
3	TABLESPOONS BROWN SUGAR, PACKED
1	CUP UNBLEACHED WHITE BREAD FLOUR

dough

2	EGGS, BEATEN
1	TEASPOON SALT
3 to 4	CUPS UNBLEACHED WHITE BREAD FLOUR

1 to 2 TABLESPOONS MELTED BUTTER

YIELDS 16 TO 18 ROLLS
PREPARATION TIME: 45 MINUTES
RISING TIME: ABOUT 2 HOURS
BAKING TIME: 25 MINUTES
COOLING TIME: 5 TO 10 MINUTES

Place the bulghur in a large heatproof bowl and cover with the boiling water. Add the butter, stir, and set aside to cool to room temperature.

Meanwhile, make the batter, or "sponge." In a small bowl, dissolve the yeast in the lukewarm water. When the bulghur has cooled for about 15 minutes, add the yeast mixture, brown sugar, and the cup of flour. Beat for 100 strokes. (Don't worry: It sounds exhausting, but it actually takes less than 3 minutes and is invigorating.) Cover the bowl with a damp towel and set it aside to rise in a warm place until the mixture bubbles, about 45 minutes.

Uncover the sponge and stir in the beaten eggs, salt, and 2 to 2½ cups of the flour to make a dough stiff enough to knead. Turn the dough out onto a lightly floured surface and knead until it is elastic, 8 to 10 minutes. Oil the bowl; then return the kneaded dough to it and turn it over to coat both sides with the oil. Cover the bowl with the damp towel and set aside in a warm, draft-free place until the dough has doubled in size, 45 to 60 minutes.

Lightly oil a large baking sheet.

Punch down the dough and turn it onto a cutting board. Divide the dough into 16 to 18 equal pieces. Roll each piece into a ball and place the balls of dough about 2 inches apart on the prepared baking sheet. Cover with a damp towel and let rise again for 20 minutes.

Meanwhile, preheat the oven to 400°.

When the rolls have risen (hallelujah!), bake for 25 minutes, or until golden and hollow-sounding when tapped. Remove from the oven and immediately brush with the melted butter. Cool for 5 to 10 minutes before serving.

"JAZZED UP" CRANBERRY SAUCE

Cranberry sauce is usually the most colorful addition to a holiday menu. Why not try this version, which is dressed up with raspberry vinegar? Our unique blending of flavors creates a sensational novelty of an oldtime classic.

½   CUP ORANGE JUICE, PREFERABLY FRESH

¼   CUP RASPBERRY VINEGAR

1   CUP SUGAR

¼   TEASPOON SALT

12   OUNCES FRESH OR FROZEN CRANBERRIES*

1   WHOLE CINNAMON STICK

SERVES 6 TO 8
PREPARATION TIME: 10 MINUTES
COOLING TIME: 30 MINUTES

* Rinse the cranberries well and discard any disreputable-looking ones.

In a medium saucepan, combine the orange juice, vinegar, sugar, and salt. Bring to a boil and stir until the sugar dissolves. Stir in the cranberries and add the cinnamon stick. Reduce the heat and simmer until the cranberries burst and the sauce is slightly thickened, 7 to 10 minutes.

Remove the cinnamon stick. Cool for about 30 minutes or refrigerate. The sauce will continue to thicken as it cools. Covered and refrigerated, it will keep for up to one week.

POLENTA DOME

Butternut squash gives this polenta a lovely pumpkin color and caramelized onions add a savory sweetness. Pour the polenta into a wide bowl rather than a tall narrow bowl; that way, the dome will firm and brown better in the oven and will slice neatly at the table. Then get out your best platter! Surrounded by our Roasted Autumn Vegetables, this is a big centerpiece of a dish—our tribute to the architecture of Italy.

For an added touch, sprinkle the finished dome with a little shredded mozzarella, Pecorino Romano, aged provolone, or extra-sharp Cheddar.

4	CUPS WATER OR VEGETABLE STOCK
1½	TEASPOONS SALT
1	TABLESPOON OLIVE OIL
2	CUPS DICED ONIONS
3	GARLIC CLOVES, MINCED OR PRESSED
2	CUPS CORNMEAL
1	MEDIUM-SMALL BUTTERNUT SQUASH (ABOUT 2 POUNDS)
1	TABLESPOON MINCED FRESH SAGE (1 TEASPOON DRIED)
2	TEASPOONS GROUND FENNEL SEEDS
½	TEASPOON GROUND BLACK PEPPER
1	CUP GRATED SHARP CHEESE (OPTIONAL)

SERVES 8
PREPARATION TIME: 40 MINUTES
COOLING TIME: 30 MINUTES
BAKING TIME: 30 MINUTES

In a covered pot, bring the water or stock and 1 teaspoon of the salt to a boil. Generously oil a 2-quart or larger bowl.

While the water heats, warm the olive oil in a heavy skillet on medium heat. Cook the onions, garlic, and ½ teaspoon of the salt for about 20 minutes, stirring frequently, until the onions are caramelized.

When the water boils, gradually pour in the cornmeal while stirring vigorously. Reduce the heat until the thickening cornmeal simmers gently. Cook, stirring frequently, until the polenta is thick and tastes done (see Note).

Meanwhile, peel and seed the squash. Use a food processor or hand grater to shred it to yield 2 cups of grated squash. Stir the squash, sage, fennel, and pepper into the sautéing onions and cook for 3 to 4 minutes. If the vegetables begin to stick, add a tiny bit of water. Cover and remove from the heat.

When the polenta is ready, stir in the sautéed vegetables. Add the cheese, if using. Pour the polenta into the prepared bowl and set it aside to cool for at least 30 minutes, until set.

Preheat the oven to 400°.

About ½ hour before serving, turn the cooled polenta dome onto an ovenproof platter or a large baking pan and bake for about 30 minutes, or until hot.

note

For a dome, the aim is a firm but pourable polenta. Finely ground cornmeal will cook in just a few minutes. Most medium-grind, fairly dark yellow cornmeals will take about 20 minutes to cook. Stone-ground and very coarse cornmeals can take up to 45 minutes. All of the varieties will probably need additions of water during cooking.

ROASTED AUTUMN VEGETABLES

Roasted vegetables are rich and satisfying. Here we've chosen the ones we like best with the Polenta Dome, but others such as baby turnips, new potatoes, or tiny whole pattypan squash all work well. If you like, try the Polenta Dome on a bed of steamed spinach and surrounded by the roasted vegetables.

Roasting may take longer than other cooking methods, but the vegetables require minimal preparation and attention. Vegetables roast best in a single layer, so for this recipe you'll need two large baking pans or several smaller ones. If the vegetables are crowded, they'll steam and a surface glaze won't form.

Potatoes, onions, and carrots take about an hour to roast to caramelized perfection. Peppers, sweet potatoes, zucchini, mushrooms, and plum tomatoes take only ½ hour. So we put the harder vegetables in the oven about ½ hour before adding the softer vegetables.

herbed garlic marinade

SERVES 8 WITH POLENTA DOME,
4 AS A MAIN DISH ALONE
PREPARATION TIME: 30 MINUTES
ROASTING TIME: 1 HOUR
TOTAL TIME: 75 MINUTES

⅓	CUP OLIVE OIL
2	TABLESPOONS BALSAMIC VINEGAR OR FRESH LEMON JUICE
5	GARLIC CLOVES, MINCED OR PRESSED
½	TEASPOON SALT
¼	TEASPOON GROUND BLACK PEPPER
1 to 2	TABLESPOONS CHOPPED FRESH ROSEMARY OR SAGE

vegetables

12	BOILING ONIONS OR 1 LARGE ONION, PEELED AND ENDS TRIMMED
1	BUNCH WHOLE TINY CARROTS WITH TOPS OR 3 MEDIUM CARROTS
2	SWEET POTATOES
12	TINY WHOLE ZUCCHINI OR 3 MEDIUM ZUCCHINI
2	RED AND/OR YELLOW BELL PEPPERS
10	OUNCES BABY PORTABELLOS OR OTHER FIRM MUSHROOMS
6 to 8	FRESH PLUM TOMATOES
	SALT TO TASTE

Preheat the oven to 450°. Lightly oil two large baking pans.

In a bowl, mix together all of the marinade ingredients.

Score the tops of the boiling onions about one-third of the way down in a tic-tac-toe pattern or thickly slice the large onion. Toss with about 1 tablespoon of the marinade to evenly coat and place on a large baking pan. If using the boiling onions, position them scored side up.

Peel the carrots. If using whole tiny carrots, cut off the tops, leaving ½ inch of green. If using larger carrots, cut lengthwise into halves and then crosswise into 2-inch pieces. Toss with about 1 tablespoon of marinade, add them to the baking pan, and roast the onions and carrots for 30 minutes.

Meanwhile, prepare the rest of the vegetables for roasting. Peel the sweet potatoes and cut them into generous bite-sized chunks or wedges. Leave tiny zucchini whole or halve them lengthwise. If using larger zucchini, trim the ends, slice into quarters lengthwise, and then cut crosswise into 2-inch pieces. Halve and core the bell peppers and cut into 2-inch squares. Trim any tough mushroom stems and cut larger mushrooms in half. Halve the plum tomatoes lengthwise.

Coat each type of vegetable with about 1 tablespoon of marinade.

When the onions and carrots have roasted for 30 minutes, stir them and lower the oven temperature to 400°. Place the newly prepared vegetables on the second large baking pan. If there isn't enough room, push the onions and carrots to one end of their pan and add the remaining new vegetables to the hot pan.

Roast all of the vegetables for 15 minutes, stir well, and continue to roast for another 10 to 15 minutes, until tender and slightly caramelized. Add salt to taste.

On a big platter, arrange the roasted vegetables around the Polenta Dome.

variation

If you prefer, shorten the oven time by first blanching the harder vegetables until just crisp-tender, then put all of the vegetables in the oven at the same time for about ½ hour.

CRISP AUTUMN SALAD

Interesting and attractive, this is a good salad to begin or end any fancy meal. The idea of Maple Mustard Dressing may startle you at first, but it's wonderful on the crisp apples and fennel and offset by the juicy grapes, nuts, and Stilton cheese. This is not just any old green salad; this one has character.

For a more casual meal another time, try it with just soup.

salad

SERVES 8
TOTAL TIME: 35 MINUTES

½   POUND MESCLUN OR SPRING MIX

3   CRISP APPLES, CORED AND THINLY SLICED

2   CUPS THINLY SLICED FENNEL BULB

24   LARGE GRAPES, HALVED AND SEEDED

¾   RED ONION, THINLY SLICED

¾   CUP TOASTED WALNUTS*

¾   CUP CRUMBLED STILTON CHEESE (ABOUT 2 OUNCES)

maple mustard dressing

3   TABLESPOONS PURE MAPLE SYRUP

1½   TABLESPOONS DIJON MUSTARD

6   TABLESPOONS APPLE CIDER VINEGAR

1½   TABLESPOONS EXTRA-VIRGIN OLIVE OIL

SALT AND GROUND BLACK PEPPER TO TASTE

* Toast walnuts in a single layer on an unoiled baking tray at 350° for about 5 minutes, until fragrant and brown.

Arrange the mesclun on individual salad plates or on a large flat platter. Top with the rest of the salad ingredients in an attractive tangle.

In a small bowl, whisk all of the dressing ingredients together with a fork. Pour over the salad and serve.

HONEY ROASTED PEARS

When the chill autumn air sets in, fresh ripe pears roasted to perfection have to be one of the season's best treats. What's extra nice is that these pears can be prepared a day or two ahead: Warmed up at the last minute, they're just as splendid.

You can make them plain and simple with butter, honey, and pear juice, or add sweet spices and (surprise!) balsamic vinegar for a sophisticated, sweet-tart flavor. Fruit connnoisseurs will insist on eating them unadorned, but adding a dollop of fresh whipped cream or a scoop of vanilla ice cream can be mighty fine, too.

8	LARGE RIPE PEARS, SUCH AS BOSC, D'ANJOU OR BARTLETT
2	CUPS UNSWEETENED PEAR JUICE*
½	CUP MILD HONEY
¼	CUP BALSAMIC VINEGAR (OPTIONAL)
½	TEASPOON GROUND GINGER (OPTIONAL)
1	TEASPOON GROUND CINNAMON (OPTIONAL)
½	CUP BUTTER

SERVES 8
PREPARATION TIME: 10 MINUTES
BAKING TIME: 35 TO 40 MINUTES
STOVE-TOP TIME: 10 MINUTES

* We like After the Fall brand. If you can't find pear juice, pear nectar will work fine. There are good organic nectars that contain only pear purée, apple juice, and ascorbic acid.

Preheat the oven to 400°. Lightly butter a 10 x 15-inch ceramic or glass baking dish or two 9-inch Pyrex pie pans.

Cut each pear lengthwise into quarters and remove the core. Place the pears skin side up in the prepared baking dish or pie pans. In a medium bowl, combine the pear juice and honey. If you like, stir in the balsamic vinegar, ginger, and/or cinnamon. Mix well and pour evenly over the pears. Dot with the butter.

Cover with aluminum foil and bake for 30 minutes; then uncover and bake for another 5 to 10 minutes, or until the pears are tender. Transfer the pears to a platter and pour their sauce into a small saucepan. Cook on high heat for about 10 minutes, until reduced by half and somewhat caramelized. Drizzle the syrupy sauce on the pears.

Serve warm or at room temperature. If stored in the refrigerator, reheat briefly in a microwave or conventional oven until the butter is melted, then serve.

PUMPKIN MAPLE PIE

Ever since pumpkin pie was served at the second Thanksgiving celebration, it's been the dessert most people gobble down on Thanksgiving Day. However, it's just as appreciated on other occasions during the fall and winter, when it's an unanticipated treat.

Maple syrup is a natural with pumpkin and creates a smooth, not-too-sweet pie. Milk with more butterfat will make a richer, creamier pie filling, but even skim milk will work.

SERVES 12 TO 16
PREPARATION TIME: 30 MINUTES
BAKING TIME: 55 TO 65 MINUTES

crust

2	CUPS UNBLEACHED WHITE PASTRY FLOUR
2	TABLESPOONS SUGAR (OPTIONAL)
½	TEASPOON SALT (OPTIONAL)
⅔	CUP CHILLED BUTTER, PREFERABLY UNSALTED
1	TEASPOON PURE VANILLA EXTRACT

6 to 8 TABLESPOONS ORANGE JUICE OR COLD WATER

filling

4	CUPS SOLID-PACK PUMPKIN (TWO 16-OUNCE CANS)*
5	EGGS
¾	CUP PURE MAPLE SYRUP
2	CUPS MILK, HALF-AND-HALF, HEAVY CREAM OR EVAPORATED SKIM MILK**
1	TEASPOON SALT
2	TEASPOONS GROUND CINNAMON
1	TEASPOON GROUND GINGER
½	TEASPOON GROUND NUTMEG

* Make sure you purchase plain pumpkin, not pie filling.

** Evaporated skim milk contains 200 calories and less than a gram of fat per cup. Sixty percent of the water has been removed from evaporated milk, which gives it a creamy rich texture. Don't confuse it with condensed milk, which is sweetened.

In a large bowl, stir together the flour, and the sugar and salt, if using. Cut the butter into small chunks and mix it into the flour mixture with a pastry cutter or your fingertips until it resembles coarse meal. In a cup, combine the vanilla and the orange juice or water. Gradually stir it into the flour mixture with a fork, until the flour is moistened and forms a dough. You may not need all of the liquid. Gather the dough into a ball and cut it into two equal pieces.

Roll out each piece of dough on a lightly floured surface to form a 12-inch circle. Transfer each circle of dough to a 9-inch pie plate. Fold the edges under and crimp them. Refrigerate the crusts until the filling is ready.

Preheat the oven to 375°.

In a large bowl, combine all of the filling ingredients and whisk until smooth. Pour into the prepared crusts and bake until the crust is golden and a knife inserted halfway between the center and the edge comes out clean, 55 to 65 minutes. Cool on a rack; then cover and refrigerate until serving time.

maple syrup

Maple syrup was derived from the "sweet waters" prized by Native Americans of the Northeast, who discovered that the sap of trees could be collected in the late winter and early spring. They found the sap of sugar maples particularly sweet and delicious. Before the advent of metal taps, Indians collected sap by making gashes in the trees, then capturing the sweet liquid in hollowed-out wooden troughs. By placing hot stones in a pot of sap to heat and reduce the water content, its sweetness could be intensified. Since sap was collected during cold months, it could also be frozen. The layer of ice that formed on top was mostly water, while the heavier part of the sap settled on the bottom. When the ice was removed, a sweeter concentrate remained.

Although there were no metal cooking vessels, sap could be boiled in birch bark containers over slow fires to make syrup and maple sugar, because birch bark does not burn as long as liquid is kept in it. When the syrup became thick as molasses, some of it could then be boiled over a slow fire until it crystallized into rock sugar, or stirred until cold to make a granulated sugar that was then formed into lumps or cakes. When Europeans introduced metal cooking vessels, Indians began using iron kettles to boil down the sap. Maple syrup ranges in color from light amber to brown. While intensely sweet, maple syrup and maple sugar have a smooth, delicate flavor and intoxicating aroma. Give thanks to the Native Americans for this treasure of the Northeastern woodlands.

VEGAN THANKSGIVING

MENU

Harvest Nuts & Seeds
Red Cabbage with Cranberries
Mushroom Filo Pastries
Mashed Potatoes & Parsnips with Caramelized Onion Gravy
Roasted Winter Squash
Apple Pecan Crumble

Woe to the parents newly informed that their son and his girlfriend, both expected home for Thanksgiving, are now eating "vegan." When he became a vegetarian, *that* required a family adjustment . . . but, really, right before Thanksgiving, the whole point of which (after gratitude, of course) is *everyone's* total enjoyment of food?

In fact, there's no need to panic. We've created a vegan Thanksgiving menu that we are certain will please all. Indeed, we have holiday menus throughout this book that are largely vegan or can become so with some artful picking and choosing from other menus.

For those who are unclear about what a vegan diet entails, it is a type of vegetarian diet based purely on foods from the world of fruits and vegetables, which includes grains and beans. In a vegan diet, no animal foods are eaten—no milk, cheese, butter, or eggs. Some vegans even demur honey, an animal product. People who eat vegan may do so for one of several reasons. Some cite health concerns: cholesterol, saturated fats, lactose intolerance. Others are repelled by the violent and exploitative treatment of animals. (There are vegans who, in addition to not eating animal foods, do not wear clothing or jewelry made from animals or their toil—no leather, silk, pearls, or feathers.) Many see a vegan diet as the most environmentally responsible way of eating. The increased use of land for livestock grazing contributes to the deforestation and erosion of the countryside. If the vast acreage now dedicated to growing animal feed were converted to agriculture for human consumption, pound for pound it could feed more people than the meat that is produced by the same land use.

At Moosewood, we are serving more and more vegan customers as well as more non-vegan diners interested in having vegan meals on a regular basis. Indeed, mainstream nutritional wisdom strongly recommends that we all eat vegan at least some of the time.

So here's a great vegan Thanksgiving menu, but how do you serve everything that needs to be piping hot without overcooking some of it? To clear your space and your mind, we recommend preparing the Apple Pecan Crumble early in the day or a day ahead. Harvest Nuts & Seeds can be made way ahead: Hide them in the freezer to save them from the nibblers. The Red Cabbage with Cranberries and the Caramelized Onion Gravy can also be made ahead of time; neither will suffer a bit. Because the roasted squash is baked at the highest temperature, we suggest baking it first and then rewarming it during the last 10 minutes that the Mushroom Filo Pastries are in the oven. Drizzle the squash with the sweet-and-sour sauce just before serving. While the filo pastries bake, prepare the Mashed Potatoes & Parsnips on the stove top and reheat the onion gravy.

By the way, some of our least stressful Thanksgivings happened when recipes were divvied up among willing family members or friends. Cooking together is fun and can add a co-creative dimension to the dinner. If everyone contributes, no one is overwhelmed. And remember, those who don't cook can always do their part at the end of the meal.

HARVEST NUTS & SEEDS

This addictive appetizer, with a coating like a delicate nut brittle, combines an abundant assortment of nuts and seeds with just the right amount of sugar and spice. Add the cayenne to taste: It can provide a nice kick without taking over.

2	TABLESPOONS VEGETABLE OIL OR BUTTER
3	TABLESPOONS PURE MAPLE SYRUP
½	CUP PINE NUTS
½	CUP CHOPPED HAZELNUTS
½	CUP SLICED ALMONDS
½	CUP RAW PUMPKIN SEEDS
½	CUP RAW SUNFLOWER SEEDS
2	TABLESPOONS BROWN SUGAR, PACKED
½	TEASPOON SALT
¼	TEASPOON PAPRIKA
⅛	TEASPOON CAYENNE (OPTIONAL)

YIELDS 4 CUPS
TOTAL TIME: 35 TO 40 MINUTES

Preheat the oven to 350°.

In a small saucepan, warm the oil with the maple syrup on medium heat for about ½ minute. Toss together the pine nuts, hazelnuts, almonds, pumpkin seeds, sunflower seeds, brown sugar, salt, and paprika in a bowl. Sprinkle in the cayenne to taste. Pour on the butter mixture and stir well to thoroughly coat the nuts and seeds. Spread them evenly (not clumped together) on an unoiled baking sheet.

Bake for 8 to 10 minutes, turn them over with a spatula, and bake until golden, 8 to 10 minutes more. Be careful not to let the mixture burn. Remove from the oven, loosen the nuts and seeds with a spatula, and allow them to cool for about 5 minutes. Store in a sealed container at room temperature or freeze for long-term storage.

RED CABBAGE WITH CRANBERRIES

This simply delicious side dish is sweet and sour with a difference—the tart accent of cranberries. The object is to have discreet, intact, bright red cranberry jewels interspersed throughout the darker maroon of the cooked red cabbage, so be careful to keep the cranberries from disintegrating.

¼	CUP VEGETABLE OIL
4	CUPS THINLY SLICED ONIONS
8	CUPS THINLY SLICED RED CABBAGE
1	TEASPOON SALT, OR TO TASTE
⅔	CUP APPLE JUICE OR CIDER
2	CUPS FRESH OR FROZEN CRANBERRIES, SORTED AND RINSED*
2	TABLESPOONS CIDER VINEGAR
2	TABLESPOONS SUGAR, OR TO TASTE

SERVES 8
TOTAL TIME: 50 MINUTES

* If using frozen cranberries, remove them from the freezer and allow them to thaw at room temperture while you prepare the ingredients and cook the onions and cabbage.

Warm the oil in a large saucepan on medium heat. Add the onions and sauté for about 10 minutes, until translucent. Add the cabbage, sprinkle with the salt, and continue to cook, stirring often, for about 15 minutes, or until the cabbage is tender.

Add the apple juice or cider and the cranberries and cook, stirring continuously for 3 to 4 minutes, just until the cranberries begin to pop. The cranberries should be tender but still hold their shape.

Remove the saucepan from the heat, stir in the vinegar and sugar, and serve immediately.

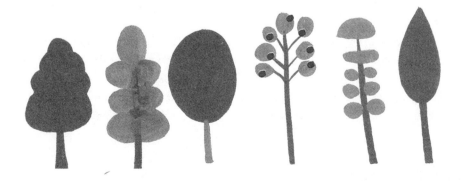

MUSHROOM FILO PASTRIES

This savory, flaky pastry with its creamy mushroom-leek filling is the perfect centerpiece for a vegan Thanksgiving. Or it can be an option for the vegetarians in your family. Just don't be surprised if *everyone* at the table helps eat them up!

The filo pastries can be made ahead of time and baked at the last minute. Just wrap them well and keep them refrigerated until about ½ hour before dinnertime. If you've never tried firm silken tofu, we think this recipe will quickly make you a fan. Its smooth, creamy texture is never chalky and is perfect for vegan fillings.

1	TABLESPOON OLIVE OIL
3	CUPS RINSED AND CHOPPED LEEKS*
½	TEASPOON SALT
8	CUPS CHOPPED MUSHROOMS (1½ POUNDS)
½	CUP DRY SHERRY
2	TABLESPOONS CHOPPED FRESH THYME
1	CAKE FIRM LOW-FAT SILKEN TOFU (12 OUNCES)
2	TABLESPOONS FRESH LEMON JUICE
2	TABLESPOONS SOY SAUCE
½	CUP OLIVE OIL
¼	TEASPOON SALT
¾	POUND FILO PASTRY (12 X 17-INCH SHEETS)

YIELDS 8 PASTRIES
PREPARATION TIME: 50 MINUTES
BAKING TIME: 25 MINUTES

* Cut off the root end of the leeks and remove any tough green leaves. Rinse the white and tender green stalks under water. Slice the leeks lengthwise in half, or into quarters if very large, and rinse again. Chop the leeks crosswise and fully submerge in a bowl of water. Transfer to a colander; then rinse a final time to completely remove all of the sand and grit.

Preheat the oven to 400°. Lightly oil two baking sheets.

Warm the oil in a large skillet. Add the leeks and salt and sauté on high heat for about 3 minutes. Reduce the heat to medium and continue to sauté for 5 minutes, stirring often, until tender. Add the mushrooms and continue to sauté for another 5 minutes, until they begin to release their juices. Stir in the sherry and the thyme and bring to a simmer. Cook, uncovered, stirring occasionally, for about 15 minutes, until the liquid has reduced and the mixture is almost dry. Remove from the heat and set aside.

Crumble the tofu into the bowl of a food processor, add the lemon juice and soy sauce, and purée until smooth and creamy. Stir the purée into the sautéed mushrooms and mix well.

In a small bowl, combine the oil and the salt. Unfold 16 sheets of filo on a dry, spacious work surface. Have the filling, the oil, and a pastry brush close at hand (see Note). Take two sheets of filo from the stack and, keeping them together, place them with their short sides facing you. Brush the top sheet lightly with oil. (The salt tends to sink to the bottom, so mix it by swirling the pastry brush each time you dip into the oil mixture.) Fold both sheets neatly in half lengthwise and brush the strip with oil. Spread ½ cup of filling from the bottom edge of the filo strip to the middle. Fold the lower right corner up and over diagonally until the bottom edge is flush with the left side and you have a triangle at the end. Brush once with oil, and then keep folding the triangle up, as you would a flag, to make a triangular pastry. Brush both sides of the finished pastry lightly with oil and place on one of the prepared baking sheets.

Repeat to make eight pastries in all. Bake for about 25 minutes, until golden brown and slightly puffed. Serve hot.

note

Unoiled filo becomes brittle when exposed to air, so it's best to be in a draft-free spot while you work and to keep a damp towel on the not-yet-used filo. An inexpensive new 2-inch paintbrush works great as a filo pastry brush.

MASHED POTATOES & PARSNIPS

We think that the promise of eating mashed potatoes is one of the primary reasons folks continue to prepare and look forward to holiday meals. Here is a creamy-tasting vegan mashed potato recipe that celebrates the tastes of autumn by incorporating the sweet musk of parsnips.

Serve it with our Caramelized Onion Gravy (opposite) and your guests will be swooning in comfort-food heaven.

10	CUPS THINLY SLICED YUKON GOLD POTATOES*
3	CUPS PEELED AND THINLY SLICED PARSNIPS
6	GARLIC CLOVES, MINCED OR PRESSED
3	TABLESPOONS EXTRA-VIRGIN OLIVE OIL
1½	TEASPOONS SALT
¼	TEASPOON GROUND BLACK PEPPER

SERVES 8 TO 10
TOTAL TIME: 45 MINUTES

* Yukon Golds whip up wonderfully creamy without the help of milk or butter.

Combine the potatoes and parsnips in a large pot with enough water to cover. Place a tight-fitting lid on the pot and bring to a boil on high heat. Reduce the heat and simmer until the vegetables are soft, about 20 minutes.

Meanwhile, sauté the garlic in the olive oil on medium-high heat, stirring constantly, for about 1 minute. When the vegetables are cooked, reserve 1 cup of the cooking liquid; then drain the vegetables and return them to the pot. Add the garlic and oil to the vegetables and mash with the cooking liquid. Stir in the salt and pepper. Serve hot.

CARAMELIZED ONION GRAVY

At Moosewood, we love creating recipes that bring a whole new perspective to time-honored customs. Nothing is more traditionally American than mashed potatoes with gravy—songs have even been written about it—but unlike most gravies, this one, made with caramelized onions and vegetarian broth, is healthful, vegan, and versatile. Try it on dishes such as tofu burgers, grilled portabello mushrooms, or omelets, too.

2	TABLESPOONS VEGETABLE OIL
6	CUPS THINLY SLICED VIDALIA OR SPANISH ONIONS
½	TEASPOON SALT
¼	TEASPOON DRIED THYME (¾ TEASPOON FRESH)
½	TEASPOON MINCED FRESH ROSEMARY
½	TEASPOON DRIED MARJORAM (1½ TEASPOONS FRESH)
¼	TEASPOON FRESHLY GRATED NUTMEG
3	TABLESPOONS SOY SAUCE
2	CUPS COMMERCIAL "NO-CHICKEN BROTH"*
¼	CUP DRY SHERRY OR MARSALA
2	TABLESPOONS CORNSTARCH
¼	TEASPOON GROUND BLACK PEPPER, OR TO TASTE

YIELDS 3 CUPS
TOTAL TIME: 35 TO 40 MINUTES

* Natural foods stores and gourmet supermarkets now carry delicious vegetarian mock chicken broths in the soup aisles, labeled "no-chicken" or "unchicken." Imagine Foods produces a good one that we can recommend. It is sold in aseptic quart packages that, when opened, will keep in the refrigerator for up to 10 days.

Warm the oil in a large saucepan on medium-high heat. Add the onions and sauté for 2 to 3 minutes, until the onions are coated with oil. Stir in the salt, thyme, rosemary, marjoram, and nutmeg. Continue to cook, uncovered, stirring often, for about 25 minutes, until limp and browned. You should have a generous cup of caramelized onions.

Add the soy sauce, 1¾ cups of the broth, and the sherry or marsala to the onions. Bring to a simmer. Dissolve the cornstarch in the remaining ¼ cup of broth and mix into the saucepan in a thin steady stream. Stir constantly for about 5 minutes, until the gravy is thickened.

Add pepper to taste.

ROASTED WINTER SQUASH

Inspired by an Italian classic, this mildly sweet-and-sour dish is easy to make, lovely to look at, and has enough lively tanginess to make it a good partner for hefty fall and winter fare. True to its origins, Roasted Winter Squash is also a good accompaniment to tomato-based dishes.

Try to find fresh mint, but in its absence, use 2 teaspoons of dried mint and sprinkle the deep orange squash with fresh parsley for a brilliant presentation.

2½	**POUNDS BUTTERNUT SQUASH OR PIE PUMPKIN**
⅓ to ½	**CUP OLIVE OIL***
	DASH OF SALT
2	**LARGE GARLIC CLOVES, MINCED OR PRESSED**
¼	**CUP RED WINE VINEGAR**
¼	**CUP BROWN SUGAR, PACKED****
2	**TABLESPOONS CHOPPED FRESH MINT**
¼	**TEASPOON SALT**
¼	**TEASPOON GROUND BLACK PEPPER**
	FRESH MINT LEAVES

SERVES 6
PREPARATION TIME: 20 MINUTES
BAKING TIME: 15 MINUTES

* **The amount of oil you'll need for the squash and the dressing will depend upon how liberally you brush the squash slices with oil.**

** **If you wish, replace the brown sugar with 3 tablespoons of mild honey.**

Preheat the oven to 450°. Oil a baking sheet.

Peel the squash or pumpkin with a potato peeler or paring knife. Cut it lengthwise through the stem end and scoop out the seeds and fibers. Set the halves cut side down, and slice crosswise into ¼-inch-thick semicircles. Brush each slice with olive oil and place it on the prepared baking sheet. Lightly salt the squash and bake for 15 minutes, until tender but still firm.

While the squash bakes, heat the remaining olive oil in a small saucepan. Add the garlic and cook for 1 minute. Add the vinegar and brown sugar and whisk until the sugar has dissolved. Add the mint, salt, and pepper and remove from the heat.

When the squash slices are baked, arrange them on a platter. Pour the dressing evenly over all and decorate with fresh mint leaves.

APPLE PECAN CRUMBLE

We decided that an autumnal fruit dessert, still warm from the oven, would be the perfect ending for our vegan Thanksgiving. The richness of the pecan topping makes it hard to believe there's no butter! If you like, both the fruit filling and the topping can be made ahead and refrigerated. That way the assembly takes just 5 minutes and you can serve the dessert fresh from the oven.

If you want a creamy flourish, serve with a vanilla soy- or rice-based frozen dessert.

fruit mixture

SERVES 8
PREPARATION TIME: 35 MINUTES
BAKING TIME: 50 TO 60 MINUTES

6	CUPS PEELED, CORED AND CHOPPED APPLES
1/3	CUP SUGAR
1	TEASPOON FRESHLY GRATED LEMON PEEL
1	TABLESPOON FRESH LEMON JUICE
1	CUP CHOPPED UNSULPHURED DRIED APRICOTS

topping

1	CUP UNBLEACHED WHITE FLOUR
1/2	CUP SUGAR
1/4	TEASPOON SALT
1	CUP CHOPPED PECANS
1/3	CUP VEGETABLE OIL

Preheat the oven to 400°.

In a large bowl, stir together the apples, sugar, lemon peel, lemon juice, and apricots and set the mixture aside. In a medium bowl, combine the flour, sugar, salt, pecans, and oil. Mix the topping with your fingers to distribute the oil evenly throughout.

Give the apple mixture a stir and divide it equally into eight ovenproof cups or ramekins at least 6 ounces in volume. Fill each cup with one-eighth of the fruit filling and gently tap its bottom on the counter to help the fruit settle. Spread a generous 1/4 cup of the topping on the fruit in each dessert cup and place the cups on an unoiled baking sheet.

Bake until the apples are tender and the topping is golden brown, 50 to 60 minutes. Serve warm or at room temperature.

note

If you prefer, spread the crumble in an unoiled 9 x 13-inch baking dish and bake, uncovered, for about 1 hour at 400°.

RAMADAN

Ramadan is the ninth month of the Islamic calendar, when the faithful abstain from food and drink from sunrise to sunset. It commemorates the month when the prophet Muhammad received the first of the revelations that make up the Koran, the holy book of Islam. Fasting during Ramadan is one of the five pillars of the Islamic faith and, in many parts of the world, anyone who is seen eating or drinking during the daytime hours is easily identified as a nonbeliever.

Although it may seem odd to create a menu for a time of fasting, the meals eaten after sunset are often very elaborate and replete with special dishes prepared only once a year. The rhythms of daily life change, sleep is often suspended, and the very air is charged with prayer and reflection. Meals are anticipated with heightened appreciation and families and friends gather to eat and spend time together.

The daily fast is broken at sundown with a meal called *ftur,* in literary Arabic *iftar,* or breaking the fast. In some places, such as Morocco, this is a light meal consisting of dates and water; in others, such as coastal Eritrea, it is the main meal of the day. The second meal is the *'asha* or *al-'isha',* and the third, just before dawn, the *s'hur* or *al-sahur.*

Islam is practiced by millions around the globe. We have selected just a few specialties, mostly from North Africa, to create a celebratory Moosewood menu in honor of Ramadan. This meal is for those from all over the world who miss home and who remember special meals with family and friends, and for all of those who share the value of remembrance.

When preparing this menu, if you like company and cooking with others, just hand out the recipes and put on some good music. However, preparation can be done ahead of time for many of the dishes. The beureks can be made and frozen until you are ready to use them. Just make sure you allow at least 2 hours for them to thaw before baking. The stock for the Shorba can also be made ahead and frozen: In fact, many of us keep a ready supply of vegetable stock in our home freezers. The filling for the Sambusas can easily be made ahead and refrigerated. The cookies can be made up to a week in advance if stored in a sealed container.

SAMBUSAS

Deep-fried pastries come in many guises and are part of numerous national cuisines. Most are filled with savory meat and/or vegetables. Ours has a flavorful tofu filling. For another vegetarian filling, see the sambusa recipe on page 512 of *Sundays at Moosewood Restaurant*.

Sambusa dough is traditionally made by hand, but we've discovered that, in this day of the global marketplace, spring-roll pastry sheets are a perfect time- and labor-saving substitute.

1	CAKE FIRM TOFU, PRESSED (16 OUNCES)*
2	TABLESPOONS OLIVE OIL
2	CUPS FINELY CHOPPED ONIONS
3	GARLIC CLOVES, MINCED OR PRESSED
1¼	TEASPOONS SALT
2	TEASPOONS GROUND CUMIN
2	TEASPOONS GROUND CORIANDER
1	TEASPOON GROUND FENNEL SEEDS
½	TEASPOON GROUND BLACK PEPPER
2	TEASPOONS MINCED FRESH ROSEMARY
1	TABLESPOON TAHINI**
1	TABLESPOON FRESH LEMON JUICE
3	TABLESPOONS UNBLEACHED WHITE FLOUR
3	TABLESPOONS WATER
12	SPRING-ROLL PASTRY SHEETS, APPROXIMATELY 8 INCHES SQUARE***
	VEGETABLE OIL FOR FRYING

YIELDS ABOUT 24 PASTRIES
PREPARATION TIME: 1½ HOURS
COOKING TIME: 20 MINUTES

* Sandwich the tofu between two plates and rest a heavy can or book on the top plate. Press for about 15 minutes, then drain the expressed liquid.

** A creamy paste made from hulled sesame seeds. It has a slightly thinner consistency than peanut butter and is available in natural food stores and well-stocked supermarkets.

*** Spring-roll pastry sheets can be found in specialty Asian markets. They come in different sizes, but Spring Home Brand 8-inch-square ones are good for this recipe. If pastry sheets are unavailable, wonton wrappers, which are available in many supermarkets, will do.

While the tofu is pressing, warm the oil in a large skillet. Add the onions, garlic, and salt and cover and cook on low heat for about 10 minutes, stirring occasionally, until the onions are translucent and quite soft. Add the cumin, coriander, fennel, and black pepper and cook for 1 to 2 minutes, stirring constantly. Crumble the pressed tofu into the skillet, add the rosemary, and cook, stirring often, for about 10 minutes, until the mixture is thoroughly hot and slightly dry. Stir in the tahini and the lemon juice and set aside.

In a small cup or bowl, mix the flour and water to form a paste. Have the spring-roll pastry sheets, the filling, the paste, and a 1-inch pastry brush close at hand. Cut the pastry sheets in half to make 24 rectangles. Place one rectangle with the short side toward you on a clean, dry work surface. Dip the brush in the paste and spread it in a ½-inch strip around all four sides. Starting at the near end, spread 2 tablespoons of filling halfway up the middle of the pastry sheet well inside the paste border. Fold the lower right corner up and over diagonally until the bottom edge is flush with the left side and you have a triangle at the end. Press the edges together to seal well. Keep folding the triangle up, as you would a flag, to make a triangular pastry.

Repeat to make 24 sambusas. They can be placed on a platter, wrapped well, and stored in the refrigerator for several hours and up to overnight before frying.

To fry the sambusas, heat 2 to 3 inches of oil in a heavy pot to about 365°. If you don't have a thermometer, heat the oil until a tiny piece of a pastry sheet dropped in the oil sizzles instantly to the surface. To make good, crispy sambusas, give them plenty of room in the pot and be sure the oil is hot. Deep-fry each pastry for 2 minutes per side, until golden brown.

Drain on paper towels and serve hot.

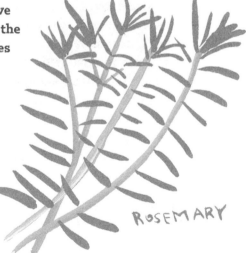

ROSEMARY

SPINACH ALMOND BEUREKS

Beurek, or *borek,* is a generic term for the many kinds of food "pockets" made throughout the Mediterranean. They can be made from filo, pie, or yeast dough, filled with most anything, then baked, steamed, or fried.

We've used a yeast dough that is easy to work with, requires only one rising, and freezes well. We had great fun playing with different fillings and have chosen this as our favorite. What could be better than spinach and feta combined with the crunchiness of almonds and the creaminess of tahini?

dough

1	TABLESPOON ACTIVE DRY YEAST
1	TEASPOON SUGAR
1	CUP WATER (105° TO 115°)
3	TABLESPOONS OLIVE OIL
1½	TEASPOONS SALT
2½ to 2¾	CUPS UNBLEACHED WHITE BREAD FLOUR

YIELDS 12 BEUREKS
PREPARATION TIME: 1¼ HOURS
RISING TIME: ABOUT 1 HOUR
BAKING TIME: ABOUT 35 MINUTES

filling

1	TABLESPOON OLIVE OIL
2	CUPS FINELY CHOPPED ONIONS
2	GARLIC CLOVES, MINCED OR PRESSED
½	TEASPOON SALT, MORE TO TASTE
¼	TEASPOON GROUND BLACK PEPPER
1	TABLESPOON GROUND CORIANDER SEEDS
10	OUNCES FRESH SPINACH, RINSED AND CHOPPED*
1	CUP CHOPPED TOASTED ALMONDS**
¼	CUP TAHINI
1	TABLESPOON FRESH LEMON JUICE
1	CUP GRATED FETA, LIGHTLY PACKED

 * Remove thick or tough stems and drain well before chopping.

** Toast almonds in a single layer on an unoiled baking tray at 350° for 5 to 10 minutes, until fragrant and golden brown. Cool before chopping.

Combine the yeast and sugar in a large bowl and stir in the water. Set aside until the mixture bubbles, about 10 minutes. When the yeast is thoroughly dissolved and foamy, add the oil, salt, and 2 cups of the flour and mix well. Form the dough into a ball, adding about ½ cup of flour as needed to form a ball.

Sprinkle some flour on a clean work surface. Knead the dough for about 10 minutes, until smooth and elastic, adding ¼ cup of flour or more if necessary. Place the kneaded dough in a lightly oiled bowl, cover with a damp towel, and set aside to rise in a warm, draft-free place until doubled in size, about 1 hour (see Notes).

While the dough rises, prepare the filling. Warm the oil in a large skillet. Add the onions, garlic, and salt and cook on medium-low heat for about 10 minutes, stirring often. Add the pepper and coriander and cook for about 5 minutes, stirring frequently, until the onions are soft; if the spices begin to stick, add a splash of water. Add the spinach, increase the heat to high, and cook for 2 to 3 minutes, stirring constantly, until the spinach is wilted but still bright green. Remove from the heat and mix in the almonds, tahini, lemon juice, and feta. Set aside.

When the dough finishes rising, preheat the oven to 350° and lightly oil a baking sheet at least 14 x 16 inches.

Punch down the dough and knead it for 2 minutes. Cut the dough into twelve equal pieces and form them into balls. On a lightly floured work surface, use your hands to flatten and stretch each ball of dough into a circle about 6½ to 7 inches in diameter. Place ¼ cup of the filling on the lower half of the circle and fold the dough up and over the filling to make a semicircle. Press the edges together with your fingers and use a fork to prick the top of each beurek in five or six places. Place the finished beureks on the prepared baking sheet.

Bake for about 35 minutes, until golden brown. Serve warm or at room temperature.

notes

You can place a large pot of very hot water in an unheated oven to make a well-insulated, warm rising place for the dough.

If wrapped well in plastic wrap and placed in freezer bags, beureks can be frozen before baking. Thaw for at least 2 hours before baking as above.

SHORBA

During Ramadan in many parts of North Africa and the Middle East, soup is an integral part of the meal that breaks the fast. There are probably as many kinds of soup as there are cooks. This simple, hearty soup has a fresh, pleasing taste and can be enjoyed any time of the year.

SERVES 4 TO 6
TOTAL TIME: 40 MINUTES

2	TABLESPOONS OLIVE OIL
1½	CUPS FINELY CHOPPED ONIONS
1	LARGE GARLIC CLOVE, MINCED OR PRESSED
1	TEASPOON SALT, MORE TO TASTE
½	TEASPOON GROUND BLACK PEPPER
1	TEASPOON GROUND CORIANDER
¼	TEASPOON GROUND CARDAMOM
½	TEASPOON GROUND CINNAMON
⅔	CUP MEDIUM-GRADE RAW BULGHUR
2	CUPS FINELY CHOPPED FRESH TOMATOES
3½	CUPS VEGETABLE STOCK OR BROTH (PAGE 408)*
1 to 2	TABLESPOONS FRESH LEMON JUICE

GRATED FETA CHEESE (OPTIONAL)
CHOPPED FRESH PARSLEY (OPTIONAL)

* If you prefer a commercially produced broth, we recommend Pacific Organic or Imagine Foods brands, in aseptically packaged boxes.

Warm the oil in a 2-quart pot. Add the onions and garlic, sprinkle with the salt, and sauté on medium heat for about 10 minutes, until the onions are soft and translucent. Add the pepper, coriander, cardamom, and cinnamon and cook, stirring constantly, for about 1 minute.

Add the bulghur and continue to stir for another 1 to 2 minutes. Add the tomatoes and the stock, cover, and bring to a boil. Reduce the heat and simmer for about 10 minutes, covered, until the bulghur is tender. Remove from the heat and stir in the lemon juice.

Serve immediately topped with feta cheese and fresh parsley, if desired.

note

The bulghur continues to absorb liquid as it sits, so you may want to add a little more stock or water when reheating the soup at a later time.

MOROCCAN SALAD

The secret to this salad is the unique tanginess of both the preserved lemon and the sumac. Nonetheless, if you don't have any preserved lemon on hand, you can still make Moroccan Salad and it will be nearly as good. Use slender scallions for the salad, so the oniony flavor is well dispersed throughout, yet not prominent. The minced herbs strike a nice balance with the lemon in the dressing and their essence lingers on the palate, leaving a refreshing aftertaste.

The salad is salty, tart, colorful, aromatic, and versatile. You can stuff it into a pita pocket along with a few "tofalafels" (tofu falafels), or serve it beside grilled fish, stuffed mushrooms, roasted vegetables, or beureks—as we do in this menu. We also love to briefly sauté a clove or two of garlic in a little of the salad's dressing and spread it on some good bread.

dressing

SERVES 4 TO 6
TOTAL TIME: 20 MINUTES

1   TABLESPOON OLIVE OIL
1   TABLESPOON MINCED FRESH OREGANO
1   TABLESPOON MINCED FRESH THYME
1   TABLESPOON GROUND SUMAC*
2 to 3 TEASPOONS FRESH LEMON JUICE

salad fixings

1   CUP PEELED, SEEDED AND DICED CUCUMBERS
1   CUP DICED FRESH TOMATOES
1   CUP DICED RED OR YELLOW BELL PEPPERS
2   TABLESPOONS MINCED SCALLIONS
½   TEASPOON SALT
2   TABLESPOONS MINCED PRESERVED LEMON PEEL, MORE TO TASTE
      (PAGE 194)

* Sumac is a seasoning available in Middle Eastern groceries and large supermarkets with an international foods section. Its tangy flavor is distinctively tasty and it quickly becomes a favorite ingredient of the newly initiated.

In a cup or small bowl, whisk together the oil, oregano, thyme, sumac, and lemon juice and set aside.

In a serving bowl, combine the cucumbers, tomatoes, peppers, scallions, salt, and preserved lemon peel. Pour the dressing on the salad and toss well. Serve at room temperature.

PRESERVED LEMONS

We are fortunate at Moosewood to have the occasional influx of new cooks who bring their own repertoires and talents to our kitchen. We would like to thank Steve Vierk for suggesting, and then making, these preserved lemons for us. We had all seen recipes that used them, but we had never tried making them until Steve gave us some to sample! It was love at first bite.

They are so simple to make and just a small amount will add a distinctive flavor to tajines, fish sauces, and our own Moroccan Salad (page 193). Preserved Lemons can sometimes be found in well-stocked Middle Eastern and North African groceries.

4 to 5 LEMONS, PREFERABLY ORGANIC*
4 to 5 TEASPOONS COARSE SALT
FRESH LEMON JUICE, AS NEEDED

YIELDS 1 PINT
PREPARATION TIME: 5 MINUTES
PRESERVING TIME:
APPROXIMATELY 6 TO 8 WEEKS

* It's good to have another lemon or two handy for juicing in case your jar needs a little extra juice to top it off.

Thoroughly wash a pint canning jar and lid or any 16-ounce jar with a tight lid. Rinse and dry the lemons. Cut each lemon three-fourths of the way through the stem end in an "X," so that the 4 quarters are still attached at the bottom end. Spoon a teaspoon of salt into the center of each lemon. Place them in the jar, pushing each in to release some of its juice. Give the jar a good shake and, if it's not filled to the very top with lemon juice, add more juice.

Place in a cool, dark cupboard for 6 to 8 weeks. Check every week or so and top off with more lemon juice as needed. They are "done" when the lemons are quite soft and almost opaque. They should then be refrigerated and will keep for several months. When cooking with preserved lemons or including them in recipes, use only the peel (discard the pulp).

SEMOLINA ALMOND COOKIES

Both almond paste and semolina are common ingredients in Middle Eastern cuisine, and folks there sometimes make homemade almond paste—a culinary ritual that's enjoyable when time permits. Here in the United States, we just buy it by the can in the baking aisle of the supermarket. It's a wonderful ingredient for baked goods, but watch out! It can also be positively addictive on its own: We know people who occasionally sneak a spoonful right from the can as a snack.

Try a bit of almond paste stuffed into dates for an instant delicacy that can be served as an appetizer or dessert.

1	CUP UNSALTED BUTTER, AT ROOM TEMPERATURE
½	CUP ALMOND PASTE (PAGE 396)
1	CUP SUGAR
1	TEASPOON SALT
2	LARGE EGGS
2	TEASPOONS PURE VANILLA EXTRACT
3	CUPS SEMOLINA*
40	WHOLE ALMONDS (ABOUT ⅓ CUP)

YIELDS 40 COOKIES
PREPARATION TIME: 10 MINUTES
BAKING TIME: 15 TO 20 MINUTES

* Make sure you use semolina that has the texture of salt, not flour.

Preheat the oven to 325°.

Beat the butter and almond paste with an electric mixer, until creamy. Add the sugar and salt and beat until smooth. Beat in the eggs and vanilla. Add the semolina and beat until well mixed.

Scoop up a heaping tablespoon of the dough and roll and shape it into an oval, about 2½ inches long (mimic the shape of an enlarged almond or tiny American football). Place it on an unoiled baking sheet and press an almond into the center of the cookie. Repeat with all of the dough, spacing the cookies about an inch apart.

Bake for 15 to 20 minutes, until the cookies are firm and the bottoms are golden brown. Cool on wire racks and store in a sealed container. The cookies will keep for about a week.

WINTER

In winter, when the earth's axis tilts away from the sun, our days are darker, shorter, and colder. During these long months of nature's dormancy, ancient peoples felt the need for rituals to encourage the sun to return to full brightness, to reassure themselves that there would be a rebirth of light and warmth and abundance. These rituals, often involving keeping watch through the night for the new sunrise, setting blazing bonfires, rolling wheels of fire, or ceremoniously lighting hearth fires, occurred on the winter solstice, the longest night of the year.

Later religious and cultural holidays were also fixed near the solstice and appropriated symbols of the sun, such as the shining halos depicted behind sacred figures, images of stars, and the golden round foods traditionally prepared at this time. And, of course, the lighting of small fires, such as candles (or twinkle lights) offers symbolic hope and an antidote to darkness.

Many of the holidays around the world at this time of year are festivals of light. Although the greater part of harsh winter still stretches ahead, after these celebrations are over we feel better prepared to finish the winter. And then, imperceptibly at first, the days do begin to lengthen and we are returned to the light.

In the cold season, more than any other time of the year, we delight in staying home. We crave indoor warmth and other domestic comforts. We take pride in provisioning our larders and creating a generous hospitality. We feel a spirit of sharing and giving. Winter celebrations are often suffused with nostalgia and imagination. There's a sense of anticipation and excitement, secrets, magic. There's a bubbling hope, however fragile, of peace on earth and goodwill among men.

Some of the greatest moments around the table come in winter. Foods are sweeter and richer. There are buttery baked goods filled with warm spices and nuts, long-roasted earthy root vegetables, and the concentrated flavors of dried fruits. Plentiful feasting and merriment abound. Sharing food at the same table is a way of bonding and encouraging fellowship.

Even those of us who don't share the religious underpinnings of the traditional winter celebrations can embrace the kinship with the past and the connection to the cycles of life. We may no longer feel the sting of winter's hunger and cold, and we may no longer engage in rituals to appease the elements; still, our survival depends on our capacity to share the fruits of the earth and live in peace and harmony.

HANUKKAH

Hanukkah, the festival of lights, was originally a Jewish solstice celebration. During the Middle Ages, it evolved into a holiday that retells the dramatic story of the Maccabees: How they saved their temple and people from annihilation and how one day's supply of sacred oil miraculously lasted for the eight days needed to rededicate the temple.

The menorah is the traditional symbol of the holiday. It is a candelabrum with eight branches plus one central holder for the *shammes* (servant) candle, which is used to light the other eight. These candles represent the miracle of the eight days of light. Each evening of the eight-day celebration, children light the family menorah: One candle for the first day, two for the next, and one more candle each day afterward. All over the world, Jewish families prepare special fried foods in remembrance of the sacred long-burning oil. Potato latkes are traditional in Eastern Europe, and versions of deep-fried doughnuts or fritters are the custom in Greece, Persia, and Israel.

In North America, it has become popular to give children *gelt,* chocolate coins wrapped in gold foil, and dreidels, spinning tops decorated with four Hebrew letters. The game of dreidel revolves around the letter that lands face up when the top stops spinning. Different letters mean the player must take away or put in more of the gelt that was distributed evenly among the players at the beginning of the game.

Not only kids love Hanukkah. Adults also eagerly await the chance to feast on latkes with applesauce and then indulge in dessert.

The best way to manage this Hanukkah menu is to make one or both of the desserts ahead of time. The Cranberry Sorbet and Homemade Applesauce are fun to make with children, so we suggest you make their preparation part of the festivities. Lastly, the much-anticipated Potato Latkes are best fried just before serving them, while your guests are chatting and their mouths are watering.

POTATO LATKES
TO CELEBRATE YOUR ROOTS

At Hanukkah time, it's exciting to gather together family and friends to eat latkes. As the house fills with the inviting smells of frying potatoes and onions, the arriving guests feast first on the fabulous aromas. So good!

There are a multitude of potato latke recipes in the world, but we set out to create colorful latkes that feature root vegetables and herbs. Although elegant enough for adults, these red, gold, and green latkes will catch children's eyes, too. Kids will never guess they're consuming vitamin-rich beets, rutabaga, and parsley.

We realize that the thought of putting rutabaga in potato latkes may be alarming, but trust us: It's a great combination. If you like, replace the rutabaga with peeled and grated butternut squash or sweet potatoes, and the latkes will still be a lovely golden color.

If your food processor has a grating blade, you can probably skim 15 minutes off the total time and be eating these latkes about 45 minutes after you get the urge to make them.

3	CUPS PEELED AND GRATED RUSSET POTATOES*
½	CUP GRATED ONIONS
2	EGGS, LIGHTLY BEATEN
¼	CUP UNBLEACHED WHITE FLOUR OR MATZO MEAL
½	TEASPOON BAKING POWDER
1	TEASPOON SALT
¼	TEASPOON GROUND BLACK PEPPER, OR MORE TO TASTE
½	CUP PEELED AND GRATED RUTABAGA
½	CUP PEELED AND GRATED BEETS
½	CUP CHOPPED FRESH PARSLEY
2	TABLESPOONS CHOPPED FRESH DILL
¼	CUP VEGETABLE OIL

YIELDS 12 LATKES
PREPARATION TIME: 30 MINUTES
FRYING TIME: 30 MINUTES
(10 MINUTES PER BATCH)

* Russet potatoes have a sturdy, starchy texture that is important for making good latkes. Their flavor holds up well when mixed with other grated vegetables. Three or four potatoes will yield about 3 cups of grated potatoes.

Line a colander with two layers of paper towels. Place the grated potatoes and onions in the lined colander. Gather together the ends of the paper towels and vigorously press out as much liquid as possible, until the grated potatoes are somewhat dry. This will help to create crisp latkes.

Transfer the drained potatoes and onions to a large bowl and stir in the eggs, flour, baking powder, salt, and pepper. Divide the mixture equally among three smaller bowls (1¼ cups per bowl). Mix the rutabaga into the first bowl, the beets into the second bowl, and the parsley and dill into the third.

Preheat the oven to 200°.

Warm the oil on high heat in a very large, heavy cast iron or nonstick skillet, until a drop of batter sizzles in the hot oil. Take one of the bowls of latke batter and drop the batter in fourths into the skillet: A scant ½ cup of batter per latke. Flatten the latkes with a spatula. Fry on both sides until brown and crisp, about 5 minutes per side. Drain well on paper towels. Transfer to a baking tray in a single layer and keep warm in the oven. Repeat with the other two bowls of latke batter to make twelve latkes in all.

Offer each person a plate with three latkes: One of each kind. Or artfully arrange the latkes on a platter either in rows by color or in a spiral of alternating colors.

Serve with Homemade Applesauce (page 202) and top with sour cream, yogurt, or our Versatile Sour Cream Sauce (page 51). Try thin slivers of lox (smoked salmon) atop the sour cream for a delicious addition.

HOMEMADE APPLESAUCE

Here is a quick and easy applesauce that's great to make with children. They can help core and chop the apples (butter knives are safe for little fingers), and most kids love mashing the cooked apples with a potato masher. Let them decide the color and flavor of the applesauce by adding their favorite berry. Will it be blueberries, strawberries, or cherries today?

5 to 6 CUPS PEELED, CORED AND COARSELY CHOPPED
APPLES, SUCH AS FUJI, GRANNY SMITH OR CRISPIN
(ABOUT 3 POUNDS)

½ CUP UNSWEETENED APPLE, APRICOT, CHERRY OR
PEACH JUICE

½ CUP BLUEBERRIES, HULLED STRAWBERRIES OR
PITTED CHERRIES (OPTIONAL)*

1 TABLESPOON FRESH LEMON JUICE
SUGAR, HONEY OR PURE MAPLE SYRUP TO TASTE

* Fresh or frozen are both fine. If using fresh fruit, rinse it well.

YIELDS 4 CUPS
PREPARATION TIME: 15 TO
20 MINUTES
COOKING TIME: 20 MINUTES

Combine the apples and fruit juice in a medium saucepan and bring to a boil. Cover and cook on low heat for 10 minutes. Stir in the berries or cherries, if using, and cook on medium heat for about 5 minutes more, until all of the fruit is very soft.

For chunky applesauce, mash the cooked fruit with a potato masher until you reach the consistency you like; then add the lemon juice and sweeten to taste. For a smooth applesauce, purée the cooked fruit and lemon juice in the blender or food processor. Add sugar, honey, or maple syrup to taste and pulse for a few seconds.

Serve warm or cold.

POPPYSEED COOKIES

At Moosewood, we try to preserve our families' best recipes by including them in our books. Moosewood cook Lisa Wichman thanks her mother-in-law, Mary Wichman, for this recipe. Mary has made these delightful, not-too-sweet cookies by the dozens for her grateful grandchildren.

For easier handling, we recommend chilling the dough for 30 minutes, but if you're in a hurry for cookies, don't bother. Serve the cookies with hot coffee, tea, or steamed frothy milk.

batter

3	EGGS
¾	CUP VEGETABLE OIL
1	CUP SUGAR
3½	CUPS UNBLEACHED WHITE FLOUR
2	TEASPOONS BAKING POWDER
¼	TEASPOON SALT
½	CUP POPPYSEEDS

topping

¼	CUP SUGAR
½	TEASPOON GROUND CINNAMON

YIELDS 3 DOZEN
PREPARATION TIME: 10 MINUTES
CHILLING TIME: 30 MINUTES
BAKING TIME: 10 TO 12 MINUTES
PER BATCH

Preheat the oven to 350°. Oil one or two baking sheets.

In a mixing bowl, beat the eggs with a whisk until just combined. Beat in the oil and sugar. In a separate bowl, sift together the flour, baking powder, and salt, then add the poppyseeds. Stir the flour mixture into the oil mixture to make a stiff dough.

Turn the dough onto a floured surface and knead several times until smooth and well mixed. Divide the dough into three balls, return them to the bowl, and refrigerate for about ½ hour. Combine the sugar and cinnamon in a small bowl and set aside.

On a floured surface, roll out one ball of dough at a time until about ¼ inch thick. Using a 3-inch cookie cutter or the rim of a glass, cut out the cookies. Place them close together on the prepared baking sheet (or sheets) and sprinkle lightly with the cinnamon sugar.

Bake for 10 to 12 minutes, until the cookies are firm to the touch and starting to brown. Cool completely on racks. Stored in a sealed container, the cookies will keep for at least a week.

HOLIDAY COOKIE EXCHANGE

Cherry Chocolate Rugalach
Cranberry Cornmeal Biscotti
Lemon Cookies
Oatmeal Chocolate Chip Cookies
Orange & Fig Cookies
Peanut Butter Cookies
Spiced Coconut Date Bars

Homemade cookies are nice any time, but during the holiday season, they come to symbolize home and happiness for many of us. These recipes are ones that we've been making with our families over the years. They're a little out of the ordinary and always a hit. Hopefully, they'll find a place in your cookie repertoire, too.

Cookies are the perfect sweet treat for drop-in guests, and they make welcome presents for neighbors, teachers, and mail carriers. A big box or decorative cookie tin filled with an assortment of delicious, homemade cookies is a good gift for a whole household. But be prepared, some of last year's recipients may start hinting in November that it's almost time for you to start baking.

Ambitious holiday baking plans, but too little time? Set up a cookie exchange with a few friends. First, everyone agrees on a dozen or so favorite cookie recipes that they would like to share. Each person bakes large quantities of two or three different kinds. This is efficient and saves shopping time, too. When you exchange cookies with everyone else, you end up with ten or twelve different kinds—much more of an assortment than you probably would have made on your own.

Making cookies with children can be a delightful experience and may create cherished memories at the same time. You spend time together, the house smells great, and you get to eat cookies fresh from the oven.

Cool cookies before storing them in sealed containers, where they will stay fresh up to for a couple of weeks. In some cases, you may want to store different types of cookies in separate containers so that their flavors won't merge. For shipping cookies, tins work best, but shoebox-sized boxes lined with wax paper or well-insulated cookie jars are fine as well. Place the container in a sturdy cardboard box surrounded by tightly packed crumpled newspaper or other packing material. All of the cookie recipes that follow make good sturdy cookies, suitable for mailing.

Delicious cookies from other sections in this book include:

Bone Cookies (page 128)
Cashew Butterscotch Bars (page 47)
Cornmeal Lemon Shortbread (page 92)
Poppyseed Cookies (page 203)
Semolina Almond Cookies (page 195)

CHERRY CHOCOLATE RUGALACH

Two of our Moosewood members have a long-standing friendly disagreement about whose mother's rugalach recipe is better. Actually, both are equally delicious, but we are secretly invested in keeping their friendly controversy alive and encourage them to make their versions again and again so that we can "compare."

Here's one of the contenders for a fussy, exquisite rugalach that's absolutely worth the bother. Winnie Stein lovingly dedicates these sumptuous morsels to her mother, who taught her, as Alice Walker says, "to honor the difficult."

The pastry dough can be prepared the night before or up to two days in advance. You can also freeze unbaked rugalach in a zippered freezer bag for up to one month; then just bake them for 5 or 6 minutes longer than usual.

pastry dough

1   CUP UNSALTED BUTTER, AT ROOM TEMPERATURE
6   OUNCES CREAM CHEESE, SOFTENED
2¾   CUPS UNBLEACHED WHITE FLOUR
¼   TEASPOON SALT

filling

¼   CUP SUGAR
1   TEASPOON GROUND CINNAMON
⅔   CUP CHILLED CHERRY PRESERVES (10-OUNCE JAR)*
½   CUP DRIED CHERRIES
¾   CUP MINIATURE SEMI-SWEET CHOCOLATE CHIPS
1   TABLESPOON UNSWEETENED COCOA POWDER
1   CUP FINELY CHOPPED ALMONDS**

glaze

1   BEATEN EGG
1   TABLESPOON MILK

      SPRINKLING OF SUGAR

YIELDS 32 RUGALACH
PREPARATION TIME: ABOUT 1 HOUR
CHILLING TIME: AT LEAST 2 HOURS
BAKING TIME: 20 MINUTES

* If the preserves have large pieces of cherries, briefly whirl in a food processor to break them up.

** If chopping almonds in a food processor or blender, add ½ teaspoon of flour to prevent the nuts from becoming pasty.

In a large bowl, cream the butter and cream cheese until light and fluffy. Add the flour and salt and knead the dough briefly until well mixed. Wrap the dough in a large sheet of wax paper to form a tight package and mold the dough into a 12-inch-long log. Chill for at least 2 hours or overnight.

When you are ready to bake the rugalach, combine all of the filling ingredients in a bowl and set aside. In a separate bowl, whisk together the egg and milk for the glaze. Line a heavy baking pan with parchment paper or lightly oil it with cooking spray.

Divide the dough into four equal pieces. Gently flatten each piece into a disk and wrap each one in wax paper. Work with one disk at a time and keep the rest refrigerated. Using a rolling pin, roll each disk between 2 sheets of wax paper into a 9-inch round. Spread one-quarter of the filling on the dough and pat down. Carefully cut each round into 8 equal pie-shaped wedges. Roll up the wedges from the wide outer edge to the center point. Place the pastries point side down on the pan about an inch apart.

Preheat the oven to 375° when you begin to work on the last disk of dough.

Brush all of the pastries with the glaze and sprinkle with sugar.

Bake for about 20 minutes, until golden brown. Carefully transfer the rugalach to a wire rack to cool completely, then store in a sealed container.

CRANBERRY CORNMEAL BISCOTTI

Tart, fresh cranberries punctuate the grainy sweetness of cornmeal in these appealing biscotti. Dunk them in espresso or hot cider. They're equally at home with the foods of Italy and New England.

¼	CUP BUTTER, MELTED
1	CUP SUGAR
3	LARGE EGGS
1	CUP FRESH CRANBERRIES, COARSELY CHOPPED*
2	CUPS UNBLEACHED WHITE FLOUR
½	CUP CORNMEAL
1	TEASPOON BAKING POWDER
½	TEASPOON SALT

YIELDS 14 BISCOTTI
PREPARATION TIME: 10 TO 15 MINUTES
BAKING TIME: 30 TO 35 MINUTES

* A food processor will chop cranberries quickly and easily.

Preheat the oven to 350°. Lightly oil a baking sheet.

In a bowl, cream the butter and sugar with an electric mixer or a wire whisk. Add the eggs one at a time, beating between each addition. Fold in the cranberries and set aside.

In a separate bowl, sift together the flour, cornmeal, baking powder, and salt. Fold the dry ingredients into the creamed mixture. Dust your hands lightly with flour and shape the dough into a ball.

Use a spatula and your floured hands to scoop the dough onto the oiled baking sheet. Form the dough into a 12 x 3-inch-diameter log shape; then press down on the log, flattening it to a thickness of about an inch. The length and width of the flattened log should be about 14 x 4 inches.

Bake on the top shelf of the oven for 25 to 30 minutes, until the dough is firm and just slightly brown. Remove from the oven and transfer the log to a cutting board. When cool enough to handle, slice crosswise into ¾-inch pieces. Lay each biscotti cut side down on the baking sheet. Bake for about 5 minutes on each side, using tongs to gently flip them. Cool on a rack.

When completely cooled, store in an airtight container. Biscotti will easily keep for a couple of weeks.

LEMON COOKIES

These crisp, light, not-too-sweet cookies have great citrus flavor. For even more zing, mix the topping the day before so the lemony flavor fully permeates the sugar. Because they're so easy to make, these cookies are a fun family project that kids will enjoy. Put some out for Santa and his helpers. Invite Rudolph the Red-Nosed Reindeer or Scrooge over for dessert.

Serve our Lemon Cookies with coffee or tea or use them to decorate your favorite ice cream or mousse.

topping

1½ TEASPOONS FRESHLY GRATED LEMON PEEL
1½ TABLESPOONS SUGAR

**YIELDS 4 DOZEN COOKIES
PREPARATION TIME: 30 MINUTES
CHILLING TIME: 1 HOUR
BAKING TIME: 7 TO 8 MINUTES
PER BATCH**

dough

1¾ CUPS UNBLEACHED WHITE FLOUR
½ TEASPOON SALT
¾ CUP SUGAR
½ CUP UNSALTED BUTTER, CUT INTO SMALL PIECES
1 TABLESPOON FRESHLY GRATED LEMON PEEL
1 TEASPOON PURE VANILLA EXTRACT
1 LARGE EGG, LIGHTLY BEATEN
1 TABLESPOON FRESH LEMON JUICE

Stir together the topping ingredients in a wide, shallow bowl and set aside.

In a food processor, combine the flour, salt, and sugar and pulse once or twice until blended. Add the butter and lemon peel and process until the mixture has the texture of coarse meal. Add the vanilla, egg, and lemon juice and blend until the dough leaves the sides of the bowl and forms a ball. Remove the dough, wrap it in plastic wrap, and refrigerate for 1 hour.

Preheat the oven to 350°.

Divide the chilled dough into four equal pieces. Working with one portion of dough at a time, roll small amounts of dough between your hands to make twelve small balls. Repeat with the remaining portions of dough. Using the bottom of a glass, flatten the four dozen balls into 2-inch circles. Press the circles firmly into the lemon-sugar topping to coat thoroughly on one side.

Place the cookies topping side up on an unoiled baking sheet and bake until golden at the edges, 7 to 8 minutes. Cool for 1 minute, and then transfer to a rack to cool completely. Store in a sealed container.

OATMEAL CHOCOLATE CHIP COOKIES

These crisp, chewy cookies are a perfect playtime dessert when the kids are home from school for the holidays or an evening snack while watching the Winter Olympics or going ice skating. Share them at the ski lodge and you'll make instant friends with whoever's warming up by the woodstove. The cookies are easy to make and freeze well. Make a double batch: We guarantee you won't be sorry.

YIELDS ABOUT 3 DOZEN 3-INCH COOKIES
PREPARATION TIME: 15 MINUTES
BAKING TIME: 25 MINUTES
COOLING TIME: 10 MINUTES

1	CUP SUGAR
½	CUP BUTTER, AT ROOM TEMPERATURE
¼	CUP VEGETABLE OIL
2	EGGS
1	TEASPOON PURE VANILLA EXTRACT
1	CUP UNBLEACHED WHITE FLOUR
½	TEASPOON SALT
½	TEASPOON BAKING SODA
2½	CUPS QUICK-COOKING OR ROLLED OATS
¾	CUP CHOCOLATE CHIPS
½	CUP RAISINS OR COARSELY CHOPPED WALNUTS OR PECANS (OPTIONAL)

Preheat the oven to 375°. Lightly oil a baking sheet.

In a large bowl, beat together the sugar, butter, and oil until light and creamy. Beat in the eggs and vanilla. Sift the flour, salt, and baking soda into the batter and mix until smooth. Stir in the oats, chocolate chips, and the raisins or nuts, if using.

Drop the batter onto the baking sheet by rounded tablespoonfuls, about 2 inches apart. We suggest baking the cookies in two batches: They will spread slightly as they bake.

Bake for 10 to 12 minutes, until the cookies are golden and crisp around the edges but still soft in the middle. Transfer to a wire rack to cool for about 10 minutes. Cool completely before storing in a sealed container.

ORANGE & FIG COOKIES

These zesty cookies are full of robust orange flavor and sweet chewy figs, and have a light airiness thanks to the single whipped egg white. The batter isn't fussy to make, so it's perfect for winter holidays when you want a special cookie fast. Serve the cookies beside vanilla ice cream topped with a drizzle of Grand Marnier for a more lavish dessert.

1	CUP BUTTER, AT ROOM TEMPERATURE
½	CUP GRANULATED SUGAR*
¼	CUP BROWN SUGAR, PACKED
1	EGG WHITE**
2	WHOLE EGGS
1	TEASPOON PURE VANILLA EXTRACT
2½	CUPS UNBLEACHED WHITE FLOUR
2	TEASPOONS BAKING POWDER
½	TEASPOON SALT
1½	CUPS MINCED DRIED FIGS (½ POUND)*
1	TABLESPOON FRESHLY GRATED ORANGE PEEL
3	TABLESPOONS FRESH ORANGE JUICE

**YIELDS 24 COOKIES
PREPARATION TIME: 20 MINUTES
BAKING TIME: 20 MINUTES**

* If you like, mince the figs in a food processor with a small amount of the sugar.

** The egg white must not contain even a speck of the yolk to whip properly. So crack an egg in half crosswise and carefully slip its yolk (without breaking it) from one half of the shell to the other, as the white drains off into a bowl.

Preheat the oven to 350°. Lightly oil two baking sheets.

In a large bowl, cream together the butter, granulated sugar, and brown sugar until smooth and fluffy. In a small bowl, beat the egg white until soft peaks form. Add the beaten white, the whole eggs, and the vanilla to the creamed butter and mix well.

In a separate bowl, sift together the flour, baking powder, and salt. Combine the wet and dry ingredients, then stir in the figs, orange peel, and orange juice.

Drop the batter by well-rounded tablespoonfuls onto the baking sheets. Bake for 20 minutes, until the cookies are just slightly brown. Remove the cookies from the baking sheets and cool on a rack.

Cool completely before storing in a sealed container.

PEANUT BUTTER COOKIES

This recipe makes big, chewy, golden brown, crunchy cookies that are delightfully sweet and peanut-y. Perfect for dunking in a glass of milk, munching with ice cream, or as a snack with hot cider or tea, they are hefty and satisfying, and they travel well.

Peanuts lend us, in America, a little taste of Africa (where they are called groundnuts and are an important food staple). One of our well-known botanists, George Washington Carver, found a gazillion hip uses for peanuts, but he couldn't top peanut butter cookies.

1	CUP BROWN SUGAR, PACKED
½	CUP SMOOTH OR CRUNCHY PEANUT BUTTER*
¼	CUP VEGETABLE OIL
1	EGG
1	TABLESPOON PURE VANILLA EXTRACT
2	TABLESPOONS LIGHT CORN SYRUP
1¼	CUPS UNBLEACHED WHITE FLOUR
½	CUP WHOLE WHEAT PASTRY FLOUR
1	TEASPOON BAKING POWDER
1	TEASPOON BAKING SODA
½	TEASPOON SALT
1 to 2 TEASPOONS WATER, AS NEEDED	

YIELDS ABOUT 30 COOKIES
PREPARATION TIME: 15 MINUTES
BAKING TIME: 10 MINUTES

* We recommend using a good, natural peanut butter, either salted or unsalted. If using unsalted peanut butter, you may want to increase the salt to 1 teaspoon.

Preheat the oven to 375°. Lightly oil a baking sheet or two.

Cream together the brown sugar, peanut butter, oil, egg, vanilla, and corn syrup. On a piece of wax paper or in a separate bowl, sift together the flours, baking powder, baking soda, and salt. Add the dry ingredients to the creamed mixture and blend thoroughly. The dough will be stiff and crumbly: If it won't hold together, add a teaspoon or so of water.

With your hands, shape and roll the dough into 1-inch balls. Place them on the baking sheet and, with the bottom of a glass, press them into flat circles. Smooth the cracked edges a little with your fingers. If you like, press the tops with the tines of a fork to give them the mark of classic peanut butter cookies. If you like them brown and crisp on top, spray a light coat of oil on the tops of the unbaked cookies.

Bake for about 10 minutes, until golden brown. Cool on a rack and store (hide) in a cookie jar.

SPICED COCONUT DATE BARS

Recipes using dates just aren't that common. There's date nut bread, the occasional stuffed date, and then—date bars. Here's a golden opportunity for date enthusiasts to sink their teeth into the pure ecstasy of these luscious vegan treats. Serve with strong coffee or hot spearmint tea.

½	CUP CHOPPED WALNUTS
2	CUPS PITTED, CHOPPED DATES
½	CUP SOY MARGARINE OR VEGETABLE OIL
½	CUP BROWN SUGAR, PACKED
1½	CUPS UNBLEACHED WHITE FLOUR
½	TEASPOON GROUND CINNAMON
	PINCH OF GROUND CLOVES
½	TEASPOON BAKING POWDER
1	CUP ROLLED OATS*
2	TABLESPOONS FRESHLY GRATED ORANGE PEEL
2	TABLESPOONS FRESH ORANGE JUICE
½	CUP UNSWEETENED GRATED COCONUT

YIELDS 16 BARS
PREPARATION: 30 MINUTES
BAKING TIME: 30 MINUTES
COOLING TIME: 30 MINUTES

* With a food processor, use regular rolled oats; by hand, use quick-cooking oats.

Preheat the oven to 350°. Oil an 8-inch-square glass baking pan.

Spread the walnuts on an unoiled baking sheet and toast in the oven for 5 to 7 minutes. Set aside. Meanwhile, combine the dates and ¾ cup of water in a small heavy saucepan and simmer for about 15 minutes, stirring occasionally, until the dates are soft.

While the dates cook, blend the margarine or oil and the brown sugar in a mixing bowl or food processor. Sift the flour, cinnamon, cloves, and baking powder into the bowl, add the oats, and mix or pulse until blended. Stir in the walnuts. The dough will be crumbly. Firmly pat about two-thirds of the dough into the baking pan to make a thin bottom crust.

Stir the orange peel, orange juice, and coconut into the cooked dates. Spread the date mixture evenly over the crust. Crumble the remaining dough over the date layer as a topping.

Bake for about 30 minutes, until the topping is golden and dark brown around the edges. Cool the bars for 30 minutes before cutting into 16 squares. In a sealed container, they will keep for up to 2 weeks.

CHRISTMAS

The desire to create beauty, warmth, and good cheer is perhaps never so widely shared as at Christmastime. People all over the world commemorate the birthday of the gentle Prince of Peace with family traditions and religious rituals that celebrate light and the spirit of giving and receiving. During the long nights of winter, we comfort ourselves with the inspiring glow of burning candles, oil lamps, twinkling stars, sparkling lights, and colorful ornaments.

But there is arguably no day of the year (with the possible exception of April 15 here in the States) that stimulates as much frantic activity—and relief when it's over. The madness of nonstop shopping can certainly get out of hand. Nevertheless, our genuine impulse to express love and appreciation does manage to shine through on this happy, hopeful, wish-fulfilling holiday.

Cooking good food to share and special treats to give away is one way to stay grounded and open your heart. There is magic in preparing food for the purpose of making merry. That pile of cookies and those decorative tarts look so wonderful that eating them is almost beside the point. Late December represents the tail end of the harvest. You can fill your home with the fragrances of cinnamon, nutmeg, orange, rum, and vanilla as well as the rich and savory aromas of onions, sage, rosemary, thyme, and smoky chestnuts, all amid the mystical scent of evergreen. Religious beliefs aren't necessary to experience joy and the spirit of loving-kindness. Let cooking at Christmastime feel like sacred alchemy.

Choose from the selections above and create a menu of vegetarian and vegan dishes that suits the tastes of your family and guests. The Chocolate Cranberry Tart is fine made a day or two ahead. The soup, stuffed yams, pearl onions, and roasted pears can all be made ahead, too, and then reheated. Roast the chestnuts during dinner.

SALMON BAKED IN PARCHMENT

These delicate and delectable salmon fillets are baked in parchment paper with a wonderful herbed shallot and white wine reduction. Once the packets are prepared, they bake very quickly, preserving the moisture of both the fish and the sauce and infusing the salmon with flavor. As they bake, the parchment packets become see-through and reveal the herb-topped fillets tucked inside. *Ooo-la-la!*

8	INCH-THICK SALMON FILLETS (ABOUT 6 OUNCES EACH)
6	TABLESPOONS BUTTER
3	CUPS MINCED SHALLOTS
3	CUPS DRY WHITE WINE
⅔	CUP CHOPPED FRESH ITALIAN PARSLEY*
3	TABLESPOONS MINCED FRESH DILL
	SALT AND GROUND BLACK PEPPER TO TASTE
8	PIECES OF 9 X 15-INCH PARCHMENT PAPER
8	FRESH ITALIAN PARSLEY SPRIGS*
8	FRESH DILL SPRIGS

* Italian parsley is the flat-leaf variety.

SERVES 8
PREPARATION TIME: 45 TO 60 MINUTES
BAKING TIME: 15 MINUTES

Gently rinse the salmon fillets in cold water, pat them dry, and set aside.

Melt the butter in a medium skillet. When the butter begins to sizzle, add the shallots and sauté on medium heat for 10 minutes, until translucent and beginning to turn golden. Pour in the wine and simmer, uncovered, for

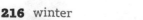

about 20 minutes, until reduced to 1½ to 2 cups of syrupy sauce. Stir in the chopped parsley and dill. Add salt and pepper to taste and set aside.

While the sauce simmers, prepare the parchment wrappers. Fold each piece of parchment paper in half crosswise to form a 9 x 7½-inch rectangle. Trim the two corners opposite the fold, rounding them, so when you unfold the parchment, you have an oval.

Preheat the oven to 350° when the shallot reduction is ready.

Now assemble the packets. Lightly butter the top of one of the oval parchment pieces. Place a fillet to one side of the center fold. Spoon 3 to 4 tablespoons of the sauce onto the fillet and top it with one sprig each of parsley and dill. Fold the parchment over the fish and crimp the open edges together: Starting at one end, carefully fold over about ¼ inch of the cut edge. Work your way around to the other end, folding small segments as you go. Fold the entire edge over a second time to form a seal and place the packet on a large unoiled baking sheet. Repeat the process for the rest of the fillets.

Bake for about 15 minutes, depending on the thickness of the fillets. Snip the packets open with scissors and serve the fillets in the parchment, or carefully remove the fillets from their packets without letting any of the sauce escape.

VEGETABLE POT PIE

This hearty, savory pie has an herbed pastry fragrant with rosemary and a rich, colorful filling. For an artful touch, use cookie cutters to cut the pie crust into festive shapes to decorate the top of the pie. Or, make a full top crust and cut slits in it shaped like large asterisks, which will open up during baking to make good-looking stars. If you have any leftover dough, cut out a large shooting star (use your imagination) and place it on top amid the other cut-out stars.

SERVES 8
PREPARATION TIME: 1¼ HOURS
BAKING TIME: 40 TO 50 MINUTES
COOLING TIME: 10 TO 15 MINUTES

1	TABLESPOON VEGETABLE OIL
1½	CUPS CHOPPED ONIONS
3	BAY LEAVES
2½	CUPS CUBED POTATOES*
1	TEASPOON SALT
1½	CUPS CHOPPED CELERY
1	CUP VEGETABLE STOCK**
2	CUPS CUT GREEN BEANS (1-INCH LENGTHS)
3	CUPS PEELED CUBED BUTTERNUT SQUASH*
2½	CUPS SLICED MUSHROOMS
3	TABLESPOONS CHOPPED FRESH PARSLEY
1½	TABLESPOONS CHOPPED FRESH DILL (2 TEASPOONS DRIED)

havarti cheese sauce

¼	CUP BUTTER
⅓	CUP UNBLEACHED WHITE FLOUR
2	CUPS VEGETABLE STOCK**
1½	CUPS GRATED DILLED HAVARTI CHEESE
	SALT AND GROUND BLACK PEPPER TO TASTE

pastry

1¾	CUPS UNBLEACHED WHITE FLOUR
1	TEASPOON CHOPPED FRESH ROSEMARY
½	CUP BUTTER
¼	CUP ICE WATER

* We recommend using Yukon Gold potatoes. Cut both the potatoes and squash into ½-inch cubes.

** No-Chicken Stock by Imagine and Roasted Vegetable Stock by Kitchen Basics are both good choices. Or try our Basic Vegetable Stock (page 408).

In a large soup pot, warm the oil. Add the onions and bay leaves and sauté for about 10 minutes on medium heat, until the onions are soft. Stir in the potatoes, salt, celery, and the cup of vegetable stock. Cover and bring to a boil; then lower the heat and simmer for 5 minutes. Add the green beans and continue to simmer for 5 more minutes. Stir in the squash and cook for another 5 to 10 minutes, until all of the vegetables are just barely tender. Add the mushrooms, parsley, and dill and cook for 3 to 4 minutes to soften the mushrooms. Remove and discard the bay leaves. Cover the vegetables and set aside.

Preheat the oven to 375°.

In a saucepan, melt the butter and whisk in the flour to make a roux. Cook for 2 minutes, stirring constantly. Whisk in the stock and cook on medium heat, whisking often, until the sauce thickens and simmers gently. Whisk in the cheese until melted and stir the sauce into the pot of cooked vegetables. Add salt and ground black pepper to taste. Pour the filling into a 9 x 13 x 2-inch baking pan or a 10-inch round deep-dish pie plate and set it aside.

Prepare the pastry. Mix together the flour and rosemary in a large bowl. Rapidly work the butter into the flour with a pastry cutter or your fingers until it resembles coarse meal. Sprinkle the ice water over the mixture a tablespoon at a time, and lightly mix it in. Push the dampened dough into the center of the bowl and form a ball.

On a floured surface, roll out the pastry to fit your baking dish. Completely cover the top and crimp the edges or arrange cut-out designs on top of the filling. If you totally cover the pie with pastry, cut a few slits in the top. That way steam can escape during baking for a crisper crust. Gaps between cut-out designs will make good "vents," too.

Bake for 40 to 50 minutes, until the crust is golden and the filling bubbly. Cool for 10 to 15 minutes before serving.

BRUSSELS SPROUTS WITH CHESTNUT BEURRE BLANC

A velvety chestnut beurre blanc gives these tiny cabbages a touch of class. Beurres blancs require care but are not technically difficult at all. Temperature is the all-important variable; the butter must be heated just enough to melt without separating. The final result will then be cohesive and creamy. This recipe yields 2 cups of sauce.

If preparing fresh chestnuts for the beurre blanc, see Roasted Chestnuts (page 225).

seasoned beurre blanc

10 FRESH OR 15 CANNED ROASTED, SHELLED CHESTNUTS*
1 to 2 TEASPOONS FRESH LEMON JUICE
¼ CUP MINCED VIDALIA OR RED ONIONS, OR SHALLOTS
4 TEASPOONS RED WINE OR BALSAMIC VINEGAR
½ CUP COLD BUTTER
¼ TEASPOON SALT, OR TO TASTE
PINCH OF GROUND BLACK PEPPER
PINCH OF GROUND NUTMEG

4 CUPS BRUSSELS SPROUTS (1½ POUNDS)
PINCH OF THYME

* Canned chestnuts work fine; ¾ pound canned equals about 1 pound fresh. Reserve their flavorful packing liquid. Look for Clément Faugier, an affordable, good-quality brand, in the baking sections of well-stocked supermarkets.

In a blender, purée the chestnuts and lemon juice with about ¾ cup of warm water or, if using canned chestnuts, with ¾ cup of their packing liquid. Use a rubber spatula to scoop the purée into a bowl and set aside.

Combine the onions, vinegar, and ¼ cup of water in a small saucepan and simmer until most of the liquid has evaporated, about 5 minutes. While the liquid reduces, cut the butter into small pieces.

Reduce the heat to very low. Add 4 or 5 pieces of butter to the saucepan and whisk until the butter has melted. Immediately lift the pan from the burner and add another handful of butter. Return the saucepan to the heat and whisk until the butter is incorporated. Repeat until all of the butter is melted; then remove from the heat. Whisk in the reserved chestnut purée, salt, pepper, and nutmeg, cover, and set aside in a warm, but not hot, place.

Remove any yellowed or bruised outer leaves from the Brussels sprouts and slice off the tough bottoms. Use small ones whole and halve large ones. Steam or blanch in boiling water seasoned with thyme for 4 to 5 minutes, until bright green and easily pierced with a knife.

Beurre blanc thickens as it sits; if needed, thin it with a small amount of water, vegetable stock, or heavy cream. Ladle the sauce over the Brussels sprouts and serve.

STUFFED YAMS

Sweet, buttery, and fruity stuffed yams with their deep orange color add richness to the sweet and savory pleasures of Christmas. Make the most efficient use of time by first getting the whole yams in the oven and then preparing the rest of the recipe ingredients while they bake.

Yams have thin and somewhat fragile jackets, so they're not quite as easy to stuff as baking potatoes. Scoop out their soft interiors carefully, leaving a lining inside the skin that will support the filling. Stuffed yams can be made ahead and refrigerated for up to two days; then just reheat them and serve. To make a vegan version, use vegetable oil instead of butter.

4	LARGE YAMS*
1½	TABLESPOONS BUTTER OR VEGETABLE OIL
½	CUP FINELY CHOPPED ONIONS
4	TEASPOONS MINCED CRYSTALLIZED GINGER
2	TABLESPOONS UNSULPHURED GOLDEN RAISINS
2	TABLESPOONS CHOPPED PRUNES
½	TEASPOON SALT
	FRESHLY GROUND BLACK PEPPER TO TASTE

SERVES 8
TOTAL TIME: 1 TO 1¼ HOURS

* The "yams" called for here are actually a type of sweet potato with brick-red skin and deep orange flesh. They are larger and longer than their paler cousins.

Preheat the oven to 450°.

Rinse the yams to remove any dirt, dry them, and place whole on an unoiled baking sheet. Bake for 45 to 60 minutes, until soft to the touch. Meanwhile, melt the butter in a heavy skillet and sauté the onions on medium heat for 8 to 10 minutes, until translucent.

Remove the cooked yams from the oven. Set on a cutting board until cool enough to handle, about 10 minutes. Cut each yam in half lengthwise, then carefully scoop out the soft interior of each half, leaving a lining of ¼ to ½ inch inside the skin. In a medium bowl, stir together the cooked yam flesh, the sautéed onions, the crystallized ginger, raisins, prunes, salt, and pepper and mix well.

Mound the filling into the hollowed yam halves and place the stuffed yams on an unoiled baking sheet (see Note). Return the yams to the oven for about 5 minutes, until thoroughly hot, and serve immediately.

note

If you're making the yams ahead of time, cover and refrigerate the stuffed, unbaked yam halves until ready to serve. Reheat the stuffed yams at 350° for 30 minutes, until piping hot, and serve.

variation

Peel the skin away from the cooked whole yams and capture all of the soft interior flesh in a bowl. Add the sautéed onions and the rest of the filling ingredients as above and mix well. Spoon the mixture into a lightly oiled casserole dish and bake at 350° for 15 to 20 minutes. Serve hot.

PEARL ONIONS BRAISED IN WINE

Here's an Italian method of cooking pearl onions which produces beautiful purple-glazed onions that are richly wine-flavored. Select pearl onions close in size with about a 1-inch diameter. You can use red or white onions—a mix is fine, too.

This recipe makes a perfect, innovative side dish for Christmas dinner or can serve as a colorful garnish. Any leftover onions can be used to boost the flavor of a soup or stew.

1½	POUNDS PEARL ONIONS
1	TABLESPOON OLIVE OIL
1	CUP RED WINE
2 or 3	BAY LEAVES
1	TEASPOON DRIED THYME
½	TEASPOON SALT
1	TABLESPOON BALSAMIC VINEGAR
1	TEASPOON SUGAR

SERVES 6
TOTAL TIME: 45 MINUTES

In a saucepan, bring about 4 cups of water to a boil. Meanwhile, slice off as little as possible of each onion's root end and discard the ends. Blanch the onions in the boiling water for just 2 minutes. Drain and rinse immediately with cold water. Peel each onion by holding it at the top end and squeezing gently; the onion should slip out of its skin through the root end. Trim the tops of the peeled onions.

Warm the oil in a cast iron or stainless steel saucepan on low heat. Sauté the onions for 3 minutes. Add the wine, bay leaves, thyme, salt, and vinegar, partially cover, and simmer for 20 minutes, shaking the pan occasionally. Add the sugar and simmer, uncovered, for about 5 minutes, until the liquid is reduced to a syrup and the onions have a hazy purple glaze. Remove and discard the bay leaves.

Serve hot.

THYME

BAY

ROASTED CHESTNUTS

Moosewood cook Tony Del Plato fondly remembers the frequent aroma of chestnuts roasting in the kitchen from Thanksgiving to Christmas. As his mother worked on the holiday preparations, she would periodically add water to the pan of roasting chestnuts while singing "chestnuts roasting on an open fire" along with Nat King Cole.

The chestnut originated in Europe and Central Asia, where it has long been a staple. Chestnut trees once grew densely from New England to the Carolinas and as far west as Michigan, but a fungal blight at the turn of the twentieth century virtually wiped out these magnificent trees in North America. There have been attempts in Florida to bring back the chestnut tree, with varieties bearing hopeful names like Heritage and Revival, but today chestnuts come primarily from Europe and from some Japanese chestnut trees grown for commercial use on the West Coast.

Chestnuts are very low-fat and can be used as appetizers and in soups and dressings. In season, choose firm, heavy nuts with shiny shells and oven roast them. We had difficulty finding good chestnuts after the winter holiday season: So get them while they're good.

24   HARD, UNCRACKED, FRESH CHESTNUTS

SERVES 4 TO 6
PREPARATION TIME: 15 MINUTES
BAKING TIME: 30 MINUTES

Preheat the oven to 400°.

On the flat side of each chestnut, carefully carve an X with the tip of a paring knife. Place the chestnuts X side down on a baking sheet or in a cast iron pan. Bake for about 30 minutes. The chestnuts are done when the shell cracks open easily when pressed between the thumb and index finger. The nut meat will feel tender.

Wrap a clean towel around the roasted chestnuts to steam them and keep them warm. To eat, squeeze them open and then peel off both the shell and the coarse membrane that covers the nut.

Serve with vermouth or sherry after dinner.

CHOCOLATE CRANBERRY TART

Cranberries and chocolate? Yes! This tart is an intensely delightful combination of flavors and textures. Sweet-tart cranberries laced with dark bittersweet chocolate bask in a rich, crisp, cookie-like almond crust. Served alone, this may be a somewhat "adult" dessert, but top it with a bit of vanilla ice cream and kids love it, too.

Because the dough must be chilled, baked, and cooled and the chocolate must cool as well, you need to start making the tart at least 3 to 3½ hours before you plan to serve it. Actual hands-on time, however, is only 35 to 45 minutes, so you can prepare something else in between, hang a few holiday decorations, catch up on email, wrap those last-minute presents, or just catch your breath.

dough

1½ CUPS UNBLEACHED WHITE PASTRY FLOUR*

¼ CUP SUGAR

½ CUP CHILLED BUTTER, CUT INTO SMALL PIECES

¼ TEASPOON SALT

1 LARGE EGG YOLK

¼ TEASPOON GROUND NUTMEG

1 TEASPOON PURE VANILLA EXTRACT

¼ CUP FINELY CHOPPED TOASTED ALMONDS**

1 to 2 TABLESPOONS COLD WATER

filling

3 CUPS FRESH OR FROZEN CRANBERRIES

1 CUP SUGAR

1 TABLESPOON CORNSTARCH DISSOLVED IN ¼ CUP WATER

1 TEASPOON FRESHLY GRATED ORANGE PEEL

½ CUP CHOPPED OR GRATED SEMI-SWEET CHOCOLATE

SERVES 12
PREPARATION TIME: 35 TO 45 MINUTES
DOUGH CHILLING TIME: 30 TO 60 MINUTES
BAKING TIME: 25 MINUTES
CRUST COOLING TIME: 1 HOUR
CHOCOLATE COOLING TIME: 15 MINUTES

* The low-protein content of pastry flour, which is milled from soft wheat, gives baked goods an especially tender crumb.

** Toast ⅓ cup of whole almonds in a 350° oven for about 10 minutes, until fragrant; then finely chop in a food processor, blender, or by hand.

Combine the flour, sugar, butter, and salt in the bowl of a food processor and pulse until crumbly. Beat together the egg yolk, nutmeg, and vanilla in a cup and pour it into the dough; pulse briefly. Add the almonds and pulse again. Add 2 to 3 teaspoons of the cold water, pulse briefly, and push the dough together with your hands. If necessary, add a little more of the water and pulse again, until the dough holds together. Form the dough into a 1-inch-thick disk, cover with plastic wrap, and chill for 30 to 60 minutes.

Meanwhile, cook the cranberries in a nonreactive saucepan on medium heat, stirring occasionally, for 2 to 3 minutes, until they begin to soften. Add the sugar and simmer until it has dissolved and the berries are juicy. Pour in the cornstarch mixture and cook for 2 to 3 minutes, stirring constantly, until the sauce thickens. Add the orange peel and remove from the heat.

Preheat the oven to 375°.

Roll the chilled dough into a circle 13 to 14 inches in diameter. Place it in a 10-inch tart pan or pie plate, pressing about an inch of the pastry up the sides and folding over the edge to make a sturdy, decorative rim. Prick the bottom and sides of the dough every 2 inches or so with the tines of a fork.

Bake for 10 minutes, then lower the heat to 350° and bake for about 15 minutes more, until the crust is golden brown and firm. Set aside to cool for about an hour.

When the crust is cool, melt the chocolate (see Note). Heat the chocolate in a double boiler until pourable. Drizzle half of the chocolate onto the crust and allow it to cool for a few minutes. Evenly spoon on the cranberry filling. Drizzle the rest of the chocolate here and there, so that the deep ruby red cranberry filling shines through. (Here's your chance to rival the great Abstract Expressionist artists of the mid-twentieth century!) Allow the chocolate to firm up before serving the tart, about 15 minutes.

note

If you have a microwave, put the chocolate in a Pyrex 2-cup measure and heat on high for 1 minute, or a little longer, until pourable. The great thing about using a measuring cup for melting the chocolate is the convenience of its pouring spout for drizzling.

KWANZA KARAMU BUFFET

Harvest Stuffed Squash
Sweet Potato Stuffed Eggplant with Spicy Peanut Sauce
Spinach Callaloo with Crabmeat
Curried Coconut Green Beans
Collard Greens & Red Beans
Apple Brown Betty with Jamaican Rum & Fruit Compote
Peanut Butter Cookies (page 212)

Kwanza is a seven-day festive observation of black heritage developed in 1966 by Maulana Karenga, a prominent African-American professor of black studies. It weaves together cultural themes and elements of various harvest festivals celebrated by people in Africa and the diaspora to create a holiday in which everyone can participate.

The word *Kwanza* means "first fruits of the harvest" in Swahili, and in keeping with the harvest-festival themes, people come together to enjoy great home cooking each night. The culmination, on December 31, is a feast called a Kwanza Karamu and it's a time to pull out all the stops and indulge in the incredible array of cuisines of the African diaspora: Caribbean, Brazilian, and other South American foods with African origins, Southern soul food, Creole and Cajun cooking, and traditional dishes from the many countries of mother Africa herself.

Kwanza feasts can be entirely or partly vegetarian and still draw upon African traditions. Take full advantage of the seasonal vegetables and fruits in your region to make an authentic homage to the harvest and use them to decorate your Kwanza table as well.

The items suggested for our buffet create a lavish spread, so feel free to choose four or five favorites from the list for your menu. Select either the Harvest Stuffed Squash or the Sweet Potato Stuffed Eggplant as the central focus. Pick two of the three side dishes and one (or both!) of the desserts.

Plan ahead. The Spicy Peanut Sauce for the eggplant and the Jamaican Rum & Fruit Compote can be prepared well in advance, stored in the refrigerator, and then reheated for serving. Peanut Butter Cookies can be baked several days ahead. On the day before the feast, make the seasoned rice and prep the spinach for the callaloo; then whip up the Coconut Green Beans, which can be reheated the next day or served chilled. That same day or early on Kwanza Karamu, make the stuffed vegetables of your choice; then, just before serving, bake them until hot. While they bake, prepare the Collard Greens & Red Beans and finish off the Spinach Callaloo. The Apple Brown Betty is best hot, so either bake it during dinner or be sure to rewarm it before serving.

To compose a complete Kwanza table, you will need these elements:

* *Mkeka*: a straw or hand-woven place mat of African or African-American design placed on a table or sideboard that has been covered with a simple black, white, or green cloth to represent tradition.
* *Mazao*: one or two baskets overflowing with seasonal fruits and vegetables.
* *Vibunzi*: ears of multicolored Indian corn, one for each child in the family, or one or more ears to symbolize all children.
* *Kinara*: a seven-branched candle holder representing Africa and her people.
* *Mishumaa Saba*: seven candles to represent the "seven principles for daily life" (page 231). Use alternating red and green candles and a central black candle because those are the colors of the black liberation flag. Light one candle each of the seven nights.
* *Kikombe cha Umoja*: a large, decorative communal cup, symbolizing unity, from which everyone can take a sip in honor of the ancestors, family, friends, community, and future generations of black people.

HARVEST STUFFED SQUASH

This is a really pretty dish with a very savory stuffing of mushrooms, bell peppers, and multi-colored rice. It makes a fine main dish for Kwanza, Thanksgiving, or any harvest meal.

We recommend butternut squash for its mellow sweetness, but any winter squash—acorn, delicata, or buttercup—can be used. There are many interesting rice blends on the market that would work in this recipe, but a simple combination of brown rice, wild rice, and walnuts makes this stuffing chewy, nutty, and handsome.

1¾	CUPS WATER
⅔	CUP RAW BROWN RICE
⅓	CUP RAW WILD RICE
	PINCH OF SALT
4	SMALL WINTER SQUASH (ABOUT 6 INCHES LONG)
3	TABLESPOONS OLIVE OIL
2	CUPS CHOPPED ONIONS
2	GARLIC CLOVES, MINCED OR PRESSED
2½ to 3 CUPS CHOPPED RED AND YELLOW BELL PEPPERS	
1	TEASPOON DRIED CRUMBLED ROSEMARY (2 TEASPOONS CHOPPED FRESH)
¾	TEASPOON SALT
	PINCH OF GROUND NUTMEG
	GROUND BLACK PEPPER TO TASTE
2	CUPS CHOPPED MUSHROOMS (A LARGE PORTABELLO IS NICE)
½	CUP GROUND WALNUTS*
¼	CUP MINCED FRESH PARSLEY
1	CUP GRATED CHEDDAR CHEESE

SERVES 6 TO 8
PREPARATION TIME: 1 HOUR
FINAL BAKING TIME: 20 MINUTES

* Pulse the nuts several times in a food processor or chop very finely with a knife to reach the consistency of coarse meal.

Preheat the oven to 400°. Lightly oil a baking sheet.

Combine the water, brown rice, wild rice, and salt in a small saucepan. Cover tightly and bring to a boil. Reduce the heat and simmer for about 40 minutes.

While the rice cooks, rinse the squash well, cut them in half lengthwise, and remove the seeds. Use about 1 tablespoon of oil to rub on the squash halves and place them cut side down on the baking sheet. Bake, uncovered, for about 30 minutes, until tender.

While the squash halves bake, sauté the onions and garlic in the remaining 2 tablespoons of oil for about 10 minutes, until the onions are translucent and slightly golden. Add the bell peppers, rosemary, salt, nutmeg, and black pepper and continue to cook for 5 minutes. Add the mushrooms and sauté just until the mushrooms are tender and release their juices. Stir in the walnuts and parsley. Remove from the heat and mix in the rice when it's cooked.

Remove the baking sheet from the oven. Turn the baked squash halves cut side up, sprinkle the cavity with salt and pepper, and mash the flesh lightly with a fork. Mound each half with about one-eighth of the rice filling and top with 2 tablespoons of the grated cheese.

Bake for 20 minutes, until thoroughly hot and lightly browned.

kwanza's *nguzo saba*, "seven principles for daily life"

* Unity (*Umoja*): to create and maintain unity in our family, community, nation, and race.

* Self-determination (*Kujichagulia*): to define, name, and speak for ourselves.

* Collective work and responsibility (*Ujima*): to work cooperatively to share and resolve the problems of people within our communities.

* Cooperative economics (*Ujamma*): to start and develop community-based businesses.

* Purpose (*Nia*): to build and develop our community for our people's success.

* Creativity (*Kuumba*): to contribute what we can to give beauty and benefit to improve our community.

* Faith (*Imani*): to believe in our people with all our heart.

SWEET POTATO STUFFED EGGPLANT

This is a richly flavorful dish, inspired by the foods of West Africa, where true yams would replace our North American sweet potatoes and where a paste of groundnuts might replace the crunchy peanut butter. It is a good example of Kwanza cookery, drawing inspiration from mother Africa and using domestic foods of the American South.

We think the sauce has a real kick to it (but we know it doesn't hold a candle to the fiery hotness of some West African cooking). Any leftover sauce keeps a *long* time if refrigerated in a sealed container. It can be thinned with tomato juice, orange juice, or plain water, and is a good condiment with rice and vegetables, as a dipping sauce, or in pita with baked tofu and spinach.

SERVES 4 TO 6
PREPARATION TIME: 1 HOUR
FINAL BAKING TIME: 10 MINUTES

stuffed eggplant

2	PURPLE EGGPLANTS (6 TO 7 INCHES LONG)
1 to 2	TABLESPOONS SOY SAUCE
3	TABLESPOONS VEGETABLE OIL
2	CUPS PEELED AND DICED SWEET POTATOES
2	CUPS CHOPPED ONIONS
	PINCH OF SALT
2	GARLIC CLOVES, MINCED OR PRESSED
1	LARGE RED BELL PEPPER, SEEDED AND DICED

spicy peanut sauce

2	TABLESPOONS VEGETABLE OIL
1½	CUPS CHOPPED ONIONS
2	TABLESPOONS GRATED FRESH GINGER ROOT
¼	TEASPOON CAYENNE, MORE TO TASTE
¾	CUP NATURAL UNSALTED CRUNCHY PEANUT BUTTER
2	TABLESPOONS SOY SAUCE
2	TABLESPOONS LIGHT UNSULPHURED MOLASSES
2	TABLESPOONS WHITE OR CIDER VINEGAR
2	CUPS TOMATO JUICE
	SALT TO TASTE
	CHOPPED SCALLIONS

Preheat the oven to 350°. Lightly oil a 9 x 13-inch baking pan.

Cut the eggplants in half lengthwise, brush the cut sides with soy sauce, and arrange them flesh side up in the baking pan. Brush lightly with some of the oil. Add ½ cup of water to the pan and cover with foil. Bake until tender, about 30 minutes.

Meanwhile, place the sweet potatoes in a saucepan with water to cover and bring to a boil; then lower the heat and simmer about 10 minutes, until just tender. In a skillet, heat the remaining oil on medium heat and sauté the onions, salt, and garlic for 5 minutes, until the onions are soft. Add the bell peppers and cook until just tender, about 5 minutes. Drain the cooked sweet potatoes. Add them to the skillet with salt and pepper to taste. Stir, cover, and set the filling aside.

For the Spicy Peanut Sauce, heat the oil in a saucepan and sauté the onions for 3 minutes on medium-high heat. Add the ginger root and cayenne and sauté for another minute. Add the peanut butter, soy sauce, molasses, vinegar, and tomato juice. Stir thoroughly to blend in the peanut butter, cover, and cook gently on medium-low heat until melted, smooth, and hot. Stir frequently so that the sauce doesn't stick to the bottom and scorch. Add salt and more cayenne to taste and set aside.

When the eggplants are baked, remove them from the oven. With the back of a spoon, gently push the flesh to the sides. Mound the filling into the eggplant shells. Return them to the oven to bake for about 10 minutes.

If you'd like smaller portions, slice each finished eggplant crosswise into two pieces. Top the stuffed eggplants generously with sauce, sprinkle with chopped scallions, and serve.

Yams and sweet potatoes are tubers of two different plants. Although true yams (which are more starchy) are now more available in the United States, the tubers we commonly call yams are usually sweet potatoes or *batatas, Ipomoea batatas.* The true yam, *Dioscorea,* can weigh up to 30 pounds and is a native staple of Africa, the Caribbean, Indonesia, Polynesia, Papua New Guinea, and other tropical areas. Sweet potatoes are thought to be native to the East Indies and the Americas.

Our American word *yam* derives from *yami, yamme,* and *eyam,* all words for true yams in various African languages. The word *nyam* means "to eat" in Gullah, the dialect of the Georgia Sea Islands. Yam cultivation and cooking savvy are among the many good things that Africans brought to the Americas. Fortunately, yam know-how works well on sweet potatoes.

the african diaspora & cooking
in the americas

The Atlantic slave trade forcibly brought people to the New World from West, Central, and East Africa from the early 1500s to the mid-1800s. Although the practice of African customs was discouraged or forbidden, African culture inevitably spread to the United States, South America, and the Caribbean, and strong African influences have fortunately survived in our language, music, dance, decorative arts—and cuisine. For the newly arrived Africans, it must have brought comfort to cook dishes that recalled the flavors of the continent left behind, and the cuisines that developed in the Americas reflect cooking styles and ingredients of African origin.

Many New World cuisines spectacularly combine the methods and flavors of African cuisine with the ingredients and styles of the indigenous peoples and the European settlers. The African custom of grilling, stewing, and deep-frying a variety of foods quickly spread. Spices that are used extensively in African cooking were right at home in the warmer climates of the New World. Some food historians credit Africans in the Americas with introducing greens and incorporating certain vegetables into the European diet.

Similarities between today's African and American dishes are abundant. The Caribbean's *coo coo* and the grits and cornmeal mush of the southern United States are direct descendants of East African *ugali* and Niger's *touo*. What is called Hoppin' John in Georgia is called *thiebou nop niébé* in Senegal.

A Yoruba dish of flour and yams or corn steamed or fried in a banana leaf is mirrored in Puerto Rico's *pasteles* and Brazil's *acaça*. Puerto Rican *sofrito*, a flavorful vegetable sauce, contains orange-red achiote (annatto) oil, which originally may have been a look-alike for the palm oil ubiquitous in West African cooking.

The fritters found all over Nigeria and Togo are also found all over the West Indies, southern United States, and Bahia. Compare barbecuing in the United States and the wood-fire grilling of Haiti with the hundreds of braziers in Abidjan producing grilled delights with spicy sauces.

African ancestors remain a strong presence in our kitchens. We are the inheritors of the extraordinary, simmering stew of rich and varied flavors and styles that is American cuisine and culture.

SPINACH CALLALOO WITH CRABMEAT

Callaloo is a green that is commonly found in Jamaican groceries. It's still not easy to find in the Ithaca area, so we often use fresh spinach instead. Spinach cooks fast and its distinct taste really shines through in this dish.

Our recipe is adapted from the traditional Jamaican preparation that combines greens with coconut milk and spices. We've added sweet, lovely basmati rice and crabmeat—but the dish does work just as well without the crab.

SERVES 6
TOTAL TIME: 1 HOUR

1	TABLESPOON VEGETABLE OIL
1	TABLESPOON BUTTER
1½ to 2	CUPS CHOPPED ONIONS
2	GARLIC CLOVES, MINCED OR PRESSED
1	TEASPOON SALT
½	TEASPOON TURMERIC
½	TEASPOON GROUND ALLSPICE
½	TEASPOON GROUND CORIANDER
½	TEASPOON DRIED THYME (1 TEASPOON FRESH)
	PINCH OF GROUND NUTMEG
½	CUP RAW WHITE BASMATI RICE
2	CUPS VEGETABLE STOCK OR WATER
20	OUNCES FRESH SPINACH
1¾	CUPS COCONUT MILK (14-OUNCE CAN)
8	OUNCES CRABMEAT (OPTIONAL) (PAGE 50)
	SALT AND GROUND BLACK PEPPER TO TASTE
	LEMON WEDGES (OPTIONAL)

In a heavy soup pot, heat the oil and butter on medium heat. Add the onions, garlic, salt, turmeric, allspice, coriander, thyme, and nutmeg. Cover and cook for 3 to 5 minutes, stirring once or twice. Add the rice and 1 cup of the stock or water. Cover and bring to a boil, then lower the heat and simmer for 20 to 30 minutes, until the rice is tender.

Meanwhile, rinse the spinach well, remove any tough stems, and coarsely chop the spinach leaves.

When the rice is cooked, stir in the remaining cup of stock or water, the coconut milk, and the crabmeat, if using. Continue to cook, but don't let the mixture boil. When hot, stir in the spinach and cook just long enough to thoroughly wilt it. Add salt and pepper to taste.

Serve in bowls with lemon wedges, if you wish.

CURRIED COCONUT GREEN BEANS

Curry spices are common ingredients in Caribbean cuisine and this simple side dish can be made spicy hot or not, using the spices that most people have on hand in their pantry. The coconut milk makes a luscious coating for the beans, and any leftovers can be served as a great snack or a tasty chilled salad the next day.

½	TEASPOON BLACK MUSTARD SEEDS (OPTIONAL)
2	TEASPOONS VEGETABLE OIL
2	ONIONS, MINCED (ABOUT 2 CUPS)
1	SMALL RED ONION, MINCED
1½	TEASPOONS GROUND CUMIN
1	TEASPOON GROUND CORIANDER
1	TEASPOON SALT
½	TEASPOON TURMERIC
¼	TEASPOON GROUND BLACK PEPPER
⅛	TEASPOON GROUND CINNAMON
⅛	TEASPOON CAYENNE OR ¼ TEASPOON RED PEPPER FLAKES, OR TO TASTE
1	POUND GREEN BEANS, TRIMMED AND CUT INTO 2-INCH PIECES (ABOUT 3¾ CUPS)
2	TABLESPOONS MIRIN OR 1 TABLESPOON BROWN SUGAR
¾	CUP REDUCED-FAT COCONUT MILK*

* We recommend Thai Kitchen brand, which doesn't have preservatives.

If using the black mustard seeds, warm the oil in a large saucepan on medium-high heat and sauté the seeds until they begin to pop. Add the onions and red onion and sauté for 5 minutes, stirring often. When the onions begin to soften, stir in the cumin, coriander, salt, turmeric, black pepper, cinnamon, and cayenne or red pepper flakes. Stir constantly for 2 minutes.

Add the green beans and mirin and cook for 2 to 3 minutes. Pour in the coconut milk, cover, bring to a simmer, and then reduce the heat to medium-low. Simmer until the beans are tender, about 15 minutes.

Serve hot.

COLLARD GREENS & RED BEANS

Hearty, healthful, and tasty, these greens and beans are easy to make, keep well, and can be reheated without any loss of flavor. For a big crowd, double or triple the recipe.

It's become fashionable to serve greens lightly sautéed, but traditionally collards are well cooked. Try them both ways and see which method you prefer. Every ingredient in this recipe can be adjusted to suit individual taste.

1	TABLESPOON VEGETABLE, OLIVE OR PEANUT OIL
2	LARGE GARLIC CLOVES, SLICED OR MINCED
1	BUNCH FRESH COLLARD GREENS, RINSED, DRAINED, STEMMED AND CHOPPED (ABOUT 10 CUPS)
2	TABLESPOONS CIDER VINEGAR
2	TABLESPOONS WATER
½	TEASPOON TABASCO OR OTHER HOT PEPPER SAUCE, MORE TO TASTE
1½	CUPS COOKED OR CANNED KIDNEY BEANS (15-OUNCE CAN, UNDRAINED)
	COARSELY GROUND BLACK PEPPER TO TASTE
	SALT TO TASTE

SERVES 4 TO 6
PREPARATION TIME: 5 MINUTES
COOKING TIME: 20 MINUTES

Heat the oil in a 2-quart saucepan and add the garlic. Add the greens, vinegar, water, and Tabasco sauce and sauté on medium heat for 5 minutes, stirring often. Cover and cook for another 5 minutes.

Add the kidney beans with ½ cup of the cooking liquid or water or, if using canned beans, add them with their liquid. Cook, covered, for about 10 minutes, until the collards are tender and everything is piping hot. Stir in pepper, salt, and more hot sauce to taste and serve immediately.

APPLE BROWN BETTY

This is a sweet, heady dessert that will warm your heart and lift your spirits. Apple Brown Betty is good all by itself, and the succulent Jamaican Rum & Fruit Compote can hold its own over vanilla ice cream. However, when the betty is combined with the compote, it's pure comfort. The insanely decadent may add a little whipped cream.

SERVES 6 TO 8
PREPARATION TIME: 25 MINUTES
TOTAL TIME: 75 MINUTES

apple brown betty

- 4   CUPS CUBED STALE BREAD*
- 3   CUPS PEELED, CORED AND CUBED APPLES
- 3   EGGS
- 3   CUPS MILK
- 2/3   CUP BROWN SUGAR, LIGHTLY PACKED
- 1   TEASPOON PURE VANILLA EXTRACT
- 1/2   TEASPOON GROUND CINNAMON
- 1/8   TEASPOON GROUND GINGER
- 1/2   TEASPOON GROUND NUTMEG
- 2   TABLESPOONS BUTTER

jamaican rum & fruit compote

- 1   CUP CHOPPED PRUNES
- 3/4   CUP CHOPPED DATES
- 1/3   CUP DRIED CHERRIES
- 1/3   CUP RAISINS
- 1   TEASPOON FRESHLY GRATED ORANGE PEEL
- 1/2   TEASPOON FINELY GRATED FRESH NUTMEG
- 1 1/2   CUPS ORANGE JUICE
- 1/4   CUP BROWN SUGAR, LIGHTLY PACKED, LESS TO TASTE
- 1   TEASPOON PURE VANILLA EXTRACT
- 2   TABLESPOONS DARK JAMAICAN RUM

* Use whole wheat, molasses, French, or challah. If you don't have stale bread, lightly toast fresh bread to dry it a bit.

Preheat the oven to 350°. Lightly butter a 9 x 13-inch baking pan or two loaf pans.

For the betty, combine the cubed bread and the apples in a bowl. In a separate bowl, whisk together the eggs, milk, brown sugar, vanilla, cinnamon, ginger, and nutmeg. Pour the custard over the bread and apples and spread the mixture evenly in the baking pan. Bake the pudding for 45 minutes, then dot with the butter and bake for another 15 minutes, until the custard has set and the bread cubes begin to brown.

While the Apple Brown Betty bakes, make the compote. In a small saucepan, combine everything except the vanilla and the rum. Cover and simmer on medium heat for 15 minutes. Stir in the vanilla and rum and heat gently for another 5 to 10 minutes. The fruit should be tender, the raisins and cherries plump, and the sauce thick. Set aside. Thin with a little orange juice before serving, if necessary.

Serve Apple Brown Betty hot, topped with a couple of spoonfuls of the warm compote.

FIRST NIGHT

Cauliflower Fritters
Tomato Bean Soup
Escarole Pie
Orange Gratin

Maybe some of us at Moosewood came of age at a low point in the history of New Year's Eve celebrations or maybe we're just showing our age, but many of us have arrived at a rather jaded attitude about that holiday. It seems to us that, for a lot of people, New Year's Eve parties in the United States just don't work so well. For adults, the often exaggerated cheer of these parties can strike a hollow chord, plus the holiday is too often fueled by alcohol. Kids may be excluded altogether from the parties, and the alternative, staying awake at home until midnight watching a raucous party on TV, isn't much fun.

Others must have felt the same, because in the late 1970s a new way to ring in the New Year was begun in Boston. Called First Night, this new holiday idea has spread to many other towns and cities in the United States. It's a quieter appreciation of family, friends, and community. There's usually a multicultural celebration of the arts, mostly organized by and starring local talent, as well as many enjoyable outdoor activities. With First Night you'll probably be relaxed in jeans and snow boots rather than in an evening gown and high heels. Of course, there's the excitement of having fun together and staying up late to welcome another year.

The simple, casual meal we suggest is filled with hearty and delicious foods. It can work either to kick off the evening, to cap the festivities as midnight approaches, or maybe as a break mid-action: A come-in-from-the-cold pause. Although you might not guess it, we've found these dishes to be quite popular with kids as well as adults.

The Tomato Bean Soup and the Escarole Pie can be made well ahead and then reheated while you fry up the fritters and pass them around. Or maybe you'd prefer to start with hot soup, served in mugs, as an instant hand and belly warmer. The sunny little dessert is ready in minutes.

Then when everyone is full and happy, you'll be ready to plunge back out into the cold. You don't want to miss the hot potato race or the Ukrainian-Ugandan jugglers!

CAULIFLOWER FRITTERS

Cauliflower is truly glorified in these delicious fritters. You may plan to present them mounded on a big platter, but they'll probably be nabbed right out of the pan. Kids beg for more without even suspecting that there's a cruciferous vegetable in there.

We serve Cauliflower Fritters as an appetizer in this meal, but they're also a great winter snack or may be served as a side vegetable.

8	CUPS CHOPPED CAULIFLOWER
5	EGGS, BEATEN
1	CUP GRATED PARMESAN CHEESE
¼	CUP CHOPPED FRESH PARSLEY
1	TABLESPOON SALT
½	TEASPOON GROUND BLACK PEPPER
½	CUP UNBLEACHED WHITE FLOUR
½ to 1	CUP OLIVE OIL FOR FRYING

SERVES 6 TO 8
PREPARATION TIME: 30 MINUTES
COOKING TIME: ABOUT 40 MINUTES
(5 MINUTES PER BATCH)

In a large pot of boiling water, blanch the cauliflower for about 5 minutes, until softened but still a little crisp. Drain well.

In a bowl, beat together the eggs, Parmesan, parsley, salt, and pepper. Stir in the drained cauliflower. Sprinkle in the flour a little at a time, stirring until well mixed.

In a frying pan on medium-high heat, warm about ½ inch of oil until a drop of water immediately sputters and evaporates. If the oil begins to smoke, turn down the heat a notch. Carefully place heaping tablespoons of the batter into the pan and fry for about 3 minutes. Turn the fritters over and continue cooking for about 2 minutes, until golden. Drain on paper towels.

Stir the batter well before frying each batch. Continue until all of the batter is used, making about thirty 3-inch fritters. The fritters are good either warm or at room temperature. If serving them warm, keep the early batches in the oven at 200° while frying the rest.

TOMATO BEAN SOUP

This recipe is simple and fast, yet it yields a big pot of hearty soup, perfect for a chilly night. It also reheats well and, next to Escarole Pie, is just about as tasty a leftover as you can get.

SERVES 6 TO 8
TOTAL TIME: 30 TO 40
MINUTES

1	TABLESPOON OLIVE OIL
3½	CUPS CHOPPED ONIONS
1	TEASPOON DRIED OREGANO
1	TEASPOON DRIED BASIL
4½	CUPS COOKED PINTO OR ROMAN BEANS* (THREE 15.5-OUNCE CANS, DRAINED)
4½	CUPS CANNED DICED TOMATOES (28-OUNCE CAN AND 14.5-OUNCE CAN)
1	TEASPOON SALT
¼	TEASPOON COARSELY GROUND BLACK PEPPER, MORE TO TASTE
	GRATED PARMESAN CHEESE (OPTIONAL)

* Roman beans (*habichuelas romanas*) are like oversized navy beans. If you prefer to substitute another bean, such as cannellini, go right ahead.

Warm the olive oil in a heavy-bottomed soup pot. Add the onions and sauté on medium-high heat for about 10 minutes, stirring frequently, until they begin to brown. Stir in the oregano and basil and add 1 cup of water. Bring just to a boil; then cover and simmer for 3 to 4 minutes, until the onions are quite soft.

In batches in a blender, purée the onion mixture with 3 cups of the beans, 3 cups of the tomatoes, and the salt. Pour the puréed mixture back into the soup pot. Stir in the remaining beans and tomatoes and cook on medium heat for 5 to 10 minutes, stirring often. Add the pepper to taste.

Serve hot, topped with grated Parmesan cheese, if you like.

ESCAROLE PIE

This big, double-crusted pizza is filled with a flavorful, savory filling and rustic southern Italian style. It's lighter than you might expect, the perfect accompaniment to the simple bean soup in this meal, and kids love it. As a leftover, it can't be beat.

Start by mixing up the pizza dough, then make the filling while the dough rises.

½   RECIPE PIZZA CRUST (PAGE 308)

SERVES 6 TO 8
TOTAL TIME: 1½ HOURS

filling

1   CUP CHOPPED SCALLIONS

3   GARLIC CLOVES, MINCED OR PRESSED

1   TABLESPOON OLIVE OIL

1   TEASPOON SALT

8   CUPS RINSED AND COARSELY CHOPPED ESCAROLE

1   CUP PITTED KALAMATA OLIVES

1   TABLESPOON OLIVE OIL

Prepare the dough for the crust.

While the dough rises, sauté the scallions and garlic in the olive oil on medium heat, for 3 to 5 minutes, stirring frequently. Add the salt and escarole and cook for about 3 minutes, until wilted. Add the olives, remove from the heat, and drain any excess liquid. Set aside.

Punch down the dough and knead it for 3 to 5 minutes. Add flour, if needed, to better work the dough. Cut the dough roughly in half; use the larger half for the bottom crust. With your hands or a rolling pin, press the dough down and out from the center and shape into a circle or a rectangle to fit a large oiled baking pan. Set aside to rise for about 15 minutes.

Preheat the oven to 450°.

Evenly spread the escarole mixture onto the bottom crust, leaving about 2 inches uncovered around the edges. Shape the other half of the dough to fit on top and lay it over the escarole. Roll the edges up, pressing with your fingers or a fork to seal. Brush the top crust with olive oil and poke several small holes through it to allow steam to escape while baking. Bake for about 35 to 40 minutes.

Cut into wedges and serve warm or at room temperature.

ORANGE GRATIN

End your meal with a sweet dessert full of vitamin C before everyone goes back out into the cold.

8   **LARGE SEEDLESS NAVEL ORANGES**
½   **CUP BROWN SUGAR, PACKED**
¼   **TEASPOON GROUND CINNAMON**
     VANILLA ICE CREAM (OPTIONAL)

SERVES 8
TOTAL TIME: 20 MINUTES

Slice off several long pieces of orange zest from one of the oranges and cut the peel into very thin slivers 2 to 3 inches long. Set aside.

Slice the rest of the peel from all of the oranges, including the white pith, and discard it. Working over a shallow, broilerproof, nonreactive baking dish, slice toward the center of each orange along the membrane on one side of a section and then flick the knife up the membrane on the other side to release the section. Sprinkle the orange sections with the brown sugar and cinnamon. Scatter the reserved slivers of orange peel on top.

Broil for about 8 minutes, until the sugar is melted and the oranges are bubbling and hot. Serve immediately, plain or on vanilla ice cream.

NEW YEAR'S DAY BRUNCH BUFFET

Best Dressed Shrimp Salad
Sweet Potato & Zucchini Hash
Savory Flan
Good Luck Lentil Salad
Campari Compote
Buttery Blueberry Coffee Cake

Different cultures around the world celebrate the new year at different times—from January to September! Before there were calendars, the new year was signaled by natural cycles, such as rain or windstorm seasons, longer days, warm weather, or harvests. And festivals honored the gods of the sky who controlled the weather.

January 1 became the official first day of the year for much of the Roman world in 1582, when Pope Gregory XIII introduced the Gregorian calendar, which matches the 365.25-day annual passage of the earth around the sun. Today, much of the world still celebrates that date. It's traditional to greet the New Year at midnight on December 31 by kissing a loved one, and to dance, sing, and toast with friends. All-night parties are not uncommon, and in some places the merriment goes on for days.

What happens December 31 to January 1 depends on where you are. Customs vary everywhere. The Scottish celebrate Hogmany with dancing, bonfires, and huge street parties. Gifts of bread and coal symbolize driving out hunger and cold. In Japan, at midnight monks ring the Buddhist temple bells 108 times, a sacred number. It is a time of forgiveness, and gifts of bamboo, for honesty, and fir tree branches, reminders of the appearance of no change in the midst of change, are exchanged. In Belgium, children write thank-you letters to their parents. Canadians break out their fiddles for energetic Quebecois music and step dancing. In Colombia, some wear yellow underwear for good fortune. In Haiti, folks stay up December 31 through the wee hours of January 1 to see the sunrise. Mexicans set off firecrackers and eat twelve grapes at midnight for luck in the new year. Masked Nigerians dust their homes and shake trees for protection from evil.

Here in Ithaca, New York, on December 31, the windows of the twin dormitory towers at Ithaca College, which can be seen from miles around, are lit up in a prescribed pattern that displays the last two digits of the old year. Precisely at midnight, students manning their dorm-room light switches change the pattern, so onlookers see the old year (say, 03) disappear and the new year (04) suddenly appear!

All of us seem anxious to mark the cyclical nature of time with a beginning and end that, of course, never really begins nor ends. Yet this marking of time can be a wonderful impetus for renewal, reflection, and resolution. Everyone wishes for health and luck in the year to come. New Year's Eve can be the perfect opportunity for a midwinter cleaning spree that partially empties the closets and drawers, making room for the new year's bounty to come. Some like to attend parties New Year's Eve; some would rather not. But whatever your partying preference, January 1 comes around in full daylight soon enough, and then it's time for breakfast—or brunch.

Brunch, which we like to think of as the best of breakfast and lunch, is a great invention. Brunch can stretch early to late—or not. So host a brunch buffet to suit your schedule. Parcel the recipes out among neighbors and ask them to drop by between 11 and 3. Supply plenty of strong coffee and tea and some sodas for the kids. Or make the food on our menu yourself and ask your guests to contribute their signature dishes or nothing at all, as they wish. Savory Flan, Good Luck Lentil Salad, and Buttery Blueberry Coffee Cake can all be made several days ahead of time. The dressings for the Best Dressed Shrimp Salad can be made on New Year's Eve day and the Campari Compote that evening. That way, when you roll out of bed New Year's Day, it won't be hard to summon up the energy to cook Sweet Potato & Zucchini Hash. Its nested eggs—ancient symbols of rebirth—make it a perfect dish for the day. Share the hash hot from the skillet with the folks at home and the first of the arrivals. Then assemble the shrimp salad and you're home free.

Play it by ear. Relax, eat, and catch up with the news on the block. Let people come and go at leisure. Call friends you never seem to see enough and invite them over on the spur of the moment. It just might become a neighborhood tradition.

BEST DRESSED SHRIMP SALAD

Lovely pink shrimp show up beautifully against a background of bright greens in this salad, and make a stylish yet quickly prepared party dish. Serve with either or both dressings: The first is alive with fire and spice, the second is creamy smooth with a touch of residual heat.

1	CUP WATER
1	POUND PEELED AND DEVEINED SHRIMP

tomato dressing

1	FRESH GREEN CHILE, SEEDED
2	GARLIC CLOVES
½	CUP CHOPPED TOMATOES
3	TABLESPOONS VEGETABLE OIL
3	TABLESPOONS FRESH LEMON JUICE
¼	TEASPOON GROUND CUMIN
¼	TEASPOON SALT

lemon dill dressing

¼	CUP PREPARED MAYONNAISE
3	TABLESPOONS FRESH LEMON JUICE
1	FRESH GREEN CHILE, SEEDED
1	TABLESPOON MINCED FRESH DILL (½ TEASPOON DRIED)

½	POUND MIXED SALAD GREENS, RINSED AND DRAINED (10 TO 12 CUPS)
	CHOPPED FRESH PARSLEY AND/OR SCALLIONS

In a medium pot, bring the water to a boil on high heat. Add the shrimp and steam until they just turn pink, about 5 minutes. Drain the shrimp and refrigerate until ready to serve.

Place all of the ingredients for the dressing (or dressings) of your choice in a blender. Purée until smooth and set aside.

Spread the greens on a large serving platter. Arrange the shrimp on the bed of greens. Either pour the dressing over the shrimp and garnish with the parsley and/or scallions, or top the salad with the garnishes and then pass the dressings separately at the table.

SWEET POTATO & ZUCCHINI HASH

This simple, colorful skillet hash makes a good brunch dish with a nice egg nested in each portion. As you prep, aim for ½-inch cubes for both the sweet potatoes and the zucchini. If you have a good-looking skillet, serve the hash at the table, right from the pan.

Pass ketchup or your favorite salsa, if desired.

4	CUPS PEELED AND CUBED SWEET POTATOES*
1½	TABLESPOONS OLIVE OIL
2	CUPS CHOPPED ONIONS
2	GARLIC CLOVES, MINCED OR PRESSED
½	TEASPOON SALT, MORE TO TASTE
¼	TEASPOON RED PEPPER FLAKES
¼	TEASPOON GROUND BLACK PEPPER
1	TEASPOON DRIED THYME
2	CUPS CUBED ZUCCHINI
4	EGGS

**SERVES 4
TOTAL TIME: 40 MINUTES**

* Two sweet potatoes cut into ½-inch cubes will yield about 4 cups.

Bring about 4 cups of water to a boil. Ease in the sweet potatoes and simmer for 5 to 6 minutes, until tender but still firm. Drain and set aside.

Warm the oil in a heavy skillet. Add the onions, garlic, salt, pepper flakes, black pepper, and thyme and sauté on medium heat for 5 minutes. Stir in the zucchini and cook for 5 more minutes. Add the drained potatoes and cook for about 5 minutes, stirring occasionally, until the vegetables are tender. Add more salt to taste.

With the back of a spoon, make four depressions, or wells, in the hash. Break an egg into each well, cover the skillet, and cook for 4 to 5 minutes on low heat, until the eggs are set and opaque.

Serve immediately.

SAVORY FLAN

Bring this smooth, richly flavored, not-sweet flan to a dish-to-pass and it's bound to fit right in with whatever else shows up. It's a good accompaniment for a crisp salad or a chunky light soup, or try it as a spread on crackers, topped with slices of black olive or slivers of red onion. Savory flans are excellent served warm, at room temperature, or chilled.

Our basic Savory Flan can be tailored to your particular taste or made with ingredients that you have on hand. To inspire your own vegetable-herb-cheese combination, browse through our variations at the end of the recipe. If you wish to make larger portions, use four 8-ounce custard cups and bake them longer—45 minutes should be about right.

10	OUNCES FRESH SPINACH, RINSED AND STEMMED*
3	LARGE EGGS
1	CUP MILK
1 to 2	TABLESPOONS CHOPPED FRESH DILL
¼	TEASPOON SALT
1	CUP GRATED SMOKED CHEDDAR OR GOUDA CHEESE

SERVES 8
PREPARATION TIME: 30 MINUTES
BAKING TIME: 30 MINUTES

* A thawed and well-drained 10-ounce package of frozen spinach can be used, in which case there's no need to cook it before puréeing.

Oil or butter eight 4-ounce custard cups and place them in a baking pan at least two-thirds as deep as the cups. Begin to bring about 1½ quarts of water to a boil.

Preheat the oven to 400°.

In a covered saucepan, steam the spinach in about ½ cup of water until wilted but still bright green. Drain well. In a blender or food processor, purée the drained spinach with the eggs, milk, dill, and salt until very smooth. Add the cheese and purée for another minute.

Pour the custard into the prepared cups. Fill the baking pan with boiling water to about halfway up the sides of the cups. Bake just until the flan is firm and a knife inserted in the middle tests clean, about 30 minutes.

Serve hot, warm, at room temperature, or chilled.

variations

* Replace the spinach with 2 cups of steamed chopped vegetables such as carrots, broccoli, or asparagus, or about 1½ cups of chopped artichoke hearts.
* Use 1 to 2 tablespoons of chopped fresh herbs, such as basil, cilantro, tarragon, or marjoram. If you use strongly flavored fresh herbs such as thyme, oregano, or rosemary, use no more than a generous teaspoonful. With dried herbs, try a level teaspoon—or less for the strong ones.
* Select any cheese you can grate that complements your choice of vegetables and herbs, but use less of the strongly flavored cheeses. Add about ½ cup of Parmesan or Gruyère, or add ¾ cup of feta and omit the salt. For less strongly flavored cheeses, such as Cheddar, Monterey Jack, or Havarti, use about 1½ cups.

GOOD LUCK LENTIL SALAD

Many European cultures include lentils in their New Year's Day celebrations. The coin-shaped appearance of the beans signifies wealth and money, so honoring the bean at the outset of the each year is believed to bring prosperity to the household. Hey, it's worth a try. At the very least, you enjoy a delicious dish, which may be abundance enough for the moment.

To save time (and time is money, as we all know), dice the vegetables while the lentils cook.

SERVES 8
TOTAL TIME: 40 MINUTES

2	CUPS BOILING WATER
1	CUP DRIED PEARS
2	CUPS BROWN LENTILS
6	CUPS WATER
3	CUPS DICED APPLES*
1	CUP DICED RED ONIONS*
1½	CUPS PEELED AND DICED CARROTS*
¼	CUP FRESH LEMON JUICE
¼	CUP OLIVE OIL
2	TABLESPOONS RED WINE OR BALSAMIC VINEGAR
1¼	TEASPOONS SALT
¼	TEASPOON GROUND BLACK PEPPER
⅔	CUP CURRANTS
	CHOPPED FRESH PARSLEY (OPTIONAL)

* Crispin or Granny Smith apples are best for this dish. Dice the vegetables and fruit into ¼-inch pieces. Two apples, two carrots, and one red onion should do it.

Pour the boiling water over the dried pears, cover, and set aside. Place the lentils and water in a soup pot, cover, and bring to a boil; then reduce the heat to low and simmer for 20 to 25 minutes, until just tender. Drain well. Meanwhile, combine the apples, red onions, carrots, and 2 tablespoons of the lemon juice in a large bowl. Toss well and set aside.

Drain and dice the dried pears, reserving the soaking liquid. Combine the pears, ⅓ cup of the pear soaking liquid, 2 tablespoons of the olive oil, the vinegar, salt, pepper, and the remaining lemon juice in a blender and purée to a thick sauce. Add some extra pear liquid, if needed.

When the hot lentils are tender and drained, add them to the bowl of vegetables and spoon in the pear sauce. Toss well. Drizzle on the rest of the olive oil and stir in the currants. Top with parsley, if you wish.

Serve immediately or store in the refrigerator for up to 5 days. Bring to room temperature just before serving.

CAMPARI COMPOTE

Here's a zesty, citrusy, sophisticated fruit salad that gets its rosy undertone from a shot of bright red Campari liqueur. Campari's flavor—dry and piercingly herbal with fruity notes and a hint of quinine—is a wonderful foil for the sweetness of grapefruit, navel oranges, and luscious, ripe pineapple. If you prefer, the salad can be made New Year's Eve night and kept covered and refrigerated until brunch the next day.

4	LARGE PINK OR WHITE GRAPEFRUIT, SECTIONED*
6	NAVEL ORANGES, SECTIONED*
2	CUPS FRESH OR CANNED PINEAPPLE CHUNKS
¼	CUP SUGAR, OR TO TASTE
2 to 4	TABLESPOONS CAMPARI

SERVES 8
PREPARATION TIME: 15 MINUTES
CHILLING TIME: 30 MINUTES

* Use a sharp knife to slice off the peel, including the white pith. Working over a bowl, slice toward the center of the orange or grapefruit along the membrane on one side of a section and then flick the knife up the membrane on the other side to release the section.

In a large bowl, combine the sectioned grapefruit and oranges and the pineapple chunks. Gently stir in the sugar and Campari. Allow to sit for about 5 minutes, until the sugar dissolves. Cover and refrigerate for 30 minutes, or until well chilled.

Serve cold.

Campari is a highly concentrated, bitter apéritif with a tangy finish. It is produced by Fratelli Campari of Milan, Italy, and is most often served on the rocks with club soda and a twist of lime. The liqueur is made of neutral grain spirits spiked with herbs and orange zest. After much research, we discovered the secret of the crimson color is natural carmine: a pigment obtained from the red dye cochineal, which is prepared from the dried bodies of the females of a type of scale insect. Who would have guessed?

BUTTERY BLUEBERRY COFFEE CAKE

Blueberries may be higher in antioxidants than any other food in the world. So they're an especially good way to start the New Year. Combined with whole grains, seeds, and nuts in a coffee cake that's so moist and creamy, it's almost like a pudding with a crunchy topping. What could be better?

Serve this cake topped with whipped Neufchâtel or sweetened yogurt cheese (see Note), if you like.

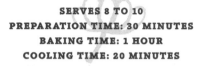

¼ CUP SESAME SEEDS (OPTIONAL)

2 CUPS FRESH OR FROZEN BLUEBERRIES

SERVES 8 TO 10
PREPARATION TIME: 30 MINUTES
BAKING TIME: 1 HOUR
COOLING TIME: 20 MINUTES

oat topping

¼ CUP BUTTER, MELTED

⅔ CUP BROWN SUGAR, PACKED

1 TEASPOON GROUND CINNAMON

1 CUP TOASTED CHOPPED NUTS*

1 CUP ROLLED OATS

⅓ CUP UNBLEACHED WHITE FLOUR

batter

½ CUP WHOLE WHEAT PASTRY FLOUR**

1½ CUPS UNBLEACHED WHITE FLOUR

2 TEASPOONS BAKING POWDER

½ TEASPOON BAKING SODA

½ TEASPOON SALT

½ CUP BUTTER, MELTED

¾ CUP BROWN SUGAR, PACKED

2 EGGS

2 CUPS NONFAT PLAIN YOGURT

1 TEASPOON PURE VANILLA EXTRACT

* Pecans, walnuts, almonds, or a mix. Toast nuts on an unoiled baking tray at 350°
for 5 to 10 minutes, until fragrant and golden brown.

** Hodgson Mill produces an organic whole wheat pastry flour in 1¾-pound packages
that can be found in well-stocked supermarkets. Bulk whole wheat pastry flour is
also available in natural food stores, health food stores, and food co-ops.

Preheat the oven to 350°.

Lightly oil a 9 x 13-inch baking pan and sprinkle with the sesame seeds, if using. Be sure to coat the bottom *and* the sides of the pan with seeds. Rinse and sort the blueberries, if using fresh. Set aside.

In a small bowl, combine all of the topping ingredients and mix well.

In a large bowl, sift together the flours, baking powder, baking soda, and salt. In a separate bowl, beat together the butter, brown sugar, eggs, yogurt, and vanilla until thoroughly blended. Briefly mix the wet ingredients into the dry ingredients with as few strokes as possible to form a uniform batter. Spread the batter evenly into the prepared baking pan. Sprinkle on the blueberries and cover with the oat topping.

Bake for 1 hour, or until a toothpick inserted in the center comes out clean. Allow to cool for 20 minutes before serving.

note

To make yogurt cheese in the traditional manner, line a colander with overlapping paper coffee filters or several layers of cheesecloth. Place the colander in a large bowl. Spoon in 2 quarts of yogurt and cover with plastic wrap. Refrigerate for 12 to 24 hours. After 3 or 4 hours or overnight, discard the liquid collected in the bowl. The yogurt will thicken to a consistency similar to soft cream cheese and should yield about 3 cups.

For our Quick Yogurt Cheese Method, reduce the amount of yogurt to 1⅓ quarts (or about 5½ cups). Set up the yogurt to drain as in the traditional method, but weight the top of the covered yogurt with a plate and a heavy object such as a can. Refrigerate for 2 hours. The weight will speed the process and produce about 3½ cups of yogurt cheese firm enough for most recipes.

Sweeten your yogurt cheese with maple syrup, honey, or sugar to taste.

SETSUBUN
(JAPANESE BEAN DAY)

Steamed Edamame in the Pod (see opposite page)
Japanese Stuffed Peppers
Asian Turnips with Wasabi
Gingered Carrots with Anjiki
Nori Rice Balls

Setsubun, meaning "seasonal division" in Japanese, is a spirited festival held on February 3, the day before their first day of spring. During the eighth century, it was customary at this time of year to chase away evil spirits with bows and arrows. In the thirteenth century, the "devils" were driven away by the noisy beating of drums and the smell of burning dried sardine heads that were hung over the front door.

Nowadays, it's popular to throw roasted beans inside one's house while shouting, "Devils out! Happiness in!" to protect the house and family from misfortune. Afterwards, everyone picks up and eats the number of beans that corresponds to his or her age plus one. It has also become traditional to throw beans in shrines and temples. As you can imagine, this lively rite of spring is especially enjoyed by families with young children.

In the northern United States and Canada, Setsubun, or Bean Day, corresponds to our Groundhog Day, when we speculate on the number of weeks of winter still to come. But with winter half over, February is never too soon to be planning a garden and looking forward to the first freshly picked asparagus and tender peas. It is certainly not too early in the year to be chasing away the winter doldrums by whisking the dust out the back door and sitting down to a light, tasty Japanese-inspired meal.

So first take a shopping trip a day or two before February 3 to pick up some edamame and any other ingredients you may need for the menu. Edamame, which are fresh young green soybeans, are one of the Asian treats that herald in the season of spring. They have only recently appeared in U.S. marketplaces, but they're quickly gathering a following. Still, they may be a novelty for the guests you've invited for Setsubun. Undoubtedly, people will be pleased by the nutty, sweet flavor of these delicate pea-like beans.

The most dependable source for edamame is the freezer section of natural food stores, Asian groceries, and most large supermarkets. Oriental Mascot and Shirakiku brands come in handy one-pound packages. Sunrich's Heart & Natural brand is certified as not genetically modified, so stock up.

When Setsubun arrives, allow about two and a half hours to prepare the meal from start to finish. First, make the Nori Rice Balls and cover them in plastic wrap so they stay soft and moist. Then prepare the Japanese Stuffed Peppers. While the peppers are baking, make the Asian Turnips with Wasabi and the Gingered Carrots with Hijiki. Cover the vegetables and keep them warm on the top of the stove.

As company arrives, steam the edamame according to the directions on the package and serve them sprinkled with a little coarse salt. Then join your guests in eating at least as many of these fresh soybeans as your age (if not three or four times more). Arrange the vegetable selections on large plates. While the first signs of spring may be weeks away, a little meal in honor of Bean Day will certainly help to shrug off the weatherman's snowy forecast.

JAPANESE STUFFED PEPPERS

Years ago, former Moosewood cook Andi Gladstone introduced us to a light, lovely Japanese custard baked with shiitake, vegetables, and shrimp called *chawan mushi*. We've been coming up with delectable variations ever since.

Our most recent version uses a combination of enoki and oyster mushrooms, with their intriguingly distinctive yet delicate flavors. We urge you to try straw mushrooms or shiitake as well, which have a chewy texture and smoky flavor. Our filling is baked in whole bell peppers, rather than in custard cups, making each serving a small meal.

6	LARGE RED, ORANGE OR YELLOW BELL PEPPERS
2	CUPS CHOPPED SCALLIONS
2½	CUPS CHOPPED FRESH ENOKI AND OYSTER MUSHROOMS (ABOUT 6 OUNCES)*
1	TABLESPOON VEGETABLE OIL
1	TABLESPOON DARK SESAME OIL
2	TABLESPOONS SOY SAUCE
12	MEDIUM EGGS
¼	CUP WATER
1	TABLESPOON CHINESE RICE WINE, DRY SHERRY OR SAKE
2	TABLESPOONS MINCED FRESH BASIL

SERVES 6
PREPARATION TIME: 25 MINUTES
BAKING TIME: 35 TO 40 MINUTES

ginger sherry sauce

¼	CUP DRY SHERRY
1	TABLESPOON DARK SESAME OIL
1	TEASPOON GRATED FRESH GINGER ROOT
2	TEASPOONS SUGAR
1	TABLESPOON RICE VINEGAR
1 to 2	TABLESPOONS SOY SAUCE
1	TEASPOON CORNSTARCH
1	TABLESPOON COLD WATER

COOKED BROWN RICE (OPTIONAL)

* Fresh straw mushrooms are also fine.

Preheat the oven to 450°.

Remove the stem ends from the bell peppers, cutting a hole about 2 inches in diameter in the tops. Remove the seeds. Sauté the scallions and mushrooms in the vegetable and sesame oils for about 2 minutes. Stir in 1 tablespoon of the soy sauce and set aside. In a bowl, gently beat the eggs with the rest of the soy sauce, the water, and the rice wine, sherry, or sake. Stir in the sautéed mushrooms and add the basil.

Stand the bell peppers upright in a small, deep-sided baking pan, arranging them side by side to support one another. Ladle the egg mixture into the pepper shells: Leave a little room at the top for the custard to expand.

Pour an inch of water into the bottom of the baking pan. Add a splash of soy sauce and cooking wine, sherry, or sake. Cover the pan with aluminum foil and bake for 30 to 35 minutes, until the custard is puffy. Remove the foil and bake for another 5 minutes, until lightly browned.

While the peppers bake, prepare the Ginger Sherry Sauce. In a small pan on medium heat, bring the sherry, sesame oil, ginger root, sugar, vinegar, and soy sauce to a low simmer. Thoroughly blend the cornstarch and cold water in a cup and stir it into the sauce. Continue to cook on low heat for about 10 minutes, stirring occasionally, until the sauce thickens slightly. Cover and set aside.

Serve the stuffed bell peppers sliced in half lengthwise and topped with Ginger Sherry Sauce. Nestle them in a bed of brown rice, if you like.

variations

* Replace the fresh mushrooms with 8 to10 dried shiitake. Soak them in 2 cups of hot water until tender and pliable. Trim off the stems and discard. Slice the caps and sauté with the scallions.
* Add 12 medium peeled and deveined shrimp and simmer for 3 minutes. Chop them into bite-sized pieces and add them to the custard. Reduce the number of eggs to 10.
* Add ½ cup of sliced water chestnuts to the scallions and mushrooms.
* Add carrots or 12 snow peas, trimmed and cut in half. Sauté with the scallions and mushrooms.

ASIAN TURNIPS WITH WASABI

This quick and quirky side dish is a warming way to serve turnips. The only out-of-the-ordinary ingredient is wasabi paste, a Japanese variety of horseradish with a spicy hot and compelling taste.

At Moosewood, we don't use already made wasabi paste (sold in tubes) because it almost always has additives—and we prefer the robustness of the wasabi powder. Once mixed with water, let the wasabi sit for 10 minutes to develop its flavor fully.

wasabi paste

SERVES 6
TOTAL TIME: 25 MINUTES

2	TEASPOONS WASABI POWDER*
2	TEASPOONS WARM WATER
1	POUND TURNIPS
1	TABLESPOON VEGETABLE OIL
2	TABLESPOONS WATER
2	TABLESPOONS SOY SAUCE
2	TEASPOONS BROWN SUGAR, LIGHTLY PACKED
1	TEASPOON TOASTED SESAME SEEDS**

SLICED SCALLIONS AND/OR SLIVERS OF RED BELL PEPPER (OPTIONAL)

* Wasabi powder can usually be found in well-stocked supermarkets and specialty grocery stores.

** Toast sesame seeds on an unoiled baking tray at 350° for 2 to 3 minutes, until fragrant and golden.

In a small bowl, combine the wasabi powder and water and set aside.

Slice off and discard the ends of the turnips and peel them with a potato peeler or paring knife. Cut them in half lengthwise, and then slice each half into thin half-moons.

Warm the oil in a skillet on medium heat, add the turnips, and sauté for about 4 minutes, until very slightly browned. Add the water, cover the pan, and steam for 6 to 8 minutes, until just tender. Meanwhile, whisk together the wasabi paste, soy sauce, and brown sugar in a small bowl.

When the turnips are ready, remove them from the heat and toss with the wasabi mixture. Stir in the sesame seeds and, if you like, top with sliced scallions and/or slivers of red bell pepper for color.

GINGERED CARROTS WITH HIJIKI

Hijiki is the most mineral-rich of all seaweeds and is especially high in calcium and iron. In Japan, it is prized as a food that adds luster to hair and enhances beauty.

This simply prepared side dish looks very pretty with its bright orange carrots and shiny black hijiki. The gingery glaze and touch of sesame oil add a depth of flavor to the carrots. To save time, cut the carrots and grate the ginger while the hijiki soaks.

SERVES 6
TOTAL TIME: 20 MINUTES

- 1/8   CUP CHOPPED DRIED HIJIKI, LOOSELY PACKED
- 1   CUP FRESH ORANGE JUICE
- 3   CUPS CARROT MATCHSTICKS (1/4 X 2 INCHES)
- 1   TABLESPOON GRATED FRESH GINGER ROOT
- 1/2   TEASPOON DARK SESAME OIL
      SALT AND GROUND BLACK PEPPER TO TASTE

Soak the hijiki in the orange juice for 10 minutes.

In a large nonreactive skillet, combine the hijiki, orange juice, carrots, ginger root, and sesame oil. Bring to a boil on medium heat; then cover and cook for 3 minutes. Reduce the heat, uncover, and simmer for about 5 minutes, until the carrots are glazed. Season to taste with salt and black pepper.

NORI RICE BALLS

How can a triangle be a ball? Don't ask us. All we know is that these cute triangular packages of rice, eaten out of hand like a sandwich, are known as rice balls. In Japan, they're sold as street food and make handy lunchbox fare. With a little practice, you can swiftly make a pile of your own. Wrap them tightly in plastic: They're best when eaten within a few hours.

Since the other dishes in this menu are highly flavored with ginger, wasabi, and dark sesame oil, plain nori rice balls make a nice complement. If you serve them alone as appetizers or alongside other mildly seasoned dishes, try them with one or both of our Two Dipping Sauces (page 359).

The ingredients for making rice balls are not difficult to find in a well-stocked supermarket with a good selection of international foods. We use Kokuho Rose sushi rice and prefer the brands of sweetened rice vinegar that are free of preservatives, such as Mutsukan, Marukan, or Asian Gourmet. Nori varies from brand to brand, but the very thin sheets labeled "roasted" or "roasted and seasoned" are the tastiest.

1½	CUPS SUSHI RICE (PAGE 401)
2	TABLESPOONS SEASONED RICE VINEGAR*
3	TABLESPOONS SOY SAUCE
½	CUP TOASTED SESAME SEEDS
6	SHEETS ROASTED OR ROASTED SEASONED NORI**

SERVES 6
YIELDS 12 RICE BALLS
TOTAL TIME: 45 MINUTES

* Or use regular rice vinegar mixed with ½ teaspoon of sugar.

** A dark green seaweed which comes dried and packaged in thin, flat rectangular sheets that often measure 8 x 7 inches. It's available in Asian groceries, natural food stores, and the ethnic section of most supermarkets.

Rinse the rice several times in cold water until the water runs clear. In a small heavy pot, bring the rice and 2 cups of water to a boil on medium heat. Turn the heat down as low as possible and simmer the rice for 15 to 20 minutes, until all of the water is absorbed. Remove from the heat and allow to steam with the lid on for 10 minutes.

Scoop the rice into a medium bowl and immediately immerse the cooking pot in cold water to soak for easy cleanup later. Stir the vinegar into the hot rice until fully absorbed. Let the rice cool for 5 to 10 minutes, stirring occasionally to help release the heat.

Meanwhile, pour the soy sauce into a cup and locate your pastry brush. Place the sesame seeds in a shallow bowl. Cut each nori wrapper diagonally in half with scissors to make 12 triangles. Set a large bowl of water nearby for rinsing your hands.

With wet hands, scoop about ¼ cup of rice into a mound that fills the palm of your hand. With both hands, squeeze the rice into a 1-inch-thick triangular shape that's smooth and flat on both sides. Brush all surfaces of the rice triangle with soy sauce and roll it in the sesame seeds. Place the rice "ball" in the center of the nori wrapper so that the points of the rice triangle bisect the sides of the nori triangle.

Rinse and dry your hands. Fold all three points of the nori wrapper toward the center of the rice ball to form a closed package. It's ok if the very tip of the rice triangle peeks out from the top. Cover the "rice ball" tightly with plastic wrap and set aside.

Repeat the process for the rest of the rice balls, being sure to rinse and shake your hands each time, so that the rice doesn't stick to your fingers.

Serve the dainty packets at room temperature.

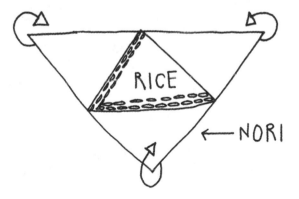

SOUTHWEST DINNER PARTY

Tomatillo Fish Soup
Light Southwestern Potato Salad
Avocado Citrus Salad
Calabacitas
Brown Sugar Poundcake (page 374)

While some snowbirds flee the chilly northern climes for sultry Florida, others are drawn to a pilgrimage. Within a few short hours, heavy gray clouds give way to sunny, clear blue skies. Arizona, New Mexico, Texas, and Utah all provide welcome respite for winter-weary northerners.

As fondness for the climate and terrain of these southwestern places grows, so does an appreciation of the cuisine. While it's true that Texans probably developed the first commercial chili powder, the basis of southwestern cuisine has moved way beyond the beans and barbecue once dubbed "Tex-Mex." The foods of this region are, in fact, a composite of many regional cuisines based on Spanish and Native American influences and are derived from indigenous plants that include corn, many varieties of chiles, tomatoes, beans, pumpkin, and squash.

By February or March the time is ripe for a taste of the contrasting sunny, sweet, and brash flavors in this menu. Warm up with Calabacitas spiked with hot peppers, garlic, and cilantro. Enjoy sweet-tart Tomatillo Fish Soup garnished with crisp tortilla chips. Cool down with a beautifully composed Avocado Citrus Salad, spruced up with fresh oranges and grapefruit. Finish the meal with a leisurely downing of some sweet, rich Brown Sugar Poundcake.

If you decide to make the Brown Sugar Poundcake and the dressing for the potato salad a day ahead, the rest of this fresh, light, cheerful meal can be easily prepared in about 2 hours. Make the Tomatillo Fish Soup first, adding the reserved poached fish just before serving. Next, make the Avocado Citrus Salad and keep it chilled in the refrigerator until ready to serve. While you're in the fridge, take out the dressing you made for the potato salad so it can warm to room temperature. Then prepare all of the ingredients for the Calabacitas. Finally, as you turn up the salsa and merengue music, cube the potatoes for Light Southwestern Potato Salad and get them simmering. Finish off the Calabacitas while the potatoes cook. Dress the potatoes and wait for the guests to arrive.

TOMATILLO FISH SOUP

This unusual, rich, and satisfying soup is a study in flavor contrasts: The tomatillo-cilantro-lime soup is tart and the chunks of fish taste sweet in that context. The color is a very pretty green. You can add yet another dimension with a garnish of crumbled tortilla chips.

Serve with Mexican, Southwest, and Caribbean foods or accompanied by a green salad and bread for an ample supper or lunch.

SERVES 4 TO 6
TOTAL TIME: 50 MINUTES

2	CUPS CHOPPED ONIONS
1	CUP CHOPPED CELERY
1	TABLESPOON OLIVE OIL
3	CUPS WATER
½	TEASPOON SALT
¾	POUND FRESH FISH FILLETS OR STEAKS*
2½	CUPS DRAINED CANNED WHOLE TOMATILLOS**
¼	CUP CHOPPED FRESH CILANTRO
2	TABLESPOONS FRESH LIME JUICE
	TORTILLA CHIPS (OPTIONAL)

* Use whichever fish is freshest at your market. For a mild flavor, try scrod, turbot, or flounder; for a more distinct flavor and firmer texture, try salmon, sea bass, or ocean trout.

** Find canned whole tomatillos in the Latin American sections of well-stocked supermarkets.

In a covered soup pot, sauté the onions and celery in the olive oil on medium heat for about 15 minutes, until very soft. Add the water and salt and bring to a boil. Carefully lower the fish into the soup pot and poach until it is cooked through and flakes easily with a fork, 4 to 8 minutes, depending upon its thickness.

With a slotted spoon, remove the fish from the broth and place it in a shallow bowl. Remove and discard any skin and bones. With a fork, flake the fish into bite-sized pieces and set aside.

In a blender, purée the soup with the drained tomatillos, cilantro, and lime juice. Return the purée to the soup pot and bring to a simmer. Stir in the flaked fish, top with tortilla chips, if using, and serve.

LIGHT SOUTHWESTERN POTATO SALAD

Warm potato salad is such a nice idea that once you try it, we're sure you'll be hooked. To save time, you can prepare the dressing ingredients and arugula while the cubed potatoes are simmering.

6   POTATOES (ABOUT 2 POUNDS)

SERVES 4 TO 6
TOTAL TIME: 25 MINUTES

dressing

¼   CUP OLIVE OIL

2   TABLESPOONS VEGETABLE OIL

2   TABLESPOONS VERY FINELY DICED SHALLOTS

1   GARLIC CLOVE, MINCED OR PRESSED

¼   CUP WHITE BALSAMIC OR CIDER VINEGAR

1   TABLESPOON FRESH LEMON JUICE (OPTIONAL)

1   TEASPOON DIJON MUSTARD

3   TABLESPOONS CHOPPED FRESH PARSLEY

2   TEASPOONS CHOPPED FRESH CILANTRO

½   TEASPOON GROUND CUMIN

½   TEASPOON GROUND CORIANDER

½   TEASPOON PAPRIKA

¾   TEASPOON SALT

¼   TEASPOON GROUND BLACK PEPPER

4   CUPS ARUGULA, RINSED AND STEMMED (OPTIONAL)*

* Or use other sharp greens, such as baby mizuna, mesclun, watercress, or a mix.

Scrub the potatoes and peel them if you wish. Cut them into ¾-inch cubes and place them in a pot with salted cold water to cover. Bring to a boil; then reduce the heat, cover, and simmer for 15 to 20 minutes, until the potatoes are just tender.

Meanwhile, in a small bowl, whisk together all of the dressing ingredients. When the potatoes are tender, drain them in a colander. While they're still piping hot, spoon them into a serving bowl, pour on the dressing, and toss well.

Serve immediately right from the bowl or on a bed of arugula or other sharp greens.

AVOCADO CITRUS SALAD

Whether you compose this light, delightful salad on a colorful platter or on individual plates, the bright field greens, pale green avocado and cucumbers, dark pink grapefruit, and golden orange segments sprinkled with nuts or seeds will exude health, beauty, and simple elegance.

dressing

SERVES 4 TO 6
TOTAL TIME: 20 MINUTES

2	TABLESPOONS FRUITY EXTRA-VIRGIN OLIVE OIL
2	TABLESPOONS FRESH LIME JUICE
1 to 2	TEASPOONS MILD HONEY
½	TEASPOON SALT
1	TABLESPOON MINCED SHALLOTS OR RED ONIONS

salad

3 to 4	CUPS MESCLUN OR MIXED FIELD GREENS, RINSED AND PATTED DRY
1	CUCUMBER, PEELED
1	RUBY GRAPEFRUIT, PEELED
2	ORANGES, PEELED
1	LARGE RIPE AVOCADO, PREFERABLY HASS
½	CUP LIGHTLY TOASTED SLICED ALMONDS, OR TOASTED PUMPKIN OR SUNFLOWER SEEDS*
	FRESHLY GROUND BLACK PEPPER

* Toast nuts or seeds on an unoiled baking tray at 350° for about 5 minutes, until fragrant and golden brown.

In a small bowl, combine the dressing ingredients and set aside. In another bowl, toss the greens with 1 to 2 tablespoons of dressing and arrange them on a platter or individual plates. Cut the cucumber in half lengthwise, scoop out the seeds, and slice crosswise into ¼-inch-thick crescents. Toss them with a little dressing and scatter them on the greens.

Section the peeled citrus fruit (see Note, opposite). Squeeze any remaining juice from the membranes of the citrus into the dressing. Arrange alternate sections of grapefruit and orange like a pinwheel or starburst over the greens. Slice around the avocado lengthwise, gently twist the halves apart, and remove the pit. Carefully cut the flesh into cubes right in the skins, scoop them out with a serving spoon, and arrange them on the salad. Drizzle the rest of the dressing over the fruit and avocado.

Sprinkle with nuts or seeds and serve with fresh black pepper.

CALABACITAS

Calabacitas is derived from the Spanish *calabaza,* which means "pumpkin" or "squash." The word *calabacitas* is often used in Mexican restaurants to describe a vegetarian filling that usually contains summer squash, corn, and something spicy hot. Our local Viva Tacqueria livens up its basic burrito with a calabacitas filling. Try it in a taco or as the base for a soup, too.

You can vary the amount of chiles and cilantro in the recipe and use frozen limas, if you like. And, in true Moosewood cross-cultural style, we have to tell you that a wok works great for making this dish!

1	TABLESPOON OLIVE OIL
2	CUPS FINELY CHOPPED ONIONS
2 to 3	GARLIC CLOVES, MINCED OR PRESSED
½	TEASPOON SALT
6	CUPS DICED ZUCCHINI
1 or 2	JALAPEÑOS OR OTHER FRESH CHILES, SEEDED AND CHOPPED
1	TEASPOON DRIED OREGANO
1	CUP FRESH OR FROZEN CORN KERNELS
1	CUP COOKED LIMA BEANS OR CANNED BUTTER BEANS
1	TABLESPOON FRESH LIME JUICE
¼ to ½	CUP CHOPPED FRESH CILANTRO

SERVES 4 TO 6
TOTAL TIME: 35 MINUTES

In a large skillet or a wok on high heat, warm the oil and sauté the onions, garlic, and salt for 3 or 4 minutes, until the onions are golden. Add the zucchini, chiles, and oregano and sauté for 3 minutes, until the zucchini begins to soften. Stir in the corn, beans, and lime juice and cook for another few minutes, until the limas are very tender and everything is hot.

Stir in the cilantro to taste and serve immediately.

note

To section the grapefruit and oranges, cut off the rind and pith. Slide a sharp knife between the segment and membrane, cutting toward the center of the fruit; then reverse the direction of the blade and slide it under the other side of the segment from the center out. The segment should fall right out.

CHINESE NEW YEAR

MENU

Mandarin Hot & Sour Soup
Tea Eggs
Chinese Long Beans
Mu Shu Vegetables
Fresh Pineapple (see opposite page)

The Chinese New Year is the most celebrated of Chinese holidays. Traditionally, it signifies the beginning of the planting season, the end of winter, and the return of longer days. The Chinese calendar follows the phases of the moon, so Chinese New Year is a different day from year to year, falling on the new moon that rises between January 21 and February 19.

Foods prepared for this holiday are more than just a good-tasting start to the New Year. Golden and round like the sun and gold coins, the foods symbolize our homage to the sun, gratitude for its return, and the coming of a prosperous and abundant year. In prerevolutionary China, women would gather ahead of time to make dumplings in large enough quantities to last for the entire holiday, when all labor would come to a complete halt. Today, firecrackers are set off to scare away all traces of negativity, and the color red, which stands for prosperity and happiness, is ubiquitous: Red lanterns, candles, dinnerware, and even chopsticks are used to set the stage for a good New Year.

The popularity and abundance of Chinese restaurants in this country is a testament to their significant influence on the way many of us eat today. Here is a style of cooking that has never relegated vegetables to a mere supporting role and that introduced tofu (bean curd) to the world a couple of millennia ago!

Chinese-American cuisine was perhaps the first non-European "ethnic" cooking to firmly establish itself on the American continent. Long before the arrival of other Asian cuisines, the neighborhood Chinese restaurant was a fixture in even small American cities. The Chinese style that took hold in the United States was heavily influenced by the Cantonese background of many of the early immigrants. The last quarter of the twentieth century enjoyed a widening of interest in all the cuisines of China: Now Chinese restaurants serve foods common to the whole country as well as regional specialties.

If your experience with Chinese-American cuisine has been as a diner rather than a cook, we hope this menu will tempt you to try your hand at creating the food. When you're the chef, you can make sure there's not too much salt or oil or any MSG. You can control the hot, the sweet, and the sour.

The hot & sour soup can be prepared the day before and gently reheated just before serving. Make the Tea Eggs ahead of time; then use them as an appetizer to snack on while you encourage your guests to join you in the kitchen for the stir-frying, which should always be done just before serving. All of the ingredient preparation for the menu can be ready to go before the guests arrive, including cutting all of the vegetables and measuring other ingredients into small dishes or bowls. With a little practice, you can quickly stir up a feast with a flair that will impress your guests no end. If you're using your only wok for the mu shu stir-fry, cook the Chinese Long Beans in a skillet just as the mu shu is nearing completion.

Fresh sliced pineapple is a refreshing and appropriate dessert. If the pineapple isn't as sweet and flavorful as it could be, jazz it up with a quick roasting, as follows: Lightly oil or spray a baking dish. Preheat the oven to 400°. Slice, core, and peel one whole ripe pineapple and place the slices in the prepared baking dish. Sprinkle with about $\frac{1}{3}$ cup of brown sugar and 2 tablespoons of rum or pineapple juice. Bake for 25 to 30 minutes, stirring once or twice. If you bake the pineapple while dinner is being served, the heady aroma wafting from the kitchen will remind people to save room for dessert. Serve the roasted pineapple at room temperature or cooled.

MANDARIN HOT & SOUR SOUP

When a crowd of friends get together at a local Chinese restaurant, the service can be amazingly fast, and occasionally a steaming, aromatic bowl of hot & sour soup ends up at the wrong place. We've noticed, however, whoever gets it is almost certain to eat it—whether they ordered it or not. One deep whiff and they're sold.

Our vegetarian version of this restaurant classic captures the traditional flavor of the soup, but we add onions and carrots for richness and color. If you have a commercial "no-chicken" broth (page 218) on hand, don't hesitate to use it for all or part of the water or stock called for in the recipe.

SERVES 4 TO 6
TOTAL TIME: 40 MINUTES

4 or 5 DRIED CHINESE BLACK MUSHROOMS, RINSED (ABOUT 1 OUNCE)

1	TEASPOON VEGETABLE OIL
1	CUP THINLY SLICED ONIONS
½	TEASPOON SALT
½	CUP JULIENNED CARROTS*
4	CUPS WATER OR BASIC VEGETABLE STOCK (PAGE 408)
3	TABLESPOONS SOY SAUCE
¼	CUP CIDER VINEGAR
¼	CUP RICE VINEGAR
⅓	CAKE SOFT TOFU (5 OUNCES)
½	CUP JULIENNED BAMBOO SHOOTS*

¼ to ½ TEASPOON FRESHLY GROUND BLACK PEPPER**

2	TABLESPOONS CORNSTARCH
2	TABLESPOONS COLD WATER
1	EGG, BEATEN (OPTIONAL)

MINCED SCALLIONS, CUT ON THE DIAGONAL

DARK SESAME OIL

* A medium-sized carrot, peeled and sliced into ⅛ x 1-inch matchsticks, will yield ½ cup. Look for bamboo shoots packed in water: They come whole or "stripped," which means already cut into matchsticks.

** ¼ teaspoon gives the soup a mild "hot" (a bit more subtle than we prefer) and ½ teaspoon makes it quite intense—for those who like truly spicy hot dishes.

Soak the mushrooms in boiling water to cover in a heatproof bowl for 20 minutes. Drain, reserving the soaking liquid.

Meanwhile, warm the oil in a soup pot on medium heat. Add the onions and salt and sauté for about 10 minutes, until the onions are translucent. Add the carrots, toss well, cover, and continue to cook for 5 more minutes, stirring now and then.

Pour in the water or stock, cover, and bring to a boil. Add the soy sauce, vinegars, and about a cup of the reserved mushroom soaking liquid; then reduce the heat to low.

Meanwhile, remove and discard the mushroom stems and thinly slice the caps. Cut the tofu into tiny cubes or matchsticks. Add the mushrooms, tofu, bamboo shoots, and pepper to the soup pot and return to a boil; then reduce the heat and simmer gently for 5 minutes.

In a small bowl, combine the cornstarch and cold water to make a paste. Ladle about ¼ cup of the hot soup broth into the bowl, blend until smooth, and then gradually add the cornstarch mixture to the soup, stirring constantly. Cook for 2 to 3 minutes, until thickened. Drizzle in the egg, if using, and cook for another minute or two.

Serve hot. Top every bowl with minced scallions and several drops of sesame oil.

DELICIOUS

TEA EGGS

Marbled eggs are traditionally served at Chinese New Year parties, and once you make them, you'll see why. They are *gorgeous*—a celebration in themselves. They taste like lightly salted hard-boiled eggs with just a suggestion of five-spice powder, and while they take longer to cook than your average hard-boiled eggs, they're well worth it.

Five-spice powder is a spicy Chinese seasoning made of ground Sichuan peppercorns, star anise, fennel, cumin, and cloves. It's available in most Asian markets.

12	EGGS
¼	CUP BLACK TEA LEAVES*
3	TABLESPOONS SOY SAUCE
2	TEASPOONS SALT
2	TEASPOONS FIVE-SPICE POWDER

SERVES 12
PREPARATION TIME: 1 HOUR
COOLING TIME: 1 HOUR

* If you don't have loose tea, tea bags are fine. Just open up enough to make ¼ cup of tea leaves.

Place the eggs in a medium saucepan with water to cover. Bring to a boil, then reduce the heat and simmer for 5 to 6 minutes. Drain the eggs and rinse with cold water until they're cool enough to handle. Tap each egg gently with the back of a spoon until the shell is cracked all over.

Return the eggs to the saucepan and add fresh water to cover. Stir in the tea leaves, soy sauce, salt, and five-spice powder and bring to a boil. Reduce the heat to a gentle simmer, cover, and cook the eggs for about 40 minutes, stirring occasionally to distribute the tea and spices throughout the boiling water.

Cool the tea eggs in the cooking liquid for about 1 hour. When you peel them, you'll discover that they're attractively covered with a lovely marbled pattern. Eat them at once or refrigerate for up to 3 days. For best flavor, serve at room temperature.

CHINESE LONG BEANS

The best reason to try this recipe is because long beans are such a handsome vegetable. The finished dish looks like it came from the kitchen of a great Chinese restaurant, yet it's quite easy to prepare.

Long beans are the immature pods of black-eyed peas. They are sold in Asian markets in looped coils and are sometimes called yard-long beans. Crunchier and less moist than green beans, they are best when stir-fried. Look for beans that are free of black spots and store in the refrigerator.

Fermented, or salted black beans, are made by steaming small black soybeans and then preserving them in salt and spices. They are sold in plastic bags and should feel soft in the bag. Store them in the pantry in a well-sealed container.

If you have trouble finding fermented beans, black bean sauce is available in most supermarkets and can be substituted with good results.

1	POUND LONG BEANS
2	TABLESPOONS FERMENTED BLACK BEANS
2	TABLESPOONS PEANUT OR OTHER VEGETABLE OIL
4	GARLIC CLOVES, CHOPPED
½	TEASPOON SALT, OR TO TASTE
¼	CUP WATER
½	TEASPOON CHINESE CHILI PASTE, OR TO TASTE
½	TEASPOON DARK SESAME OIL

SERVES 4 TO 6
TOTAL TIME: 15 MINUTES

Trim and discard the ends of the long beans and cut the beans into 6-inch lengths. Rinse the fermented black beans very well; then drain and coarsely chop them.

Warm the oil in a wok or frying pan on high heat, until it just begins to smoke. Add the long beans and toss them in the hot oil for about 1 minute. Add the black beans and toss for a few more seconds. Stir in the garlic, salt, water, and Chinese chili paste and continue to stir-fry for 2 minutes.

Remove from the heat. Add the sesame oil, toss once more, and serve immediately.

MU SHU VEGETABLES

The three defining elements of mu shu "pancakes" are (1) a stir-fry of vegetables, (2) a warm wheat wrapper to roll them in, and (3) sweet yet savory hoisin sauce. Our recipe uses easy-to-find vegetables, and we think you won't miss the exotic Chinese ingredients often used in mu shu dishes. The vegetables can be cut with the shredding blade of a food processor or very thinly sliced by hand.

Prepare all of the ingredients and place them in bowls near the stove to facilitate stir-frying. Then you won't accidentally overcook the vegetables while bumbling around the kitchen hunting for the next ingredient.

Try these savory pancakes accompanied by rice that's enlivened with a bit of dark sesame oil and some toasted sesame seeds and chopped scallions.

SERVES 4
TOTAL TIME: 45 MINUTES

egg strips

½ TEASPOON DARK SESAME OIL
½ TEASPOON VEGETABLE OIL
2 EGGS, LIGHTLY BEATEN

vegetable filling

3 TABLESPOONS DRY SHERRY
3 TABLESPOONS SOY SAUCE
3 TABLESPOONS RICE VINEGAR OR CIDER VINEGAR
3 TABLESPOONS HOISIN SAUCE
1½ TABLESPOONS VEGETABLE OIL
3 GARLIC CLOVES, MINCED OR PRESSED
2 TABLESPOONS GRATED PEELED FRESH GINGER ROOT
1¼ CUPS SHREDDED CELERY
2 CUPS SHREDDED GREEN OR CHINESE CABBAGE
2 CUPS SHREDDED RED AND/OR GREEN BELL PEPPERS
1 CUP MUNG BEAN SPROUTS
⅓ CUP FINELY CHOPPED SCALLIONS

4 TEN-INCH FLOUR TORTILLAS
 HOISIN SAUCE

Warm the sesame and vegetable oils in a heavy 10-inch skillet or wok. Add the beaten eggs and tilt the pan to distribute. When the egg is set, flip with a spatula and cook 1 to 2 minutes on the other side, then remove to a plate. Roll up the egg pancake and cut it crosswise into thin strips. Set aside.

Combine the sherry, soy sauce, vinegar, and hoisin sauce in a bowl. Set aside.

Warm the oil in a wok or large heavy skillet, add the garlic and ginger root, and cook for about a minute. Add the celery, cabbage, and bell peppers and stir-fry on high heat for 3 to 4 minutes. Stir in the mung sprouts, scallions, and the sherry mixture. Continue to stir-fry on high heat for 1 more minute, or until the vegetables are crisp-tender. Remove from the heat, drain any excess liquid, and transfer to a warm serving bowl. Add the reserved strips of egg, mix well, cover, and set aside.

Stack the tortillas, wrap them in a paper towel, and heat in a microwave oven for 1 minute. Or, wrap them in aluminum foil and bake at 300° for 10 minutes in a preheated oven.

To serve, offer the filling, the tortillas, and a small bowl of hoisin sauce. Then spread as much hoisin sauce as you like on a warm tortilla, spoon on a cup of the filling, roll it up, and enjoy.

variation

Replace the egg with thin strips of seasoned baked tofu or tofu kan or with your favorite brand of seitan.

VALENTINE'S DAY

CANDIES

Traditional folklore is full of foods thought to stimulate or strengthen ardor. Garlic and onions qualify but may not be your first choice for Valentine's Day, and precious, rare, or expensive foods, such as saffron and caviar, have often been associated with lustful behavior. Other foods have been deemed aphrodisiacs because of their appearance; among them oysters, carrots, bananas, eggplant, melons, asparagus, mushrooms, and figs. If these foods suggest a romantic menu to you, be our guest.

Us? We'll take chocolate. This symbol of love and passion out of legend, folklore, and Hershey, Pennsylvania, may actually be good for the heart. Researchers in the Netherlands recently found that chocolate, and especially milkless dark chocolate, contains high levels of catechins—antioxidant-like substances that may fight cancer and heart disease. In addition, chocolate contains a stimulant, phenylethylamine, which is very similar to chemicals released by the body during lovemaking.

Chocolate confections can be easy to make. The ones we like best certainly are, so the recipients are invariably thrilled way out of proportion to the effort invested by the cook. These candy recipes require neither exact temperature control nor tempering of chocolate. A couple of them are one-step operations.

SPECIAL DAY CHOCOLATES

These chocolates, adapted from a recipe by Jacques Pépin, are very pretty, and there's plenty of room for invention; they can be confected on the spur of the moment with any good chocolate and almost any fruit and nut filling. Even the youngest children can help to make, taste-test, and parcel out the goodies. Including fresh fruit makes the candies especially delicious and unusual, but they'll only keep for a day—hence the name.

To make the candies, you'll need the small fluted foil or paper candy cups available in the candy section of most grocery stores. Candied violets are available at confectioners' shops, specialty stores, and often in supermarkets. If you can't find them, oh well, no purple flowers on top.

7	OUNCES BITTERSWEET, MILK OR WHITE CHOCOLATE
16	PISTACHIOS, PEANUTS, ALMOND SLICES OR PIECES OF PECAN OR WALNUT
16	DRIED CHERRIES OR CRANBERRIES
4	DRIED APRICOTS OR FIGS, CUT INTO QUARTERS
16	RAISINS
16	CANDIED VIOLETS
4	FRESH STRAWBERRIES, CHERRIES OR GRAPES, QUARTERED (OPTIONAL)

YIELDS 16 CANDIES
PREPARATION TIME: 20 MINUTES
CHILLING TIME: 1 HOUR

Coarsely chop the chocolate. Place it in a heatproof glass measuring cup, set the cup in a small saucepan of hot water (see Note), and melt the chocolate on low heat for about 1 minute, stirring until smooth.

Double up 32 small fluted cups to make 16 sturdy candy cups. Arrange them on a flat plate or in an 8-inch-square pan. Pour the melted chocolate into the cups. Lightly press the nuts, dried fruits, candied violets, and fresh fruit pieces partially into the chocolate. Try to coat the cut sides of the fresh fruit pieces with chocolate without completely submerging them. Be sure to let the pretty candied violets float on top.

Chill until set, about 1 hour. Store tightly covered in the refrigerator. The fresh fruit candies will keep for only a day. The nut and dried fruit candies will keep for 2 weeks.

note

You can also use a double boiler or a microwave oven.

CHOCOLATE-FILLED DRIED FIGS

This is a simple, but inspired, lush confection to savor slowly with a full-bodied cup of coffee or tiny glass of dessert wine. Although the liqueur is optional, we recommend using it, since its flavor enriches the chocolate. Our proportions in this recipe give you a little fig with your chocolate. For fig enthusiasts, who would prefer more fig per chocolate, just cut the chocolate ganache into smaller pieces and stuff more figs than we call for here.

8   OUNCES HIGH-QUALITY BITTERSWEET OR
    SEMI-SWEET CHOCOLATE

½   CUP HEAVY CREAM

1 to 2 TABLESPOONS COFFEE-, ORANGE- OR ANISE-FLAVORED LIQUEUR
    (OPTIONAL)

40   LARGE, PLUMP DRIED CALIMYRNA OR SMYRNA FIGS (1½ POUNDS)

YIELDS 40 OR MORE STUFFED FIGS
PREPARATION TIME: 30 MINUTES
CHILLING TIME: AT LEAST 2 HOURS

In a nonstick saucepan or in the top of a double boiler, heat the chocolate, heavy cream, and optional liqueur for 3 to 4 minutes, stirring frequently, until the chocolate melts. Pour the chocolate ganache mixture into an 8-inch-square glass baking dish or 9-inch glass pie plate and refrigerate for several hours, until firm.

Slice off any hard stems from the dried figs. Starting from the stem end, cut about two-thirds of the way down through the center of each fig. Cut the chilled chocolate ganache into 40 (or more) pieces. Gently widen the opening in each fig, scoop out a piece of ganache with a teaspoon, insert it in the fig, and then push the sticky cut edges of the fig back together so that a rim of chocolate shows.

Chocolate-Filled Dried Figs can be made up to a week ahead and stored in a tin or other sealed container in the refrigerator.

CHOCOLATE CRUNCH

This recipe is unsurpassed as a certain kid-pleaser. What better "glue" than chocolate to bind these crisp rice cereal, raisin, and nut candies? Store them, tightly covered, in a cool dry place, and serve at room temperature for the best flavor and texture. If your cool spot warms up and the Chocolate Crunch begins to soften, refrigerate it just long enough to harden.

14   OUNCES MILK CHOCOLATE
1   CUP CRISP RICE CEREAL
1   CUP RAISINS
½   CUP TOASTED CHOPPED PEANUTS OR PISTACHIOS, OR PEANUT
     BUTTER CHIPS

YIELDS ABOUT 40 PIECES
PREPARATION TIME: 15 TO 20 MINUTES
CHILLING TIME: 1 HOUR

Melt the chocolate in a metal bowl over a small pot of simmering water, stirring until smooth. Remove from the heat and stir in the cereal, raisins, and nuts or peanut butter chips.

Spread the mixture evenly into an 8 x 8-inch glass pan or drop it by spoonfuls into neat little heaps onto paper plates or a tray lined with wax paper, foil, or parchment paper.

Chill until firm, about 1 hour. If you poured the chocolate mixture into a pan, cut it into squares. If you made little mounds, they should pop off the paper when firm. Serve at room temperature.

CHOCOLATE APRICOTS

While we realize that "moist dried fruit" is an oxymoron, dried apricots generally tend to be moister than many other dried fruits, and that makes them perfect for this chewy, succulent treat. The softness of the apricots also makes it easy to find and manipulate the opening where the nuts are inserted. And almonds are perhaps the easiest nuts to stuff in because of their pointed ends.

With the two contrasting colors of chocolate, these are truly tempting and good-looking treats, yet more nutritious than your average candy.

30   DRIED APRICOTS, PREFERABLY UNSULPHURED

30   TOASTED ALMONDS, HAZELNUTS OR PISTACHIOS*

3.5 OUNCES SEMI-SWEET CHOCOLATE

3.5 OUNCES WHITE CHOCOLATE

YIELDS 30 CANDIES
PREPARATION TIME: 35 MINUTES
CHILLING TIME: 40 TO 55 MINUTES

* Toast nuts in a single layer on an unoiled baking tray at 350° for 5 to 10 minutes, until fragrant and golden brown. If you like, double the number of pistachios and put two in each apricot.

Squeezing gently, loosen the open edge of each apricot and insert a nut (or perhaps two pistachios). Squeeze the edges together again to seal. In two double boilers (see Note), melt each of the chocolates separately, stirring until smooth.

Drop 15 stuffed apricots, 5 at a time, into the dark chocolate, turning to coat completely. Remove them with small tongs and gently shake off the excess chocolate over the pan. Reserve the leftover chocolate for decorating later. Place the chocolate-coated apricots an inch apart on paper plates or on a dish lined with wax paper.

Use the same procedure to dip the remaining 15 apricots into the white chocolate. Place all of the coated apricots in the freezer for 10 minutes or in the refrigerator for about 25 minutes, until partially firm.

Gently remelt the leftover chocolates separately. Remove the coated apricots from the freezer or refrigerator and arrange on a serving plate. Drizzle the two melted chocolates in lines over the whole plate of apricots, à la Jackson Pollock.

Refrigerate until the chocolate is firm, about 30 minutes. Store, tightly covered, in the refrigerator until serving time. The candies will keep for up to 2 weeks.

note

You can also melt the chocolates in a microwave oven or use two metal bowls over simmering water.

variation

For a more uniform look, dip a fork into the white chocolate and press the tines onto the top of a dark chocolate-coated apricot to create a combed stripe decoration. Do the same with the dark chocolate on the white chocolate-coated apricots.

ESPRESSO TRUFFLES

These truffles, laced with liqueur, are foolproof yet sophisticated and not too sweet.

Forming truffles and coating them with the cocoa and confectioners' sugar is inevitably a rather messy job. Your fingertips and eventually your palms will be covered with chocolate. It's worth it, but plan to have the answering machine pick up the phone.

8	OUNCES SEMI-SWEET CHOCOLATE
½	CUP HEAVY CREAM
1	TABLESPOON INSTANT ESPRESSO POWDER
2	TABLESPOONS CHOCOLATE OR MOCHA LIQUEUR, SUCH AS KAHLÚA
¼	CUP UNSWEETENED COCOA POWDER

2 to 3 TABLESPOONS CONFECTIONERS' SUGAR (OPTIONAL)

YIELDS 24 TRUFFLES
PREPARATION TIME: 20 MINUTES
CHILLING TIME: 1 TO 2 HOURS

In a double boiler or in a small bowl set over a pot of barely simmering water, melt the chocolate with the cream and instant espresso powder. Stir for a few minutes until smooth and remove from the heat. Stir in the Kahlúa or other liqueur. Pour into a pie plate or an 8-inch-square glass baking pan and chill until firm, 1 to 2 hours.

When the mixture is chilled and firm, spread the cocoa on a plate. Scoop up rounded spoonfuls of the truffle mixture and shape into 24 balls by rolling briefly between the palms of your hands (see Note). Roll each ball in the cocoa powder and dust with confectioners' sugar, if desired.

Place each truffle in a small fluted paper cup, or store the truffles in a cookie tin lined with wax paper and separate the stacked layers with wax paper, too. Tightly covered and refrigerated, these truffles will keep for at least 2 weeks.

note

If you prefer, cut the chocolate into 24 squares and then roll the squares into balls.

HAZELNUT TRUFFLES

The warm, buttery taste of hazelnuts pairs perfectly with chocolate. So simple. So divine. These are perfect with a steaming cup of coffee or a celebratory glass of dessert wine, maybe shared in front of the fire late in the evening on Valentine's Day.

16 OUNCES BITTERSWEET, SEMI-SWEET OR MILK CHOCOLATE

¾ CUP HEAVY CREAM

¼ CUP FRA ANGELICO OR OTHER HAZELNUT LIQUEUR

1½ CUPS HAZELNUTS

YIELDS 48 TRUFFLES
PREPARATION TIME: 30 MINUTES
CHILLING TIME: 1 TO 2 HOURS

In a double boiler or in a bowl set over a pot of barely simmering water, melt the chocolate with the cream. Stir for a few minutes until smooth. Add the liqueur and mix well. Divide the mixture evenly into two pie pans or two shallow 8- or 9-inch-square glass pans. Refrigerate until firm, 1 to 2 hours.

Meanwhile, toast the hazelnuts in a 325° oven for about 10 minutes, until browned and fragrant. Roll the nuts in a clean, dry kitchen towel to remove some of the skins. In a food processor or blender, coarsely grind the nuts. Set aside on a plate.

When the chocolate mixture is chilled and firm, work with one pan of it at a time and keep the other refrigerated. Scoop up rounded spoonfuls of the chocolate, roll each briefly between the palms of your hands, and shape into twenty-four 1-inch balls. Repeat with the remaining pan (see Note). Roll each truffle in the ground hazelnuts.

Place each truffle in a small fluted paper cup, or store the truffles in a cookie tin lined with wax paper and separate the stacked layers with wax paper, too. Tightly covered and refrigerated, these truffles will keep for at least 2 weeks.

note

If you prefer, cut each pan of chocolate into 24 squares and then roll the squares into balls.

TIBETAN-AMERICAN LOSAR DINNER

MOOSEWOOD

Tibetan-style Seitan Burritos
Choklay's Home Fries with Tibetan Hot Sauce
Spicy Cabbage Salad
Tibetan-style Chai
Kheer (page 155)

A small enclave of about twenty Tibetans arrived in Ithaca in 1992. Because they came as immigrants, they had to set about making a living immediately in order to support themselves and eventually reunify their families, a process that sometimes took seven years or more. They brought with them skills as teachers, cooks, artists, shopkeepers, woodworkers, bookkeepers, loan counselors, and hotel managers. But, in the same way most immigrants make their way, the Tibetans accepted work wherever they could find it, which is how several of them came to Moosewood.

Many of these folks have gone on to become established presences in the restaurant and in other businesses in Ithaca. Palden C. Oshoe is now a translator and artist who teaches at Namgyal Monastary. Karma Dorjee works at Snow Lion Publications, a distributor of Tibetan Buddhist books and materials. Nyima Dhondup, who is employed at Cornell, continues to work also at Moosewood, where he graciously serves customers and willingly helps out wherever most needed. Choklay Lhamo, who had her own restaurant business in India, quickly became an innovative force in our kitchen, creating many new recipes during her years at Moosewood. And although Choklay is now just an occasional visitor, Tashi Dhondup still faithfully runs the dishwashing operation as if it were a well-oiled Mercedes, and the Sunday ethnic menu board is impeccably illustrated week after week by Dhondup Dorjee.

In addition to their diverse work skills, the Tibetans brought their traditional holiday celebrations to Ithaca, and some have become popular community events. The Tibetan word *Losar* means "new year" and Tibetans, like Americans, celebrate the start of the new year once every twelve months. Rather than keeping track of personal birth dates, Losar was once considered every Tibetan's birthday! According to the Tibetan calendar, Losar falls on the new moon that follows the first full moon of February. So depending on the year and the cycle of the moon, Losar will always be in February or March. The day before Losar is traditionally a day for intensive cleaning—making way for the new. Then, the custom in Tibet is to celebrate Losar for the next *three* days. The first day is a day to connect with family at home. The second day, everyone shares festivities with their friends and relatives, traveling from home to home. The third day is an entertainment day in which one attends parties, shows, or other events that interest them.

The night before the first Tibetan new year celebration in Ithaca, Choklay crafted two hundred *momo* (the nickname for Tibetan dumplings) plus a spicy tomato dipping sauce called *sibhen*. They were a hit. Now Losar has become an annual Tibetan cultural day, held at our local community center, with traditional Tibetan song and dance, monks in debate, colorful carved butter sculptures, and mandala sand-painting. Long tables laden with beautiful traditional handicrafts are offered for sale. Door prizes are distributed among the hundred or more guests, who help themselves to a buffet of delicious Tibetan food.

Here's your chance to experience Tibetan-American cuisine. To make this menu most manageable, prepare the Kheer, the Tibetan Hot Sauce, and the filling for the Tibetan-style Seitan Burritos a day ahead. Then, a few hours before guests arrive, make the Spicy Cabbage Salad. While the salad marinates, assemble the burritos and have them oven-ready. Finally, sauté Choklay's Home Fries, then cover them with foil and keep them warm on the back of the stove while the burritos bake. When the burritos are done, reduce the oven temperature to low and keep both the burritos and home fries warm until serving time. For dessert, accompany the chilled Kheer with juicy, ripe mango slices and Tibetan-style Chai, a wonderful sweet spiced tea.

TIBETAN-STYLE SEITAN BURRITOS

Choklay Lhamo invented this dish one night at Moosewood when the menu planner had suggested burritos as one of that evening's selections. Choklay smiled and said, "Okay, I will make burritos Tibetan-style."

The filling she made uses ingredients found in Tibetan dumplings: Ginger, garlic, cabbage, onions. As with the dumpling fillings, the vegetables are skillfully sliced into mere shreds, and the garlic and ginger are finely minced, too. Savoy cabbage is particularly nice for this dish.

Serve with Choklay's Home Fries and Tibetan Hot Sauce (pages 290–91).

2	CUPS THINLY SLICED ONIONS
2	TABLESPOONS VEGETABLE OIL
2	TABLESPOONS MINCED GARLIC
3	TABLESPOONS GRATED FRESH GINGER ROOT
1	TEASPOON SALT
4	CUPS THINLY SLICED OR SHREDDED CABBAGE
1 to 2	TEASPOONS ASIAN CHILI PASTE, TO TASTE
2	CUPS PEELED AND GRATED CARROTS
1½	CUPS SLICED SEITAN (1 X ¼-INCH STRIPS)
1	TEASPOON DARK SESAME OIL
6	FLOUR TORTILLAS (11 INCHES ACROSS)

SERVES 6 TO 8
PREPARATION TIME: 45 MINUTES
BAKING TIME: 15 MINUTES

Preheat the oven to 350°. Lightly oil an 8-inch-square baking dish.

In a wok or a heavy skillet, sauté the onions in the oil on medium heat for about 5 minutes, until just soft. Add the garlic, ginger root, and salt and cook for 1 to 2 minutes. Stir in the cabbage and cook, stirring frequently, until the cabbage is limp.

Add the chili paste, carrots, and seitan and cook for about 10 minutes, until the vegetables are soft and somewhat browned. Add a little water to prevent sticking, if needed. At the very end, sprinkle the sesame oil over the vegetables and remove the pan from the heat.

Divide the filling among the tortillas, roll them up, and place them seam side down in the baking dish. Cover the dish tightly with aluminum foil and bake for about 15 minutes, until hot. Serve immediately.

accommodating change

For Tibetans in exile, adaptation plus tradition equals survival. After being forced from their homeland by the Chinese government, Tibetans have established communities in India, North America, Europe, and other areas around the world. In these places of refuge, most Tibetans have taken care to transplant their language, cuisine, customs, and religious beliefs. They've participated in their new communities while working to preserve their culture, which may or may not survive the oppression and upheavals of the twentieth century. They have been resourceful and exceedingly patient in every regard. And every Losar, the Tibetans express their gratitude, or *tashi delek*, by ceremoniously giving people flowing, pure white silk neck scarves.

Tibetans who move from place to place adapt their traditional recipes to ingredients available in their new locales. For example, many dishes incorporate the spices and flavors of the regional cuisines of India, where the majority of Tibetans settled after fleeing Tibet. Lemon, ginger, garlic, soy sauce, chili pepper, cilantro, and mint are now commonly used in Tibetan cooking. Butter, which in Tibet is made from thick, yellow, yak milk, was always considered a source of protein. Here, where yak milk is unheard of, Tibetans use butter made from cow's milk in their tea. In our Tibetan American Losar menu, many Indian influences and Moosewood adaptations are apparent.

It may come as a surprise to discover that some meat is a customary part of the Tibetan diet. While Buddhists do not usually sanction the killing of animals, the severe climate and short growing season on the Tibetan plateau compel the people living there to supplement their diet of vegetables, fruit, grains, and butter with meat. Because eating fish or chicken sacrifices so many animal lives, small creatures are rarely eaten. However, one cow can feed many people, so beef is considered an acceptable source of protein.

CHOKLAY'S HOME FRIES

Choklay's home fries are delicious, spicy, and turmeric-tinted. The larger amount of red pepper flakes—or more—would suit most Tibetans' taste; less intrepid palates should season to taste.

SERVES 6
TOTAL TIME: 45 MINUTES

2	QUARTS WATER
1	TEASPOON SALT, MORE TO TASTE
4	CUPS PEELED AND CUBED POTATOES (1-INCH CHUNKS)
2	TABLESPOONS VEGETABLE OIL
2	CUPS CHOPPED ONIONS
2	TABLESPOONS MINCED OR PRESSED GARLIC
½ to 1	TEASPOON DRIED RED PEPPER FLAKES
1	TEASPOON TURMERIC
1	TEASPOON PAPRIKA

In a soup pot, bring the water and salt to a boil and add the potatoes. Keep the heat high and when the water boils again, drain the potatoes, cover, and set aside.

In a heavy skillet or a wok, warm the oil on medium heat. Add the onions and garlic and sauté until the onions are soft, 5 to 6 minutes. Stir in the red pepper flakes, turmeric, and paprika. Add the potatoes and continue to sauté on medium heat until they soften, brown, and start to become crisp. If the potatoes stick to the bottom of the skillet, add a little water.

Serve hot.

TIBETAN HOT SAUCE

This fiery sauce, called *sibhen* in Tibetan, has ingredients similar to those in a tomato salsa, but much more finely chopped to give it a more sauce-like character. The soy sauce deepens and darkens the color to a rich burgundy red.

Tibetan Hot Sauce will add a rich spiciness to bean dishes, chili, enchiladas, burritos, frittatas, and casseroles. Try it on the Bell Pepper & Asparagus Frittata (page 334).

2	CUPS CHOPPED FRESH TOMATOES
½	CUP CHOPPED SCALLIONS
2	GARLIC CLOVES, MINCED OR PRESSED
½	TEASPOON TABASCO OR OTHER HOT PEPPER SAUCE*
1	TABLESPOON SOY SAUCE
2	TABLESPOONS CHOPPED FRESH CILANTRO
2	TABLESPOONS CHOPPED FRESH MINT

YIELDS ABOUT 2 CUPS
PREPARATION TIME: 20 MINUTES
SITTING TIME: 30 MINUTES

* Or use minced fresh chiles, and adjust the hotness to your palate.

With a sharp knife or in a food processor, finely chop the tomatoes and place them in a small bowl. Stir in the scallions, garlic, Tabasco sauce, soy sauce, cilantro, and mint. Set aside at room temperature for 30 minutes or longer before serving so that the flavors will mingle.

Stored in a sealed container and refrigerated, the hot sauce will keep for about a week.

SPICY CABBAGE SALAD

Make this salad as spicy as you like by adding Asian chili paste to taste. Presalting the cabbage and allowing it to drain creates a crisp, mildly flavored salad—an optimum setting for the flavorful and spicy seasonings. Draining time is about 2 hours, so remember to prepare the cabbage ahead.

5 to 6 CUPS GRATED GREEN CABBAGE

1½ TEASPOONS SALT

1 TEASPOON GRATED FRESH GINGER ROOT

¼ to ½ TEASPOON ASIAN CHILI PASTE

2 TEASPOONS DARK SESAME OIL

1 TABLESPOON BROWN SUGAR, PACKED

2 TEASPOONS RICE VINEGAR

2 TEASPOONS SOY SAUCE

2 TABLESPOONS MINCED SCALLIONS

SERVES 6
PREPARATION TIME: 10 MINUTES
DRAINING TIME: 2 HOURS

Place the cabbage in a colander, toss with the salt, and set the colander in the sink. Let it stand at room temperature for about 2 hours.

Rinse the cabbage with cool running water and drain well, pressing out some of the liquid. Mix together the ginger root, chili paste, sesame oil, brown sugar, vinegar, soy sauce, and scallions in a large bowl. Add the drained cabbage to the bowl and toss well with the seasonings.

Serve at room temperature or chilled.

TIBETAN-STYLE CHAI

Traditionally, Tibetans drink butter tea, but they also enjoy Indian spiced tea, or chai. At Namgyal Monastary, in downtown Ithaca, the monks serve chai and a snack every Friday after the early evening community meditation.

This is a full-bodied tea with a balanced blend of "sugar and spice and everything nice." Although the spices have an essential presence, they aren't at all overpowering, and the tea flavor shines through. Many Tibetans like their tea very strong with lots of milk. You can adjust the amount of tea, milk, and sugar in the recipe according to your own taste.

Serve this simple, delicious chai with dessert at the end of the meal. Or forget about dessert: The tea itself is filling enough to be totally satisfying.

5	CUPS WATER
1/3 to 1/2	CUP CHOPPED FRESH GINGER ROOT*
1	TEASPOON CARDAMOM SEEDS
3	WHOLE CINNAMON STICKS
4	TEA BAGS OR 4 TEASPOONS LOOSE BLACK TEA, SUCH AS ORANGE PEKOE OR DARJEELING
4	CUPS MILK
1/2	CUP SUGAR

SERVES 6
YIELDS 7½ CUPS
TOTAL TIME: ABOUT 25 MINUTES

* Peel the ginger or not, as you like. If you enjoy a little extra spicy kick to your tea, use the larger amount of ginger.

In a large covered pot, bring the water, ginger root, cardamom, cinnamon, and tea to a boil. Reduce the heat, uncover, and simmer for 10 to 15 minutes. Add the milk and sugar and return to a boil; then lower the heat and simmer for 5 more minutes. Strain and serve.

Store leftover chai in a sealed container in the fridge. Gently reheat the tea as necessary.

NEW ORLEANS MARDI GRAS DINNER

Menu

Baked Creole Ratatouille
Olive Butter Spread
Best Dressed Shrimp Salad (page 248)
Cajun Dirty Rice
Puff Pastry with Strawberries

Ash Wednesday marks the beginning of Lent, the penitential period of forty days before Easter, when observant Christians abstain from all meat and poultry. The day before Ash Wednesday, liturgically known as Shrove Tuesday, is a time to confess your sins and be forgiven or "shriven." Customarily, people celebrate their cleansed consciences until Tuesday at midnight when they don the repentent spirit and fasting discipline of Lent.

The French dubbed Shrove Tuesday *Mardi Gras,* which translates as "Fat Tuesday," an appropriate name considering the extravagant feasting that often takes place that day. It's the culmination of the period the French and Cajuns call "Carnival," which begins Twelfth Night (January 6) and ends midnight on Mardi Gras (exactly 46 days before Easter). Perhaps it's no surprise that the word "carnival" comes from the Latin *carnem levare,* "to take away meat."

New Orleans has one of the most spectacular Mardi Gras parades in the world, often considered the "Greatest Free Show on Earth." People in nineteenth-century costumes dance in the streets to jazz marching bands, processions of masked dancers and decorated vehicles can be seen for miles, and beads or trinkets spray from lavish floats into the huge crowds of over a million people.

So why is New Orleans the Mardi Gras hot spot? For starters, on March 3, 1699, Pierre le Moyne landed at the mouth of the Mississippi and named the spot Pointe du Mardi Gras in honor of the day of his arrival. Years later, many French-speaking peasants from Acadia were forced out of their Bay of Fundy homesteads by England and they reunited in New Orleans. These Acadiennes, nicknamed Cajuns, transformed the medieval French begging ritual of their ancestors into the present-day rural Cajun tradition of the Mardi Gras Run. In France, poor people disguised in masks would travel from castle to castle singing and dancing in exchange for food. Today, Cajuns sprint from house to house carrying skillets laden with favorite homemade dishes. Without a doubt, food is a major focus of any New Orleans–style carnival celebration, with some foods, such as gumbo, almost a must.

Gumbo is derived from the West African name for okra, *guingombo,* and a dish with okra is integral to any Mardi Gras feast. So in keeping with tradition, our Baked Creole Ratatouille contains a generous helping of okra. To make this menu in an unhurried, laid-back style, start on Monday. Whip up the Olive Butter Spread and tuck it in the fridge. Whisk together the dressing, rinse the greens, and cook the shrimp for the salad; then store each component in its own container and refrigerate. Cook the fruit for the puff pastry dessert and chill it overnight.

On Fat Tuesday, thaw the puff pastry in the morning. About 2 hours before you serve the meal, assemble the ingredients for the ratatouille and the Cajun Dirty Rice. Preheat the oven, get the rice cooking, and set a timer to remind you when it's ready. Chop all of the garlic, bell peppers, and tomatoes needed for the ratatouille and dirty rice and set aside those for the rice. Finish the Creole Ratatouille, slip it into the oven to bake, and then concentrate on sautéeing the vegetables for the rice. Remove the Olive Butter Spread and cooked fruit from the fridge to warm to room temperature. When the Baked Creole Ratatouille comes out of the oven, pop in the pastry shells. Meanwhile, set out the Olive Butter Spread appetizer tray, assemble the Best Dressed Shrimp Salad, stir together the Cajun Dirty Rice, and start working up your appetite. The pastry shells will be ready to fill just before you sit down to eat (or, if you prefer, take a breather after dinner and fill them then).

BAKED CREOLE RATATOUILLE

When Europe, West Africa, and the Caribbean set up a trade triangle in the sixteenth century, Creole cooking was born. The cuisine is characterized by glorious combinations of ingredients and invites experimentation. We start with a classic French ratatouille and add Caribbean, Italian, and Spanish ingredients. Then we layer the dish for an appealing casserole effect. If you like, include chayote, a type of summer squash called *mirliton* in New Orleans.

It's best to cut all of the vegetables into ½-inch pieces or cubes for even roasting. To save time, cube and salt the eggplant, then prepare the next six ingredients; while they all roast, prepare the rest of the ingredients. Serve on rice topped with Parmesan cheese, if you like.

6	CUPS CUBED, SALTED EGGPLANT*
2	CUPS CHOPPED RED ONIONS
1	CUP CUBED YELLOW SQUASH
2	CUPS SLICED FRESH OKRA**
2	CUPS CUBED ZUCCHINI
3	CUPS CHOPPED BELL PEPPERS (TWO COLORS IS NICE)
2	SMALL CHAYOTE, PEELED AND CUBED (OPTIONAL)
5	TABLESPOONS OLIVE OIL
3	CUPS CUBED TOMATOES
1	CUP CHOPPED SCALLIONS
1	TABLESPOON MINCED OR PRESSED GARLIC
1 to 2	JALAPEÑO PEPPERS, SEEDED AND MINCED
¼	CUP CHOPPED FRESH BASIL
1	TABLESPOON CHOPPED FRESH THYME
1	TABLESPOON FRESH LEMON JUICE
1	TABLESPOON CIDER VINEGAR
1	TEASPOON SALT, OR TO TASTE
¼	TEASPOON GROUND BLACK PEPPER

SERVES 4 TO 6
PREPARATION TIME: 1¼ HOURS
FINAL BAKING TIME: 40 MINUTES

* Sprinkle the eggplant cubes with salt, and set aside for about 20 minutes.

** Frozen okra also works fine. Slice it while still frozen; thawed, it's very slippery.

Preheat the oven to 375°. Lightly oil a 7 x 11 x 3-inch baking pan.

Rinse the eggplant in a colander, drain, and thoroughly dry on paper towels. In a bowl, toss together the eggplant, red onions, squash, okra, zucchini, bell peppers, and chayote, if using, with 2 tablespoons of the olive oil. Spread the vegetables in a single layer on one or two baking trays. Roast for 40 minutes, until the vegetables are softened and their edges browned.

Meanwhile, combine the tomatoes, scallions, garlic, jalapeños, basil, thyme, lemon juice, vinegar, salt, black pepper, and the remaining 3 tablespoons of olive oil in a bowl. Set aside to marry the flavors while the other vegetables are roasting.

When the roasted vegetables are ready, layer half of them into the prepared baking pan and top with half of the seasoned tomatoes. Layer on the remaining roasted vegetables and finish with the rest of the tomatoes. Cover and bake for 40 minutes, until hot. Serve immediately.

OLIVE BUTTER SPREAD

Moosewood cook Susan Harville has an unassuming generous nature and is prone to greet even unexpected visitors with some new concoction from her fridge. So it's no surprise that she's the source of this unabashedly rich and irresistible dish. The spread is easy to make, especially now that pitted kalamata olives are available in the supermarket. Serve it with a glass of red wine as the appetizer for this vegetable-filled Mardi Gras dinner.

YIELDS 1½ CUPS
TOTAL TIME: 10 MINUTES

1   CUP UNSALTED BUTTER, AT ROOM TEMPERATURE
½   CUP FINELY CHOPPED PITTED KALAMATA OLIVES,
     MORE TO TASTE
1   TEASPOON MINCED GARLIC
1   TABLESPOON MINCED FRESH PARSLEY
     SALT TO TASTE
     WHOLE LEAVES OF BELGIAN ENDIVE*
     TOASTED THIN ROUND SLICES OF BAGUETTE OR GARLIC BREAD*

* Use either or both, as you wish. A ½-pound head of Belgian endive will yield 16 to 20 leaves. Add some sliced cherry tomatoes or slivers of red bell pepper as garnishes to offset the richness of the spread, if desired.

In a medium bowl, cream the butter with a fork until smooth. Add the chopped olives, garlic, parsley, and salt to taste. Mix well. Mound about 1 teaspoon of olive butter at the base of each Belgian endive leaf and/or spread it on toasted baguette slices. Serve at room temperature.

Olive Butter will keep, covered and refrigerated, for up to 2 weeks.

CAJUN DIRTY RICE

Dirty rice, a Southern classic, is traditionally made with chicken livers and gizzards. Our version uses chewy seitan and lots of vegetables with Cajun spices and is quite quick when made with white rice. We sometimes add a squeeze of lemon or lime just before serving.

1½	CUPS RICE*
½	TEASPOON DRIED THYME
2	TEASPOONS PLUS 1 TABLESPOON OLIVE OIL
6	GARLIC CLOVES, MINCED OR PRESSED
2½	CUPS WATER OR VEGETABLE STOCK
2	CUPS MINCED ONIONS
1	CUP MINCED BELL PEPPERS, ANY COLOR(S)
½	CUP MINCED CELERY
½	TEASPOON SALT
1	CUP DICED TOMATOES, FRESH OR CANNED WITH JUICE
8	OUNCES SEASONED SEITAN, FINELY CHOPPED (ABOUT 1½ CUPS)
2	TEASPOONS DRIED OREGANO
2	TEASPOONS DRIED BASIL
1	TABLESPOON SOY SAUCE
	PINCH OF CAYENNE OR SPLASH OF TABASCO OR OTHER HOT SAUCE
	SALT AND GROUND BLACK PEPPER TO TASTE
	MINCED FRESH CHIVES, SCALLIONS, PARSLEY OR BASIL (OPTIONAL)
	GRATED SMOKED CHEDDAR CHEESE OR SOUR CREAM (OPTIONAL)

* *Choose either long-grain white rice or brown basmati rice. The brown rice takes about 20 minutes longer to cook, but can provide a more flavorful backdrop.*

Combine the rice, thyme, 2 teaspoons of the oil, and half of the garlic in a heavy pot with a tight-fitting lid. Cook for 1 to 2 minutes on medium heat, stirring constantly. Add the water or stock, cover, and bring to a boil; then reduce the heat to low and cook until the water is absorbed and the rice tender, about 20 minutes for white rice, 40 minutes for brown rice.

While the rice cooks, heat the remaining tablespoon of oil in a large skillet. Sauté the onions, bell peppers, celery, salt, and the rest of the garlic on medium-high heat, stirring often, for 10 to 15 minutes, until the onions are translucent. Add the tomatoes, seitan, oregano, and basil and cook for 5 more minutes, or until all of the vegetables are tender.

Stir in the soy sauce, cayenne or Tabasco sauce, and salt and black pepper to taste. Mix in the hot cooked rice. Serve with your choice of toppings.

PUFF PASTRY WITH STRAWBERRIES

If you have puff pastry and fruit in your freezer, you can create a last-minute elegant dessert anytime. The fruit can be thawed ahead and served chilled or warm. Using fresh fruit is also fine, but it will increase the prep time a bit. If you like, top with fresh whipped cream or vanilla ice cream.

4	CUPS SLICED FRESH OR FROZEN STRAWBERRIES*
⅓	CUP SUGAR, MORE TO TASTE
½	TEASPOON PURE VANILLA EXTRACT
½	TEASPOON FRESHLY GRATED LEMON OR ORANGE PEEL (OPTIONAL)
½	TEASPOON GROUND CINNAMON (OPTIONAL)
1	TABLESPOON CORNSTARCH
6	PUFF PASTRY SHELLS (10-OUNCE PACKAGE)**

SERVES 6
PREPARATION TIME:
ABOUT 15 MINUTES
BAKING TIME: 20 MINUTES

* Or use cherries, peaches, raspberries, blackberries, or blueberries. Thaw the fruit, if using frozen. Two pounds of frozen strawberries yields 4 cups of sliced fruit.

** Or use half of a 17.3-ounce package of puff pastry sheets (see Note).

Preheat the oven to 375°.

In a nonreactive saucepan, combine the strawberries, sugar, and vanilla. If using, stir in the citrus peel and cinnamon. Dissolve the cornstarch in 1 tablespoon of water and stir it into the fruit. Simmer gently just until the mixture thickens and the fruit sauce becomes clear. The strawberries should still be chunky. Set aside to cool.

Bake the puff pastry shells according to the directions on the package, until puffed and golden. Cool slightly. Fill each cooled pastry cup with about ⅔ cup of the fruit mixture and serve.

note

If using puff pastry sheets, thaw one sheet according to the directions on the package. Cut it into six 3 x 4-inch rectangles. On a lightly floured surface, roll each rectangle into a 5- to 6-inch square. Fit each square into a standard muffin tin cup and fold in the edges to form a little pastry cup. Bake for about 20 minutes, or until puffed and golden.

SPRING

It was a lover and his lass,

With a hey, and a ho,

and a hey nonino,

That o'er the green corn-field

did pass

In the spring time, the only

pretty ring-time,

When the birds do sing,

hey ding a ding, ding;

Sweet lovers love the spring.

—William Shakespeare,
As You Like It

Hope springs eternal! Green things growing once again—what a welcome sight! Spring is rebirth—dewy, refreshing, inspiring, a strength-ening of faith. Tender, baby vegetables are just around the corner and the good earth never lets us down. Springtime brings up the shiny leaves of spinach, Swiss chard, and sweet multihued salad greens. Spring gardens radiate the savory scent of chives and the stimulating fragrance of spearmint, and bring us the clean crunch of parsley and the snap of spicy green onions. Snow peas and asparagus can be picked and, pretty soon, plump, zesty radishes. A little later, the strawberries come.

Cooking at Moosewood feels different in the spring. There is no season that makes cooks more reverent, because the perfection of these beautiful herbs, vegetables, and berries demands a gentle, light touch and a restraint in cooking. Blanching sugar snaps and sautéing Swiss chard, we feel lighter on our feet. There's no need to gild the lily.

There's so much to celebrate around here. We welcome the first brave little snowdrops, crocuses, and forsythia, and appreciate the May apples and delicate pink and white trillium along the shady wildflower walks. April brings buttery yellow and white jonquils and daffodils, then cheerful tulips. May presents elegant irises, tall vermilion poppies, and the wild purple and white phlox that roam and scatter themselves all along the banks of roads, creeks, and the inlet. We're a lucky bunch. If we can't find reasons to celebrate in Spring—well, shame on us.

In the following section, we offer you a few good excuses to enjoy yourself, some traditional, some unconventional. You'll find menus here for well-known celebrations: A Mother's Day Tea, a Passover Seder, and a Cinco de Mayo Dinner. But we also have included simple menus for a Greek Easter Dinner Party, a Birthday Breakfast in Bed, and a Pizza & Sundae Party. So let yourself go, with a hey nonino!

BIRTHDAY BREAKFAST IN BED

MENU

Chai Smoothie
Chocolate Waffles with Strawberry Sauce

Breakfast in bed
Breakfast in bed,
Is there a finer way to be fed?

Even if this meal never makes it to the bedroom, it is the pinnacle of luxury. Chocolate waffles for breakfast? You betcha. After all, this is a birthday. What better occasion to eat dessert first?

Actually, these cocoa waffles are only mildly sweet, and the strawberry topping is a delicious summer fruit sauce. The Chai Smoothie, our beverage of choice, makes a spicy and refreshing counterpoint, with some protein thrown in for good measure.

To best coordinate this meal, steep the tea for the smoothie and set it in the freezer to chill, or chill it in the refrigerator the night before. Next prepare the strawberry sauce and the waffle batter. When the batter is ready for the waffle iron, remove the tea from the freezer. Make the waffles and keep them warm on an oven rack while you blend the smoothie. Transfer the waffles to a platter, put the strawberry sauce in a shallow bowl, and pour the smoothie into a pitcher. Assemble everything on a tray, put a rose in a vase, and warm up your pipes for a robust rendition of "Happy Birthday to You."

CHAI SMOOTHIE

Chai, a stimulating Indian spiced tea, is the inspiration for this refreshing smoothie. Unlike traditional chai, this beverage is caffeine-free. So if you're having it for breakfast, you can have your tea and coffee, too.

2	CELESTIAL SEASONINGS BENGAL SPICE TEA BAGS
¼	CUP PURE MAPLE SYRUP
4	ICE CUBES
1	CUP NONFAT PLAIN YOGURT
½	CUP ORANGE JUICE
1	TEASPOON PURE VANILLA EXTRACT
	PINCH OF SALT (OPTIONAL)

SERVES 2 TO 4
YIELDS ABOUT 3 CUPS
STEEPING TIME: 10 MINUTES
CHILLING TIME: AT LEAST 30 MINUTES
PREPARATION TIME: 15 MINUTES

Bring 1¼ cups of water to a boil and remove from the heat. Immerse the tea bags in the hot water, press the tea bags with the back of a spoon to begin the steeping process, then steep the tea, uncovered, for 10 minutes.

Remove the tea bags, add the maple syrup, and stir well to dissolve the syrup completely. Chill the sweetened tea. A relatively quick method is to pour the tea into a shallow bowl or baking dish and put it in the freezer for about 30 minutes. Or, if you have time, just refrigerate it for several hours or overnight.

When the tea is cold, crush the ice cubes in a blender, add the yogurt, chilled tea, orange juice, and vanilla. Blend for 30 seconds, until frothy, and pour into a chilled pitcher. Taste and add a shake of salt, if desired.

Serve within 10 minutes of preparing. Leftover Chai Smoothie separates when it sits and must be whisked or reblended just before serving.

CHOCOLATE WAFFLES WITH STRAWBERRY SAUCE

These are extravagant, deep chocolate waffles for a special brunch. Top them with some of our Easy Strawberry Sauce, with whipped cream, or with other fresh fruit. Make them even fancier with one of our other suggested variations. These waffles can also make a good dessert served with ice cream.

easy strawberry sauce

YIELDS ¾ CUP SAUCE AND
6 BELGIAN WAFFLES
TOTAL TIME: 30 TO 45 MINUTES

1½ CUPS FRESH STRAWBERRIES, RINSED, STEMMED AND SLICED*

2 TABLESPOONS SUGAR

1 TEASPOON CORNSTARCH*

1 TEASPOON COLD WATER

waffles

1 CUP UNBLEACHED WHITE FLOUR

¼ TEASPOON BAKING SODA

⅓ CUP UNSWEETENED COCOA POWDER

½ CUP SUGAR

½ TEASPOON SALT

1 CUP BUTTERMILK OR MILK

3 TABLESPOONS BUTTER, MELTED

1 TEASPOON PURE VANILLA EXTRACT

2 EGGS, SEPARATED

* If using frozen strawberries, increase the cornstarch to 2 teaspoons.

Combine the strawberries and sugar in a saucepan. Bring to a boil on medium heat, stirring constantly, then reduce the heat to low. In a small cup, dissolve the cornstarch in the cold water and stir into the strawberries. Simmer for about 30 seconds, stirring constantly, until the juice is clear and thickened. Remove from the heat and set aside.

Preheat a waffle iron. If there is a temperature setting, set it on medium.

In a large bowl, sift together the flour, baking soda, cocoa, sugar, and salt. Mix thoroughly. In another bowl, combine the buttermilk or milk, melted butter, vanilla, and egg yolks. In a third bowl, beat the egg whites with clean beaters or a whisk until stiff but not dry and set aside. Stir the buttermilk mixture into the dry ingredients without overmixing. Gently fold in the beaten egg whites.

Scoop the batter into the preheated waffle iron with a ½-cup measure for six waffles. Bake according to the directions for your waffle iron.

Serve immediately, topped with the strawberry sauce, or keep warm by placing directly on the rack of a 200° oven until all of the waffles are made.

variations

When combining the wet and dry ingredients, you can also mix in any of the following: ¼ teaspoon of pure almond extract, 2 tablespoons of coarsely ground chocolate chips, 2 tablespoons of coarsely ground nuts, or ½ teaspoon of freshly grated orange peel. You can grind the chocolate chips and nuts in several batches in a spice grinder for a fine, even texture.

PIZZA & SUNDAE PARTY

Homemade Pizza Crust & Toppings
Your Favorite Bottomless Bowl of Fresh Salad Greens (page 368)

For Sundaes:
Classic Caramel Sauce
Easy Strawberry Sauce (page 304)
Bittersweet Chocolate Sauce
Wet Walnuts
Whipped Cream
Sundry Sundae Toppings

Long gone are the birthday parties where a bunch of kids in frilly dresses, pressed trousers, and party hats sat around a table eating cake and ice cream and then played pin the tail on the donkey.

Today, more often than not, birthday parties are raucous affairs filled with activities and events. Some are like a day in Vegas, with magicians, martial artists, and exotic animals. Parties are held at the cineplex, in bowling alleys, and arcades. Parents spend hours dreaming up treasure hunts, art projects, and superhero games to keep everyone (including themselves) involved and entertained.

Here's an idea to add to the list. We know a lot of kids who enjoy helping out in the kitchen, plenty who are finicky about their food, but few who don't like pizza and ice cream. At this party, kids get to make their own pizzas and sundaes, just the way they like them.

For the pizza part of the party, you'll need pizza dough, baking trays, a variety of toppings, and one or two long tables. Nine round pie crusts, each 8 inches across, can be formed from our pizza dough recipe, but if you're short on time, ready-to-shape pizza dough is available in many supermarkets and is even sold at some neighborhood pizzerias. Boboli-type crusts will also work. We've provided dough weights in our recipe so you'll know what to ask or look for if you need to purchase your dough.

If you're very adventurous, lightly flour one of the tables and let the kids roll out their own pizza crusts. Some very interesting-shaped pizzas will probably emerge. Remember to transfer the kids' crusts to baking pans before they top them with goodies; it will be impossible afterwards. If you're more practical-minded, roll out the pizza crusts ahead of time and place them on oiled baking sheets.

Next, herd everyone over to table number 2, where you've set out the toppings in large bowls and platters. For the 5- to 8-year-old set, spooning on sauce, scattering some vegetables, and sprinkling cheese on their pies might be the limit. Older kids can participate more by grating cheese, slicing vegetables, and preparing other toppings. (For you kids-at-heart, there are also topping ideas for adult pizza soirées.) When the pizza masterpieces are complete, slide them in the oven, four or five at a time, and bring out the salad and beverages. Our thin-crusted pizzas bake for such a short time that almost instant gratification is close at hand.

When everyone's ready for dessert, you can count on sundaes. We listed all of the ice cream toppings that popped into mind, but as we're sure you've noticed, new soda fountain flavors, combinations, and ingredients seem to appear continuously from nowhere. Food allergies, especially to milk and milk products, are not uncommon these days. Nor are concerns about saturated fat. Fortunately, other frozen dessert choices exist. Look for frozen yogurts, soy- and rice-based frozen desserts, ice milks, sherbets, and sorbets. Because you're going all out with toppings, keep the ice cream choices simple: Vanilla and chocolate, with maybe one fruity flavor thrown in. For an adult sundae party, you might offer coffee- or mocha-flavored ice cream and include a liqueur or two in your topping assortment.

Pizza and sundae parties offer great before-and-after photo opportunities. Don't forget the washcloths.

HOMEMADE PIZZA CRUST & TOPPINGS

This simple pizza dough has no added fat, requires only one rise, and yields a tasty, thin, crisp crust with the most basic equipment: An oven and some large baking sheets. It depends on using mostly all-purpose flour with just a little whole wheat bread flour. After the dough rises and is punched down, it can be refrigerated for up to 4 hours before being shaped into crusts.

The dough can also be frozen after rising. Punch it down and either roll it out or form a ball to be rekneaded and rolled out into the desired shape after thawing. It takes about 2 hours at room temperature for a ball of dough to defrost. After rekneading (adding flour if needed) and rolling out thawed dough, let it rise for about a half hour before baking.

There will be enough dough to make 8 or 9 individual pizzas or 4 regular-sized ones. You could also opt for 2 large sheet pizzas with a patchwork of toppings. If time is short and you want to use commercially prepared dough, you will need 3¾ pounds of dough (about 6½ ounces for each individual crust).

To serve a party of eight simultaneously, you will need at least two 18 x 13-inch pans, which fit in a standard oven and will hold two 9-inch pies each (see Note). When the first 4 pizzas are ready, it will only be 10 to 12 minutes before the next 4 are out of the oven, so everyone can eat their hot pizzas together.

See the box on page 310 for some great topping ideas.

yeast mixture

YIELDS NINE 8-INCH, EIGHT 9-INCH, OR FOUR 12- TO 14-INCH CRUSTS
PREPARATION TIME: 20 TO 30 MINUTES
RISING TIME: 1 HOUR
BAKING TIME: 10 TO 12 MINUTES

3	CUPS HOT WATER (100° TO 115°)*
1	TABLESPOON ACTIVE DRY YEAST (NOT FAST-ACTING)*
2	TABLESPOONS UNBLEACHED WHITE FLOUR
2	TABLESPOONS MILD HONEY

dough ingredients

5	CUPS UNBLEACHED WHITE FLOUR
2	CUPS WHOLE WHEAT BREAD FLOUR
1	TABLESPOON SALT

CORNMEAL FOR DUSTING

* Active yeast foams when dissolved. If it doesn't foam, your dough won't rise. Go back to the store for fresher yeast.

Mix together the water, yeast, flour, and honey. Stir to dissolve the yeast and let rest for 5 to 10 minutes. The mixture should foam and become creamy.

In a large bowl, combine 4½ cups of the white flour with the whole wheat flour and salt. Add the yeast mixture and stir for 1 to 2 minutes, until the flour is uniformly moist and can be formed into a ball.

Lightly flour your hands and the countertop. Knead the dough with the heels of your hands for about 5 to 8 minutes by repeatedly pressing the ball flat, folding it in half, and pressing again. This dough is not stiff, but soft and slightly sticky. Sprinkle a tablespoon of flour at a time on the counter as needed, so the dough doesn't tear or stick to your hands or the counter. When you have a smooth ball of dough, place it in a lightly oiled bowl and cover with plastic wrap. Set aside to rise in a warm, draft-free place until doubled in size, about 1 hour.

While the dough is rising, prepare the toppings of your choice.

When the dough is finished rising, preheat the oven to 500°.

Now lightly flour the counter, punch down the dough, and knead for 1 to 2 minutes. Divide the dough into nine equal balls. (If you wish to freeze the dough, now is the time. Place each ball in its own zippered freezer bag.) Sprinkle a cutting board with cornmeal, set five of the dough balls aside on it, and cover them with a towel. Oil two 18 x 13-inch baking sheets.

Working with the four remaining dough balls one at a time, place each ball on a lightly floured surface, flatten it, and sprinkle with a little flour. With a rolling pin, press down and out from the center of the dough to make an 8-inch-wide crust. Put the four crusts on the prepared baking sheets and let loose the kids (or kids-at-heart) to pile on their favorite toppings. Finish with a sprinkling of cheese.

Bake the pies for 8 to 10 minutes, until the crust is golden and the cheese melted. With a spatula, slip the baked pizza pies directly onto the oven racks and bake for 1 to 2 minutes more, to crisp the bottom crust. Slide the baked crusts onto large platters.

While the first four pizzas bake, roll the remaining balls of dough into crusts. As soon as the first batch of pizzas are off the baking trays, put the second batch on the trays, top away, and bake. In almost no time, the second batch will be out of the oven and ready to eat, too.

note

More pies can be baked simultaneously by lining your oven racks with unglazed clay tiles and preheating them in a 500° oven for about an hour. The pies can then bake directly on the tiles for about 10 minutes.

plenty o' pizza toppings

Here are a few of our favorite ideas to get your creative and appetitive juices flowing. Experiment with wild combinations, if you dare.

for kids

Tomato sauce

Grated cheese: Mozzarella, Parmesan, Romano, Cheddar

Raw vegetables: Sliced tomatoes, peppers, zucchini, mushrooms

Cooked vegetables: Steamed or sautéed spinach, broccoli

Soy sausage, soy pepperoni, vegetarian meatballs (Yves brand is good)

for older kids and adults

All of the above toppings

Pesto, tapenades

Grated or sliced cheeses: Asiago, Fontina, feta, fresh mozzarella, chèvre

Roasted eggplant, roasted garlic cloves

Sautéed or caramelized onions

Sautéed broccoli rabe, escarole, kale, or other greens

Sun-dried tomatoes

Artichoke hearts

Pepperoncini

Pitted olives

Chopped fresh herbs

Anchovies

Shrimp

CLASSIC CARAMEL SAUCE

Browned white sugar has a distinctive, ambrosial flavor and fragrance, and this sauce is rich, sweet, and buttery without using heavy cream. Be sure to use a heavy saucepan to avoid scorching the caramel.

Try the sauce on ice cream, crêpes, waffles, pancakes, bread, or rice puddings, and on poached or baked apples or other fruit.

1	CUP SUGAR
3	TABLESPOONS WATER
1½	TEASPOONS CORNSTARCH
1	CUP HALF-AND-HALF
¼	CUP UNSALTED BUTTER, CUT INTO SMALL PIECES
1	TEASPOON PURE VANILLA EXTRACT

YIELDS 1½ CUPS
TOTAL TIME: 30 MINUTES

In a small heavy saucepan, stir the sugar and water until the sugar is somewhat dissolved. Cook on medium-high heat, uncovered and *without stirring* (resist the urge!), for 10 to 15 minutes, until the syrup begins to turn golden brown, bubbles, and is fragrant.

Meanwhile, in a small bowl, thoroughly mix the cornstarch with 2 tablespoons of the half-and-half and set aside.

When the syrup browns, remove the pan from the heat, and gradually pour in the rest of the half-and-half. The mixture will sputter and hiss and begin to form a solid mass. Immediately return the pan to medium heat, whisking vigorously for 5 to 10 minutes. The sauce may froth and expand, but just keep whisking until the sugar mass melts again and the sauce is a uniform consistency.

When the sauce is smooth, cook and stir for 4 more minutes, until it thickens slightly, then gradually whisk in the butter pieces. When the butter has melted, add the cornstarch mixture, lower the heat, and simmer for 1½ minutes. Remove from the heat and stir in the vanilla.

Serve the sauce warm or chill in a sealed container. The sauce will keep in the refrigerator for up to 4 or 5 weeks. To serve, rewarm it in a double boiler over boiling water, zap it in a microwave oven, or stir it constantly in a saucepan on medium-low heat.

BITTERSWEET CHOCOLATE SAUCE

Chocolate sauce recipes abound and there's probably not a truly bad one among them. Here's one that we're especially partial to for its satiny texture and the depth of the bittersweet chocolate. Leftover sauce keeps well in the refrigerator and can be reheated in a hot water bath or microwave oven.

Bittersweet chocolate is packaged in bars with ½-ounce markings for easy measuring. Supermarkets variably stock these bars in the baking section or the candy aisle, or both. We recommend Ghirardelli, Callebaut, and Hershey's Special Dark.

1	CUP HEAVY CREAM
2	TABLESPOONS UNSALTED BUTTER
¼	CUP LIGHT CORN SYRUP
10	OUNCES BITTERSWEET CHOCOLATE, FINELY CHOPPED*

YIELDS 2¼ CUPS
TOTAL TIME: 10 TO 15 MINUTES

* Or grind it in the bowl of a food processor.

In a small saucepan, combine the cream, butter, and corn syrup. Bring to a boil on medium-high heat. Remove from the heat, add the chocolate, cover, and allow to sit for 5 minutes. Whisk into a uniform, dark, creamy sauce.

This sauce solidifies when refrigerated, so store it in a microwave-safe container or one that can be placed in a hot water bath. One minute in the microwave oven or several in the double boiler will return the chocolate to a sauce.

WET WALNUTS

We have been serving Wet Walnuts on ice cream for as long as Moosewood has been in business. Easy as pie? Way easier.

1½	CUPS TOASTED CHOPPED WALNUTS*
1	CUP PURE MAPLE SYRUP

YIELDS 2½ CUPS
TOTAL TIME: 5 MINUTES

* Toast walnuts on an unoiled baking tray at 350° for about 5 minutes, until fragrant and golden brown.

Stir the nuts into the syrup. Heat in a small saucepan, if desired.

WHIPPED CREAM

We make this foolproof recipe daily at Moosewood—sometimes several times a day, it's so good.

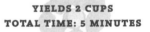

1   CUP HEAVY CREAM
1   TEASPOON PURE VANILLA EXTRACT
2   TABLESPOONS PURE MAPLE SYRUP*

YIELDS 2 CUPS
TOTAL TIME: 5 MINUTES

* Or use 3 tablespoons confectioners' sugar.

Whip the cream in a mixing bowl with an electric or rotary mixer until soft peaks form. Take care not to overbeat or your cream will turn to butter. Fold in the vanilla and maple syrup.

Serve at once or refrigerate for up to 2 days.

sundry sundae toppings

Here are more ideas for topping and decorating ice cream to your heart's content.

Chopped nuts

Salted peanuts

Fresh or frozen (and thawed) berries

Sliced ripe bananas

Sliced ripe peaches

Crushed pineapple

Shredded unsweetened coconut (toasted is nice)

Chocolate chips

Butterscotch chips

Sprinkles

Crumbled cookies

Miniature marshmallows or Fluff

Crumbled pretzels

Miniature candies

GREEK EASTER DINNER PARTY

MENU

Greenest Green Salad
Roasted Baby Artichokes
Vegetable Pastitsio
Baklava with Hazelnuts

Food plays an important part in the observance of religious holidays in many parts of the world. When Moosewood friend Lara Kelingos visited Greece, her grandfather's native country, she brought back stories of some Eastertime festivities there. The devout who follow the Greek Orthodox tradition abstain from eating meat, fish, milk, butter, cheese, and eggs for forty days before Easter Sunday. When it's time to break the fast, the dishes that are offered are beautiful and richly flavored. In some villages, children explode firecrackers outside of the church during midnight Mass. Afterwards, everyone breaks the fast with an abundant feast, dances until dawn, sleeps for a few hours, and gathers again for a delicious late-morning brunch.

In Greece, many of the ingredients used in dishes prepared for Easter feasting have a special significance. Lentils symbolize the tears of the Virgin Mary, wheat signifies everlasting life, almonds and raisins are served to wish guests a sweet life, and pomegranate seeds bespeak a wish for prosperity. Hard-boiled eggs are dyed red to symbolize the blood of Jesus and then baked in the shape of a cross on the top of a lovely braided bread called *tsourek*. People also play a game with the red eggs. They are banged together, end to end, to find the strongest egg, and the person with an uncracked egg is supposed to have good luck in the coming year.

A dinner party with food inspired by a Greek Easter menu is a perfect way to celebrate the arrival of spring in North America. Here we use some traditional ingredients in fresh-tasting spinach salad and lemony baked baby artichokes. Our sumptuous, meatless pastitsio, made with eggplant and lentils, will receive raves, and our baklava features hazelnuts for a new version of a well-known and much-loved dessert.

We have some suggestions to make the preparation of this meal easier and more efficient. The pastitsio can be made a day or so ahead and baked on the day of your dinner party. Or if you prefer, cook the lentils and prepare the béchamel and vegetable sauces ahead of time. Refrigerate everything until you are ready to assemble and bake the casserole.

The hazelnuts for the baklava can be toasted, ground, mixed with the sugar and orange peel, covered with plastic wrap, and stored until you are ready to bake. Put the baklava in the oven after the pastitsio has baked for 20 to 25 minutes. While they bake, prepare and boil the artichokes and make their marinade. When you remove the baklava and pastitsio from the oven, increase the temperature to 450° and roast the artichokes while the pastitsio sets up and the baklava cools. You should have just the right amount of time to prepare the Greenest Green Salad and to cut some tulips and daffodils to decorate your table.

GREENEST GREEN SALAD

We've composed the greenest salad we can imagine—from the spinach to the olives and grapes—to honor spring. The dressing celebrates the classic Greek ingredients yogurt, mint, and dill and includes some of the feathery leaves from the fennel bulb. These often-ignored, subtle, anise-scented fronds can be minced like an herb or used whole as a garnish.

1	FRESH FENNEL BULB WITH FRONDS
1	CUCUMBER
10	OUNCES FRESH SPINACH (8 CUPS, PACKED)
1	CUP WHOLE SEEDLESS GREEN GRAPES
1	CUP PITTED PICHOLINE, MANZANILLA OR OTHER BRINE-CURED GREEN OLIVES

SERVES 6 TO 8
YIELDS 1⅓ CUPS DRESSING
TOTAL TIME: 20 MINUTES

fennel yogurt dressing

⅓	CUP PLAIN LOW-FAT YOGURT
3	TABLESPOONS RED WINE VINEGAR, MORE TO TASTE
2	TABLESPOONS CHOPPED FRESH DILL
2	TABLESPOONS CHOPPED FRESH MINT
2	TABLESPOONS CHOPPED FRESH FENNEL FRONDS
1	TEASPOON SUGAR
½	TEASPOON SALT
⅔	CUP OLIVE OIL

MINT

Slice off the top of the fennel bulb and reserve a few fronds for the dressing. Remove any tough or bruised outer layers from the bulb and then cut it in half lengthwise. Remove the fennel core if it isn't tender, then cut each half crosswise into thin slices. Peel the cucumber, slice it in half lengthwise, scoop out the seeds, and cut the halves crosswise into thin crescents. Toss the cucumber and fennel slices together and set aside.

Stem the spinach, rinse well, and spin or pat dry. Slice the spinach into thin ribbons and arrange on a large serving platter. Scatter the fennel and cucumbers over the spinach, and dot with the grapes and olives.

Combine the yogurt, vinegar, dill, mint, chopped fennel fronds, sugar, and salt in a blender and purée just enough to mix well. While the blender is still whirling, gradually add the olive oil in a thin, steady stream. Purée for about 10 seconds, or until the dressing is pale green and flecked with herbs.

Pass the dressing at the table, or pour it on the salad and toss just before serving. Store extra dressing in a sealed container in the refrigerator.

ROASTED BABY ARTICHOKES

Like their full-sized cousins, baby artichokes make an elegant appetizer or side dish. These babies have a limited season, so think of this dish when the California harvest is rolling in to market. In Ithaca, that's in early spring and again in the autumn.

24   BABY ARTICHOKES

cooking sauce

½   CUP OLIVE OIL

¼   CUP FRESH LEMON JUICE

3   TABLESPOONS BALSAMIC VINEGAR

2   GARLIC CLOVES, MINCED OR PRESSED

2   TEASPOONS GROUND FENNEL SEEDS

¼   TEASPOON SALT

⅛   TEASPOON COARSELY GROUND BLACK PEPPER

SERVES 6 TO 8
PREPARATION TIME: 30 MINUTES
BAKING TIME: 25 MINUTES

Preheat the oven to 450°.

To cook the baby artichokes, bring a large pot of water to a boil. Use a stainless steel knife to cut off the top one-quarter of the artichokes and trim the stems to about an inch. Bend back the outer green leaves and snap them off at the base until you reach the yellow leaves. Trim the remaining green from the base.

Boil the baby artichokes for 10 to 20 minutes, until a leaf can be pulled out easily. Drain upside down. Meanwhile, in a blender or small bowl, mix all of the cooking sauce ingredients until smooth.

In an 8-inch-square glass or stainless-steel baking pan, arrange the drained artichokes upright, side by side, and pour the cooking sauce over them. Roast for 20 to 25 minutes, basting occasionally, until very tender.

VEGETABLE PASTITSIO

This hearty Greek casserole was adapted from a recipe in *The Vegetarian Epicure,* one of our favorite cookbooks in Moosewood Restaurant's early years. We still serve pastitsio regularly, and our customers still love it. It will dirty half of the pans in your kitchen, but we vouch for the fact that it's worth it. To speed things up, make the béchamel sauce or cook the lentils a day ahead.

SERVES 6 TO 8
PREPARATION TIME: 1¼ HOURS
BAKING TIME: 40 TO 50 MINUTES

lentils

- ½ CUP DRIED LENTILS, RINSED
- 3 CUPS WATER
- 1 GARLIC CLOVE
- 1 BAY LEAF

vegetable sauce

- 2 TABLESPOONS OLIVE OIL
- 1 CUP DICED ONIONS
- 2 to 3 GARLIC CLOVES, MINCED OR PRESSED
- 4 CUPS CUBED EGGPLANT (1-INCH PIECES)
- 1 CUP DICED GREEN OR RED BELL PEPPER
- ¼ CUP DRY RED WINE
- 1 TEASPOON GROUND CINNAMON
- ½ TEASPOON DRIED OREGANO
- ½ TEASPOON DRIED MARJORAM
- 3 CUPS UNDRAINED CANNED TOMATOES, CHOPPED (28-OUNCE CAN)
- ¼ CUP CHOPPED FRESH PARSLEY
  SALT AND BLACK PEPPER TO TASTE

noodle layer

- 8 OUNCES WIDE EGG NOODLES
- 2 TEASPOONS OLIVE OIL
- ½ CUP GRATED PARMESAN CHEESE

béchamel sauce

- 3 TABLESPOONS BUTTER
- ¼ CUP UNBLEACHED WHITE FLOUR
- 2 CUPS MILK, HEATED TO JUST BELOW SCALDING
  PINCH OF NUTMEG
- ¼ TEASPOON SALT OR TO TASTE
- 3 EGGS, LIGHTLY BEATEN

cheeses

1   CUP GRATED FETA CHEESE
¼   CUP GRATED PARMESAN CHEESE

In a saucepan, bring the lentils, water, garlic, and bay leaf to a boil. Reduce the heat to low, cover, and simmer for 30 to 40 minutes, until tender. Add water, if necessary, to prevent sticking. When the lentils are tender, remove the garlic clove and bay leaf and drain any excess liquid. Discard the bay leaf. Mash the garlic clove and stir it back into the lentils. Set aside.

While the lentils cook, heat the oil in a large saucepan and sauté the onions and garlic for about 5 minutes, until the onions are translucent. Add the eggplant, bell peppers, wine, cinnamon, oregano, and marjoram; cover and cook on low heat for about 10 minutes, stirring often. Add the tomatoes, parsley, salt, and black pepper and continue to cook on low heat for 15 to 20 minutes, until the vegetables are very tender. Stir the cooked lentils into the vegetable sauce and set aside.

Meanwhile, bring a pot of salted water to a boil, add the egg noodles, and cook for 8 to 10 minutes, until just al dente. Drain and toss with the olive oil and Parmesan cheese. Cover and set aside.

Melt the butter in a small heavy saucepan. Whisk in the flour and cook for 1 to 2 minutes, stirring constantly. Gradually add the hot milk and continue to whisk for several minutes, until the sauce thickens. Remove from the heat, add the nutmeg and salt, and then stir in the beaten eggs. Set aside.

Preheat the oven to 350°. Oil a 3-quart, 9 x 13-inch baking dish.

To assemble the pastitsio, spread half of the vegetable sauce in the bottom of the baking dish. Layer half of the noodles on next and top with half of the feta. Repeat the layers of vegetable sauce, noodles, feta. Evenly spoon all of the béchamel sauce on top and finish with the Parmesan cheese.

Cover and bake for about 25 minutes; then uncover and bake for another 15 to 25 minutes, until bubbly and golden on top.

variation

We use lentils to replace the ground meat traditionally used in pastitsio. Instead of lentils, try simmering 1½ to 2 cups of crumbled firm tofu, diced seitan, or one of the meat substitutes available in natural food stores, such as Gimme Lean, right in the vegetable sauce.

BAKLAVA WITH HAZELNUTS

The popular Greek pastry baklava is made mostly of nuts and layered with papery thin sheets of buttered filo dough to hold it together. It's often cut into diamond or triangle shapes, the center of each piece studded with a whole clove. In this recipe, we use hazelnuts instead of the traditional walnuts or almonds, and we cut the baklava into triangles.

4	CUPS HAZELNUTS
¼	CUP BUTTER
2	TABLESPOONS SUGAR
2	TEASPOONS FRESHLY GRATED ORANGE PEEL
1	TEASPOON GROUND CINNAMON
⅔	POUND FILO DOUGH*
16 to 32	WHOLE CLOVES

YIELDS 16 TRIANGLES
PREPARATION TIME: 1 HOUR
BAKING TIME: 35 TO 40 MINUTES

syrup

2	CUPS WATER
1½	CUPS SUGAR
	SLICED PEEL OF 1 ORANGE
1	WHOLE CINNAMON STICK
2	TABLESPOONS ORANGE JUICE
2	TABLESPOONS MILD HONEY

* You can find 1-pound packages of filo in the frozen foods section of well-stocked supermarkets.

Preheat the oven to 350°.

Spread the hazelnuts on a large unoiled baking sheet and toast them in the oven for about 10 minutes. Remove and set aside to cool. In a small saucepan, melt the butter on low heat and set aside.

When the nuts are cool, knead them in a large tea towel to remove some of the loose skins. In a blender or food processor, finely grind the nuts with the sugar. In a medium bowl, mix together the ground nuts, grated orange peel, and cinnamon and set aside.

Using a pastry brush, lightly brush some melted butter in a 9 x 13-inch glass baking pan. Unfold the filo, lay the stack next to the baking pan, and have the melted butter and the pastry brush nearby. Working quickly, fold a sheet of filo in half crosswise and fit it into the bottom of the pan; trim the edges, if necessary. Brush the top of the folded filo sheet lightly with butter. Layer on 4 more folded and buttered filo sheets. Evenly spread on one-third of the nut mixture and layer 2 more folded filo sheets on top, each brushed with butter. Repeat with one-third of the nut mixture, 2 folded and buttered filo sheets, the remaining one-third of the nut mixture, and, finally, 5 folded and buttered filo sheets.

With a sharp knife, deeply score the baklava in half lengthwise and into quarters crosswise to make 8 rectangles. Then score each rectangle in half on the diagonal to make a total of 16 triangular pieces. Anchor each triangle in the center with 1 or 2 whole cloves. Bake for 35 to 40 minutes, until the top is light brown and somewhat puffed.

While the baklava is baking, heat the water, sugar, orange peel, and cinnamon stick in a small, heavy non-reactive saucepan. Simmer for 15 to 20 minutes, until the syrup thickens a little and is reduced to about 1¾ cups. Cool and strain the syrup. Stir in the orange juice and honey.

When you remove the baklava from the oven, pour the syrup over the top, especially along the scored lines. Before serving, recut the pieces with a sharp paring or serrated knife.

Baklava is best eaten the first day, but it can be covered and stored at room temperature for 3 or 4 days or frozen for up to 1 month.

PASSOVER SEDER

Food is an essential element of every Jewish holiday, but it is especially important during Passover. The flight from Egypt demanded a quickly prepared unleavened bread, or *matzo,* which is the centerpiece of Passover meals. Tradition dictates that no leavened bread or foods made from wheat, barley, rye, oats, or spelt (and legumes, for some Jewish sects), can be eaten, and not even a crumb of these should be found in the cupboards—ensuring a good spring cleaning.

The seder is the ritual meal at which the Passover story is recited by the participants. Specific foods with symbolic meaning for the holiday are arranged on a special seder plate. Salt water is evocative of the tears of slavery. Green herbs, such as parsley, are dipped into the water as a sign of the rebirth of spring. The roasted egg is a universal symbol of emerging life, and a roasted lamb shank is representative of sacrificial offerings at the ancient temple in Jerusalem. Bitter horseradish is a reminder of the difficulty of oppression. And a delicious fruit, nut, and wine mixture, called haroset, recalls the mortar used by the slaves to build the Pharaohs' pyramids. It is traditional to invite guests who are new to the holiday to share in this joyous but bittersweet occasion that acknowledges the strength and fragility of the human condition.

The dietary restrictions of Passover have been the catalyst for an array of dishes that give culinary character to the holiday. In this menu, we've suggested a variety of recipes that include matzo or matzo meal. For a lighter menu, offer either the soup or the casserole along with the delicious Salmon Baked in Parchment (page 216) and finish with one of the Passover desserts. A green salad and Haroset will add refreshing balance to the meal.

A meatless Passover meal can require a bit of preparation. But if everyone who comes brings a part of the meal, then no one person needs to spend a lot of time cooking and there will still be plenty to eat. Just pass out the recipes and write the time of the seder on the calendar.

If you're working alone, however, here's how to prepare our Passover menu. Make the Haroset, the Garlic Peppercorn Stock for the Matzo Ball Soup, and the chilled matzo ball dough the day before. The Hazelnut Chocolate Torte and the fruit filling for the Passover "Brown Bubbie" can also be prepared ahead and stored.

On Passover, first prepare the dishes that will be baked and plan to have them in the oven while the soup broth and matzo balls are cooking. All of the baked dishes use the same oven temperature and will be ready around the same time—give or take 10 minutes. With the stock and matzo ball dough already made, you can bring the pot of salted water to a simmer and simultaneously begin the soup broth in a second pot. The matzo balls and the soup broth will both take about the same amount of time to simmer. While the soup and baked dishes are cooking, toss together a green salad with our Citrus Herb Vinaigrette (page 369).

Set the table, try not to swoon from the awesome aromas as the baked dishes come out of the oven, take off your apron, and wait for the doorbell to ring.

MATZO BALL SOUP

Traditionally served at Passover, this soup is brothy and usually served with few or no vegetables. Our Moosewood version, embellished with carrots, celery, and asparagus, glorifies spring, the season that Passover celebrates.

The matzo ball dough needs to chill for at least an hour or overnight, so get it in the refrigerator before you prepare the ingredients for the soup. You'll still have plenty of time to finish the soup before it's time to simmer the matzo balls.

We leave it to you: Season the matzo balls with your favorite fresh herbs. Our Garlic Peppercorn Stock is absolutely perfect for this soup and we recommend that you make it earlier in the day or the night before. The stock will give you a welcome spring tonic of healthful garlic.

matzo balls

SERVES 6 TO 8
TOTAL TIME: 1½ HOURS

4	EGGS, LIGHTLY BEATEN
3	TABLESPOONS VEGETABLE OIL
2	TABLESPOONS WATER
¼	CUP CHOPPED FRESH HERBS*
1	CUP MATZO MEAL
½	TEASPOON SALT
½	TEASPOON GROUND BLACK PEPPER

soup broth

1	TABLESPOON VEGETABLE OIL
2	CUPS CHOPPED ONIONS
1	CUP CHOPPED CELERY
1	TEASPOON TURMERIC
1	CUP PEELED AND CHOPPED CARROTS
½	TEASPOON DRIED THYME
2	TABLESPOONS CHOPPED FRESH DILL
8	CUPS GARLIC PEPPERCORN STOCK (PAGE 408)
2	CUPS INCH-LONG ASPARAGUS PIECES
1½	TEASPOONS SALT
	GROUND BLACK PEPPER TO TASTE
	DILL SPRIGS (OPTIONAL)

* A mix of dill, parsley, and chives is nice.

In a bowl, beat together the eggs and oil. Whisk in the water until well blended. Stir in the herbs and then add the matzo meal, salt, and pepper. Mix to form a uniform batter. Cover and refrigerate for at least 1 hour.

Meanwhile, warm the oil in a soup pot. Sauté the onions, celery, and turmeric on medium-high heat for about 10 minutes, until the vegetables just begin to soften. Add the carrots, thyme, dill, and stock, cover, and bring to a boil; then lower the heat and simmer for 15 minutes. Stir in the asparagus and salt and cook for 5 minutes, until tender. Add black pepper to taste.

When the matzo dough has almost finished chilling, bring 3 quarts of salted water to a simmer. For the lightest matzo balls, do not roll or shape them. Scoop up chilled batter with a teaspoon (table utensil) and use your finger to carefully push the batter into the simmering water. Repeat until all of the batter is used. Cover the pot and simmer for about 30 minutes, until the balls are firm yet tender.

Spoon several matzo balls into each bowl, ladle on the hot soup broth, and, if you wish, garnish with dill sprigs.

HAROSET

Haroset is a ritual dish served at the Passover seder. It symbolizes the mortar that the Jews used to build the pyramids in Egypt. At a seder, it can be sandwiched between two pieces of matzo along with horseradish or bitter herbs and called a Hillel sandwich—named for Rabbi Hillel, the great Jewish teacher.

Jews from all over the world make haroset from their local ingredients. Our version features apricots and dates, typical of the Sephardic Jews of North Africa.

1	CUP PEELED, CORED, AND DICED APPLES
1	TABLESPOON MILD HONEY
⅓	CUP ORANGE JUICE, PREFERABLY FRESH
3	TABLESPOONS PASSOVER WINE*
½	CUP RAISINS OR DRIED APRICOTS
½	CUP DATES
½	TEASPOON GRATED FRESH GINGER ROOT
½	CUP TOASTED ALMONDS**
½	TEASPOON GROUND CINNAMON
	FRESH LEMON JUICE, TO TASTE (OPTIONAL)

YIELDS ABOUT 2 CUPS
TOTAL TIME: 15 MINUTES

* We like a not-too-sweet red wine, but use the Passover wine of your choice.

** Toast almonds in a single layer on an unoiled baking tray at 350° for 5 to 10 minutes, until fragrant and golden brown.

In a bowl, combine the apples, honey, orange juice, and wine and set aside. In a food processor, briefly pulse the raisins or apricots, dates, ginger root, almonds, and cinnamon, until coarsely chopped. Stir the dried fruit mixture into the apple mixture. Refrigerate until ready to serve. Add a squeeze or two of lemon, if you like.

MATZO CASSEROLE

Cousin to a rich frittata and offspring of matzo brei, this casserole is a welcome part of a multi-dish Passover seder. Or, try it as the main course for lunch. Matzo is available year-round, so enjoy it anytime. Matzo farfel, a crumbled flaked matzo, will make a lighter casserole.

2	TABLESPOONS OLIVE OIL
2	CUPS CHOPPED ONIONS
4	MATZOS OR 2½ CUPS MATZO FARFEL
10	OUNCES FRESH SPINACH, RINSED AND STEMMED
4	CUPS SLICED MUSHROOMS
	DASH OF SALT
1	TABLESPOON CHOPPED FRESH DILL (1 TEASPOON DRIED)
2	TABLESPOONS NEUFCHÂTEL OR CREAM CHEESE
4	EGGS, LIGHTLY BEATEN
½	CUP MILK
½	TEASPOON SALT
¼	TEASPOON GROUND BLACK PEPPER
1½	CUPS GRATED MONTEREY JACK CHEESE

SERVES 6
PREPARATION TIME: 25 MINUTES
BAKING TIME: 30 TO 35 MINUTES

Preheat the oven to 350°. Lightly oil a 9 x 12-inch baking dish.

Heat the oil in a saucepan and sauté the onions for about 10 minutes, stirring occasionally until lightly browned.

Meanwhile, crumble the matzos into 1-inch pieces (or use the farfel), soak in a bowl of water for 2 or 3 minutes, drain, and set aside. Blanch the spinach in a small amount of boiling water for 1 to 2 minutes, until wilted. Drain well, pressing out as much liquid as possible, chop, and set aside.

When the onions are golden brown, add the mushrooms to the saucepan, sprinkle with salt, and cook for 3 to 4 minutes, until softened. Add the blanched spinach, dill, and Neufchâtel and cook for about 3 minutes, stirring to melt the cheese evenly. Cover and remove from the heat.

In a bowl, whisk together the eggs, milk, salt, and pepper and set aside.

Spread half of the soaked matzo in the bottom of the prepared baking dish. On top, layer half of the vegetable mixture. Evenly pour on half of the egg custard and top with half of the cheese. Repeat the layers: matzo, vegetables, custard, cheese.

Bake uncovered for 30 to 35 minutes, until the eggs are set and the casserole is firm.

HAZELNUT CHOCOLATE TORTE

Here is a rich Passover dessert that is scrumptious enough to make any time of the year. The torte's fudgy interior is surrounded by a thin crust, and we serve it right from the baking dish. If you prefer to remove it to a serving plate, be sure to line the baking dish with parchment paper or wax paper—or use an 8-inch springform pan.

1½ CUPS WHOLE HAZELNUTS
⅔ CUP SEMI-SWEET CHOCOLATE CHIPS
1⅓ CUPS SUGAR
⅓ CUP WATER
¼ CUP MATZO MEAL
    PINCH OF SALT
5 LARGE EGGS, SEPARATED*

    FRESH WHIPPED CREAM (OPTIONAL)

SERVES 6 TO 8
PREPARATION TIME: 20 MINUTES
BAKING TIME: 50 TO 55 MINUTES

* The egg whites must not contain even a speck of the yolk to whip properly. If you're using the same beater for the egg whites as for the chocolate mixture, be sure it's clean and dry.

Preheat the oven to 350°. Generously oil an 8-inch-square baking dish.

Toast the hazelnuts in a single layer on an unoiled baking sheet in the oven for 10 minutes, until fragrant and lightly browned. Briskly rub them with a clean towel to partially remove the skins.

While the nuts toast, combine the chocolate, ⅓ cup of the sugar, and the water in a small saucepan. Warm on low heat, stirring often, until the chocolate melts. Set aside. When the nuts are ready, pulse them in the bowl of the food processor until finely ground. Add the matzo meal, salt, and the remaining sugar and process until well mixed.

In a mixing bowl, lightly beat the egg yolks. Stir in the melted chocolate and nut mixtures and set the batter aside. In a separate bowl, beat the egg whites until stiff peaks form. Gently fold about one-third of the beaten egg whites into the batter; then fold in the rest in three batches and pour into the prepared baking dish.

Bake for 50 to 55 minutes, or until the cake pulls away from the sides of the pan and a knife inserted in the center comes out clean.

Serve with lightly sweetened whipped cream, if desired. Covered and stored at room temperature, the torte will keep for up to 4 days.

PASSOVER "BROWN BUBBIE"

Moosewood's Jewish version of brown betty uses matzo meal and no flour or leavening in accordance with Passover dietary guidelines. This is a homey, simple dessert with the ever-loved flavors of fruit, spice, and nuts. The fruit filling, if made ahead, will keep for 1 to 2 days when stored in a sealed container in the refrigerator.

filling

6   CUPS PEELED AND SLICED PEARS
½   CUP SUGAR
½   CUP RAISINS
2   TEASPOONS GROUND CINNAMON
¼   TEASPOON GROUND NUTMEG
1   TABLESPOON FRESH LEMON JUICE

topping

1   CUP MATZO MEAL
⅓   CUP SUGAR
1   CUP CHOPPED TOASTED WALNUTS*
1   TABLESPOON MELTED BUTTER OR VEGETABLE OIL
1   TEASPOON PURE VANILLA EXTRACT
¼   TEASPOON SALT

* Toast walnuts in a single layer on an unoiled baking tray at 350° for about 5 minutes, until fragrant and golden brown.

SERVES 6 TO 8
PREPARATION TIME: 20 MINUTES
BAKING TIME: 40 MINUTES
COOLING TIME: 15 MINUTES

Preheat the oven to 350°. Lightly oil an 8 x 10-inch glass baking pan.

In a bowl, combine all of the filling ingredients and pour them into the prepared pan. In a separate bowl, mix together all of the topping ingredients. Sprinkle the topping evenly over the filling.

Bake, uncovered, for 40 minutes, or until the fruit is tender and the topping is slightly browned. Cool for at least 15 minutes before serving. Enjoy, bubbeleh.

MOTHER'S DAY TEA

MENU

Mimosas, champagne punch, or herbal iced tea
Smoked Salmon Spread
Spring Green Salad with creamy chive dressing
Bell Pepper & Asparagus Frittata
Green Beans with Shallots
Chocolate Angelfood Cake

Believe it or not, Mother's Day is not the invention of a greeting card or florist cartel. On the contrary, mothers have been honored for millennia both as individuals and as symbols. The Greeks and Romans each held an annual spring festival dedicated to their respective deities, Rhea and Cybele: The divine mothers of their pantheons of immortals. With the spread of Christianity, this tribute to a maternal icon of protection and spiritual nourishment transmuted into a holy day honoring Mary and the Mother Church. By the 1600s in England, the celebration was an amalgam called Mothering Sunday, observed on the fourth Sunday of Lent.

The practice on Mothering Sunday was to visit one's mother parish on that day, but it was more notably seen as an opportunity for servants and apprentices to make their often long trips home to visit their mothers. They brought with them small tokens of affection and, usually, a "mothering cake." Mothering cakes differed across Great Britain. Some were sweet grain puddings, like rice puddings, only made with wheat. Some were savory pancakes, like the Scottish "Carlings." Others were steamed, baked, and iced fruitcakes called "simnel cakes."

The most direct antecedents of our American Mother's Day are rooted in the efforts of three nineteenth-century women. Each championed a holiday that would express and recognize concerns that they believed were most urgently felt by mothers. Pacifist and poet Julia Ward Howe called for a Mother's Day when women would speak out for peace, and she held annual Mother's Day meetings at her home in Massachusetts. Anna Reese Jarvis of rural West Virginia organized a yearly "Mother's Work Day" as a way to increase public awareness of the poor health conditions in her Appalachian community. To honor her mother's work and the work of mothers everywhere, it was Ms. Jarvis's daughter, also named Anna, who led the lobbying effort of businessmen, community leaders, and congressmen to establish Mother's Day as a national holiday, which it became with the signing of a 1914 congressional bill.

So make this meal for your mother on Mother's Day, but don't stop there. Why wait another year to tell your mom how much she means to you? Have a Mother's Day feast whenever you have the chance to be together and feel like celebrating.

This "tea" can be taken at any time of day: brunch, lunch, or supper. The Smoked Salmon Spread and the Chocolate Angelfood Cake can be made a day ahead. Just remember to bring the spread to room temperature before serving. The Spring Green Salad can be made while the frittata is baking in the oven.

SMOKED SALMON SPREAD

Smoking adds a wonderful, almost enigmatic, dimension to food. A small bit of a smoked ingredient in a recipe seems to satisfy a not-oft-discussed, culinary appetite for mystery. Many supermarkets carry 8-ounce containers of smoked nova salmon pieces, which are a good deal less expensive than a whole piece of smoked salmon or lox.

This spread is an elegant starter on crostini, assorted crackers, or party-sized pumpernickel or rye bread. Or, serve it at the brunch table with bagels. We recommend a mini-food processor for making this spread most easily.

8	OUNCES SMOKED SALMON, CUT INTO SMALL PIECES
½	CUP UNSALTED BUTTER, SOFTENED
½	CUP NEUFCHÂTEL CHEESE
2	TABLESPOONS CHOPPED FRESH CHIVES
2	TABLESPOONS CHOPPED FRESH TARRAGON
4 to 6	TEASPOONS FRESH LEMON JUICE
2	TEASPOONS PREPARED WHITE HORSERADISH
⅛	TEASPOON GROUND BLACK PEPPER OR TO TASTE

YIELDS 1½ CUPS
TOTAL TIME: 15 MINUTES

Process all of the ingredients in a mini-processor, food processor, or blender until smooth and, well, salmon-colored (see Note). Serve immediately or store in a closed container in the refrigerator.

If made ahead of time, it's best to remove the spread from the refrigerator an hour before serving and bring to room temperature. When cold, the spread has the consistency of cold butter; at room temperature it's luscious and creamy.

Covered and refrigerated, the spread will keep for up to 4 days. For longer storage, you can freeze it for up to 1 month; then bring to room temperature and stir well before serving.

note

If you use a blender, you'll need to stop and scrape down the sides several times to reach a smooth consistency.

SPRING GREEN SALAD

Tender lettuce greens, watercress, and herbs are the main event in this salad, so we decided not to upstage it by adding any other salad fixings. A touch of dressing and it's complete. Then again, if you crave contrast, prop a few radish roses on the border of each salad. What's Mother's Day without roses?

creamy chive dressing

SERVES 4
YIELDS ¾ CUP DRESSING
TOTAL TIME: 15 MINUTES

2	TEASPOONS RED WINE VINEGAR
3	TABLESPOONS WATER
¼	CUP SOUR CREAM
¼	TEASPOON SUGAR
⅛ to ¼	TEASPOON SALT
⅛	TEASPOON GROUND BLACK PEPPER
6	TABLESPOONS VEGETABLE OIL
2	TABLESPOONS SNIPPED CHIVES

salad

4	CUPS BABY LETTUCE, A MIXED ASSORTMENT
2	CUPS WATERCRESS OR ARUGULA, TOUGH STEMS REMOVED
1½	TABLESPOONS CHOPPED FRESH TARRAGON
2	TABLESPOONS CHOPPED FRESH DILL
8	RADISHES (OPTIONAL)*

* To make radish roses, neatly slice away the top greens and root end. Then cut a deep "X" into the radish top, but stop just short of cutting all the way through its bottom end. Immerse the radishes in iced water; they'll open in about 45 minutes.

Combine the vinegar, water, sour cream, sugar, salt, and pepper in a blender. Purée briefly, then add the oil in a gradual steady stream, until the dressing is uniform and creamy. Stir in the chives. Pour the dressing into a cruet and, if not using immediately, chill it in the refrigerator.

Rinse all of the greens; then pat or spin dry. Toss with the herbs and serve on individual plates, in a shallow wooden bowl, or on a medium-sized platter. Decorate with radish roses, if you like.

Pass the dressing at the table.

BELL PEPPER & ASPARAGUS FRITTATA

Here's a rich, flavorful frittata that can be cooked on the stove top (moister) or in the oven (airier). We couldn't decide which one was better, and we know you'll want to make this frittata more than just once, so here are both methods. Maybe *you* can choose a favorite.

6	EGGS
½	CUP RICOTTA CHEESE
2	TABLESPOONS WATER
1	TABLESPOON CHOPPED FRESH PARSLEY
1	TABLESPOON CHOPPED FRESH MARJORAM (1 TEASPOON DRIED)
1	TEASPOON SALT
¼	TEASPOON GROUND BLACK PEPPER
2	CUPS ASPARAGUS PIECES (½-INCH LENGTHS)*
2	TEASPOONS OLIVE OIL
1	LARGE RED OR YELLOW BELL PEPPER, CUT INTO ¼-INCH MATCHSTICKS
½	CUP DIAGONALLY SLICED SCALLIONS
¼	CUP GRATED PARMESAN CHEESE

SERVES 4 TO 6
PREPARATION TIME: 30 MINUTES
STOVE-TOP COOKING TIME: 15 MINUTES; OR BAKING TIME: 30 MINUTES

* About 1 pound of asparagus trimmed and chopped will yield 2 cups.

In a large bowl, whisk together the eggs, ricotta, water, parsley, marjoram, salt, and black pepper. Blanch the asparagus in boiling water to cover for 2 to 3 minutes. Drain and plunge into cold water, then drain again and set aside.

Heat the oil in a 10-inch ovenproof skillet on medium-high heat and sauté the bell peppers for about 7 minutes, stirring often. Add the scallions and continue to cook for 1 more minute, until crisp-tender. Stir in the asparagus.

Now choose either the stove-top or oven method and proceed.

Stove-top Method: Stir the egg mixture into the sautéed vegetables, cover, and cook on medium-high heat for 5 minutes. Preheat the broiler. Reduce the stove burner's heat to low and continue to cook until the frittata is almost set, 5 to 10 minutes more. Sprinkle the Parmesan on the top of the frittata and place under the broiler for 1½ to 2 minutes, until bubbly and beginning to brown. Loosen with a spatula, slide onto a plate, and serve immediately.

Oven Method: Preheat the oven to 350°. Transfer the sautéed vegetables to an oiled 9-inch-square baking dish. Pour the egg mixture over the vegetables and sprinkle the Parmesan on top. Bake for about 30 minutes, until golden and set. Cool on a rack for a few minutes before serving.

GREEN BEANS WITH SHALLOTS

The shallot crisps, which top the green beans, can be made several hours ahead, but don't leave them where they will tempt your guests, or they might disappear before you've had a chance to cook the beans.

The beans may be served hot or at room temperature. When serving them hot, add the shallot crisps at the last minute; otherwise, the hot beans will steam and soften the shallots and eliminate their appealing, crunchy contrast.

1   CUP VEGETABLE OIL
3½   CUPS SLICED SHALLOTS (ABOUT 1 POUND)*
2   POUNDS GREEN BEANS, STEMMED
1   TABLESPOON OLIVE OIL
       SALT AND GROUND BLACK PEPPER TO TASTE

* Cut them into thin rings.

SERVES 8
TOTAL TIME: 40 MINUTES

Bring a large covered pot of salted water to a boil.

Meanwhile, warm the oil in a large cast iron skillet until very hot, but not smoking. Add the shallots and fry for 2 to 4 minutes, stirring frequently, until evenly golden brown. If your skillet isn't large enough to hold all of the shallots in a single layer, fry the shallots in two batches. Pay close attention: If even a few get too dark too fast, all of them can taste burned.

Pour the shallots and oil through a fine mesh strainer or remove the shallots from the oil with a slotted spoon. Reserve the flavorful oil for another use. Spread the shallots on paper towels to drain and crisp. Set aside at room temperature until ready to serve the beans.

When the water boils, cook the green beans until tender, 5 to 8 minutes. Drain the beans, place them in a serving bowl, and sprinkle them lightly with the olive oil, salt, and pepper.

Serve hot or at room temperature, topped with the shallot crisps.

CHOCOLATE ANGELFOOD CAKE

Dark and chocolaty, yet light as foam, this cake served with fresh, chunky strawberry sauce is a perfect surprise for Mother's Day. Although the balsamic vinegar is optional, it deepens the color of the strawberries in a rather amazing way, making them glisten like jewels. The cake can be made one day, cooled and wrapped, and then enjoyed the following day.

The loftiness of an angelfood cake depends on beating the egg whites with utensils that are spotless and free of oil. Store the yolks in a closed container in the refrigerator and use within 2 or 3 days for custard or hollandaise sauce, or add 1½ teaspoons of salt or sugar per cup of yolks and freeze for up to several months in an ice cube tray wrapped in plastic (for easy retrieval of small amounts).

This cake really requires a pan with a removable bottom. Otherwise, you'll have to carve the cake out of the pan, which will ruin the presentation, although it'll taste just as good.

cake

⅓	CUP UNSWEETENED COCOA POWDER
¾	CUP UNBLEACHED WHITE PASTRY FLOUR*
½	TEASPOON SALT
1½	CUPS SUGAR
12	EGG WHITES, AT ROOM TEMPERATURE (2 CUPS)**
1	TEASPOON CREAM OF TARTAR
1	TEASPOON PURE VANILLA EXTRACT

SERVES 12
PREPARATION TIME: 25 MINUTES
BAKING TIME: 45 TO 50 MINUTES
COOLING TIME: 1½ TO 2 HOURS
EQUIPMENT: 10-INCH TUBE PAN WITH A REMOVABLE BOTTOM

strawberry topping

1	QUART STRAWBERRIES, RINSED AND HULLED
¼	CUP SUGAR
½	TEASPOON BALSAMIC VINEGAR (OPTIONAL)

* Milled from soft wheat, pastry flour, with its low protein content, gives baked goods an especially tender crumb.

** The egg whites must not contain even a speck of the yolk to whip properly. So crack an egg in half crosswise and carefully slip its yolk (without breaking it) from one half of the shell to the other, as the whites drain off into a bowl. To bring the eggs to room temperature, place them in a bowl, cover them with warm water, and allow to soak for about ½ hour.

Preheat the oven to 350° and place the oven rack in the bottom third of the oven.

Sift the cocoa, flour, salt, and ¾ cup of the sugar into a large bowl and set aside. In another very large bowl, beat the egg whites until thick and foamy. Add the cream of tartar and vanilla and continue beating until soft peaks form. Scrape down the sides of the bowl. Then beat in, a little at a time, the remaining ¾ cup of sugar at high speed, stopping only occasionally to scrape the sides of the bowl.

When the whites are glossy and stiff, gently fold in the sifted ingredients with a large wire whisk until well incorporated into the whites. The batter should be soft and fluffy. Pour the batter into a tube pan with a removable bottom.

Bake for 45 to 50 minutes, until the top of the cake springs back slightly when touched. Remove the cake from the oven, immediately turn it upside down on a rack, and cool completely.

When cool, loosen the cake by carefully running a knife around all of the edges. Hold the removable center piece to lift and separate the cake from the bottom. Transfer the cake onto a flat serving platter. Cover tightly with plastic wrap until ready to serve.

About an hour before serving the cake, slice the strawberries. Transfer one-third of the berries to a bowl and add the sugar and, if you wish, the vinegar. Mash well with a large spoon. Stir in the rest of the sliced strawberries and allow the sauce to sit for at least an hour.

Cut the cake gently with a serrated knife using a sawing motion. Serve each slice with a generous spoonful of the strawberry topping.

CINCO DE MAYO

Tamale Pie
Stewed Cardoons
Nopalitos Salad
Black Bean & Citrus Salad
Strawberry Chocolate Quesadillas

Mexicans love a party! There are literally hundreds of Mexican festivals packed into each calendar year, and Cinco de Mayo, or the Fifth of May, is one of the most widely celebrated. Today, Mexicans in both Mexico and the United States participate in activities organized for this day of remembrance. For those proud of Mexico's heritage, the holiday has become much more than just an excuse to party.

Exactly how you celebrate Cinco de Mayo depends on where you live. In the neighborhood of Peñón de los Baños in Mexico City, there is a re-enactment of the 1862 battle in which the outnumbered and poorly equipped Mexican soldiers, under the leadership of General Zaragoza, held the forts at Puebla de Los Ángeles, Mexico, against Napoleon III's French navy. In other towns throughout Mexico, families, children, and teens gather to make music, dance, and play games. Rows of street vendor stalls line the roads near the town squares, or *zócalos,* and the unmistakable aroma of *mole poblano,* a thick, spicy sauce representative of Mexican cuisine, is everywhere. Popular mariachi bands and shows add to the widespread gaiety. People make noise or keep rhythm with whistles, horns, and rattles. Often circus-style fairs are set up with rides and games of luck or skill.

Many U.S. cities also come alive on Cinco de Mayo. In Los Angeles, as many as 500,000 people of Mexican descent gather in the streets outside City Hall to join in the all-day event, in which Mexican dignitaries are guests of honor. The red, white, and green of the Mexican flag is echoed in colorful decorations as well as in vibrant traditional costumes that include ruffled dresses, fancy vests and knickers, and wide full-circle skirts. Mexican orchestras, famous musicians, and local bands play both Mexican patriotic songs and popular dance music. Trained performers and novices alike show off their footwork and expertise with castanets.

In San Francisco, the holiday has developed into a festival that honors Mexican nationalism. Pageants, speeches, songs, and parades are all in Spanish, and the celebrants emphasize "La Raza," "Bronze Culture," and the homeland of the Aztlán—the ancient Aztec domain of northern Mexico and the U.S. Southwest. Children take part in theatrical plays written for the occasion, and throngs of Mexican Americans attend the festivities at the city's Civic Center. The song lyrics of "Cielito Lindo" certainly describe the joyous sentiment of the day: "Sing, don't cry. For with singing, the heart becomes happy."

On Cinco de Mayo, people either patronize their favorite Mexican restaurants, go to parks with picnic baskets of Mexican food, or invite family or friends to gather at home for dinner. So if you'd like to celebrate in style, try out this tasty Mexican menu. With a little advance preparation, it's a cinch. The Black Bean & Citrus Salad only improves with age, so make it a day or two ahead. Choose either the Stewed Cardoons or the Nopalitos Salad and whip together the dish while the Tamale Pie is baking. Have the ingredients for the quesadillas handy, but be sure to let everyone have a breather before dessert. Serve the Strawberry Chocolate Quesadillas straight out of the pan with a good strong coffee or rich espresso.

TAMALE PIE

Anna Thomas says of this authentic Mexican dish, ". . . it's a delicious casserole and has its own place in the culinary scheme of things." We agree. Whether you like it spicy hot or mild, it's a luscious combination of flavors and textures.

Cut both types of potatoes into ¾-inch cubes; a consistent size ensures even cooking. While the vegetables simmer, you can prepare the wet and dry topping ingredients in separate bowls and have them ready. That way, when the vegetable stew is finished, you just mix the topping together and bake.

You'll need a 10-inch skillet or a baking dish at least 8 inches square for this casserole. If you use an ovenproof skillet for cooking the stew, it can go straight from the stove to the oven—a one-pot preparation that can't be beat.

Serve topped with your favorite salsa, sour cream, and slices of ripe avocado sprinkled with fresh lemon juice and salt.

SERVES 6
PREPARATION TIME: 50 MINUTES
BAKING TIME: 30 TO 35 MINUTES

pie

2	CUPS CHOPPED ONIONS
2 or 3	GARLIC CLOVES, MINCED OR PRESSED
½	TEASPOON SALT
1	MINCED FRESH GREEN CHILE, SEEDED FOR A MILDER "HOT" *
1	TABLESPOON VEGETABLE OIL
2	TEASPOONS GROUND CUMIN
2	CUPS WATER
1	CUP STEMMED AND DICED GREEN BEANS
2	CUPS CUBED POTATOES
2 to 3	CUPS PEELED AND CUBED SWEET POTATOES**
1	TABLESPOON FRESH LIME OR LEMON JUICE
1	CUP GRATED CHEDDAR CHEESE

topping

1	CUP CORNMEAL
2	TABLESPOONS UNBLEACHED WHITE FLOUR
1½	TEASPOONS BAKING POWDER
½	TEASPOON BAKING SODA
½	TEASPOON SALT
½	CUP FRESH OR FROZEN CORN KERNELS
½	CUP DICED RED BELL PEPPERS
2	TABLESPOONS MINCED FRESH CILANTRO

2	EGGS, BEATEN
½	CUP BUTTERMILK
2	TABLESPOONS VEGETABLE OIL

* Or use 2 teaspoons minced chipotles in adobo sauce, which are smoked hot peppers in a spicy thick tomato purée.

** Or use carrots or butternut squash.

Preheat the oven to 350°. If you're not using an ovenproof skillet, lightly oil an 8-inch-square baking pan.

In an ovenproof skillet or soup pot, sauté the onions, garlic, salt, and chile in the oil until the onions start to brown, about 10 minutes. Stir in the cumin. Add the water, green beans, potatoes, and sweet potatoes and bring to a boil. Reduce the heat and simmer for about 20 minutes more, until the vegetables are tender. Stir in the lime or lemon juice, transfer the stew to the prepared baking pan, if using, and sprinkle on the cheese.

In a bowl, stir together the cornmeal, flour, baking powder, baking soda, salt, corn, bell peppers, and cilantro. In a separate bowl, combine the eggs, buttermilk, and oil. Fold the wet ingredients into the dry ingredients just until mixed. Pour the topping over the stew and cheese and spread to cover evenly.

Bake for about 30 minutes, until a knife inserted in the topping comes out clean. Serve hot.

PARTY

STEWED CARDOONS

Silvery green cardoons look a little like giant, slightly spiny celery with 12- to 25-inch stalks, but they're actually members of the thistle family and related to artichokes, which they resemble in taste. Cardoons are a popular offering in South America, France, and Italy. They are appearing more often now in the United States in well-stocked supermarkets.

Cooking cardoons as suggested in most traditional recipes is a load of work. They're often boiled for as long as 2½ hours, then floured and fried, and *then* oven-braised with a cheese or cream sauce. We've considerably simplified both the ingredients and the procedure for a much easier dish that allows the mild, artichoke-like flavor to shine through.

1	BUNCH CARDOONS (2½ TO 3 POUNDS)
½	FRESH LEMON
1	TABLESPOON SALT
2	TEASPOONS OLIVE OIL
2	GARLIC CLOVES, MINCED OR PRESSED
3½	CUPS STEWED TOMATOES (TWO 14.5-OUNCE CANS)
½	CUP SLICED BLACK OLIVES
2	TEASPOONS CAPERS
1	TEASPOON DRIED OREGANO
	PINCH OF HOT PEPPER FLAKES, MORE TO TASTE

SERVES 6
PREPARATION TIME: 25 MINUTES
FINAL SIMMERING TIME:
20 MINUTES

Bring a large pot with 5 quarts of water to a boil.

Meanwhile, trim the base of the cardoons. Discard tough, fibrous, wilted, or discolored outer stalks and the small leafy inner stalks. With a paring knife, strip away the top leaves and any green jagged leaves on the edges of the healthy stalks. Remove any fibrous strings from the larger ribs, just as with celery. Slice the larger ribs in half lengthwise and rub any cut edges with the lemon half. Cut the stalks into 2-inch pieces.

Squeeze the lemon into the heating water and add the salt. When the water boils, add the cardoons, lower the heat to a rapid simmer, and cook for 15 to 20 minutes, until tender—a skewer or thin sharp knife should easily pierce the cardoons.

While the cardoons cook, make the sauce in a pot large enough to hold them. Heat the olive oil and sauté the garlic for 1 minute, until golden. Stir in the tomatoes, olives, capers, oregano, and hot pepper flakes. Keep the sauce warm on low heat. When the cardoons are tender, drain them in a colander. Stir them into the sauce and simmer gently for 20 minutes.

NOPALITOS SALAD

Nopalitos are small pads, or leaves, of the pear cactus. They are very popular in Mexico, where they are part of the traditional cuisine and are sold both fresh and in jars. We sauté the cactus pads lightly in olive oil and season them with lemon, jalapeño, and cilantro to make a refreshing and delicious salad.

Serve plain or on fresh, crisp greens.

8	OUNCES FRESH NOPALITOS*
2	TABLESPOONS OLIVE OIL
	DASH OF SALT
2	RIPE TOMATOES, CHOPPED
½	CUP CHOPPED SCALLIONS
1	JALAPEÑO OR OTHER CHILE, MINCED AND SEEDED FOR A MILDER "HOT"
2	TABLESPOONS CHOPPED FRESH CILANTRO
2	TABLESPOONS FRESH LEMON JUICE

SERVES 6
TOTAL TIME: 30 MINUTES

* If you can't find fresh nopalitos, look in the Mexican section of the supermarket for nopalitos strips in jars or cans and drain them. Most nopalitos in markets are already cleaned and spineless. If yours aren't, use a potholder mitt to hold the nopalitos and shave the needles out with a sharp knife: Slice in the direction that the spines are pointing.

Remove the spines from the nopalitos, if necessary. Rinse the nopalitos and cut them into long strips. In a skillet, heat 1 tablespoon of the oil, add the nopalitos, and sprinkle with salt. Sauté on medium heat until the nopalitos are tender and beginning to deepen in color, about 5 minutes.

In a bowl, stir together the sautéed nopalitos, the remaining tablespoon of oil, the tomatoes, scallions, chile, cilantro, and lemon juice.

BLACK BEAN & CITRUS SALAD

This delicious salad is a favorite at Moosewood Restaurant, and it's a good dish-to-pass item, too. The vegetable-bean combo with its tart citrus bite is especially refreshing on a warm day. More and more people are realizing the value of regularly including low-fat, protein-rich beans in their diets. This is one great way to add them to your usual weekly repertoire.

3	CUPS COOKED BLACK BEANS (TWO 15-OUNCE CANS)
1	CUP FRESH, FROZEN OR CANNED CORN KERNELS
1	TOMATO, CUBED
½	CUP CHOPPED RED ONION
1	RED BELL PEPPER, SEEDED AND DICED
2	ORANGES, PEELED, SECTIONED AND CUT INTO SMALL PIECES*
1	GRAPEFRUIT, PEELED, SECTIONED AND CUT INTO SMALL PIECES*
1	RIPE HASS AVOCADO, CUBED**
½	CUP CHOPPED FRESH CILANTRO
1	CUP COOKED RICE (OPTIONAL)

SERVES 6
TOTAL TIME: 30 MINUTES

dressing

¼	CUP FRESH LIME JUICE
2	TABLESPOONS FRESH LEMON JUICE
2	GARLIC CLOVES, PRESSED OR MINCED
3	TABLESPOONS VEGETABLE OIL
1	TABLESPOON GROUND CUMIN
½	TEASPOON SALT

* Use a sharp knife to slice off the peel, including the white pith. Working over a bowl, slice toward the center along the membrane on one side of a section and then flick the knife up the membrane on the other side to release the section.

** Slice around the avocado lengthwise, twist the halves apart, and remove the pit. Carefully cut the flesh into cubes right in the skins and scoop out with a spoon.

Rinse and drain the beans. Blanch the corn in boiling water to cover for 3 to 5 minutes, until just tender. Drain well. In a large bowl, toss together the beans, corn, tomatoes, onions, bell peppers, orange and grapefruit pieces, avocado cubes, cilantro, and rice, if using. In a small bowl, whisk together all of the dressing ingredients. Toss the salad with the dressing.

Serve right away or refrigerate. Black Bean & Citrus Salad will keep, covered, in the refrigerator for 3 or 4 days.

STRAWBERRY CHOCOLATE QUESADILLAS

This simple dessert can be created in almost no time at all. If fresh strawberries are not available, use canned pineapple instead. We suggest eating these charmingly gooey delights with a knife and fork!

3	CUPS THINLY SLICED FRESH STRAWBERRIES
½	TEASPOON GROUND CINNAMON
¼	CUP CONFECTIONERS' SUGAR
6	FLOUR TORTILLAS (8 INCHES ACROSS)
	VEGETABLE OIL
¾	CUP CHOCOLATE CHIPS

SERVES 6
TOTAL TIME: 15 MINUTES

Combine the strawberries, cinnamon, and 3 tablespoons of the confectioners' sugar in a bowl. Leaving a ½-inch border at the edges, spread half a cup of the strawberry mix on one half of each of the tortillas.

Brush two large heavy skillets with oil and heat until hot but not smoking. Place one tortilla in each skillet and put 2 tablespoons of the chocolate chips on the plain half of each tortilla, leaving a border of about 1½ inches at the edges. Cook for about 2 minutes, until the chocolate melts. Fold the tortilla in half and press the edges together with a spatula. Remove the quesadillas from the skillets and repeat the procedure with the remaining two pairs.

Serve immediately, dusted with the remaining confectioners' sugar and sliced in half.

ANY TIME

OF YEAR

While some festive foods smack of a particular season, there are others that we eat all year-round, never mind the weather. Depending upon where you live and your personal preferences, you probably have your own set of year-round special foods.

We consider this "Any Time of the Year" section a little treasure trove of extras—dishes that come in handy as part of a larger menu or as solo snacks or even as gifts. Most use ingredients that are likely to be accessible nationwide during any season whatsoever. The section is arranged in three parts:

1. Appetizers, Dips & Dressings
2. Eight More Cakes
3. Food as a Gift.

Browse through all of the recipes. Maybe you love the Greek Easter Dinner Party menu, but you'd like an appetizer, too. Green Skordalia could be just the ticket! Looking for a dressing that will utilize your just-before-the-frost herb harvest? Check out the Dressings for Every Season. Use this section to add flexibility to your celebratory menu planning or just pluck up a single recipe to try on the spur of the moment. And, yes, that recipe for Dog Biscuits is for real (for dogs, that is), although if it happens to be April Fool's Day . . .

APPETIZERS, DIPS & DRESSINGS

In almost any menu, the addition of either finger foods or a simple soup or salad is always welcome. So here's a smattering of eclectic recipes that we wouldn't want you to be without. These little dishes can add that final touch to a festive spread. You'll find two soups, six hors d'oeuvres as different as can be, seven distinctive dips, one luscious topping, and over a half-dozen dressings.

Although soup is sometimes the main component of a luncheon or simple supper, it also makes a great starter for what's to come. Serve the soup in discrete portions in small glass bowls or decorative china. Here we've included recipes for one refreshing cold soup and one hot brothy one, which can be dressed up with noodles or enjoyed without. Use them to suit your taste as a complement to any meal.

Appetizers are bite-sized finger foods that stave off hunger and whet the appetite. Although small, they're often "pretty as a picture" or, as the translation of the French *hors d'oeuvres* suggests, miniature works of art. They can also make great snacks or act as a side dish to a light meal. Dips are especially versatile and can be eaten with crudités, spread on crackers or toast, stuffed into a pita pocket or baguette, or used to complete a salad combo plate.

We have developed some dressings tied to specific seasons by their ingredients and others that you'll want to make almost any time. All of them take only minutes to whip up. A perky green salad or fresh steamed vegetable can come alive instantly with just a drizzle of the right dressing. If you keep a few ready-to-go in the fridge, they'll be there the moment a spark of inspiration strikes. Choose a dressing that complements the main dish you plan to serve. Having a hearty stew? Try a light lemony dressing. Cheesy casserole? Maybe a fruity dressing would be nice. Serving low-fat stuffed vegetables? A savory dressing is a must.

Each recipe has our suggestions for a variety of ways to use it, and we're sure you'll come up with many more ideas of your own. Finishing touches to a menu can make all the difference in the world. That extra bit of caring never goes unnoticed.

LIGHT SAFFRON FISH SOUP

Our simple, saffron-scented, Provençal-style tomato broth is divine when just cooked: The tomatoes still have that fresh smack and the scallions and parsley are still bright green. Nevertheless, it makes a great leftover and can become a full meal when ladled on rice vermicelli or angel hair pasta.

Different pastas require different cooking times, so check the directions on the package and read our note on cooking rice vermicelli. You should plan to begin cooking the pasta so that it's cooked, drained, and still quite warm when the soup is ready.

Try any fresh, inexpensive, or seasonal fish at your seafood counter—trout, flounder, tilapia, haddock, scrod—you get the idea.

2	TABLESPOONS OLIVE OIL
2	CUPS DICED ONIONS
2	GARLIC CLOVES, MINCED OR PRESSED
¼	TEASPOON DRIED THYME
1	TEASPOON SALT
3	CUPS WATER
1	POUND SKIN-ON FISH FILLETS, BONES REMOVED
2	CUPS CHOPPED FRESH TOMATOES
	GENEROUS PINCH OF SAFFRON
2	TABLESPOONS MINCED SCALLIONS
2	TABLESPOONS MINCED FRESH PARSLEY
	SALT AND GROUND BLACK PEPPER TO TASTE

SERVES 6 TO 8
TOTAL TIME: 40 MINUTES

8 to 10 OUNCES ANGEL HAIR PASTA OR RICE VERMICELLI* (OPTIONAL)
    LEMON OR LIME WEDGES

* Dried rice vermicelli, often called rice sticks or rice noodles, are thin, string-like noodles sold in 8- or 14-ounce cellophane-wrapped packages. Look for them in Asian markets or in the Chinese section of supermarkets.

In a covered soup pot on medium-low heat, warm the olive oil and then cook the onions, garlic, thyme, and salt until the onions are very soft, about 15 minutes. Add the water and bring to a boil.

Ease in the fillets and simmer until the fish flakes easily off the skin, 5 to 10 minutes, depending on the type and thickness of the fish. With a slotted spoon, transfer the fillets to a bowl and remove and discard the skin. Return the fish pieces to the soup and add the tomatoes, saffron, scallions, and parsley. Simmer for about 5 minutes. Add salt and pepper to taste.

If using, cook the angel hair pasta until al dente or the rice vermicelli (see Note). Whichever noodle you use, it should be ready when the soup is done. Divide the pasta into individual, shallow, wide bowls and ladle on the soup.

Be sure everyone squeezes fresh lemon or lime juice on their portion before digging in.

note

Package directions often say to just soak the noodles in water, but we've discovered it's best to immerse the noodles in a large pot of boiling water and as soon as the water returns to a boil, remove the pot from the heat. Let the vermicelli sit for about 5 minutes, until al dente. Then drain in a colander.

If you have any leftover cooked rice noodles, toss them with a little oil, cover, and store in the refrigerator. To reheat, immerse the noodles briefly in boiling water.

AVOCADO ORANGE SOUP

This soup is all about texture. Its velvety, rich creaminess is a perfect counterpoint to spicy dishes. If you like, serve from a large glass bowl to show off the soup's cool, light green color and let your guests serve themselves in espresso or demitasse cups for perfect-sized portions.

4	AVOCADOS, PREFERABLY HASS
2	TEASPOONS SALT
4	TEASPOONS SUGAR, MORE TO TASTE
¼	CUP FRESH LEMON JUICE
3	CUPS NONFAT PLAIN YOGURT
1	CUP REDUCED-FAT COCONUT MILK*
1	QUART ORANGE JUICE
¾	TEASPOON GROUND CINNAMON
¾	TEASPOON GROUND CARDAMOM

SERVES 8
TOTAL TIME: 25 MINUTES

TOASTED UNSWEETENED GRATED COCONUT (OPTIONAL)**

* Sometimes, no matter how vigorously you shake the can of coconut milk, it remains separated. If that happens, pour the contents into a bowl and whisk until smooth.

** To toast coconut, spread it on an unoiled baking tray and toast at 350° in a toaster or conventional oven for 2 to 3 minutes, until lightly golden.

Slice the avocados lengthwise around the center, twist the halves apart, and remove and discard the pits. Score the avocado flesh of each half in a crisscross pattern right in the skin, and then scoop out the cubes with a spoon into a large bowl. Add all of the remaining ingredients. Purée in batches in a blender until smooth.

Serve cold, garnished with coconut, if desired.

TWO OLIVE HERB SPREADS

These piquant and crunchy spreads are great for crackers and can add pizzazz to your favorite sandwiches. They are also wonderful as a filling for toasted pita pockets or crêpes. We especially like them in socca, a Provençal-style crêpe made with chickpea flour, which Moosewood cook Kip Wilcox introduced to the rest of us about ten years ago.

YIELDS ABOUT 3½ CUPS
OF EACH SPREAD
TOTAL TIME:
15 TO 20 MINUTES

kalamata & sun-dried tomato

⅔   CUP SUN-DRIED TOMATOES, SOFTENED*
1   CUP CHOPPED FRESH TOMATOES
1   LARGE GARLIC CLOVE
1   TABLESPOON OLIVE OIL
1   TABLESPOON MINCED FRESH ROSEMARY
1   CUP PITTED KALAMATA OLIVES
½   CUP CHOPPED TOASTED ALMONDS**

green olive & cilantro

1½   CUPS PITTED GREEN OLIVES
½   CUP PACKED CHOPPED FRESH CILANTRO
½   CUP PACKED CHOPPED FRESH PARSLEY
1   CUP CHOPPED TOASTED PECANS OR WALNUTS**
1   LARGE GARLIC CLOVE
3   TABLESPOONS OLIVE OIL
2   TABLESPOONS FRESH LEMON JUICE
⅛   TEASPOON CAYENNE, OR TO TASTE

* In a heatproof bowl, cover the sun-dried tomatoes with boiling water, soak for about 15 minutes, until softened, then drain.

** Toast nuts in a single layer on an unoiled baking tray at 350° for 5 to 10 minutes, until fragrant and golden brown.

For each spread, place all of the ingredients in the bowl of a food processor and whirl until well blended. Stored in a sealed container, each spread will keep for up to 10 days. Serve at room temperature.

BAKED EGGPLANT DIP

This Middle Eastern–style dip was inspired by a spread served at Brous & Mehaffey, one of Ithaca's most popular gourmet delis and bakeries. Simple yet lively, our eggplant dip is a good candidate for crudités and sesame crackers, and it makes a delectable filling for a pita pocket.

It's also tempting as a sauce on hot pasta topped with fresh mozzarella or as a dressing for a chilled chunky pasta salad made with fusilli or farfalle.

2	EGGPLANTS (ABOUT 1 POUND EACH)
2	TABLESPOONS OLIVE OIL
½	TEASPOON SALT, OR TO TASTE
¼	CUP SUN-DRIED TOMATOES (NOT OIL-PACKED)
2	CUPS CHOPPED ONIONS, PREFERABLY VIDALIA OR RED ONIONS
2	GARLIC CLOVES, MINCED OR PRESSED
1	TABLESPOON GROUND CUMIN
1½	CUPS CHOPPED FRESH TOMATOES
2	TABLESPOONS FRESH LEMON JUICE
¼	CUP CHOPPED FRESH PARSLEY
	PINCH OF GROUND BLACK PEPPER

YIELDS 4 CUPS
TOTAL TIME: 1 HOUR

Preheat the oven to 450°.

Cut each eggplant in half lengthwise, brush the pulp with a little of the olive oil, and sprinkle lightly with salt. Place the halves face up in a baking pan. Bake, uncovered, for 35 to 45 minutes, until very soft. Remove from the oven to cool.

While the eggplant bakes, soak the sun-dried tomatoes in boiling water to cover for about 15 minutes, until softened. Meanwhile, heat the remaining oil in a medium skillet and sauté the onions until translucent, about 10 minutes. Add the garlic and cumin and sauté for 1 to 2 more minutes.

Drain and chop the sun-dried tomatoes. Add them with the fresh tomatoes and a little salt to the skillet and cook on medium heat for 4 minutes, until the tomatoes become saucy. Remove from the heat.

When the eggplant halves are cool enough to handle, scrape the flesh away from the skin into a small bowl. Discard the skin. In a food processor or in batches in a blender, purée the eggplant with the tomato mixture and the lemon juice. Transfer to a bowl, add the parsley and pepper, and mix well. Add more salt to taste.

Serve at room temperature or refrigerate and serve chilled.

ASIAN BEAN CURD SPREAD

This invigorating spread is spicy with Chinese mustard and ginger and deepened with hoisin sauce and dark sesame oil. It's at its best when made with silken tofu and chilled for 15 to 20 minutes before serving. It can be served immediately, however, and soft tofu will also work.

Chinese hot mustard is available as both a powder and a paste. We recommend finding a powder with just one unadulterated ingredient: mustard powder. It's easy to mix with water and tastes like real Chinese mustard. We haven't liked the flavor of the pastes we've tried, and most contained a lot besides mustard flour: Vinegar, sugar, salt, wheat flour, garlic, oil, and spices—and, unfortunately, additives and preservatives. So shop around and find a powder or good-quality paste that you like. Its flavor makes or breaks this dish.

We make our spread in a food processor, but it's also very easy to use a potato masher—and then, if you want a smoother consistency, purée the mashed spread in a blender.

Serve with vegetable sticks, rice cakes, or sesame crackers.

1	TABLESPOON CHINESE MUSTARD POWDER
1 to 1½	TABLESPOONS WATER
1	CAKE SILKEN OR SOFT TOFU (16 OUNCES), CRUMBLED
1	TABLESPOON HOISIN SAUCE*
1	TABLESPOON SOY SAUCE
1	TEASPOON DARK SESAME OIL
1	TEASPOON GRATED FRESH GINGER ROOT, MORE TO TASTE
¼	CUP FINELY CHOPPED SCALLIONS
	BLACK SESAME SEEDS (VERY PRETTY)

YIELDS GENEROUS 2 CUPS
TOTAL TIME: 15 MINUTES

* For a slightly different flavor, replace the hoisin sauce with plum sauce.

Mix together the Chinese mustard powder and enough of the water to make a soft paste. Combine the tofu, hoisin sauce, soy sauce, sesame oil, ginger root, and Chinese mustard in the bowl of a food processor. Whirl until creamy, stopping to scrape down the sides with a spatula if necessary. Add the scallions and whirl briefly just to mix. Add more ginger root to taste.

Spoon into a serving bowl and stir in or top with black sesame seeds.

variation

This recipe, made with silken tofu, can double as a tasty dressing for greens or vegetables. Just add 1 tablespoon of rice vinegar and 1 tablespoon of water.

GREEN SKORDALIA

Skordalia, sometimes seen spelled Skorthalia, is a pungent Mediterranean garlic paste, and it's like aioli's counterpart in the world of potatoes. The mashed potatoes provide a base for the raw garlic, much like the mayonnaise in aioli does. This wonderful concoction can be spread on little toasts as simple hors d'oeuvres, whisked into soups for added zing, dolloped on steaming hot vegetables, or served as a dip for crudités. It also makes a nice sandwich spread (hold the mayo).

While most skordalias are white and sometimes flecked with bits of green herbs, this skordalia is bright green thanks to the addition of nutritious kale, which we blend right in. Skordalia is most often served at room temperature or slightly warmed.

2 CUPS IDAHO OR RUSSET POTATOES, PEELED AND QUARTERED (ABOUT 1 POUND)

3 to 4 CUPS STEMMED AND CHOPPED KALE

6 to 8 GARLIC CLOVES, MINCED OR PRESSED (OR FEWER FOR THE FAINT-HEARTED)

¾ CUP PLAIN NONFAT YOGURT

¼ CUP OLIVE OIL

2 TABLESPOONS WHITE WINE VINEGAR*

1 TABLESPOON FRESH LEMON JUICE

1 TEASPOON SALT

⅛ TEASPOON GROUND BLACK PEPPER

½ CUP FINELY CHOPPED ALMONDS OR PINE NUTS (OPTIONAL)

* If white wine vinegar is unavailable, red wine vinegar will work, too.

YIELDS ABOUT 3½ CUPS
TOTAL TIME: 40 MINUTES

Place the potatoes in a large saucepan, cover with plenty of water, cover the pan, and bring to a boil on high heat. When the water boils, reduce the heat to medium-low, cover, and simmer for 25 to 30 minutes, until soft.

Meanwhile, blanch the kale in boiling water for 5 to 7 minutes, until very tender. Drain and set aside.

When the potatoes are soft, drain them, reserving the cooking liquid. Mash the potatoes and add them to the food processor (see Note) with the steamed kale, garlic, yogurt, olive oil, vinegar, lemon juice, salt, and pepper. Process to a smooth, thick, spreadable paste, adding a little of the reserved cooking liquid only if needed. Transfer to a serving bowl, and stir in or top with the nuts, if desired.

Depending on the size of your food processor, you may need to process the skordalia in batches.

If using a blender, it's batches for sure. First purée all of the ingredients except the mashed potatoes and the nuts to make a smooth sauce. In two or three batches, combine the potatoes and sauce in the blender. Add reserved cooking liquid as needed, stopping to scrape down the sides of the blender with a spatula. Purée until well mixed.

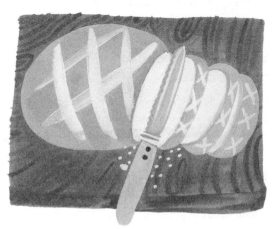

FILO BITES

While filo pastry is not a traditional Chinese ingredient, we love the way it complements the gingery broccoli-tofu-black bean filling in this dish. Our recipe makes twenty-four bite-sized triangular pastries. If you want to serve one large pastry per person as a main dish, you can fold two stacked whole filo sheets neatly in half lengthwise and use ½ cup of filling per triangle.

1½ CUPS CHOPPED CHINESE BROCCOLI*

1 CAKE FIRM TOFU, CRUMBLED (12 OUNCES)

½ CUP FINELY CHOPPED SCALLIONS

2½ TABLESPOONS CHINESE BLACK BEAN SAUCE*

2 TEASPOONS GRATED FRESH GINGER ROOT

2 TABLESPOONS DARK SESAME OIL

2 TABLESPOONS VEGETABLE OIL

⅔ POUND FILO PASTRY (12 X 17-INCH SHEETS)

1 TABLESPOON SESAME SEEDS

SERVES 12 AS AN APPETIZER
PREPARATION TIME: 40 MINUTES
BAKING TIME: 25 TO 30 MINUTES

* Chinese broccoli and Chinese black bean sauce are available in well-stocked super-markets or Asian groceries. Use only the tops and tender stems of the broccoli. If Chinese broccoli is unavailable, use regular broccoli or broccoli rabe.

In a saucepan, blanch the broccoli in about 1 cup of lightly salted boiling water until just tender, about 4 or 5 minutes. Drain. While the broccoli is cooking, combine the tofu, scallions, black bean sauce, and ginger root in a bowl. Stir in the drained broccoli and mix well.

Preheat the oven to 350°. Lightly oil a baking sheet.

Combine the sesame oil and vegetable oil in a small bowl. Unfold 12 sheets of filo on a clean, dry working surface. With kitchen shears, cut all of the filo sheets lengthwise into quarters and make a stack of the forty-eight 3 x 17-inch strips. Have the filling, the oil, and a pastry brush nearby (see Note). Take two filo strips from the stack and orient them short side facing you. Brush the top strip with oil. Place 2 tablespoons of filling at the near end of the stacked strips. Fold the lower left corner of the filo strips up and over the filling, so the bottom edge is flush with the right side and forms a triangle. Keep folding as you would a flag, to make a triangular pastry. Brush both sides with a little oil, place seam-side down on the pre-pared baking sheet, and sprinkle with a few sesame seeds.

Repeat to make twenty-four pastries in all. Bake for 25 to 30 minutes, until puffy and golden. Serve at once, while hot and crispy.

note

Unoiled filo becomes brittle once exposed to air, so work quickly in a draft-free spot or keep a damp towel on the not-yet-used filo while you work. A new inexpensive 2-inch paintbrush works great as a filo pastry brush.

TWO DIPPING SAUCES

These sauces are perfect for our Filo Bites. They can be quickly and easily prepared and add zest to any Asian-style meal. Stir them into plain rice or a soup or stew that needs a little flavor boost. A little sauce can make a big difference.

scallion sauce

¼	CUP MINCED SCALLIONS
1	TABLESPOON GRATED FRESH GINGER ROOT
2	TABLESPOONS PEANUT OR OTHER LIGHT OIL
2	TABLESPOONS RICE VINEGAR
½	TEASPOON SALT, OR TO TASTE

YIELDS ½ CUP
TOTAL TIME: 10 MINUTES

In a small bowl, whisk together all of the ingredients. Add salt to taste and serve.

hot & sweet sauce

2	TABLESPOONS SOY SAUCE
2	TABLESPOONS WATER
2	TEASPOONS DARK SESAME OIL
2	TEASPOONS RICE VINEGAR
2	SPLASHES OF HOT PEPPER SAUCE OR ½ TEASPOON CHINESE CHILI PASTE WITH GARLIC (OPTIONAL)
1	TEASPOON SUGAR

YIELDS ⅓ CUP
TOTAL TIME: 5 MINUTES

In a small bowl, combine all of the dipping sauce ingredients and serve.

SWEET POTATO POT STICKERS

Dumplings that are sautéed after simmering do tend to stick to the bottom of a wok or skillet—hence, the name pot stickers. But sautéing really enhances the flavor, so just be sure to keep them moving.

A smooth, gingery, spicy-hot sweet potato filling contrasts pleasantly with the crunch of water chestnuts in these Chinese-style dumplings. They're good with our Two Dipping Sauces (page 359) or as wontons in a brothy soup. After trying them, you may just end up as stuck on pot stickers as we are!

Our recipe fills about 30 wonton wrappers. If you don't want to stuff and cook them all at once, the filling will keep in the refrigerator for 2 to 3 days. Boiled pot stickers can be frozen for up to 3 or 4 months, then thawed and stir-fried whenever the urge arises.

filling

YIELDS ABOUT 30
TOTAL TIME: 70 MINUTES

2½	CUPS PEELED AND CUBED SWEET POTATOES
1	TABLESPOON GRATED FRESH GINGER ROOT
1	GARLIC CLOVE, MINCED OR PRESSED
½	CUP DICED WATER CHESTNUTS
¼	CUP MINCED SCALLIONS
½	TEASPOON CHINESE CHILI PASTE WITH GARLIC
½	TEASPOON SALT
1	TWELVE-OUNCE PACKAGE WONTON WRAPPERS (ABOUT 50)
1 to 2	TABLESPOONS CORNSTARCH
	VEGETABLE OIL, FOR STIR-FRYING

Bring the sweet potatoes and enough water to cover to a boil in a small saucepan. Cover and cook until soft, about 10 minutes. Drain and mash thoroughly. Combine with the ginger root, garlic, water chestnuts, scallions, chili paste, and salt. Set aside.

Prepare a dry work surface. Arrange nearby a stack of wonton wrappers covered with a damp cloth, a small bowl of water, a baking sheet dusted with the cornstarch, and a clean dry cloth.

Place each wrapper on the dry surface with one of the corners pointing toward you (a diamond shape). Mound a scant tablespoon of filling just below the center of the wrapper. Dip a finger in the water and moisten its two upper edges. Take the bottom point up to the top point to form a triangle and press gently to seal the moistened edges. Arrange the pot stickers on the baking sheet with a little space between them and cover with the dry cloth.

Bring a large pot of salted water to a boil and ease in about 15 pot stickers —or more if you have a giant pot. Return the water to a simmer and cook just until the dumplings float to the top. Remove with a sieve and drain well. Repeat with the remaining pot stickers (see Note).

Quickly stir-fry the pot stickers in a hot wok or heavy skillet with about a tablespoon of oil for each batch. Fry just long enough to make them crispy and golden brown. Serve at once.

note

At this point, the pot stickers can be stored in the refrigerator for 2 to 3 days before you complete their cooking by stir-frying them. Place them on a platter with a little space between them to prevent their sticking together and cover with plastic wrap.

VEGETABLE-WRAPPED SUSHI ROLLS

You can make colorful, bite-sized, sushi without nori. We like using thin, 3- to 4-inch-long slices of carrot and unpeeled cucumber as wrappers.

1	RECIPE UMEBOSHI SUSHI INGREDIENTS (PAGE 70)	
8	CARROTS, PEELED	
6	UNWAXED CUCUMBERS, UNPEELED	

SERVES ABOUT 16
TOTAL TIME: 1½ HOURS

Make the rice mixture as described on page 70. Meanwhile, blanch and chop the spinach. Dice the bell pepper and avocado (forget about matchsticks) and blanch the bell pepper pieces for about 2 minutes, until bright red. Stir the lemon juice, umeboshi plum paste, and all of the chopped vegetables into the cooked rice mixture. Set aside.

Trim the ends from the carrots and cucumbers. Slice them lengthwise to get four thin but sturdy 4-inch-long slices from each carrot or cucumber. Blanch the slices in lightly salted boiling water for about 1 minute, until just pliable. Be sure not to overcook them.

If your vegetable slices aren't as wide as you'd like your roll to be, overlap two slices side by side to create the size desired. Shape the rice filling into small cylinders and wrap the vegetable slices around them. Place them on a serving platter seam side down.

Offer the dipping sauce on the side.

TOFU ALMOND BALLS

These tofu balls are the essence of simplicity: Little gems of protein you'll want to gobble right up. Serve them to tofu skeptics with pasta and tomato sauce for a rapid change of attitude or try them in a pita, on a salad, or as a simple snack.

Since they don't require any bread crumbs to bind them, they are suitable for folks on wheat-free diets. If you like ground fennel, use our suggested amount; if you're not sure, use a bit less to start.

⅔	CUP ALMONDS
1	TABLESPOON OLIVE OIL
2	CUPS DICED ONIONS
3	GARLIC CLOVES, MINCED OR PRESSED
1	TEASPOON SALT
1½	TEASPOONS GROUND FENNEL, OR TO TASTE
½	TEASPOON GROUND BLACK PEPPER
1	CAKE FIRM TOFU (16 OUNCES), PRESSED*
¼	CUP CHOPPED FRESH BASIL, PACKED

YIELDS 24 SMALL BALLS
PREPARATION TIME: 25 TO 30 MINUTES
BAKING TIME: 30 TO 40 MINUTES
COOLING TIME: 5 MINUTES

* Sandwich the tofu between two plates and rest a heavy weight (can or book) on the top plate. Press for about 15 minutes; then drain the expressed liquid from the bottom plate.

Preheat the oven to 400°. Generously oil a baking sheet.

Spread the almonds on an unoiled baking sheet and bake in the oven until fragrant and toasted, about 5 to 7 minutes. Cool for a few minutes, then grind them in a food processor or a blender until finely chopped. Set aside.

In a small saucepan, warm the oil. Add the onions, garlic, salt, fennel, and pepper. Cover and cook on low heat for 10 to 15 minutes, stirring occasionally. When the onions are juicy and very soft, remove them from the heat and set aside.

Mash the tofu in a bowl with a potato masher or crumble and squeeze it with your hands. Mix in the seasoned onions, ground almonds, and basil. Shape the mixture into balls using ⅛ to ¼ cup for each one and place them on the prepared baking sheet.

Bake for 30 to 40 minutes, until firm and golden brown. To help them hold their shape better, cool on the baking sheet for 5 minutes before removing.

PUFF PASTRY CHEESE STRAWS

Next time you serve a soup or salad, add some novelty with these cheese straws. Twisted puff pastry is automatically festive-looking, the "straws" taste great, and they are unquestionably a clever idea for a party appetizer. It doesn't take long to make enough for either several small meals or one large get-together.

1	SHEET OF FROZEN PREPARED PUFF PASTRY*
½	CUP GRATED PARMESAN CHEESE
2	TABLESPOONS CHOPPED FRESH BASIL
1	GARLIC CLOVE, MINCED OR PRESSED

YIELDS ABOUT 20 STRAWS
PREPARATION TIME: 45 MINUTES
BAKING TIME: ABOUT 10 MINUTES

* **Find frozen puff pastry in the supermarket freezer aisle near the frozen breads and desserts.**

Allow the puff pastry to thaw at room temperature for about 20 minutes.

Preheat the oven to 425°. Lightly oil a baking sheet.

In a small bowl, mix together the Parmesan, basil, and garlic. Place the sheet of puff pastry on a lightly floured surface and sprinkle evenly with half of the cheese mixure. With a rolling pin lightly dusted with flour, gently roll the cheese into the pastry dough. Fold the pastry sheet in half lengthwise, sprinkle on the rest of the cheese mixture, and roll it into the surface to form a rectangle about 5 inches wide. Cut the pastry sheet crosswise into about ten ½-inch-wide strips. Separate each strip into its two layers to make 20 strips.

Twist each strip several times and place on the baking sheet. Bake for 8 to 10 minutes, until golden. Cool on the baking sheet for a minute and then transfer to a wire rack to cool completely.

Stored in an airtight container, the cheese straws will keep for several days.

BASIL

FRIED SAGE LEAVES

Large, fresh sage leaves coated in batter and fried are an unusual and delicious Italian appetizer, nice with a glass of Chianti or dry white wine. Figure on five or six leaves per person: They go down easy and can disappear quickly. The batter can be made 2 to 3 hours before you actually fry the leaves; cover and refrigerate until you're ready to cook.

batter

SERVES 6 TO 8
TOTAL TIME: 45 TO 50 MINUTES

1	EGG
1	CUP ICE WATER
1	TEASPOON CORNSTARCH
1	CUP UNBLEACHED WHITE FLOUR
1	TEASPOON SALT
¼	TEASPOON GROUND BLACK PEPPER
1	TEASPOON FRESHLY GRATED LEMON PEEL (OPTIONAL)

2 to 3 CUPS VEGETABLE OIL FOR FRYING*

36 to 40 FRESH SAGE LEAVES (1 TO 3 INCHES LONG, RINSED AND THOROUGHLY DRIED)

* The oil used for frying the shallot crisps in Green Beans with Shallots (page 335) can be reused here, if you wish.

Beat the egg in a bowl and stir in the ice water. Add the cornstarch, flour, salt, and pepper and stir briskly with a fork until smooth. If you wish, stir in the grated lemon peel. Set aside until the rinsed leaves are dry enough to fry.

Pour 1½ to 2 inches of oil into a heavy 7-inch saucepan or skillet, and warm on medium-high heat until hot but not smoking, 350° on a candy thermometer.

Dip the sage leaves, four at a time, into the batter and drop them into the hot oil. The oil will bubble and crackle. Fry the leaves for about 45 seconds on each side, until golden brown, being careful not to splash the oil as you turn them over. Remove them with tongs or a slotted spoon and place on paper towels to drain. Repeat in batches with the remaining leaves.

Serve hot or warm.

SAGE
LEAVES

CASHEW CREAM

Here's our version of a rich vegan treat served at Millennium restaurant in San Francisco. Use it as you would sour cream: To add creaminess to a sauce, to garnish a stew or soup, and as a dip.

⅔ CUP TOASTED CASHEWS*
1 TABLESPOON LIGHT MISO
2 TABLESPOONS FRESH LEMON JUICE
⅔ to 1 CUP WATER
  SALT TO TASTE

YIELDS ¾ CUP
TOTAL TIME: 5 TO 10 MINUTES

* Toast cashews in a single layer on an unoiled baking tray at 350° for 3 to 5 minutes, until fragrant and golden brown.

In a food processor or, preferably, a blender, purée the nuts, miso, lemon juice, and enough of the water to make a smooth, desirable consistency. Add salt to taste.

Chill for 30 minutes before serving. Cashew Cream keeps refrigerated in a tightly covered container for 4 or 5 days.

ANCHOVY DRESSING

Those of us who eat fish at Moosewood occasionally get an irresistible urge for anchovies. When that happens, this dressing can really satisfy. It's assertive and lemony, with the bold, unapologetic flavor of those small, herringlike sea fish. So if the penchant for anchovies strikes you, try this out. Serve on well-rinsed mesclun or a mixture of other beautiful lettuces. It's important to spin or pat dry the lettuce so that the dressing will coat the greens well.

4 to 10 ANCHOVY FILLETS, DRAINED*
1 GARLIC CLOVE, MINCED OR PRESSED
¾ CUP EXTRA-VIRGIN OLIVE OIL
¼ CUP FRESH LEMON JUICE

YIELDS 1 CUP
TOTAL TIME: 5 TO 10 MINUTES

* A 2-ounce can holds eight to ten fillets. If you like, add the anchovies to the blender one at a time until you reach the strength you prefer. We like using the entire can.

Combine the anchovy fillets, garlic, oil, and lemon juice in a blender and purée until completely smooth. Stored in a sealed container in the refrigerator, the dressing will keep for up to 1 week.

NO-EGG CAESAR DRESSING

Fans of thick, creamy salad dressing, rejoice! This rich-tasting dressing, sharp and perky with garlic, mustard, and lemon, is as smooth and pleasingly unctuous as can be. It's a tasty alternative to traditional Caesar dressing and has less cholesterol. If you have nori on hand, its briny flavor will add that "essence of the sea" quality, and you won't miss the anchovies a bit. Although the seaweed is optional, we really urge you to try it.

In addition to its distinctive dressing, the traditional Caesar salad is composed of roughly torn romaine and croutons. Baby romaine is becoming increasingly available at the market and is also a nice option.

YIELDS ABOUT 1 CUP
TOTAL TIME: 10 TO 15 MINUTES

½   CUP SOFT CRUMBLED TOFU*

¼   CUP FRESH LEMON JUICE

3   TABLESPOONS GRATED PARMESAN OR ROMANO CHEESE

2   GARLIC CLOVES, MINCED OR PRESSED

1   TABLESPOON FINELY CRUSHED TOASTED NORI (OPTIONAL)**

1½ TEASPOONS WORCESTERSHIRE SAUCE (PAGE 403)

½   TEASPOON DIJON MUSTARD

¼   TEASPOON SALT

    GROUND BLACK PEPPER TO TASTE

⅓   CUP OLIVE OIL

* Soft tofu works best here: It blends smooth yet has body.

** Dried nori, which is usually pressed into thin sheets and packaged, can be found in most Asian markets and the ethnic section of well-stocked supermarkets. Half of a standard 8 x 7-inch sheet will yield 1 tablespoon finely crushed. Toast the nori by waving it for a minute or less over a gas flame or candle; then crumble it with your fingers and/or crush with a mortar and pestle into tiny pieces that resemble ground black pepper.

In a blender or food processor, purée the tofu, lemon juice, Parmesan cheese, garlic, nori, if using, and the Worcestershire sauce, mustard, salt, and pepper until well combined. Gradually drizzle in the oil in a thin steady stream and continue to purée until smooth and thick.

This eggless dressing will keep in a sealed container in the refrigerator for about a week.

DRESSINGS FOR EVERY SEASON

Here are a range of tasty, distinctive vinaigrettes, each with a particular ingredient or emphasis that makes it shine. Some of them use the specialty oils and vinegars that are in every supermarket these days. Branch out and try a few of them. Drizzle these dressings on a variety of greens and jot down the pairings you like best.

ZIPPY SOUTHWEST DRESSING (autumn)

Here's a unique dressing one of us invented while at Bodhi Manda Zen Center in New Mexico. It uses some ingredients popular in the southwestern United States. The spicy jalapeño pepper gives this vinaigrette a real lift, making it especially good on potato salads and pasta salads. For a milder "hot," just remove the seeds from the jalapeño. If you can't find champagne vinegar or don't happen to have any on hand, red wine vinegar will work fine, too.

½	CUP OLIVE OIL
¼	CUP NONFAT PLAIN YOGURT
1	TABLESPOON CHAMPAGNE VINEGAR
1	TABLESPOON FRESH LEMON JUICE
1	JALAPEÑO PEPPER, DICED
2	TABLESPOONS CHOPPED FRESH MINT*
1	TABLESPOON CHOPPED FRESH CILANTRO
½	TEASPOON GROUND CUMIN
½	TEASPOON GROUND CORIANDER
½	TEASPOON SALT
½	TEASPOON FRESHLY GRATED LEMON PEEL (OPTIONAL)

YIELDS ABOUT 1 CUP
TOTAL TIME: 10 MINUTES

* Or use a scant tablespoon of dried mint. The contents of 1 peppermint tea bag works surprisingly well.

Combine the oil, yogurt, vinegar, lemon juice, jalapeño, mint, cilantro, cumin, coriander, and salt in a blender and purée until smooth. If you wish, stir in the lemon peel. Refrigerated in a sealed container, this dressing will keep for up to a week.

SAVORY SHALLOT VINAIGRETTE (winter)

The shallots never completely disappear in this dressing, even with lots of blending—and that's that. They provide a sweet-savory accent that complements the clean taste of the champagne vinegar. Whirl the dressing in a blender before serving to evenly distribute the shallots.

3   TABLESPOONS PEELED AND DICED SHALLOTS
½   TEASPOON CHOPPED FRESH MARJORAM
¼   TEASPOON FRESH THYME LEAVES
⅔   CUP OLIVE OIL
3 to 4 TABLESPOONS CHAMPAGNE VINEGAR
1   TEASPOON SUGAR
½   TEASPOON SALT
     GROUND BLACK PEPPER TO TASTE

YIELDS 1 SCANT CUP
TOTAL TIME: 15 MINUTES

In a saucepan, sauté the shallots and herbs in a little of the oil for 3 to 5 minutes on medium-high heat. Stir constantly, until the shallots begin to brown. Purée them with the remaining oil, 3 tablespoons of the vinegar, the sugar, salt, and pepper for about 30 seconds. Add vinegar to taste. The dressing will keep, refrigerated, for up to 5 days.

CITRUS HERB VINAIGRETTE (spring)

Refreshing and light, this dressing relies on the bright flavor of fresh oranges, lemons, and herbs. The specialty oil adds a lovely but subtle nutty undertone.

½   CUP OLIVE OIL
2   TABLESPOONS HAZELNUT OR WALNUT OIL
¼   CUP ORANGE JUICE
2   TABLESPOONS FRESH LEMON JUICE
2   TEASPOONS CIDER VINEGAR
1   TABLESPOON CHOPPED FRESH PARSLEY
1   TABLESPOON CHOPPED FRESH TARRAGON
2   TEASPOONS CHOPPED FRESH CHIVES
¼ to ½ TEASPOON SALT TO TASTE

YIELDS ABOUT 1 CUP
TOTAL TIME: 15 MINUTES

Combine the oils, citrus juices, and vinegar in a blender and purée until smooth. Whisk in the herbs and salt. Shake well before serving. Refrigerated in a sealed container, this dressing will keep for 4 or 5 days.

RASPBERRY MINT VINAIGRETTE (summer)

Mint adds a subtle undertone to this light, fruity dressing and gives it a pleasant cooling effect on the palate. The mint flavor deepens with time. If you prefer pure raspberry flavor and color, omit the mint and it's just as delicious. This vinaigrette is gorgeous on greens.

⅓	CUP FRESH OR FROZEN RASPBERRIES
¼	CUP RASPBERRY VINEGAR
⅔	CUP VEGETABLE OIL
1	TEASPOON SUGAR
¼	TEASPOON SALT
	DASH OF GROUND BLACK PEPPER, MORE TO TASTE
1	TABLESPOON FRESH MINCED MINT (OPTIONAL)

YIELDS 1 CUP
TOTAL TIME: 10 MINUTES

Combine the raspberries, vinegar, oil, sugar, salt, and pepper in a blender and purée until smooth. If you wish, stir in the mint. Refrigerated in a sealed container, this dressing will keep for up to a week.

MELLOW MISO VINAIGRETTE (year-round)

Here's the perfect dressing for a salad that's part of an Asian menu, and it's a great choice for vegans as well. The miso provides a rich, salty flavor and contains highly beneficial digestive enzymes. If you prefer the sesame seeds to be less prominent, crush them in a spice grinder or with a mortar and pestle before adding them to the blender. Use this versatile vinaigrette to transform yesterday's leftover side vegetables into today's delicious lunch salad.

¾	CUP PEANUT OIL
¼	CUP RICE VINEGAR
2	TABLESPOONS LIGHT MISO
2	GARLIC CLOVES, MINCED OR PRESSED
1	TEASPOON FRESHLY GRATED GINGER ROOT
1	TEASPOON TOASTED SESAME SEEDS

YIELDS 1 CUP
TOTAL TIME: 10 TO 15 MINUTES

Combine all of the ingredients in a blender and purée until quite smooth. Refrigerated in a sealed container, this dressing will keep for at least a week. Shake or reblend just before serving.

BUTTERMILK VINAIGRETTE (year-round)

If fresh dill is in season or if it's available at the supermarket or in your kitchen herb pot, then it's a good time to try this creamy dressing.

YIELDS 1 CUP
TOTAL TIME: 10 MINUTES

- ⅓ CUP BUTTERMILK
- 1 TABLESPOON RED WINE VINEGAR
- 1 TEASPOON HORSERADISH
- 1 TABLESPOON CHOPPED FRESH DILL
- 1 TABLESPOON CHOPPED SCALLIONS
- ½ TEASPOON SUGAR
- ¼ TEASPOON SALT
- ⅛ TEASPOON GROUND BLACK PEPPER, OR TO TASTE
- ½ CUP VEGETABLE OIL

Briefly purée the buttermilk, vinegar, horseradish, dill, scallions, sugar, salt, and pepper in a blender for about 10 seconds. With the blender still on, gradually add the oil in a thin steady stream, until the dressing is smooth and creamy. Refrigerated in a sealed container, this dressing will keep for 4 or 5 days.

THYME

EIGHT MORE CAKES

Winemaker's Grape Cake
Brown Sugar Poundcake
Chocolate Ganache Birthday Cake
White Chocolate & Fig Poundcake
Vegan Chocolate Gingerbread
Frosted Carrot Cupcakes
Almond Cake with Peaches
Chocolate Pudding Cake

"If I knew you were comin',
I'd have baked a cake,
baked a cake,
baked a cake!"

Want to make today a special occasion? Well, then, bake a cake! A pie may be nice, pudding is pleasant, we all like cookies, and yet, it's cake that signals a truly festive event. So here we've gathered recipes for six more of our favorite cakes. Some, like Chocolate Ganache Birthday Cake, are big and impressive-looking and will feed a crowd. Others, like Vegan Chocolate Gingerbread or Frosted Carrot Cupcakes, are fun, fast, and less fancy. They all taste great and none of them is difficult to make. The simpler ones can be dressed up with your best frosting or glaze and decorated with flowers or whatever reflects the occasion.

WINEMAKER'S GRAPE CAKE

Inspired by the breads and cakes traditionally served during grape harvests in Italy and France, this light, not-too-sweet cake features the fruits of the harvest: Grapes, wine, and olive oil.

3	CUPS SEEDLESS PURPLE OR RED GRAPES, STEMMED
4	EGGS, SEPARATED*
1/3	CUP EXTRA-VIRGIN OLIVE OIL
1	CUP BROWN SUGAR, PACKED
1/2	TEASPOON SALT
1	TEASPOON PURE LEMON EXTRACT
1/2	CUP DRY RED WINE, DRY SHERRY OR MARSALA
2	CUPS UNBLEACHED WHITE PASTRY FLOUR
1	TEASPOON BAKING POWDER
1	TEASPOON MINCED FRESH ROSEMARY (OPTIONAL)

1 to 2 TABLESPOONS SUGAR

SERVES 12 TO 16
PREPARATION TIME: 30 MINTUES
BAKING TIME: ABOUT 1 HOUR
COOLING TIME: 15 MINUTES

* Crack an egg in half crosswise and carefully slip its yolk (without breaking it) from one half of the shell to the other, as the whites drain off into a bowl. The egg whites must not contain even a speck of the yolk to whip properly.

Preheat the oven to 350°. Butter and flour a 10-inch springform pan.

Rinse the grapes and set them aside on a kitchen towel to dry. With an electric mixer, beat the egg whites in a mixing bowl until stiff, but not dry, and set aside. In a separate bowl, beat the olive oil and brown sugar with the electric mixer for 1 minute, until lightened in color. Beat in the egg yolks. Add the salt, lemon extract, and wine, and beat until smooth.

In a separate bowl, stir together the flour, baking powder, and rosemary, if using, and add to the batter. Beat until smooth. With a rubber spatula, gently fold in the beaten egg whites and half of the grapes and pour the batter into the prepared pan.

Bake for 20 minutes. Remove from the oven, arrange the rest of the grapes on top of the cake, and sprinkle the sugar over all. Bake for another 40 to 45 minutes, until the top is lightly browned and feels firm to the touch. Transfer to a rack to cool for about 15 minutes.

Run a knife around the outside of the cake and remove the outer ring of the springform pan. Loosen the cake from the bottom of the pan and transfer it to a platter. Serve warm or at room temperature.

BROWN SUGAR POUNDCAKE

Gorgeous to look at and moist, this dense, plain poundcake has just the right amount of crackly sugar topping. And who doesn't like cinnamon sugar? Can't wait for a big deal occasion to make it? Serve it at a Saturday afternoon See-My-Just-Weeded-Garden Party with a pot of hot strong tea, or provide the impetus for a musical or theatrical soiree and invite everyone back for a late-night dessert garnished with fresh fruit.

cake

2	CUPS BUTTER, AT ROOM TEMPERATURE
3	CUPS BROWN SUGAR, PACKED
6	EGGS
2	TEASPOONS PURE VANILLA EXTRACT
2	TEASPOONS BAKING POWDER
4	CUPS UNBLEACHED WHITE PASTRY FLOUR
½	CUP MILK OR HEAVY CREAM

SERVES 16 TO 24
PREPARATION TIME: 25 MINUTES
BAKING TIME: 75 TO 80 MINUTES
COOLING TIME: 20 MINUTES
GLAZING TIME: 10 MINUTES

glaze

½	CUP CONFECTIONERS' SUGAR
3	TABLESPOONS BROWN SUGAR, PACKED
2	TABLESPOONS MILK OR WATER

cinnamon sugar topping

3	TABLESPOONS BROWN SUGAR, PACKED
1	TEASPOON GROUND CINNAMON
½	TEASPOON GROUND NUTMEG

Preheat the oven to 350°. Butter a 10-inch bundt pan and dust it with flour (see Note).

Using an electric mixer, cream the butter and brown sugar until light. Add the eggs and vanilla and beat until fluffy. In a separate bowl, stir together the baking powder and flour. With the mixer on low speed, add the flour mixture in two batches, alternating with the milk. Beat until well blended, another minute or so.

Scrape the batter into the prepared pan and bake for about 75 minutes, or until a knife inserted into the center comes out clean. The cake should be golden brown, firm, and pulling slightly away from the pan.

While the cake bakes, prepare the glaze and topping. In a small bowl, mix all of the glaze ingredients together until smooth. In a cup, stir together the brown sugar, cinnamon, and nutmeg for the topping and set aside.

When the cake is done, cool upright on a rack for 10 minutes and then invert onto a serving plate, leaving the baking pan in place for another 10 minutes before removing it. Then apply the glaze and topping while the cake is still warm. Using a pastry brush, quickly coat the surface of the cake with the glaze and immediately sprinkle the topping on the moist glaze. Carefully tip the cake a bit while sprinkling, so that sugar will adhere to the sides as well as the top.

note

To remove excess flour from the sides of the pan, tap the pan a couple of times on the counter and discard the flour that falls out. If you missed a spot with the butter, you'll be able to see it now and correct it.

CINNAMON

CHOCOLATE GANACHE BIRTHDAY CAKE

Over the years, we've baked many a chocolate layer cake at Moosewood; this one is emerging as everyone's favorite for birthdays. Special occasions deserve a dessert with both visual impact and sumptuous taste and texture. This cake is tall, impressive, moist, light, and very chocolaty.

We use Dutch-processed cocoa for deeper color and flavor. American-style cocoas will also work but they yield a less intense flavor and redder color. Ganache is a simply made truffle-like cream—perfect for a cake that aims to fulfill your every chocolate dream.

cake

SERVES 10 TO 16
PREPARATION TIME: 1 HOUR
BAKING TIME: 20 TO 25 MINUTES

1	CUP BOILING WATER
¾	CUP UNSWEETENED DUTCH-PROCESSED COCOA
¾	CUP UNSALTED BUTTER, AT ROOM TEMPERATURE
2¼	CUPS BROWN SUGAR, PACKED
3	EGGS, LIGHTLY BEATEN
1	TEASPOON PURE VANILLA EXTRACT
2½	CUPS UNBLEACHED WHITE FLOUR*
½	TEASPOON BAKING SODA
½	TEASPOON SALT
⅔	CUP BUTTERMILK

ganache

¾	CUP HEAVY CREAM
4½	OUNCES SEMI-SWEET CHOCOLATE, CHOPPED INTO SMALL PIECES OR CHIPS
1	TABLESPOON COFFEE OR HAZELNUT LIQUEUR (OPTIONAL)

mocha frosting

1	TABLESPOON INSTANT COFFEE GRANULES DISSOLVED IN 1 CUP HEAVY CREAM**
⅓	CUP CONFECTIONERS' SUGAR
1	TABLESPOON UNSWEETENED COCOA

* Sift flour onto a large piece of wax paper or a clean surface before measuring. Use a large spoon to gently fill a measuring cup: Do not pack. Level with a knife.

** Before whipping, stir the instant coffee granules into the cream until they are thoroughly dissolved.

Preheat the oven to 350°.

Lightly butter the bottoms of three 9-inch round cake pans. Fit each pan with a circle of wax or parchment paper; then butter and flour the paper and sides of the pans. In a small heatproof bowl, gradually whisk the boiling water into the cocoa to form a smooth paste; cool in the refrigerator.

Beat the butter until creamy. Add the brown sugar in two batches, beating after each addition with an electric mixer for 1 to 2 minutes, until fluffy. Blend in the eggs one at a time in a slow steady stream. Beat in the vanilla.

In another bowl, sift together the measured flour, baking soda, and salt. Stir the buttermilk into the cocoa paste to form a sauce. With the mixer on low speed, add the flour mixture and cocoa sauce to the egg mixture alternately in thirds. Scrape down the sides of the bowl after each addition. Mix just until the flour is incorporated and the batter smooth: Overbeating at this stage will develop the gluten in the flour and toughen the cake.

Pour one-third of the batter into each of the three prepared cake pans and smooth the tops with a spatula. Bake until a knife inserted in the center tests clean, 20 to 25 minutes. Cool on a rack in the pans for 10 minutes; then turn out onto a rack, turn right side up, and cool completely.

While the cake layers are baking, prepare the ganache and the frosting. Bring the cream to a simmer in a small heavy-bottomed saucepan. Whisk in the chocolate and heat gently until it fully melts. Add the liqueur, if using. Pour the ganache into a bowl and refrigerate for about 30 minutes, whisking every 10 minutes. Avoid overchilling. It's ready when it spreads easily without being either stiff or runny.

For the Mocha Frosting, whip the flavored heavy cream with an electric mixer or whisk until soft peaks form. Add the sugar and cocoa and whip just until stiff peaks form. Don't overbeat or you'll make butter. Chill.

To assemble the cake, place one cooled layer on an attractive serving plate. Spread half of the ganache on top, then add a second cake layer. Spread on the rest of the ganache and top with the third layer. Frost the top and sides with the Mocha Frosting. Serve immediately or cover and refrigerate.

variation

For a vanilla-flavored frosting, omit the coffee and the cocoa and add 1 teaspoon of pure vanilla extract.

WHITE CHOCOLATE & FIG POUNDCAKE

The entrancing aroma and taste of cocoa butter pervades this lovely, fine-grained cake speckled with bits of figs. We like to serve such a dense, rich cake with strong coffee, espresso, or a good black tea like Barry's Irish Gold.

cake

SERVES 16
PREPARATION TIME: 25 MINUTES
BAKING TIME: 60 TO 70 MINUTES
COOLING TIME: 40 MINUTES

1	CUP BUTTER, AT ROOM TEMPERATURE
2	CUPS SUGAR
5	LARGE EGGS
2	TEASPOONS PURE VANILLA EXTRACT
3½	CUPS UNBLEACHED WHITE PASTRY FLOUR
2	TEASPOONS BAKING POWDER
¼	CUP MILK
1	CUP WHITE CHOCOLATE CHIPS*
2	CUPS DICED DRIED FIGS**

glaze

⅓	CUP WHITE CHOCOLATE CHIPS OR 2 OUNCES WHITE CHOCOLATE
1½	TABLESPOONS MILK OR HEAVY CREAM

* Or use 6 ounces of finely chopped or grated white chocolate. In the bowl of a food processor, this is an easy task: Just cut the chocolate into chunks and whirl.

** 12 ounces of figs will yield 2 cups of chopped pieces about the size of blueberries.

Preheat the oven to 350°. Generously butter and flour a 10-inch bundt pan.

Using an electric mixer, cream the butter and sugar until well blended. Add the eggs and vanilla and beat until light and fluffy. Sift together the flour and baking powder. Add about half of the flour mixture to the batter and beat well. Mix in the milk, then add the remaining flour and beat well. By hand, fold in the chocolate and figs.

Pour the batter into the prepared pan and bake for 60 to 70 minutes, until the cake pulls away from the sides of the pan and a knife inserted into the center tests clean. Cool the cake in the pan on a rack for about 10 minutes. Invert the cake onto a plate, remove the pan, and cool completely.

In a very small saucepan on low heat, melt together the chocolate and the milk or cream. Stir constantly to prevent scorching. Use a pastry brush to evenly coat the surface of the cake with the melted white chocolate.

VEGAN CHOCOLATE GINGERBREAD

Want old-fashioned comfort on a damp, chilly day? Here's a quick, reliable adaptation of our Six-Minute Chocolate Cake, a much sought-after dessert at Moosewood Restaurant among customers and staff alike. In this version, we spike the chocolate with traditional gingerbread spices. We figure, ya gotta love chocolate and ginger.

Vegan Chocolate Gingerbread will keep, covered, for 2 or 3 days, but it's best when served the first day. We like it with tea, hot cider, or mulled wine.

SERVES 8
PREPARATION TIME: 30 MINUTES
BAKING TIME: ABOUT 30 MINUTES

⅓	CUP UNSWEETENED COCOA POWDER
1⅓	CUPS UNBLEACHED WHITE FLOUR
½	TEASPOON BAKING SODA
½	TEASPOON SALT
1	TEASPOON GROUND CINNAMON
2½	TEASPOONS GROUND GINGER
1	CUP BROWN SUGAR, PACKED
1	CUP STRONG BREWED COFFEE, COOLED TO ROOM TEMPERATURE
½	CUP VEGETABLE OIL
¼	CUP COARSELY CHOPPED CRYSTALLIZED GINGER (OPTIONAL)
2	TABLESPOONS CIDER VINEGAR

Preheat the oven to 375°. Oil an 8-inch-square baking pan and dust it with cocoa or flour.

Sift the cocoa, flour, baking soda, salt, cinnamon, ginger, and brown sugar into a large bowl. In a 2-cup measure, combine the coffee and oil. With a spoon or a whisk, beat the liquid into the dry ingredients. Stir in the crystallized ginger, if using, and then quickly stir in the vinegar.

Pour the batter into the prepared pan and bake for about 30 minutes, or until a toothpick inserted in the center of the cake comes out clean.

FROSTED CARROT CUPCAKES

Cupcakes are fun for kids' parties, and they're faster to bake than large cakes. Pineapple, ginger, and coconut give a tropical flair to these perennial favorites. While carrot cakes are traditionally made with oil, olive oil is not the usual choice. Use regular olive oil, which has a very subtle, mildly fruity flavor; extra-virgin olive oil may be too assertive. The frosting adds sweetness and a more festive quality, but the cupcakes are good plain, too.

YIELDS 12 CUPCAKES
PREPARATION TIME: 25 MINUTES
BAKING TIME: 25 TO 30 MINUTES
COOLING TIME: 20 MINUTES

wet ingredients

1	CUP PEELED AND FINELY GRATED CARROTS, PACKED
1	CUP UNSWEETENED CRUSHED PINEAPPLE (8-OUNCE CAN, WELL DRAINED)
1	CUP BROWN SUGAR, PACKED
2	LARGE EGGS, LIGHTLY BEATEN
⅔	CUP OLIVE OIL
½	CUP UNSWEETENED GRATED COCONUT (PAGE 397)
1	TEASPOON FINELY GRATED PEELED FRESH GINGER ROOT
1	TEASPOON PURE VANILLA EXTRACT

dry ingredients

2	CUPS UNBLEACHED WHITE FLOUR
1	TEASPOON BAKING POWDER
½	TEASPOON BAKING SODA
½	TEASPOON SALT
½	TEASPOON GROUND CINNAMON
¼	TEASPOON GROUND NUTMEG

vanilla cream cheese frosting

2	TABLESPOONS UNSALTED BUTTER, AT ROOM TEMPERATURE
¼	CUP NEUFCHÂTEL OR CREAM CHEESE, AT ROOM TEMPERATURE
⅔	CUP CONFECTIONERS' SUGAR
1	TEASPOON PURE VANILLA EXTRACT

Preheat the oven to 350°. Butter a standard 12-cup muffin tin or fill with paper liners.

Combine the wet ingredients in a large bowl. (Reserve the pineapple juice for another use—or just drink it!) Using a large spoon, mix the ingredients together until well blended. In another bowl, sift together the dry ingredients. Stir them into the wet ingredients and mix just until all of the flour is moistened and incorporated.

Pour the batter in twelve equal portions into the prepared muffin cups. Bake for 25 to 30 minutes, until a knife inserted in the center of the largest cupcake comes out clean. Cool the cupcakes for 3 or 4 minutes; then remove them from the tin and allow to sit on a rack for about 20 minutes.

To prepare the frosting, cream together the butter and Neufchâtel or cream cheese in a food processor bowl or with an electric mixer. Add the confectioners' sugar and vanilla and beat until smooth.

When the cupcakes have cooled completely, frost them.

ALMOND CAKE WITH PEACHES

The flavor of almonds naturally balances the taste of luscious fresh peaches in this moist, not-too-sweet cake. We prefer pure almond paste to marzipan, which can be sugary sweet. Almond paste is found in the baking aisle of most supermarkets. Our favorite brand is Odense. Solo makes a good one, too.

batter

8	OUNCES ALMOND PASTE
1	CUP UNSALTED BUTTER, AT ROOM TEMPERATURE
1	CUP SUGAR
5	EGGS
1	TEASPOON PURE VANILLA EXTRACT
½	CUP MILK
1	CUP UNBLEACHED WHITE PASTRY FLOUR

SERVES 8 TO 12
PREPARATION TIME: 15 MINUTES
BAKING TIME: 50 MINUTES
COOLING TIME: 20 MINUTES

whipped cream

1	CUP HEAVY CREAM
1	TEASPOON PURE VANILLA EXTRACT
2	TABLESPOONS CONFECTIONERS' SUGAR

fruit

8 to 10	RIPE PEACHES, PEELED AND SLICED*
1	TABLESPOON SUGAR

* The safest way to slice peaches is to halve them, remove the pit, peel each half, and then slice.

Preheat the oven to 350°. Butter and flour a 9-inch round cake pan.

Using an electric mixer, cream together the almond paste, butter, and sugar until smooth and light. Add the eggs and vanilla and beat well. On low speed, add the milk and then the flour, mixing just until combined.

Pour the batter into the prepared pan and bake until a toothpick inserted in the center comes out clean, about 50 minutes. Cool for 20 minutes on a rack; then remove from the pan and turn out onto a serving plate.

Whip the cream until stiff. Fold in the vanilla and confectioners' sugar and refrigerate until ready to serve. Toss together the peaches and sugar in a bowl. Arrange wedges of cake on individual plates. Top each with a dollop of whipped cream, draped with a large spoonful of peach slices.

CHOCOLATE PUDDING CAKE

This is a rich, gooey pudding with a fudgy cake layer on top. It's low in fat and vegan when made with soy milk. We predict it will disappear instantly, once sighted.

There is an uncanny sense of kitchen magic at work with this cake. When you follow the recipe, it seems strange—as if it won't work. But the results will surprise and please you. This is a great cooking project to do with children, who will enjoy both the making and devouring of it.

Top with berries, vanilla ice cream, frozen yogurt, or fresh whipped cream, if desired.

1	CUP GRANULATED SUGAR
½	CUP UNSWEETENED COCOA POWDER
1	CUP UNBLEACHED WHITE FLOUR
2	TEASPOONS BAKING POWDER
½	TEASPOON BAKING SODA
¼	TEASPOON SALT
½	CUP SOY MILK OR MILK
¼	CUP VEGETABLE OIL
1	TEASPOON PURE VANILLA EXTRACT
½	CUP BROWN SUGAR, PACKED
1½	CUPS BOILING WATER

SERVES 6 TO 8
PREPARATION TIME: 20 MINUTES
BAKING TIME: 20 TO 25 MINUTES
COOLING TIME: 15 MINUTES

Preheat the oven to 350°. Oil a 9 x 13-inch glass baking pan.

In a mixing bowl, combine ¾ cup of the granulated sugar and ¼ cup of the cocoa with the flour, baking powder, baking soda, and salt. Mix well. Stir in the milk, oil, and vanilla and beat well to form a thick batter. Spread the batter in the prepared pan.

In a separate bowl, mix together the brown sugar with the remaining ¼ cup of granulated sugar and cocoa powder. Sprinkle the mixture evenly on top of the batter in the pan. Pour the boiling water over the top.

Bake until the pudding cake is set around the sides and the top is loose and slightly bubbly, 20 to 25 minutes. Cool in the pan for about 15 minutes before serving: The pudding layer thickens nicely as it sits.

Serve warm or at room temperature.

FOOD AS A GIFT

Homemade food as a gift is sweet-hearted and thoughtful, often unique, and always welcome. Like other handcrafted gifts, it is of you as well as from you. The recipient is bound to feel special and will appreciate the time, effort, creativity, and thoughtfulness that went into its making. And for so many of us, food resonates love.

Often, the primary expenditure on homemade gifts is time, but presents of food can be made for many simultaneously. It takes about the same amount of time to make three dozen muffins as one dozen, or a quart of tapenade as a pint. And don't discount the bonus of a fragrant kitchen.

There's no need to wait for a holiday. Since most of us have so little time to cook, food is always a welcome present. Do you know someone who moans about no time for breakfast? Leave a tin of homemade granola on her doorstep. Present a new neighbor with a basket of dried pasta, a jar of homemade sauce, and a hunk of aged cheese. Include some freshly made dressing or flavored oils and vinegars and some specialty olives and she may be tempted to eat her greens. The gift of some pesto or salsa can inspire a busy friend to cook and maybe even invite you over.

Food can also give comfort. Prepare something for a friend far from home. Roast chestnuts for a displaced New Yorker. Take a box of grits and a wedge of cheddar to a friend from the South. Help out someone who has dietary restrictions. Make a big pot of vegetable soup, which is naturally low-fat and low-calorie. Is your valentine vegan? Present a delicious Vegan Chocolate Gingerbread and clinch it with a batch of heart-shaped goodies (Dog Biscuits) for their "best friend."

When it comes to food, we have lots of ideas. Give a gift that indulges the sweet tooth—confections, cakes, cookies, preserves, and fruit butters—you'll find plenty of recipes in this book. For the adventurous epicure in your life, make a gift of exotic ingredients or unusual foods and beverages. Go to the produce section and look for white asparagus, golden kiwis, exotic mushrooms, or carambola (star fruit). Mix and match homemade treats with purchases. Pair special teas, coffees, wines, or liqueurs with homemade cookies, biscotti, quickbread, or scones. Box some jars of different salsas and include a tortilla press and a package of masa harina. To celebrate a birthday, anniversary, or major achievement, create your own sampler box of our Special Day Chocolates. Do you have a friend who loves to bake? Prepare a package of parchment paper, a selection of pure extracts, and bittersweet Belgian chocolate.

Half the fun of preparing gifts of food is the packaging and decorating. There are multicolored plastic wraps and too many ribbons to use in a lifetime. There are affordable, beautifully colored and faceted bottles for flavored oils and vinegars, and maybe more cookie cutters than varieties of cookies. There are sturdy bake-and-serve gift pans for quickbreads and brownies, available in round, square, loaf, and mini-loaf sizes (order through kingarthurflour.com or www.surlatable.com). Thrift shops are gold mines for tins of every imaginable size, shape, and color, as well as a good source for interesting bottles, jars, cruets, and baskets.

When shipping food, seal it well and pack it with as much protection as possible. Double-box items or place them in a tin and then pack in a box with lots of filler: Try air-popped popcorn in place of Styrofoam peanuts or bubble wrap. When you make a gift of food, don't forget to include a copy of the recipe!

more gift foods

Below is a list of recipes that you'll find on the pages of other celebratory menus in the book. All of them make good gifts.

Cheddar Shortbread Hearts (page 76)

Chocolate Candies (pages 279–285)

Cilantry Almond Pesto (page 33)

Classic Southern Italian Figs (page 78)

Harvest Nuts & Seeds (page 178)

Homemade Applesauce (page 202)

Jerk Sauce (page 29)

Mango Cranberry Chutney (page 149)

Mojo Sauce (page 28)

Olive Butter Spread (page 297)

Pan de Muerto (page 137)

Preserved Lemons (page 194)

Roasted Chestnuts (page 225)

Tomato Lime Pesto (page 77)

Two Olive Herb Spreads (page 353)

Vegan Chocolate Gingerbread (page 379)

holiday cookies as gifts

Almost all of these delectable, travel-hardy sweets can be found in the Holiday Cookie Exchange section (pages 204 to 213). The recipes that are elsewhere have an exact page reference below.

Baklava with Hazelnuts (page 320)

Cashew Butterscotch Bars (page 47)

Cherry Chocolate Rugalach

Cornmeal Lemon Shortbread (page 92)

Cranberry Cornmeal Biscotti

Lemon Cookies

Oatmeal Chocolate Chip Cookies

Orange & Fig Cookies

Peanut Butter Cookies

Poppyseed Cookies (page 203)

Semolina Almond Cookies (page 195)

Spiced Coconut Date Bars

PEAR RASPBERRY PRESERVES

If you've never made your own preserves, you're in for a treat. Preserve-making does not require a knowledge of calculus or complex equipment. For old-fashioned, cooked-down preserves, all you'll need is a wide, heavy, flat-bottomed pot and a couple of hours to tend it lovingly.

Because our preserves use markedly less sugar than standard commercial recipes, they don't have the translucent, high-gloss appearance and sticky texture of most. However, we've come to prefer their rustic appearance and fresh mouthfeel.

This Pear Raspberry Preserves recipe can be used as a template for making any kind of preserves. We use very slightly underripe pears: A sweeter fruit might call for less sugar. You can always add a bit of fresh lemon juice at the end, if the fruit itself does not supply that satisfying sweet-tart balance.

These preserves, without the aid of sterilized jars or canning, keep for 3 weeks, tightly lidded and refrigerated. For information on canning and sealing, and other fascinating information about the art of making preserves, see *Lost Arts: A Celebration of Culinary Traditions,* by Lynn Alley, Ten Speed Press. This recipe can be halved to make an ample amount for home use.

11 to 12 CUPS PEELED, CORED AND CHOPPED
    ANJOU PEARS (6 POUNDS)

2   CUPS RASPBERRIES

¾ to 1 CUP SUGAR

1 to 2 TEASPOONS FRESH LEMON JUICE (OPTIONAL)

YIELDS EIGHT 4-OUNCE JARS
TOTAL TIME: 2½ TO 3 HOURS

Combine the pears, raspberries, and sugar in a 10-inch, heavy, flat-bottomed pot. Stir on high heat until the fruit expresses a couple of inches of juice and begins to boil. Reduce the heat to low and simmer, uncovered, stirring frequently to prevent sticking and scorching.

Pears are very juicy and will need to simmer and reduce for close to 2 hours. As the liquid reduces and the fruit thickens, stir more attentively. For a uniform texture, mash the fruit with a potato masher or purée in the bowl of a food processor. Add lemon juice to taste, ladle into jars, and chill before using.

WINTER SQUASH BUTTER

Apple butter is deservedly beloved by many, but we prefer our spicy squash take on this popular spread. Go into your kitchen on a dreary fall or winter day and make up a batch to brighten your meals for weeks to come. Not too sweet, with a warm, deep flavor, this can be a vegan and low-fat alternative to butter or cream cheese.

Use Winter Squash Butter as a breakfast spread with muffins and scones or try it as a topping on oatmeal or waffles. It's perfect on cornbread with skillet beans for supper. We even like it as a simple dessert served with a nut bread. A jar of it tied festively with ribbon makes a great gift.

2½ to 3 POUNDS WHOLE WINTER SQUASH*	
½ CUP BROWN SUGAR, PACKED	
¼ TEASPOON SALT	
1 TEASPOON GROUND CINNAMON	
¼ TEASPOON GROUND NUTMEG	
¼ TEASPOON GROUND GINGER	
⅛ TEASPOON GROUND CLOVES	
1 TABLESPOON FRESH LEMON JUICE	

YIELDS ABOUT 3 CUPS
PREPARATION TIME: 15 MINUTES
BAKING TIME: 45 MINUTES
COOKING TIME: 20 MINUTES

* We recommend delicata, butternut, acorn, kuri, or pumpkin, but pumpkin must be puréed with a blender or food processor—not by hand.

Preheat the oven to 375°.

Halve and seed the squash. Place the halves cut side down on a lightly oiled baking sheet. Bake for about 45 minutes, until the squash feels soft when poked with a knife. Remove from the oven and set aside to cool.

When cool enough to handle, scoop the soft pulp into a blender, food processor, or mixing bowl; be careful not to include any of the rind. Stir the remaining ingredients into the squash. Purée the mixture until smooth or mash by hand with a potato masher and then whisk vigorously with a wire whip.

Transfer the puréed squash to a nonreactive, heavy pot. Bring to a simmer on medium heat; then reduce the heat to low and cook, stirring frequently, for about 20 minutes. The mixture will be quite thick and hold a soft shape when done. Add more lemon juice or brown sugar to taste, if needed.

Cool and serve, or store refrigerated for up to 3 weeks. For long-term storage, squash butter can be frozen in small batches and then thawed. For gifts, "can it" in jars using safe canning techniques.

the p's and q's of salt & pepper

Salt highlights and enhances the taste of just about everything, even sweet things. It's used to draw out juices from vegetables like eggplant and to pickle or preserve vegetables, cheeses, fish, and meats. Salt is either mined from the earth or distilled from seawater. It is 40 percent sodium, 60 percent chloride, and, when unprocessed, it's surprisingly full of trace minerals.

Table salt is mined from the earth and processed. Its natural iodine is lost as a result. In an effort to address the widespread occurrence of thyroid goiters caused by insufficient iodine in the diet, the twentieth-century practice of re-fortifying processed salt with iodine was instituted. *Iodized salt* is now commonplace. *Sea salt* has a superior flavor to processed salts and retains its beneficial minerals, including iodine. *Kosher salt* comes in coarse crystals and is less salty than sea salt or table salt.

You may want to sample several of the unusual salts now available in specialty food shops: Crystalline and mild French fleur de sel, sel gris—a large-grained grey salt from the northern coast of France, black lava and red clay salts from Hawaii, Peruvian pink salt, English Maldon sea salt, and smoked Danish salt. Many of these are gaining popularity with chefs in America.

Pepper is the fruit of *piper nigram*, a perennial vine native to southern India that has been used for thousands of years. It grows best within 15 degrees of the equator and thrives with tropical heat, plenty of rain, and shade from direct sunlight.

Green, black, and white pepper each have a distinct look and taste. All three are berries of the same plant but harvested at different stages of growth. Green peppercorns are picked when young, green, soft, and aromatic. They can be sprinkled directly onto food or mashed into a paste, and they'll soon turn black unless frozen or preserved in brine. Black peppercorns are picked green and dried. They have a complex, hotter, sweeter taste than either green or white peppercorns. White peppercorns are harvested when fully ripe, soaked to remove their red outer skins, and dried. They have a mild flavor. Intensely flavored Sichuan pepper, or anise pepper, used in Chinese cuisine, is from an altogether different plant and looks like a dried red flower, not a peppercorn.

Because they contain volatile oils, peppercorns quickly lose flavor and aroma once crushed or ground. We recommend cracking whole peppercorns with a mortar and pestle or grinding them in a pepper mill or spice grinder. The resulting flavor is warm, intense, and far superior to already ground pepper.

A SALT & PEPPER SAMPLER

A great gift for a cook (or from a cook) can be a sampler box of a variety of specialty salts and peppers. Since almost everyone uses salt and pepper regularly, you can give it to anyone, even the person who has everything, and know it will not go to waste.

Look for decorative and colorful salts and peppers in gourmet food shops and select an array of them. Then whip up our seasoned salt recipes and put them in pretty jars to add an even more personal touch to your gift box. Pop in a couple of designer shakers or grinders for a little added pizzazz.

THREE SAVORY SEASONED SALTS

garam masala

To add authentic flavor to Indian and Caribbean-style stews, soups, or curries, add garam masala to taste. When briefly sautéed with onions or other vegetables in ghee, an Indian clarified butter, the flavor and aroma of the spices intensify.

1	THREE-INCH PIECE OF WHOLE CINNAMON STICK
2	TABLESPOONS CORIANDER SEEDS
1	TABLESPOON CUMIN SEEDS
1	TABLESPOON BLACK PEPPERCORNS
1	TEASPOON CARDAMOM SEEDS
1	TEASPOON WHOLE CLOVES
½	TEASPOON FENNEL SEEDS
1	TEASPOON COARSE KOSHER SALT OR SEA SALT

YIELDS 6 TABLESPOONS
TOTAL TIME: 35 MINUTES

Preheat the oven to 200°.

Put the cinnamon stick in a small plastic bag and crush it into small pieces with a rolling pin. Place the crushed cinnamon, coriander, cumin, peppercorns, cardamom, cloves, and fennel on an unoiled baking sheet and bake for 30 minutes. Stir once or twice during baking.

Remove the spices from the oven, cool, and pulverize in a spice grinder. Mix in the salt. Store in a glass jar in a cool place and use within a few months.

gremolata

Embodying the essential flavor of the classic Milanese seasoning mixture, gremolata seasoned salt can add piquant flavor to pastas, risottos, vegetable stews, and frittatas. Sprinkle on fish, asparagus, marinated vegetables, or roasted potatoes.

½ TEASPOON COARSE KOSHER SALT OR SEA SALT
1 TABLESPOON FRESHLY GRATED LEMON PEEL
1 GARLIC CLOVE, MINCED OR PRESSED
  PINCH OF SAFFRON (OPTIONAL)
½ CUP MINCED FRESH PARSLEY

YIELDS ABOUT ¼ CUP
TOTAL TIME: 5 MINUTES

In a small bowl, stir together all of the ingredients. Gremolata is best prepared fresh for immediate use. Leftover gremolata should be well covered, refrigerated, and used within 1 week.

gomashio

For classic Japanese flavor, sprinkle Gomashio on rice, baked tofu, grilled fish or vegetables, broiled eggplant, or miso soup.

1 TEASPOON COARSE KOSHER SALT OR SEA SALT
5 TABLESPOONS BLACK OR WHITE SESAME SEEDS

YIELDS ½ CUP
TOTAL TIME: 5 MINUTES

In a heavy skillet, toast the salt and sesame seeds until the seeds start to pop. Cool. Grind in a spice grinder. Store in a cool place in a glass jar and use within 2 weeks.

PARSLEY

STOUT IRISH GINGERBREAD

Myoko Maureen Vivino put on her Irish jig shoes and danced around the kitchen to make this "fortified" version of gingerbread. This is serious gingerbread: Spicy and not too sweet—definitely not cupcakes! The recipe makes two loaves, since we thought that while you were at it, you might as well make one as a gift, too. It's the perfect Saint Patrick's Day present.

Although beer isn't a common bread ingredient, oatmeal stout adds a great touch to this recipe. Oatmeal stout is a sweet, full-bodied dark ale brewed with rolled oats and roasted barley. Two widely distributed brands are Young's of London and Samuel Smith's. Samuel Adams also has a nice stout that works fine in this recipe, and, of course, there's Guinness Stout.

1	CUP OATMEAL STOUT OR GUINNESS STOUT
1¼	CUPS DARK UNSULPHURED MOLASSES (NOT BLACKSTRAP)
1	CUP BUTTER, AT ROOM TEMPERATURE
1½	CUPS BROWN SUGAR, PACKED
3	LARGE EGGS, BEATEN
3	CUPS UNBLEACHED WHITE FLOUR
2	TEASPOONS BAKING POWDER
½	TEASPOON BAKING SODA
¼	TEASPOON SALT
2	TABLESPOONS GROUND GINGER
2	TEASPOONS FRESHLY GRATED NUTMEG
1	TEASPOON GROUND CINNAMON
½	TEASPOON GROUND CLOVES
	PINCH OF GROUND BLACK PEPPER

LIGHTLY SWEETENED FRESH WHIPPED CREAM

YIELDS 2 LOAVES
PREPARATION TIME: 25 MINUTES
BAKING TIME: 60 TO 70 MINUTES
COOLING TIME: 10 MINUTES

Preheat the oven to 350°. Butter two 9 x 5-inch loaf pans and dust with flour.

In a large saucepan, bring the stout and molasses to a boil; then set aside to cool. In a large bowl, cream together the butter and brown sugar. Beat in the eggs. In a separate bowl, sift together the flour, baking powder, baking soda, salt, and spices. Mix the dry ingredients into the wet in two or three batches, alternating with the cooled molasses mixture, to make a smooth batter.

Pour the batter into the prepared loaf pans and bake for 60 to 70 minutes, until a knife inserted in the center comes out with just a few moist crumbs. Cool in the pan for about 10 minutes and then turn out onto a rack. Serve topped with fresh whipped cream.

BEST VEGAN DATE NUT BREAD

We experimented (and ate) many versions of this quickbread in our quest for a moist, delicious bread containing no animal products yet having a really good crumb. This low-fat recipe was the hands-down winner. We gobbled it up and so will you.

Our vegan date nut bread makes a good gift: Wrapped in plastic and foil, it stays fresh for up to a week. Bring it as a hospitality gift the next time you go visiting.

1	CUP WHOLE WHEAT PASTRY FLOUR*
1	CUP UNBLEACHED WHITE PASTRY FLOUR**
1	TEASPOON BAKING SODA
½	TEASPOON SALT
½	TEASPOON GROUND CINNAMON
¼	TEASPOON FRESHLY GRATED NUTMEG
⅓	CUP VEGETABLE OIL
¼	CUP BROWN SUGAR, PACKED
⅔	CUP ORANGE JUICE
1	TABLESPOON FRESHLY GRATED ORANGE PEEL
½	CUP UNSWEETENED APPLESAUCE***
½	CUP CHOPPED PITTED DATES
½	CUP CHOPPED WALNUTS

SERVES 8 TO 10
PREPARATION TIME: 25 TO 30 MINUTES
BAKING TIME: 45 TO 50 MINUTES
COOLING TIME: 10 TO 25 MINUTES

* Well-stocked supermarkets often carry Hodgson Mill organic whole wheat pastry flour. Also widely available in bulk at natural food stores.

** Milled from soft wheat, white pastry flour, with its low protein content, gives baked goods an especially tender crumb.

*** Mott's brand "natural" applesauce is unsweetened and has no preservatives; it's pure apples and water. Or try our Homemade Applesauce (page 202).

Preheat the oven to 350°. Spray or lightly oil an 8½ x 4½–inch loaf pan.

Sift together the flours, baking soda, salt, cinnamon, and nutmeg into a large bowl. In another bowl, whisk together the oil, brown sugar, orange juice, and orange peel. Stir the wet ingredients into the dry ingredients until well combined. Mix the applesauce evenly into the batter; then fold in the dates and walnuts. Spoon into the prepared loaf pan.

Bake for 45 to 50 minutes, until the top is brown and a knife inserted into the center comes out clean. Cool in the pan for 10 to 25 minutes; then turn out onto a wire rack. Allow to cool thoroughly for easier slicing.

CURRANT & WALNUT BISCUITS

Walnuts, currants, and maple syrup lend their earthy sweetness to this recipe, which makes either a slew of drop biscuits or a pan of cornbread (see Variation). The batter has just enough cornmeal in it to provide a pleasantly crunchy texture. The amount of maple syrup is up to you.

The biscuits, with their craggy, uneven crust and nice brown edges, are best fresh and hot—or split and reheated in a toaster oven.

1½	CUPS UNBLEACHED WHITE FLOUR
½	CUP FINELY GROUND YELLOW CORNMEAL
3	TEASPOONS BAKING POWDER
½	TEASPOON BAKING SODA
1	SCANT TEASPOON SALT
1	CUP CHOPPED WALNUTS
1	CUP CURRANTS
½	CUP BUTTER
¼ to ½	CUP PURE MAPLE SYRUP
1	CUP BUTTERMILK

YIELDS 18 BISCUITS
PREPARATION TIME: 25 TO 30 MINUTES
BAKING TIME: 15 MINUTES

Preheat the oven to 350°. Lightly butter two baking sheets.

Sift together the flour, cornmeal, baking powder, baking soda, and salt in a large bowl. Mix in the walnuts and currants and set aside.

In a small saucepan, melt the butter on low heat. Add the maple syrup. Make a well in the dry ingredients and stir in the maple-butter mixture and the buttermilk, until just combined. Drop the batter by ¼ cups onto the prepared baking sheets, spacing the biscuits at least 1 inch apart.

Bake for about 15 minutes, or until firm to the touch and lightly golden. Serve warm—with butter, if desired.

variation

To make a 9-inch square pan of cornbread instead of biscuits, butter the pan and lightly dust it with flour. Spread the batter evenly into the prepared pan and bake at 350° for 20 minutes. Well covered, the cornbread stays moist and will keep for a week. Try it dabbed with Winter Squash Butter (page 388) for a special treat.

DOG BISCUITS

Moosewood cooks Joan Adler and Dave Dietrich baked an experimental half batch of these canine treats and offered two to each of their dogs, Nicky and Chloe. The dogs wolfed them down. Satisfied with the success of the biscuits, Joan and Dave went about their day, leaving twenty more biscuits on the cooling rack. When they returned later, only four biscuits were left. We don't need Sherlock Holmes to solve this case of "The Disappearing Dog Biscuits."

biscuits

YIELDS 48 BISCUITS 1½ INCHES
IN DIAMETER
PREPARATION TIME: 10 TO 15 MINUTES
BAKING TIME: 20 MINUTES
HARDENING TIME: 30 TO 60 MINUTES

⅔ CUP BROWN RICE FLOUR

1⅔ CUPS UNBLEACHED WHITE FLOUR

½ CUP BREWERS' (NUTRITIONAL) YEAST

½ CUP WHEAT GERM

3 TABLESPOONS VEGETABLE OIL

2 GARLIC CLOVES, MINCED OR PRESSED

2 TABLESPOONS SOY SAUCE

1 CUP WATER

topping

1 TABLESPOON SOY SAUCE

1 TABLESPOON VEGETABLE OIL

Preheat the oven to 400°. Lightly spray a baking sheet with oil or line it with either parchment paper or a brown paper bag cut to fit.

In a large bowl, mix the flours, brewers' yeast, and wheat germ. In a small bowl, whisk together the oil, garlic, soy sauce, and water. Add the wet ingredients to the dry and mix until well combined.

Turn the dough out onto a lightly floured surface and knead for 2 to 3 minutes. Flour the surface again and roll out the dough to about a ⅜-inch thickness. Cut into shapes using a cookie cutter or the rim of a glass. Arrange the biscuits close together on the prepared baking sheet: Almost touching is ok because they don't spread. Whisk together the topping ingredients and brush on the tops of the biscuits.

Bake for 20 minutes. Let the biscuits cool in the turned-off oven for 30 to 60 minutes, so they get crunchy. (We no longer recommend cooling on a rack—ahem!) When cool, store in a jar or sealable plastic bag.

(P.S. If you use cute cookie cutters, be sure to warn the kids!)

glossary of ingredients

ALMOND PASTE is a sublime mash of ground blanched almonds, sugar, and liquid (usually glucose or glycerin)—with almond extract sometimes added. Almond paste is used in cakes, cookies, and confections. Marzipan is a type of almond paste, but it has more finely ground almonds than regular almond paste. Almond paste is available in the baking aisle in cans or plastic rolls. Reseal and store in the refrigerator. If it hardens, warm briefly for 5 minutes in a warm conventional oven or 5 seconds in a microwave oven, until pliable.

ARUGULA Originally a staple in southern Italian cooking and harvested wild, arugula has become a standard addition to salads in both Europe and North America. Also known as *ruchetta, rucola,* or "garden rocket," this calcium-packed green grows year-round and its sweet, tender little leaves can be harvested within three weeks of planting. Left to mature, the leaves become more peppery and sharp-tasting and will add piquancy to salads, soups, and dressings. With its stems immersed in water, arugula will keep for a few days in the refrigerator. Before using, submerge arugula in water and rinse thoroughly several times to remove any embedded dirt.

BELGIAN ENDIVE Popular as a raw salad green and a nice complement to arugula, radicchio, and watercress, Belgian endive has tightly packed, silvery white leaves edged in very pale yellow that form a small, oval head. A member of the chicory family, it has a succulent, clean, crisp, refreshing flavor. Strangely enough, it's cultivated in the dark. Choose heads with smooth, unspotted outer leaves and rinse lightly before using. It will keep in a perforated plastic bag in the refrigerator for at least 1 to 2 days.

BROCCOLI RABE *(broccoli di rape, rapini, rappi)* A strong and bitter type of broccoli with a small flower-head used frequently in Italian cuisine. Be sure to rinse it thoroughly before using, since it's often grown in sandy soil. Select bunches with slender, flexible stems and no yellow leaves or flowers.

CAPERS are tiny, green buds of a flowering Mediterranean plant with a sharp, piquant flavor. Labor-intensive harvesting, processing, and importing all drive up their price. They are packaged either in a vinegar-based brine or in sea salt. At Moosewood, we prefer the less salty, brine-packed variety. Rinse capers well before using and, for the best flavor, add toward the end of cooking.

CHESTNUTS have been a low-fat staple of Europe and Central Asia for generations: There is even a Tuscan chestnut museum attesting to their long history. The chestnut trees that once flourished in the United States were destroyed by an early-twentieth-century fungal blight. Today chestnuts sold in this country are primarily from Europe and Japan.

Choose firm, heavy nuts with shiny, blemish-free, mahogany shells. They are best when freshly imported during the winter holiday season. Store the nuts in a cool, dry place and refrigerate shelled nuts in a container. See our recipe for Roasted Chestnuts (page 225).

CHÈVRE *(goat cheese)* is made from goat's milk using a process similar to almost all fresh cheeses and is most often ripened by surface mold. This soft, young, mild cheese is occasionally seasoned with black pepper or herbs. It requires no pasteurization because goats don't carry the tuberculosis bacterium, and it can sometimes be tolerated by people who are lactose intolerant.

CHINESE CHILI PASTE (*chili paste with garlic*) is a deep red, saucy condiment that can spark up almost any Asian dish. Supermarkets stock a wide variety of chili pastes and most include crushed, fermented chiles, salt, soy oil, and garlic. The simpler the ingredient list, the better. Look for bottled brands without preservatives. Tightly capped and refrigerated, Chinese chili paste keeps indefinitely.

COCONUT In this book, we haven't used fresh coconut meat, but several of our recipes call for unsweetened dried coconut flakes or coconut milk. Contrary to its name, coconut milk is neither the liquid in a fresh coconut nor the sweetened coconut cream used in tropical beverages and mixed drinks. It's actually the smooth, thick, rich-flavored liquid made by puréeing water and grated coconut and then straining it. It comes canned in regular and reduced-fat versions, and some brands are free of preservatives and additives. Once opened, it will keep for about 3 days, covered and refrigerated. Frozen, it lasts indefinitely.

Unsweetened coconut flakes are available in Indian, Caribbean, or Southeast Asian groceries, natural food stores, and many supermarkets. We avoid the very sweet "sweetened shredded coconut" in the supermarket baking section: Too sugary and not coconutty enough.

CRYSTALLIZED GINGER Much like candied fruit, crystallized ginger is made of ginger root pieces coated with granulated sugar or sugar syrup—a preservative process that dates back to medieval times. Its hot, sweet flavor is quite

different from either fresh ginger root or dried ginger. Look for it with the spices, or in the baking aisle or Asian section of the supermarket.

FENNEL Fresh fennel bulb, or "Florence fennel," is a curious-looking vegetable with a sweet anise/licorice flavor and crunchy texture. Sometimes labeled anise at markets, fresh fennel has a large, white edible bulbous bottom with green celery-like stalks topped by feathery fronds. The bulb can be sliced raw into salads, cooked as a side dish, or added to stews. The fronds make nice garnishes.

FETA CHEESE is a sharp, white, salty cheese similar to the Balkan cheese Teleme. It's made with either goat, sheep, or cow's milk and is available in tins, jars, plastic, or loose in salty brine. This creamy cheese melts well into a casserole, but is also excellent grated and sprinkled atop a dish—and a little gives a lot of added flavor. Most American-made feta is lower in fat than Cheddar, provolone, Swiss, or Muenster.

GARAM MASALA Like curry powders, garam masala is a mixture of roasted, ground spices that can vary according to taste and purpose. Convenient blends are available in the herb and spice aisle or the specialty foods section of Asian markets and most supermarkets. Store in a tightly sealed container in a cool, dark place and use within 3 months for best results.

If you'd like to make your own, here's one of our favorite recipes: 6 inches of crushed cinnamon stick, ¼ cup of coriander seeds, 2 tablespoons of cumin seeds, 2 tablespoons of black peppercorns, 1½ teaspoons of whole cloves, 1 tablespoon of cardamom seeds, and 1½ teaspoons of fennel seeds. Heat all of the spices on an unoiled baking tray at 200° for a half hour; cool and grind.

HOISIN SAUCE This Chinese condiment is traditionally spread on thin mu shu pancakes that are filled with stir-fried vegetables and rolled. Hoisin sauce is a deep chocolate-colored purée with a smooth, thick texture and a sweet but slightly tangy and spicy flavor. It contains soybeans, sugar, vinegar, and spices.

JICAMA can vary in weight from ½ to 6 pounds! Clean-tasting and mildly sweet, this tuber from Mexico and the Amazon has a somewhat spherical shape and coarse brownish skin. Its crunchy, translucent white, apple-like flesh is high in potassium, low in sodium, and good raw or cooked. Jicama combines well with fruit, vegetables, or seafood. Select thin-skinned specimens—by far the tastiest and most tender. Store whole jicama unwrapped in a dry spot in the refrigerator. Once cut, it will keep wrapped in plastic for about a week.

KALAMATA OLIVES (*calamata*) are delicious, meaty, purplish-black olives marinated in wine vinegar and then often packed in olive oil and vinegar. Look for them in specialty and Greek groceries and the delicatessen section of well-stocked supermarkets.

LENTILS are a staple in Europe, the Middle East, the Mediterranean, and India. They are high-protein, quick-cooking, sulphur-free legumes that contain calcium, magnesium, sodium, potassium, and other nutrients. Red lentils are available whole or split, cook faster when split, and transform into a gorgeous golden purée when cooked. The familiar brown lentils maintain their color and must simmer for 30 to 40 minutes. Lentils also make flavorful crunchy sprouts.

MASCARPONE belongs to the broadest category of cheese, which is "soft cheeses." This sweet, 75% fat, creamy white cheese is produced in Lombardy, Italy, as a by-product of making Parmesan.

MATZO Hebrew tradition requires special foods for Passover, and matzo is one of the four special foods. Unleavened, thin, and flat, these 6-inch square wheat crackers are available boxed in the kosher section of the supermarket. Matzo farfel is crumbled matzo. Finely ground matzo, or matzo meal, is used in ceremonial Jewish Passover dishes as a thickener in place of flour and bread crumbs.

MESCLUN is derived from the French word for "mixture" and it always consists of some combination of peppery, sweet, and bitter young greens. One nice blend could be red mustard, arugula, frisée, baby spinach, and mizuna. Commercial blends are colorful and ready to use, but expensive. Try mixing them with other less expensive leaf lettuces and chopped romaine for a good-looking salad at a reasonable price.

MIRIN Used to season marinades, sauces, dressings, and glazes, this Japanese rice cooking wine has a lovely sweet flavor. Both hon-mirin and aji-mirin are widely available, but hon-mirin is considered to be of higher quality. It is brewed from sake, sweet rice, and rice malt, while aji-mirin is a wine fortified with salt, fructose, and corn syrup. If you're out of mirin, a mixture of ⅔ dry sherry to ⅓ sugar can be substituted. Find mirin in Asian groceries and the ethnic section of supermarkets. Store in a cool, dry place.

MISO is made by fermenting soybeans, often with a grain such as rice, barley, or wheat. The color and flavor of this salty condiment both depend on the grain used and the length of fermentation. The lighter the color, the milder and sweeter the taste. Dark misos are very salty and very strong. Miso is a versatile ingredient. We use it in salad dressings, spreads, and as a bouillon in selected soups. Miso will keep for months in a closed container in the refrigerator. It can be purchased at natural food stores and where Asian foods are sold.

MOZZARELLA (FRESH) Soft, mild, white cheese that is most often formed into balls of varying sizes. Domestic fresh mozzarella is most often made from whole cow's milk. The gold standard, however, is crafted from buffalo milk or a combination of buffalo and cow's milk. For a special occasion, this melt-in-your-mouth variety is worth seeking out. Also, locally made cow's milk mozzarella, often sold loose at deli counters, can taste fresher and creamier than the packaged, mass-marketed brands. We serve fresh mozzarella with juicy tomatoes, assertive tapenades, or sliced and drizzled with a good olive oil and fresh herbs. It will keep for 3 to 5 days in water in a closed container in the refrigerator.

MUNG BEAN SPROUTS Slender, white, and crunchy, these sprouts are ideal salad and sandwich ingredients and a textural and nutritious addition to Asian soups, stir-fries, and stews. Sprouts are easy to "farm" right in your kitchen and provide a year-round source of fresh protein and vitamin C. Store mung sprouts in a tightly closed plastic bag in the refrigerator. Look for sprouts that are bright white and crisp. Available in well-stocked produce departments and where Asian produce is sold.

NEUFCHÂTEL is a creamy, white, unripened cheese similar in taste and consistency to cream cheese. Domestic Neufchâtel has about a 20% lower milk fat content than cream

cheese and can often replace cream cheese when a reduced-fat cheese is desired. But by definition, Neufchâtel is not necessarily a lower fat cheese. French Neufchâtel, which originated in the Normandy town of the same name, varies widely in fat content, with some versions approaching the 45% to 50% milk fat content of American cream cheese. Neufchâtel is usually located in the dairy case near the cream cheese.

NORI See pages 262 and 367.

OILS are a form of liquid fat used to prevent sticking and to add body, flavor, and a rich smoothness to foods. Store oils away from light and use while fresh. Toss out old, rancid specimens. Oils high in monounsaturated fat are healthiest for regular consumption.

OLD BAY SEASONING This spice blend was developed in the Chesapeake Bay area of Maryland to season the plentiful seafood that abounds there. At Moosewood, we use Old Bay Seasoning on all types of fish and seafood and in chowders, stews, slaws, and dressings. It's available in the spice and/or seafood section of many supermarkets.

PARCHMENT PAPER A stiff, translucent paper that is impervious to moisture or fats. Use parchment paper to line pans and protect tender baked goods and confections from sticking. Enclose julienned vegetables and fish in parchment and bake to a moist and delicate finish. Available almost anywhere that kitchen and baking supplies are sold.

PRESERVED LEMONS See page 194.

RICE is a popular grain worldwide and is now grown in tropical, equatorial, and temperate zones across the continents. Raw rice can be stored for months in a tightly capped container in a cool, dark place. Rice that retains its bran, such as brown rice, must be used soon after purchase or refrigerated to prevent rancidity. Rice is always eaten cooked and can be served hot, at room temperature, or cold. See below for basic cooking instructions.

Arborio Rice is an Italian short-grain, starchy white rice used in risottos. It's highly absorbent, but the process of cooking it and adding water is a gradual one. Ultimately, it creates a smooth, creamy base without sacrificing its firm satisfying kernel.

Basmati Rice grows in the foothills of the Himalayas and has slender, long grains that are aged for up to a year before being sold. Its nutty flavor, sweet fragrance, and smooth texture make it an appealing choice. Basmati rice is available in natural food stores and often found in well-stocked supermarkets. Domestic brands are Texmati and Calmati.

Brown Rice An excellent rice with a chewy texture and full-bodied flavor, brown rice has only the hull removed—the bran and germ are retained along with nutrients and a light brown hue. It is available in long-grain, medium-grain, and short-grain varieties: The shorter the grain, the more small, plump, and moist the cooked kernels will be. Long-grain is good when a slightly dry, fluffy rice is preferred. Medium- and short-grain are perfect for Asian dishes eaten with chopsticks.

Carnaroli Rice is one of the choice, oval, short-grain white rices that's classified as "superfino" and used for risotto. It has a hard, glass-like exterior, is resistant to rapid liquid absorption, and produces a creamy and coherent risotto. Other risotto rices are arborio, vialone nano, and baldo.

Jasmine Rice is a creamy, Thai long-grain rice with a distinctive aromatic fragrance. It can be found in Asian markets or in the international section of large supermarkets.

Sushi Rice is a short-grain, slightly glutinous white rice perfect for making sushi. It's available in the Asian section of well-stocked supermarkets and in Asian specialty shops.

Sweet Sticky Rice (*glutinous rice, sticky rice, sweet rice, sweet glutinous rice*) An Asian rice with plump, white grains that become translucent when cooked. It is used most often in Asian sweets and is widely available in Asian markets as well as some supermarkets.

White Rice is also known as polished rice because it has been processed to remove both its hull and bran. "Enriched" white rice has thiamine, niacin, and iron added to it. It is sold in long-grain, medium-grain, and short-grain varieties. All are quick-cooking.

Wild Rice is not a rice, but the slim seeds of an aquatic grass related to the rice plant. Some is hand-harvested wild and some is cultivated in rice paddies. For reasons of both taste and cost, we use it in combination with other rice or grains. Look for organic wild rice in natural food stores.

COOKING RICE Rinse and drain the grains. If you like, sauté briefly in a small amount of oil for 3 to 4 minutes, stirring constantly. Add water, cover, and bring to a boil; then lower the heat and gently simmer until tender.

Basmati Rice To 1 cup of rice, add 1¾ cups of water; cook brown basmati for 35 to 40 minutes and white basmati for about 15 minutes.

Brown Rice *(long grain and short grain)* Use 1¾ to 2 cups of water to 1 cup of rice, a little less water for larger amounts of rice. Cook for 40 to 50 minutes, 50 minutes for larger quantities.

Jasmine Rice Cook according to the directions for white basmati.

Sticky or Glutinous or Sweet Rice Sticky rice cooks quickly in a 1 to 1 proportion of rice to water. Likewise, Black Thai rice.

Sushi Rice Allow the kernels to rest for a short time after rinsing and draining, and then cook for about 20 minutes.

White Rice Use 1¾ to 2 cups of water (depending on the softness desired) to 1 cup of rice. Cook for 20 minutes.

RUTABAGA This globe-shaped root vegetable in the cabbage family has pale orange flesh and a sweet, mild taste. Rutabagas are generally the size of a grapefruit with light orange skin that deepens to magenta at the stem end. The skin is usually waxed and so must be peeled before cooking. It will keep for up to 2 weeks in the refrigerator when wrapped in plastic.

SEITAN Mildly seasoned with tamari, spices, or vegetable bouillon, this chewy, protein-rich wheat gluten is traditionally used as a meat substitute in Asia and has become a popular ingredient internationally in vegetarian cookery. Mild-mannered seitan can be added to stews, sauces, and fillings of any ethnicity. The vegetarian seitan industry is also pre-seasoning seitan for use as ready-made sandwich fillings. Look for seitan wrapped in plastic in the refrigerated section of natural food stores or in cans in Asian markets.

SESAME OIL Expressed from hulled and roasted sesame seeds, this rich, dark oil is most frequently used in Asian cooking. Because of its robust flavor, dark sesame oil is used sparingly, as a condiment. Like all oils, it's vulnerable to rancidity and, if not used frequently, will keep best refrigerated. Look for it where Asian foods are sold.

SHALLOTS are a mild, sweet member of the onion family with small bulbs cloved like garlic. Store as you would onions, in a well ventilated, uncrowded, dark, dry bin. Shallots are available in net bags where produce is sold.

SHIITAKE are succulent, woodsy-tasting mushrooms that originated in Japan, but are now produced in a number of states across the U.S. Although fresh shiitake are increasingly available, we use dried shiitake almost exclusively because of their year-round availability and affordability. All shiitake are expensive, but the concentrated flavor of dried mushrooms gives more bang (well, a different bang) for the buck. When using dried mushrooms, soak in hot water for 20 to 30 minutes, cut away and discard the tough stems, and then slice the caps for cooking. We filter the soaking liquid and use it with the mushrooms. Purchase shiitake where Asian foods are sold.

SUMAC A staple spice in the Middle East, sumac has the taste and mouthfeel of citrus and, not surprisingly, is high in vitamin C. Sumac is dried and ground from a brick-red berry grown on an indigenous Middle Eastern bush. The spice can be used to good effect in marinades, salad dressings, tajines, and fish. Look for sumac where Middle Eastern and North African spices are sold.

SUN-DRIED TOMATOES Tomatoes, like fruit (which, botanically speaking, they are), can be dried to a familiar yet densely and differently flavored end. Sun-dried tomatoes are chewy, slightly sweet, and astringent. The addition of a small amount of chopped sun-dried tomatoes can uniquely pep up polenta, mashed potatoes, rice pilaf, or any creamy pie or strudel filling. Some sun-dried tomatoes come packed in oil and are ready to use, but we prefer the lower-fat, dry-packed tomatoes, even though they require a 20-minute tenderizing bath in hot water. We also favor the taste of tomatoes preserved with salt (rinse before soaking) over ones that are treated with sulfites. Sun-dried tomatoes are available in the Italian section of the supermarket and at gourmet food stores.

TOFU *(bean curd)* is a high-protein soy product with a creamy, cheese-like texture. It is sold in cakes that can vary in weight and is often water-packed. Look for it in the dairy section or vacuum-packed in the Asian aisle. At home, refrigerate opened tofu in water in a covered container, change the water daily, and use within a week.

Firm Tofu has a dense texture good in dishes where you want cubes or triangles of the tofu to remain intact after baking, sautéeing, or stir-frying. Use when making fillings for stuffed vegetables or when freezing the tofu.

Frozen Tofu can be grated in a food processor or with a hand grater to make a crumbly, chewy product good for stuffings, soups, and stews. Use immediately: Defrosted frozen tofu is highly perishable. To freeze tofu, slice a cake vertically into four equal pieces and place in a baking dish; loosely cover with wax paper and freeze until solid, 3 to 4 hours or overnight.

Silken Tofu *(Japanese-style tofu)* is made with a higher ratio of soybeans to water than regular tofu, which gives it a higher protein and fat content. With its unobtrusive flavor and creamy, delicate texture, it performs well in dairyless desserts, drinks, and dressings, producing a thick, smooth, velvety purée. "Lite" silken tofu with a reduced fat content is also available.

Soft Tofu has a texture that falls between the density of firm tofu and the creaminess of silken tofu. It is excellent cubed and simmered in brothy soups and stews and blended into sauces, dips, spreads, and purées. Soft and silken tofus are best for desserts.

Tofu-Kan Once found only in Chinatowns across the U.S. as five-spice bean curd, tofu-kan—a baked, seasoned tofu—is now made in cottage industries all over the country using a wider range of spices and recipes. With its slightly smoky flavor and satisfying chewy, dense texture, it's perfect in soups, salads, sandwiches, sautés, and fillings. Look for these ready-to-slice-and-eat products in natural food stores and Asian markets.

UMEBOSHI See page 70.

VINEGAR can be made from the sugar in many fruits, grains, and natural sweeteners and has been used for centuries—the earliest written record dates back to 5000 B.C.E. The Babylonians made vinegar from dates, the Asians from rice, the southern Europeans from grapes, and the early American colonists from apples. In the mid-1600s the French commercialized the production of wine vinegar, and in Italy the finest balsamic vinegar is regarded as a national treasure.

Balsamic Vinegar Dark, syrupy, and complexly flavored, balsamic vinegar is a favorite for salads, sauces, vinaigrettes, and marinades and can be poured directly on fresh fruit with surprisingly delightful results.

Champagne Vinegar has a delicate flavor and a slightly lower acidity than other wine vinegars. It's perfect for fruit and herb vinegars.

Cider Vinegar is a traditional North American vinegar made from apple cider and is used as an all-purpose flavoring.

Distilled White Vinegar is clear-colored, has a crisp bite, and is produced from diluted distilled alcohol. It's appropriate in Chinese dipping sauces, good for pickling, and cheap and effective for general household cleaning.

Raspberry and Fruit Vinegars are usually made from wine or Champagne vinegars that have been combined with macerated fruit and then filtered.

Rice Vinegar This slightly sweet, mild vinegar made in China and Japan from rice wine has a lower acidity than most other vinegars.

Sherry Vinegar A slightly sweet, medium brown, aromatic vinegar from Spain, delicious when paired with nut oils.

Wine Vinegar Red wine vinegar is excellent in robust vinaigrettes and in combination with shallots, garlic, and strong herbs such as rosemary, oregano, and thyme. White wine vinegar pairs well with tarragon, basil, chives, and cilantro.

WORCESTERSHIRE SAUCE A sassy, sweet, and spicy condiment developed at the behest of a colonial English governor who yearned for the tastes of southern Asia. Classic Worcestershire sauce contains molasses, anchovies or sardines, garlic, sugar, tamarind, soy sauce, vinegar, and spices. Edward and Sons' Trading Company produces a tasty vegetarian version called the Wizard's Worcestershire Sauce, available in natural food stores.

vegan dishes

Many more people these days are choosing to eat a diet based only on plant foods. All of the following recipes adhere to vegan guidelines and contain no animal products, dairy products, or honey.

appetizers, dips & drinks

Asian Bean Curd Spread
Baked Eggplant Dip
Cashew Cream
Chipotle Tofu (page 66)
Filo Bites
Harvest Nuts & Seeds
Nori Rice Balls
Peach Fizz
Piña Colada Slush
Raspberry Fizz
Roasted Chestnuts
Sambusas
Summer Rolls with Peanut Sauce
Sushi-Stuffed Mushrooms
Sweet Potato Pot Stickers
Tofu Almond Balls
Tofu Skewers with Peanut Sauce
Two Olive Herb Spreads
Two Summer Citrus Coolers
Two Olive Herb Spreads*
Umeboshi Sushi
Vegetable-Wrapped Sushi Rolls

salads

Black Bean & Citrus Salad
Black-eyed Pea Salad
Caribbean Rice & Bean Salad
Cauliflower Green Olive Salad
Good Luck Lentil Salad
Light Southwestern Potato Salad
Mango Jicama Salad
Mexican Lime Cumin Slaw
Moroccan Salad

Nopalitos Salad
October Bitter Sweet Salad
Saucy Asian Noodle Salad
Spicy Cabbage Salad

side dishes

Asian Turnips with Wasabi
Baked Beets on Greens
Black Bean & Chocolate Chili
Cajun Dirty Rice
Calabacitas
Caramelized Onion Gravy
Chinese Long Beans
Choklay's Home Fries
Curried Coconut Green Beans
Gingered Carrots with Hijiki
Green Beans with Shallots
Greens with Cashews
Grilled Curried Corn on the Cob
Homemade Applesauce
Indian Vegetable Pancakes
"Jazzed Up" Cranberry Sauce
Jenny's Mom's Eggplant
Mango Cranberry Chutney
Mashed Potatoes & Parsnips
Pearl Onions Braised in Wine
Quick Cucumber Pickle
Red Cabbage with Cranberries
Roasted Baby Artichokes
Roasted Winter Squash
Sautéed Broccoli Rabe
Spanish Chickpeas
Spicy Grilled Corn on the Cob
Stuffed Yams

soups

Curried Squash & Apple Soup
Mandarin Hot & Sour Soup
Shorba
Tomato Bean Soup

main dishes

Baked Creole Ratatouille
Barbecued Tofu & Vegetables
Classic Burger with Pesto Marinade (page 82)
Collard Greens & Red Beans
Mushroom Filo Pastries
Polenta Dome
Red Lentils & Rice
Roasted Autumn Vegetables
Roasted Squash with Corn & Beans
Sweet Potato Stuffed Eggplant
Tibetan-style Seitan Burritos

dressings & sauces

Cilantro Almond Pesto
Citrus Herb Vinaigrette (page 369)
Jerk Sauce
Mellow Miso Vinaigrette (page 370)
Mojo Sauce
Raspberry Mint Vinaigrette (page 370)
Savory Shallot Vinaigrette (page 369)
Tibetan Hot Sauce
Tomato Dressing (page 248)
Tomato Lime Pesto
Two Dipping Sauces
Two Super Rubs

desserts & breads

Apple Pecan Crumble
Best Vegan Date Nut Bread
Campari Compote
Chocolate Apricots
Chocolate Pudding Cake
Classic Southern Italian Dried Figs
Cranberry Sorbet
Orange Gratin
Passover "Brown Bubbie"
Puff Pastry with Strawberries
Special Day Chocolates
Spiced Coconut Date Bars
Strawberry Chocolate Quesadillas
Vegan Chocolate Gingerbread

gift foods

Dog Biscuits
Pear Raspberry Preserves
Preserved Lemons
Three Savory Seasoned Salts
Winter Squash Butter

half-hour hands-on dishes

Here's a helpful list for when time is short. The dishes that can be completed in 30 minutes or less are indicated by an asterisk (*). Most cooks should be able to get the other ones on the list ready for either the oven, stove top, or refrigerator in about a half hour. Then you can just relax or take care of other tasks while the meal bakes, simmers, or chills.

appetizers, dips & drinks

Asian Bean Curd Spread*
Bedeviled Eggs*
Cashew Cream*
Chai Smoothie
Cheddar Shortbread Hearts
Cheese Crisps*
Crabmeat Corn Spread*
Grapes & Gorgonzola*
Olive Butter Spread*
Peach Fizz*
Piña Colada Slush
Raspberry Fizz
Roasted Chestnuts
Smoked Salmon Spread
Stuffed Mushrooms
Stuffed Tomato & Cucumber Bites*
Tibetan-style Chai*
Tofu Almond Balls
Tofu Skewers with Peanut Sauce
Tomatoes & Arugula on Toast*
Tropical Fruit Kabobs*
Two Olive Herb Spreads*
Two Summer Citrus Coolers*

salads

Avocado Citrus Salad*
Best Dressed Shrimp Salad*
Black Bean & Citrus Salad*
Black-eyed Pea Salad
Blue Cheese Potato Salad*
Boston Bean Salad*

Caribbean Rice & Bean Salad*
Cauliflower Green Olive Salad
Greenest Green Salad*
Light Southwestern Potato Salad*
Mango Jicama Salad
Mexican Lime Cumin Slaw*
Moroccan Salad*
Nopalitos Salad*
October Bitter Sweet Salad*
Red Cabbage Slaw
Spicy Cabbage Salad
Spring Green Salad*

side dishes

Asian Turnips with Wasabi*
Baked Beets on Greens
Brussels Sprouts with Chestnut Beurre Blanc*
Chinese Long Beans*
Gingered Carrots with Hijiki*
Greens with Cashews*
Grilled Curried Corn on the Cob
Haroset*
Homemade Applesauce
"Jazzed Up" Cranberry Sauce
Quick Cucumber Pickle
Roasted Baby Artichokes
Roasted Winter Squash
Sautéed Broccoli Rabe*
Savory Flan
Spanish Chickpeas*
Spicy Grilled Corn on the Cob
Stewed Cardoons

soups

Avocado Orange Soup*
Potato Leek Soup
Summer Cucumber Melon Soup*
Tomato Bean Soup

main dishes

Barbecued Tofu & Vegetables
Bell Pepper & Asparagus Frittata
Collard Greens & Red Beans*
Crab Cakes
Japanese Stuffed Peppers
Matzo Casserole
Potato Latkes to Celebrate Your Roots
Roasted Autumn Vegetables

dressings & sauces

Anchovy Dressing*
Cilantro Almond Pesto*
Dressings for Every Season*
Jerk Sauce*
Mojo Sauce*
No-Egg Caesar Dressing*
Tibetan Hot Sauce
Tomato Lime Pesto*
Two Dipping Sauces*
Two Super Rubs*
Versatile Sour Cream Sauce*

desserts & breads

Almond Cake with Peaches
Apple Brown Betty
Best Vegan Date Nut Bread
Bittersweet Chocolate Sauce*
Bone Cookies
Brown Sugar Poundcake
Buttery Blueberry Coffee Cake
Campari Compote
Chocolate Angelfood Cake
Chocolate Crunch
Chocolate-Filled Dried Figs

Chocolate Pudding Cake
Chocolate Soufflé Cake
Classic Caramel Sauce*
Classic Southern Italian Dried Figs
Cornmeal Lemon Shortbread
Cranberry Cornmeal Biscotti
Cranberry Sorbet
Currant & Walnut Biscuits
Espresso Truffles
Frosted Carrot Cupcakes
Fruit Cobbler
Hazelnut Chocolate Torte
Hazelnut Truffles
Honey Roasted Pears
Kheer
Lime Frozen Yogurt
Oatmeal Chocolate Chip Cookies
Orange & Fig Cookies
Orange Gratin*
Pan de Muerto
Passover "Brown Bubbie"
Peanut Butter Cookies
Plum (or Pear) Torte
Puff Pastry with Strawberries
Pumpkin Maple Pie
Red, White & Blue Parfait*
Semolina Almond Cookies
Special Day Chocolates
Spiced Coconut Date Bars
Stout Irish Gingerbread
Strawberry Chocolate Quesadillas*
Vegan Chocolate Gingerbread
White Chocolate & Fig Poundcake
Winemaker's Grape Cake

gift foods

Dog Biscuits
Preserved Lemons
Three Savory Seasoned Salts*
Winter Squash Butter

HOMEMADE VEGETABLE STOCKS

While many soups and stews can be made with plain water, most taste even better when made with stock—and brothy soups, especially, can really benefit from the added flavor of a stock. Here are two of Moosewood's most often used stocks: Basic Vegetable Stock and Garlic Peppercorn Stock. Choose the one that best suits your needs.

basic vegetable stock

YIELDS ABOUT 8 CUPS
PREPARATION TIME: 20 MINUTES
COOKING TIME: ABOUT 1 HOUR

10	CUPS WATER
2	ONIONS, QUARTERED
2	SWEET POTATOES OR 4 CARROTS, PEELED AND QUARTERED
2	POTATOES, SCRUBBED AND THICKLY SLICED
2	CELERY STALKS AND/OR 1 CUP MUSHROOM STEMS
2	GARLIC CLOVES, SMASHED
2	FRESH PARSLEY SPRIGS
1	BAY LEAF
4	ALLSPICE BERRIES
4	WHOLE BLACK PEPPERCORNS
½	TEASPOON SALT

garlic peppercorn stock

10	CUPS WATER
3	WHOLE HEADS OF GARLIC, BROKEN INTO CLOVES
2	POTATOES, SCRUBBED AND THICKLY SLICED
2	CARROTS, PEELED AND QUARTERED
3	CELERY STALKS, COARSELY CHOPPED
¼	TEASPOON WHOLE BLACK PEPPERCORNS
4	FRESH PARSLEY SPRIGS
3	BAY LEAVES
½	TEASPOON SALT
¼	TEASPOON DRIED THYME

For the stock you select, combine all of the ingredients in a large soup pot, cover, and bring to a boil on high heat. When the water boils, lower the heat and, still covered, simmer for about 1 hour.

Allow to cool slightly; then strain the stock through a sieve or colander. Use immediately or refrigerate it in a sealed container for up to 4 days, or freeze it for up to 6 months.

index

CONVERSION CHART

Equivalent Imperial and Metric Measurements

American cooks use standard containers, the 8-ounce cup and a tablespoon that takes exactly 16 level fillings to fill that cup level. Measuring by cup makes it very difficult to give weight equivalents, as a cup of densely packed butter will weigh considerably more than a cup of flour. The easiest way therefore to deal with cup measurements in recipes is to take the amount by volume rather than by weight. Thus the equation reads:

1 cup = 240 ml = 8 fl. oz.   ½ cup = 120 ml = 4 fl. oz.

It is possible to buy a set of American cup measures in major stores around the world.

In the States, butter is often measured in sticks. One stick is the equivalent of 8 tablespoons. One tablespoon of butter is therefore the equivalent to ½ ounce/15 grams.

LIQUID MEASURES

Fluid Ounces	U.S.	Imperial	Milliliters
	1 teaspoon	1 teaspoon	5
¼	2 teaspoons	1 dessertspoon	10
½	1 tablespoon	1 tablespoon	14
1	2 tablespoons	2 tablespoons	28
2	¼ cup	4 tablespoons	56
4	½ cup		110
5		¼ pint or 1 gill	140
6	¾ cup		170
8	1 cup		225
9			250, ¼ liter
10	1¼ cups	½ pint	280
12	1½ cups		340
15		¾ pint	420
16	2 cups		450
18	2¼ cups		500, ½ liter
20	2½ cups	1 pint	560
24	3 cups		675
25		1¼ pints	700
27	3½ cups		750
30	3¾ cups	1½ pints	840
32	4 cups or 1 quart		900
35		1¾ pints	980
36	4½ cups		1000, 1 liter
40	5 cups	2 pints or 1 quart	1120

SOLID MEASURES

U.S. AND IMPERIAL MEASURES		METRIC MEASURES	
Ounces	Pounds	Grams	Kilos
1		28	
2		56	
3½		100	
4	¼	112	
5		140	
6		168	
8	½	225	
9		250	¼
12	¾	340	
16	1	450	
18		500	½
20	1¼	560	
24	1½	675	
27		750	¾
28	1¾	780	
32	2	900	
36	2¼	1000	1
40	2½	1100	
48	3	1350	
54		1500	1½

OVEN TEMPERATURE EQUIVALENTS

Fahrenheit	Celsius	Gas Mark	Description
225	110	¼	Cool
250	130	½	
275	140	1	Very Slow
300	150	2	
325	170	3	Slow
350	180	4	Moderate
375	190	5	
400	200	6	Moderately Hot
425	220	7	Fairly Hot
450	230	8	Hot
475	240	9	Very Hot
500	250	10	Extremely Hot

Any broiling recipes can be used with the grill of the oven, but beware of high-temperature grills

EQUIVALENTS FOR INGREDIENTS

all-purpose flour—plain flour
baking sheet—oven tray
buttermilk—ordinary milk
cheesecloth—muslin
coarse salt—kitchen salt
cornstarch—cornflour

eggplant—aubergine
granulated sugar—caster sugar
half and half—12% fat milk
heavy cream—double cream
light cream—single cream
parchment paper—greaseproof paper

plastic wrap—cling film
scallion—spring onion
shortening—white fat
unbleached flour—strong, white flour
zest—rind
zucchini—courgettes or marrow